## William Berger

# WAGNER WITHOUT FEAR

William Berger was born in California and studied Romance languages and music at the University of California at Santa Cruz. He worked for five years at the San Francisco Opera Company, where he acquired for the company's recorded music collection and translated for visiting performers. He has taught language at Baruch College in New York City. He contributed to James Skofield's libretto for *The Dracula Diaries*, an opera with music by Robert Moran, and has just completed the libretto for *The Wolf of Gubbio*, with the composer Patrick Barnes. Mr. Berger currently lives in New York and is at work on a performance piece, *Karajan's Wake*.

# WAGNER
## WITHOUT
## FEAR

*Learning to Love—and Even Enjoy—*
*Opera's Most Demanding Genius*

◆

## WILLIAM BERGER

VINTAGE BOOKS
A DIVISION OF RANDOM HOUSE, INC.
NEW YORK

To the memory of

Chris DeBlasio
(1959–1993),
whose solo reading of *Das Rheingold* at the piano—including all
vocal parts—remains the best performance I've ever attended

A VINTAGE ORIGINAL, FIRST EDITION, OCTOBER 1998

*Copyright © 1998 by William Berger*
*Maps copyright © 1998 by JoAnne Metsch*

Library of Congress Cataloging-in-Publication Data
Berger, William, 1961–
Wagner without fear: learning to love—and even enjoy—opera's
most demanding genius / by William Berger.—1st ed.
p. cm.
"A Vintage original"—t. p. verso.
ISBN 0-375-70054-4
1. Wagner, Richard, 1813–1883. Operas. 2. Opera. 3. Wagner,
Richard, 1813–1883. I. Title.
ML410.W13B47 1998 98-19825
782.1'092—DC21 CIP

*Author photograph © Blaise Hayward*
*Book design by JoAnne Metsch*

www.randomhouse.com

Printed in the United States of America

2 4 6 8 10 9 7 5 3 1

# CONTENTS

◆

### PART THREE: EXPLORING WAGNER

# PREFACE

◆

This book has been brewing for years. I have always loved sharing my enthusiasm for opera in general and Wagner in particular with anyone who didn't run away fast enough.

The house where I grew up was musical in that records held pride of place, and Saturday mornings and afternoons were reserved for radio broadcasts from the Met. Opera was available, and my parents were only too happy to answer questions, but no one was forced to take music lessons, and Verdi and Wagner were right beside the Beatles and the Stones on the record shelf. You weren't allowed to talk while music was playing, but discussion afterward was encouraged. Requests for records as presents were promptly and cheerfully granted. Other than this excellent environment, there's no particular reason why I should be devoted to this stuff. I'm not a musicologist. I have no particular devotion to German culture. And I am from Los Angeles, which is not famous for its devotion to the classics. . . .

Growing up in L.A. was actually an advantage in nurturing my love for the present subject. Although it was perceived as a cultural wasteland a generation ago (and not without reason), the "do your own thing" ethic was all-pervasive and even extended to such antisocial perversions as opera. The overall *Zeitgeist* among my peers was along the lines of "Dude! This Brünnhilde babe is totally awesome, but can we listen to some rock now?" Nor was my partiality to hard rock entirely separate in my mind from my budding interest in opera. I learned to appreciate intensity in music, that there's a difference between "pure music" and music as theater, that each genre of art comes with its own norms and clichés, and that there is endless pleasure in debating the meaning of obscure lyrics in difficult music. (This last bit of knowledge served me well in later years. Even considering the problems presented by the German language, the libretto of *Tristan* is simplicity itself compared to the lyrics of Led Zeppelin.) I was greatly aided by the absence of cultural traditions and institutions telling me that an appreciation for opera meant I was expected to cease associating with my cohorts and commence taking tea every afternoon at precisely four o'clock. Some of my friends, amazed to discover that dragons and flying horses did not originate in early 1970s album cover art, asked questions, listened with me, and became fellow travelers down this unique road.

The moment of truth came when I was seventeen. For a variety of reasons, I found myself living in Vienna for a few months that winter. With nary a beach nor a palm tree to be found, I went to the Opera, which seemed like the only thing to do there. I knew some Wagner, but did not know *Tristan* beyond the Prelude and *Liebestod*, and my German was firmly in the *"mit Schlag, bitte"* stage. I could not even read the synopsis. I was, like the protagonists in Act I, at sea. Was this a problem? On the contrary—I was blown away. The process of *making* it make sense had thrills of its own.

An incident that night confirmed my devotion. After the second act, a music student in standing room was deriding the performance at full voice to the shuffling audience. An elderly Viennese lady took exception to this critique and whacked him over the head with her tastefully beaded purse. A Soviet officer, attempting to restore decorum, made the mistake of laying hands on the lady, and a riot erupted: punches flew and socialites cast programs and debris from their boxes. The police arrived and within minutes all was forgotten among the heel-clicking and hand-kissing in the magnificent foyer.

I asked a stately lady for an explanation of what had occurred. After translating the student's tirade and explaining the people's lingering resentment at post-occupation Soviet officers in Austria, she added,

"You must understand the nature of *Tristan und Isolde*. It is a drug. It can open your eyes, ease your pain, even save your life. But if you keep indulging in it, it will make you insane." I was hooked.

And so it continued, in San Francisco, in Seattle, in Mexico City, in Berlin, but mostly in New York, where I learned that people have . . . opinions. Sometimes I worked in the opera world, sometimes not, but that's where I went in the evenings no matter what, and that's where I found answers and antidotes to our strange world. For me, the information presented on the operatic stage is a combination of psychological handbook and scriptural revelation. Since I am constitutionally incapable of keeping exciting discoveries to myself, I have been apt to talk about this stuff a lot, and that eventually led to this book.

You see, I don't believe that opera, even Wagner, need be marginalized as a peculiar taste. One day, as I was writing this book, my Walkman died and I persuaded the excellent managers of the Gym at the Pines (Fire Island, N.Y.) to let me play *Siegfried* on their sound system. They were intrigued, but the gym emptied faster than the Met's matinee audience at intermission. That little experiment was not repeated, but I remain convinced that the Forging Song, with its relentless 9/8 beats, has a future in the discos. Nor is this to be filed under that heinous term "crossover," since, as I see it, there's neither a "there" nor a "here" to be bridged. Opera, thank God, is a popular art form, available to anybody, with only a few pointers necessary.

Which is not to denigrate expertise. The research necessary even for a relentlessly nonacademic work like this is astounding, and I have been greatly helped by musicians, musicologists, opera people, and specialists in such varied fields as psychoanalysis and the German language. In addition to these experts, I must also thank the many friends and family who have contributed input and tolerated me for the last two years. Among these people, experts, opera lovers, and friends, I must name the following: First and foremost are Frances Berger of the Metropolitan Opera and Rich Lynn, the two most perfect Wagnerites I know. Others, listed alphabetically, are Marty Asher (of Vintage Books), Ramón Berger, Anthony Tirado Chase, Connie Coddington (Metropolitan Opera), Scott Curry

(Hochschule für Musik, Berlin), Ed De Bonis, Julie Doughty, Arthur Fox, André Gauthier (BMG Records), David Groff, Walter Havighurst, William Hoffmann, Audrey Kunstler, Dr. Lawrence Maas, Vinnie Maniscalco, Stephen J. Miller, Aronnora Morgan, Maya Nikolic (Writers House), Rose Rescigno, Anthony Roncalli, Esq., Lou Rufalo, Tina Ryker (Seattle Opera), Thom Saporita, Tom Spain, Judy Zecher (Metropolitan Opera), and Al Zuckerman (Writers House).

PART ONE

APPROACHING

WAGNER

# Welcome to the Art
# of Richard Wagner

◆

Richard Wagner (1813–83) was the most controversial artist who ever lived. To make matters even more interesting, the medium he worked in was opera, which is probably the most bizarre art form ever to achieve wide popularity. But the extreme reactions to the mention of Wagner, from swoons of approval to grunts of disgust, are not limited to opera people. His impact on modern thought has been tremendous. Devotees of history, politics, psychology, and literature, as well as artists and musicians of all kinds, all have a great deal to say about him. Eventually, anyone with an interest in the modern world must come to terms with Wagner.

This can be quite intimidating to the nonexpert who just wants to know what all the fuss is about. The opera fanatic, the musicologist, and the philosopher, for example, each have their own way of understanding Wagner, with specific vocabularies and clichés. The language employed quickly becomes so arcane that the rest of us feel left out. After reading some of the extravagant tracts written about Wagner, what sensible person could be blamed for judging the whole subject better left untouched? But this is a great loss, and entirely unnecessary. With a little preparation, anyone can enjoy the great pleasures of Wagner's operas. His ultimate genius was as a master of the theater, and truly great theater is never intended solely for a select few.

The fact of the matter is that Wagner's operas are extremely *popular*, and, contrary to many predictions a generation ago, their popularity is growing. Recordings, broadcasts, and simultaneous translations in the opera house have all played a role in this growth. Even *The Ring of the Nibelung*, Wagner's four-day-long epic once performed only at his private festival in Germany, is receiving quality, sold-out performances in mid-sized North American cities barely large enough to support major league sports franchises.

There are many good reasons for wanting to know something about Wagner's operas. Perhaps you attended a performance, and were bewildered. Is it possible that those few thousand other people in the house applauding wildly at the end were really interested, or were they all just trying to look as if they were? Conversely, maybe you heard a bit of the music in a concert, on the radio, or even on a movie soundtrack, and were intrigued. You may be attending a performance in spite of yourself—a blind date, or a social or business commitment, perhaps—and you want to give it a chance, since you'll be stuck there for several hours anyway. Or it may, initially, have nothing to do with a live performance. Maybe your shrink keeps referring to "Isolde's love-death" or your mate mentions your "Tannhäuser complex," and you want more insight. Whatever your motives (more on that word later), the pleasures of Wagner are accessible to anybody.

It will, however, take a bit of groundwork. Why shouldn't it? Imagine this: You take a person from a faraway country off his first plane flight to America directly to a baseball game. You tell him to enjoy it, but he is not allowed to ask any questions, or even speak, during the whole game. You say you'll be glad to answer any questions after the game. By then, the befuddled guest will most likely be so bored and alienated he'd be just as happy never to hear the subject of baseball mentioned again. If, in addition, the announcements and the scoreboard were in German, the situation would be perfectly analogous to attending a performance of Wagner with no advance preparation. Absurd as this sounds, this is roughly how many people have first been exposed to Wagner.

How, then, does one approach these giants of the stage? There is already a vast literature on the subject of Wagner. In fact, more books are listed in the Library of Congress catalog under his name than any other besides Jesus Christ. The great majority of these volumes, however, assume a prior knowledge of his work. The supposed "Introductions" to Wagner's operas tend to be involved musical analyses—interesting, for sure, but greatly slanted to musicians and other experts. There are also literally thousands of books concerning tangential aspects of Wagner: the political, the cultural, the psychological, and so on, ad infinitum. This is not accidental. Wagner himself wrote extensively about music in general and his own works in particular. Much of what he wrote is now accepted as standard, especially about performance ideals, while much of it is so hateful and revolting it cannot be approached without disgust. The ink has poured ever since. These volumes are worthy of attention, but they do not provide access to the works themselves. The many excellent "Introduction to Opera" books available all cop out on the subject of Wagner. After providing the reader with the stories of the operas and little more, they tend to refer the unfortunate newcomer into the existing Wagnerian literature snake pit.

The library books and the lecture halls confuse the subject, while only the operas themselves make perfect, gut-level sense. This, then, is a guide to comprehending and enjoying the operas of Richard Wagner. It is a sort of road map through a delightful but very foreign country. Once you are comfortable getting around in the world of Wagner's operas, you will find that the journey never needs to end, as "wonder upon wonder appears." Many people who do not even care for opera in general find themselves appreciating Wagner. At the very least, Wagner provides you with some of the most exhilarating and satisfying musical and theatrical experiences available. At most, his art is key to understanding the world we live in.

There is much you will not find in this volume. There are no musical analyses here. The comments, interspersed throughout the synopses of the operas, sometimes take a look at the music in terms of drama, but the reader who has the ability and the inclination to study the scores is encouraged to do so elsewhere. Likewise, psychological reflections are restricted to personal observations or references to other books written by people who are qualified to make such analyses. The same is true for the political implications of the works. The subsequent history of Wagner's art in our world is only outlined to the extent that it directly affects our initial contact with Wagner.

In general, this book only looks obliquely at the great singers of Wagnerian opera. There are anecdotes concerning some, but I have avoided the colossal temptation to include rhapsodic digressions on the artistry of Nilsson, Vinay, and many others. Even the brief discography toward the end of the book addresses conductors and recording quality more than the qualities of individual singers. There are exceptions when it was crucial to compare one singer's conception of a role to another's, but anyone who has debated voices with opera fans will no doubt agree that I have been reserved on this volatile and highly individual subject. My aim has been to interest people more in the operas themselves rather than to control people's experience of them.

What you will find here is a basic summary of the life of Wagner, a look at each of his mature operas as a guide to comprehending them in performance (live or otherwise), a summary of issues stemming from these works, a guide to the diverse writings available for deeper study of the subject, and a personal selection of instances of Wagner's influence in our everyday culture. This book is intended for use by people to penetrate the difficulties and impediments presumed to surround these great works, which are as entirely imaginary as the magic fire surrounding the Valkyries' rock.

## OPERA AND MUSIC DRAMA—WEIRD AND WEIRDER

Opera is a charged word, implying a phenomenon belonging to social no less than musical history. In Wagner's day as well as our own, the word conjured images of a bejeweled and affected audience with questionable musical acumen and a taste for glitz. Wagner fought against the typical opera audience of his day like a crusader, and many of the reforms that we take for granted in the modern theater were his innovations.

Ultimately, though, we must regard his mission in this respect as a failure, since opera as an experience has not changed all that much in the last hundred years, Wagnerian reforms notwithstanding. Composers of today can be heard bemoaning the fact that their genius must be laid out for people incapable of appreciating it, just as they griped a hundred, two hundred, and probably five thousand years ago. And yet they keep writing operas.

So did Wagner. For all his battles with opera companies in Dresden, Paris, Vienna, and Munich, did he ever seriously consider expressing himself in other musical forms? For all his carping, one must wonder why he didn't chuck the whole medium. He might have written oratorios, which are unstaged vocal concert pieces for orchestra, chorus, and soloists, usually of a sacred nature. Händel's *Messiah* is the definitive example. Berlioz, that influential giant of nineteenth-century music, did this. When his opera *The Damnation of Faust* proved unstageable, he simply dispensed with the operatic trimmings and announced that the work was an oratorio.

Wagner did actually write one oratorio, *Das Liebesmahl der Apostolen* ("The Love Feast of the Apostles"), which was performed with success in Dresden in 1845. It calls for a chorus of 1,200, assuring its impossibility in subsequent performance. He tended to regard this work as a study for *Parsifal*, and never sought to have it performed again.

The fact is that Wagner, for all his supposed superiority, had fallen in love with the magic of opera as a unique art form, just as people continue to do today. When King Ludwig of Bavaria came to Wagner's rescue, throwing open the State Treasury to finance his operas, the later works still proved all but unproduceable in existing theaters. Their correspondence at this stage is fascinating. Ludwig is always eager to see Wagner's works, and Wagner is always obsessed with production quality. Strangely, it never seems to have occurred to them to present unstaged concert versions of the new works. This is something we take for granted today, and it was not unknown at that time. Ludwig's detractors point out that the romantic and delusional king was at least as interested in the sets, costumes, lighting, and special effects as he was in the music, but the point is that Wagner himself was equally adamant about fully staged performances. This is a point that bears repeating, especially to the "pure music" types, for whom the "operatic" aspect of these works is something to be endured for the sake of the Philistines.

## OPERA: WHAT, EXACTLY, IS IT?
### A Brief Outline for the Nonexpert

At first glance, this must look like a remarkably dumb question. Everybody knows what opera is, don't they? Isn't that the place where overdressed people go to hear overweight performers sing overwrought music from long ago? As apt a description as that may be, it is not a good definition of the art form known as opera. Few people indeed could define the medium of opera, so don't feel bad if you aren't among them.

Opera is a form of drama (not music) in which the words are sung rather than spoken.

Stories are told in song in every culture around the world. Some traditions are quite elaborate, with series of songs, solos and choruses, dance, mime, and nonvocal musical instruments. But there is no beast quite like opera in the European sense. For the opera-free individual who is approaching Wagner from the point of view of intellectual or cultural history, it will be necessary to have an understanding of this unique medium and its special properties before proceeding. (The next chapter is directed at the casual operagoer who is now ready to tackle Wagner's operas.)

Opera was born in Florence in 1597, and its origins are important to those who wish to know Wagner, who was obsessed with defining and redefining the genre. A group of educated art lovers in Florence formed a *camerata*, a sort of chat group where they could explore their various artistic interests. One of their favorite topics was the theater of ancient Greece. They were aware that Greek drama had a musical element central to it. Indeed, musical instruments appeared to have been used by the Greeks to accompany the spoken words. The rhythm of poetic meter being inherent in the speeches, one could conjecture that these dramas were more sung than spoken.

What if a drama were to be produced in this way? What would be the result?

To this day, nobody knows what musical scale was used by the Greeks in Aeschylus's time, and even the sound of the spoken language is open to wide interpretation. We will probably never know. The genius of the *camerati* lay in their choice not to waste any time worrying about authentic Greek music, but to approach the *spirit* of Greek dramas within their own musical and linguistic idiom. A poet named Ottavio Rinuccini supplied the words to the mythological story of Daphne, written in Italian according to the form of Greek drama, with monologues, dialogues, and choruses. A notable composer of church and secular music named Jacopo Peri wrote musical accompaniment, very lightly scored so the words would remain clear and primary.

We can only conjecture the result from secondary evidence, since all traces of this first performance are lost, but we may be allowed to imagine these creators staring at each other in wonder at their hybrid creation. They did not even know what to call their piece, and they named it an *opera in musica*, a "work in music." The *libretto* (Italian for "little book," referring to the words) was published in 1600 and again in 1604, which testifies to the immediate popularity of the piece. In 1600, Peri wrote a second opera, *Eurydice* (another Greek myth), presented as part of the wedding festivities for Maria dei Medici and King Henri IV of France. A fellow member of the *camerata* named Caccini wrote another opera for the same event, which featured Caccini's daughter Francesca in a lead role. Caccini wrote some florid music to display Francesca's vocal abilities, scandalizing the "purists" who insisted on the importance of the text over flashy music, but the die was cast.

What is striking about this story is how all the elements that would define the world of opera were present right at the beginning. The debates about words versus music, the purist ideal versus innovation (or decadence), an odd connection to ancient Greek art, the acceptable level of vocal showmanship, and the clash of egos, all emanating from a bastard art form, have filled the opera world for the subsequent four hundred years. Another important feature of opera seems to have been present right from the start—the expense of producing it, evidenced by the royal patronage. All these issues would be central to Wagner's life work.

So what was all the fuss about? What was it about those first few operas that captured people's imaginations so thoroughly? There are several factors. The first is that opera can dramatize situations that can only be described by other media. In plays, two people who speak at the same time cannot be understood by the audience. In opera, there is the duet, which allows two characters to express themselves simultaneously. Opera can even portray two characters who are saying or thinking opposing feelings at the same time, thus giving us in the audience an overview of the entire situation. Nor does this paradigm need to stop at two people. The various expressions of several individuals can be combined at once, and even contrasted against large segments of their society represented by the various divisions of the chorus. Italian nineteenth-century composers were especially good at this.

Opera is also uniquely able to portray conflicting emotions within a single character. Where Shakespeare must use thousands of words to show us how Hamlet is divided against himself, an opera composer can contrast words, sung melody, and the various instruments in the orchestra to show the same situation in a matter of minutes. A famous example of this is found in *Iphigénie en Tauride* by Christoph Willibald von Gluck, a composer adored by Wagner. In that opera, the tenor languishes in prison, singing to himself words to the effect of "I'm fine—no, really! I'm fine!" while the nervous figures in the strings tell us he's actually a wreck. Wagner, it will be seen, exploits this feature of the operatic form to the fullest in characters like Isolde, Hans Sachs, and, especially, Mime, whose "public" personae are often in conflict with their inner selves.

The voice of the individual is the basic unit of operatic currency. It is, in the final analysis, what matters most. A certain type of voice has become standard in opera houses, a powerful, agile voice whose intensity has never been permitted in church music, popular songs, or concert singing. Why? The operatic framework of drama allows us to believe in the extremes of the human condition, and therefore the voice. Opera, while capable of the most nuanced subtleties, can tackle the really big questions of the human experience in ways that a three-minute song cannot. To express its full potential, the medium of opera relies on words, music, and visual presentation.

## THE ETERNAL PROBLEM OF WORDS AND MUSIC: AN OVERVIEW

The genius of the *camerati* that "invented" opera is apparent in, among other things, their choice to create a work in their own language rather than one in classical Greek, which could only be understood by scholars. All languages have found expression in song, but the Italian language has always had a special connection to music. For the dramatic expression necessary to the newly created form of opera, Italian was perfect. The clarity of the vowel sounds and the inherent consonant-vowel-consonant-vowel structure of the language made the words comprehensible through the music, while the built-in rhymes and metric pliability made Italian a delight for the librettist.

Which is all very well and good, except that only a tiny fraction of the world's population speaks Italian. How, then, could people beyond the Alps approach this medium? Here, roughly, were the choices:

1. Learn Italian.
2. Read a libretto during the performance, with the Italian on the left and your own language on the right, and try to follow.
3. Ignore the words entirely, and trust in the music and the stage action to convey the meaning.
4. Perform the work in translation, thereby losing the direct link between words and music but at least knowing what's going on.
5. Pretend you know Italian, and hope you are laughing or crying in all the right places.
6. Dispense with Italian opera altogether and create an opera in your own language.
7. Denounce all opera as a waste of time.

Interestingly, this problem has continued unabated to the present day, complicated by the fact that the works in question are now in German, French, Russian, Czech, English (in all its varieties), Spanish, and several other languages, as well as the old standby, Italian. It's a big problem.

In the early eighteenth century, Georg Friedrich Händel, a German, wrote his operas in Italian for audiences in London. The Londoners went wild, causing the more sober upstanding segments of xenophobic English society to deride them for spending money on effete foreign entertainment presented in a language they didn't understand. The language charge was not really fair, since we must remember that the audiences of that time sat in fully lit theaters and were in the habit of following the Italian with the help of their trusty libretti. In any case, the baroque style in opera, no less than in the visual arts, dictated that one should never say with one gesture what can be said in a hundred. Anyone who has sung in a community *Messiah* is familiar with Händel's habit of repeating a single line of verse dozens of times, and in his operas he was even more, well, baroque. Thus when the stage lovers sing, for example, *"Addio, amore mio! Addio per sempre!"* twenty-seven times in a row, moving toward opposite ends of the stage to the sad accompaniment of the oboe, even the most nonlinguistic dolt in the audience can comprehend that they are not commencing a love affair.

The "follow-along-with-a-libretto" approach to opera in a foreign language was successful for many years, until "guess who" came along and eliminated this option. Among Wagner's radical reforms in opera was a demand for a darkened auditorium, concentrating people's attention on the stage and eliminating the fabled distractions in the audience itself. Technological history was thus very obliging to Wagner in creating electricity just in time for him to put it to this handy use. People have insisted on darkened auditoriums ever since, but something was lost.

When Toscanini conducted the Italian premiere of *Tristan* at La Scala in 1897, he insisted on giving the opera in the original German and dimming the lights. The audience was annoyed. How on earth were they to know what was going on?

Of course, there has always been, and there still is, the option of performing opera in translation. The arguments in favor of opera in translation always sound entirely sensible on paper: the audience can understand the words, have a more direct experience of the piece, and not be made to feel uncultured or ignorant by the hateful polyglot elite. Government-funded opera has always leaned toward translations, since the bureaucrats can more easily convince themselves that they are providing "popular" entertainment for their public (which lets you know what they think of the imaginative capabilities of their publics). Comic opera, it is argued, is especially appropriate in translation, since the audience is meant to laugh along with the stage action. Only snobs and killjoys would insist on comic opera being performed in a language the audience does not understand.

Which is all perfectly logical, except that the medium in question is opera, where logic, per se, holds no place. Opera in translation is, at best, a compromise. The mystical union of word and music is lost. This may sound arcane, but it's true. This is most apparent to English-speakers when they hear very familiar popular songs, such as a Beatles' song, sung in translation. It just doesn't ring right.

Each of the solutions to the problem of opera in a foreign language outlined above has been tried at various times with varying degrees of success. In the early seventeenth century, Austrian composers began creating operas in German, but the public largely ignored them and continued to flock to Italian operas. The French were the first outside of Italy to get on their own somewhat shaky feet. The Germans lagged behind, much to the irritation of German composers. Wagner claimed that the standards of production in German opera houses in his youth were atrocious, and we have every reason to believe him. Either one heard German singers singing Italian words they didn't understand, and making a big mess out of them, or one heard horrid German translations that were inherently at odds with great Italian poetry. Think of the witty refrain to Leporello's Catalogue Aria in *Don Giovanni*, an opera that ruled the stage in Wagner's youth. The number of female conquests the Don has racked up in Spain alone is *"mill' e tre,"* a thousand and three. The German for this is *"drei und ein tausend."* Clearly, the German requires a different musical setting.

Beethoven inspired many of his time by composing a German opera, *Fidelio*. Carl Maria von Weber followed with *Der Freischütz*, and Germans saw that they could, after all, compose operas in their own language, as long as they didn't try to imitate Italian music directly. Wagner was very insistent that the words gave birth to the music. Not only did he insist on writing in German, but he felt he was the only person who could write the words of his own operas, since there was, in his mind, no separation between the word and the sound.

This is the basis of the whole issue known as "music drama." Wagner began to think of his works as being so far evolved beyond the conventional operas of his time, when he saw nobody caring about the union of words and music and everyone only interested in florid vocal fireworks, that he couldn't even bear to call his creations "operas." Subsequent generations have seen less of a difference between these two definitions. The field of world music has become so vast that "music dramas" look a whole lot like "operas" in the great scheme of things. Yet there was a reason this was once such an issue.

Wagner's librettos are not studied these days as masterpieces of German literature, as he assumed they would be, and few composers since Wagner have emulated him in writing their own words—unless we look to the wide realm of popular music. In any case, there is a remarkable unity of word and sound in Wagner's work. Even people who don't understand German can understand this fact. Nowadays, simultaneous translations in the theater have largely, though not entirely, replaced the option of singing in translation, and the audience has benefited. However, Wagner's words can be murky and obscure. Often they are employed more for their sound than their actual meaning. With Wagner, even more than other opera composers, it is imperative to know what is supposed to be happening on stage. Armed with a little knowledge, anyone can derive a profound experience from these works, no matter how "foreign" they appear at first.

# The Strange Life and Career
## of Richard Wagner

◆

The drama surrounding Richard Wagner begins, appropriately enough, before birth. We know he was born on May 22, 1813, in the city of Leipzig. His legal father was Friedrich Wagner, a police official, and his mother was Johanna, daughter of a baker. Wagner states in his autobiography that he was baptized two days after his birth, but records show that the event occurred three months later. In the interim, Johanna was visiting an actor-painter friend of her husband's named Ludwig Geyer. Geyer enjoyed intimate relations with the Wagner family, although the exact level of this intimacy is much debated. When Friedrich Wagner died in December 1813, Geyer took responsibility for the family. He and Johanna were married the following August.

No one would care which of these two buddies sired little Richard, except that Wagner himself wondered about it (all but one of Wagner's operatic heroes are fatherless in one form or other), and that Geyer is traditionally regarded as a Jewish name in Germany. This, and the fact that the Wagner/Geyers lived in the Jewish quarter of Leipzig, is enough for some biographers to explain Wagner's obsessive and hysterical anti-Semitism as a form of self-loathing. If only it were all that simple.

We know that Geyer was, in any case, the only father Richard ever knew, since Friedrich did not even leave a portrait of himself behind.

Geyer was a man of the theater, and he moved the family to the city of Dresden, capital of the kingdom of Saxony, in 1817. The children all began to take part in theater life in one form or another. Young Richard attended school, but his imagination was only fired in the theater.

There was less of a distinction between theater and opera in that time and place. For one thing, they were invariably in the same building, and "singers" on one night often were "actors" on another, since the pay was pretty miserable. Also, music figured prominently in dramas. The abundance of German "incidental music" of that period, of which Felix Mendelssohn's music for A Midsummer Night's Dream is the most famous example, demonstrates this. Richard began writing epic plays; he tells us he studied music merely so he could write his own incidental music. The quest for the "Total Work of Art" had begun.

Wagner downplays his musical training in his autobiography, claiming that he studied basics and counterpoint for a mere six months before he surpassed his teacher. Naturally he wanted people to think that his genius was born full-grown out of his own soul with no help from others, but it is still apparent that he had less formal training than any of the other men known as "great composers."

Wagner wrote several orchestral pieces, including a symphony that received warm applause in Leipzig in 1833, and an opera, Die Feen ("The Fairies"), which was never performed in his lifetime. On the strength of his compositions, he received a conducting job in Würzburg, and then at the theater of Magdeburg. The fragmentation of Germany into dozens of separate little countries was a disaster politically and economically, but it meant that every small town had a theater and a musical life of its own, as compared to united France, where everything tended to occur in the capital. Two interesting experiences awaited Wagner in Magdeburg.

## ROUGH DEBUTS AS COMPOSER AND HUSBAND

Wagner composed a second opera, *Das Liebesverbot* ("The Ban on Love"), based on Shakespeare's *Measure for Measure*, and he prepared the Magdeburg theater for its premiere. Everything went wrong. A grand total of three people (all Jewish, incidentally) bought tickets for the performance. Directly before the curtain was scheduled to rise, the husband of the prima donna thought this would be a good time to confront her with her extramarital activities, which included the opera's star tenor. An actual fistfight broke out backstage. The three people in the audience were informed that *Das Liebesverbot* was postponed. It never saw the light of day in Wagner's lifetime, either. Few people today have anything positive to say about this work, and while *Die Feen* contains some lovely music, *Das Liebesverbot* has been consigned to the music schools, if anywhere.

The second interesting development in Magdeburg was Minna Planer. She was a pretty, emotional actress a few years older than Wagner who traveled about with her "younger sister" (actually, her illegitimate daughter). Their relationship was shaky from the start. Minna always wanted a stable home life. From that point of view, she couldn't have made a worse choice of husband.

Wagner followed Minna to Königsberg, where she had an acting job and where Richard promised to find some work. (You won't find Königsberg on the map. It's now a gray, concrete-filled post-socialist question mark on the Baltic Sea named, for the moment, Kaliningrad.) They were married in November 1836, bickering right through the wedding ceremony. In the following months, Minna was underwhelmed by Richard's efforts to find work, as she would remain for the rest of her life, and promptly split town with a well-off businessman. After a few weeks of cat and mouse, they decided to reunite. Minna joined her husband in Riga, where he had actually landed a job as music director.

## RIGA

Riga was the capital of the Russian province of Livonia (present-day Latvia), with a sizable German colony dating from the Middle Ages that congregated around the theater. Minna withdrew from the stage to keep house while Wagner, it was said, worked wonders with the small orchestra. He also noted three features of the theater itself: the auditorium was steeply raked and very dimly lighted, and the orchestra pit was at a lower level. Wagner told people that if he ever participated in the design of an ideal theater, he would remember these qualities.

Although the theater kept him busy enough, the sleepy town gave Wagner plenty of time to work on *Rienzi*, a five-act grand opera in the style of the very popular French operas of the time, notably by the German-Jewish composer Giacomo Meyerbeer. Based on an English novel, *Rienzi* told the story of the fourteenth-century Roman commoner who united the people against corrupt nobles and briefly resurrected the republic before being assassinated. Wagner conceived a ripping spectacle, including a ballet, climaxing in a big onstage fire. Riga, obviously, was no place to stage *Rienzi*.

## ACROSS EUROPE

Two years in Riga were enough for the Wagners, and they concluded it was time to play the "big game," which could only mean Paris. Friends advised them that their application for a passport would be advertised, by law, in the papers, bringing an avalanche of debt collectors who would block their exit. Why not sneak over the border to Prussia, make a fortune in Paris, and pay off all their debts afterward? Wagner loved the idea, and he, Minna, and their big Newfoundland dog Robber made for the border.

What followed was one of the most famous episodes of their frantic lives. After hiding out in a smugglers' den of Polish Jews, the three ran across the wide ditch marking the border, evading the Cossack patrols whose orders were to shoot to kill, even after fugitives had crossed over. The dog, luckily, remained silent through the adventure. They were met on the other side by a friend in a light carriage, and took back roads to the coast to avoid creditors in Königsberg. The carriage turned over on one of these roads, luckily throwing Wagner into a heap of manure but injuring Minna, who may have been made infertile by the accident. Finally, they made their way to the Baltic port of Pillau, where a small merchant ship, the *Thetis*, was waiting to depart for London.

The presence of Robber made a sea voyage, rather than overland journey, the sole option. The *Thetis* took almost a month to make the trip, fighting storms the whole way. Wagner claimed much of the music for *The Flying Dutchman* was inspired by this harrowing journey, including echoes of the sailors' cries off the fjord cliffs of Norway. Scholars have pointed out that Wagner may have been self-dramatizing a bit, but the trip clearly made a large impression on him. He never boarded another sailing ship in his life. A few years later, the *Thetis* sank with all hands.

After a week in the awesome metropolis of London, where linguistic limitations hampered the Wagners' sightseeing, they boarded a steamer for the French side of the channel. Wagner visited Meyerbeer at the seaside resort of Boulogne, received letters of introduction, and moved on to modest quarters in Paris.

## PARIS, ACT ONE

Two things are clear about Wagner's early years in Paris: he was enormously impressed by the level of musical production and performance there, and he was equally embittered by his own tepid reception. Beyond this, it is very difficult to make sense out of these murky years. In his autobiography Wagner lies repeatedly about this period, since he wanted to minimize the effect any non-German music had on him. Meyerbeer was all the rage at the great Paris Opéra, and there is every indication that he went out of his way to help the young Wagner, to whom the truth was always incidental. Wagner believed that the entire musical establishment of Paris, which he perceived as Jewish, was out to get him, and he ended up writing about them in paragraphs that rank among the most disgraceful words ever penned by an artist. To make some money while in Paris, Wagner wrote several articles for German music journals, which are actually quite lucid and interesting. He also did musical hackwork. This involved making solo-instrument reductions of popular operatic melodies, and Wagner resented working on such "trash" as Donizetti. The work was foisted upon him by the music publisher Maurice Schlesinger, who was Jewish and "too powerful to offend." This, at least, is how he chose to remember it twenty years later. The truth seems to be that Wagner begged Schlesinger for the work.

In any case, Wagner did not have an easy time of it in Paris, though he managed to write *The Flying Dutchman* at this time. *Das Liebesverbot* was accepted for production at the Théâtre de la Renaissance, which promptly went bankrupt before they were able to perform it (Wagner was convinced Meyerbeer knew this would happen). Minna did wonders at home with no money. Robber, the dog who escaped from Riga with them, ran away, evading Wagner months later when their paths crossed. The one positive relationship of this time was with Samuel Lehrs, a fellow "Bohemian" and good friend to Wagner, who always remembered him with great warmth. Lehrs, interestingly, was Jewish.

Meanwhile, Wagner's huge Meyerbeerian grand opera *Rienzi* was accepted for production in Dresden. *Dutchman* was shortly after accepted by Berlin, largely through the influence of Meyerbeer. Wagner realized his future lay in Germany, and he and Minna took the five-day stagecoach ride to Dresden.

## DRESDEN

*Rienzi*, despite its insane length of nearly six hours, was a huge hit in Dresden. Several performances were given, as was the custom, each a greater success than the one before. When the position of Royal Kapellmeister became vacant, Wagner was enthusiastically named to it. This involved directorship of all music in the theater, palace, and church, and Dresdeners were proud of the level of culture in their elegant, Italianate city.

Minna was thrilled to have an employed husband at last, and if Wagner bucked against the idea of wearing servant's livery (as was expected of salaried musicians at that time), she loved her new status as the Frau Kapellmeisterin of royal Dresden. Now, if only Richard would do his job, not upset everybody, and write more operas people could enjoy . . .        .

Not likely. Wagner began to feel underappreciated perhaps ten minutes into his new job, a feeling he would retain to the end of his life even after he became the most celebrated musician in the world. But Dresden gave him some reason for dissatisfaction. Theater life was in disarray everywhere in those years, having lost the old aristocratic patronage and not yet having achieved modern systematization. *Dutchman* was produced in 1843, since Berlin had been dithering with it and Dresden wanted another hit from its almost-native son.

*Dutchman* received a decent if not fanatical response, being an entirely different creature from the conventional *Rienzi*. *Tannhäuser* appeared in 1845. This work left the audience even more bewildered, being farther even than *Dutchman* from typical opera of the time. Though Wagner was happy with his excellent lead singers, the production values of the theater left him dissatisfied. With his typical monomaniacal energy, Wagner submitted a thorough plan for the restructuring of the Saxon state theater system. It called for an enlarged orchestra, more rehearsal time, the establishment of music schools and scene shops, and much more. The motive behind this, of course, was to ensure better performances of the works of Richard Wagner, and all the new system needed was huge funding from the State Treasury. Self-serving as it all was, almost everything in Wagner's plan was absolutely right and logical. Pensions, minimum wages, and sick leave for employees, from prima donnas to janitors, were included as necessary improvements. The plan was trashed, and many at court labeled Wagner an ungrateful malcontent. The king of Saxony personally rejected the idea of closing the theater for two or three nights a week (as Wagner had suggested, to have more rehearsal time and better performances) for the sensible reason that there was absolutely nothing else to do in Dresden if the theater wasn't open.

Any chance for a rapprochement between Wagner and the government was gone by 1848. Far from letting himself become more docile and writing more operas people liked, as Frau Wagner hoped, Wagner was beginning to conceive of an opera on a whole different level from anything ever seen. In 1848 he wrote a *Sketch of the Nibelung Myth as Basis for a Drama,* in which he outlined his idea for a sort of festival where the people (all of them) would celebrate their heritage and art, as he imagined was done in ancient Athens. He also saw how this could be done in a musical sense, and produced the outline of *Siegfrieds Tod,* which would become *Götterdämmerung,* and, eventually, the massive, four-part epic *Ring of the Nibelung.* To create this new spectacle, he proposed to invent a new relationship between words, music, and staging, but it would require a new sort of effort on the part of the audience as well. The world, rather than just the theater of Dresden, would have to change. Wagner had become a revolutionary.

## 1848

It's hard to fathom the degree of Wagner's involvement with the revolutionary movement of the late 1840s, since he tried like hell to downplay it in later years when he depended on royal patronage. We know he became friends with the famous Russian anarchist Mikhail Bakunin, who arrived in Dresden at this time, and Wagner was busy writing revolutionary pamphlets through this period. His political pronouncements at this point reflect the confused times as well as his confused mind. At one point, he advocated overthrowing the Saxon monarchy and establishing a republic—with the king of Saxony as its first president! No writer of comic operettas could have topped this solution.

Talk turned to action all over Europe in 1848. The French monarchy was overthrown for, presumably, the last time, and there were revolutions in virtually every country on the continent. The German states proposed a united constitution, which the Saxon government appeared to approve. Dresdeners watched events with cautious optimism, and quietly armed themselves, a process in which Wagner was involved. The heady times were too much for him to ignore, and he began preaching revolution more blatantly in pamphlets and speeches. He called loudly for utter destruction of the old to make way for the new.

The "old," inconveniently, did not wish to be swept aside so easily, and reaction set in across Europe. The revolution broke out in Dresden after Easter 1849, just as it was dying out around the rest of the continent. The armed citizens rose up and appeared to sweep the government away. Wagner held a legal position in the Communal Guard, which was intended to keep order in such an event. He always maintained he had only done his Guard job according to the law, but it was clear that he was caught up in the excitement. He was seen shouting encouragement from the bell towers to the marauding revolutionaries below. Prussian troops arrived early in May, and the revolt was quelled. Many revolutionaries, real or suspected, were shot on the spot. An order was issued for Wagner's arrest. He escaped from Saxony and showed up in nearby Weimar, where Franz Liszt was installed as a music director. It is worth digressing a bit at this point to take a look at the extraordinary man Wagner turned to at this point in his life.

## FRANZ LISZT

Liszt was born in 1811 in the village of Raiding, which was part of Austria at the time, later to become part of Hungary. (Central Europe is filled with towns whose countries shift borders under them, as recent history continues to show.) His father, who managed an estate for the fabulously wealthy Eszterhazy family, and his mother were of German and Austrian descent and spoke only German. Liszt did not recreate himself as a Hungarian until years later. The child Franz was endowed with a peerless gift for piano playing. After years of hard work, the local Eszterhazys gave the young prodigy some chances to show his abilities and sent him to their even richer relatives in Vienna. The Vienna Eszterhazys decided Franz was too great even for their city, and promptly sent him with his father off to Paris to conquer the musical world.

In Paris he gave virtuoso concerts, at which he began to affect colorful Hungarian details of costume. Liszt was learning that there was more to being a famous musician than talent, and being Hungarian in no way hurt his audience appeal. A celebrity was born. Although only fourteen, he loved the attention. As he matured, attention became adulation, and Liszt found himself chased by a wide variety of women. Half the time he returned their ardor, the rest of the time he spoke of becoming a priest. Then he met Marie d'Agoult, who was a story in herself.

She was born in 1805 into the old French aristocracy, even though her maternal grandfather was of the apparently Jewish Frankfurt banking family of Bethmann (this interesting fact is missing from many biographies of Wagner, Liszt, and even Cosima). Married off to the decrepit Count d'Agoult in 1828 in an impossibly chic ceremony attended by the king and queen of France, Marie soon tired of married life and sought her thrills in Paris nightlife. When she met the irresistible Liszt in 1833, sparks flew. He was always awed by the nobility, and Marie was beautiful to boot. They were living together within a few months, and moved out of Paris. For years they wandered all over France, Switzerland, Italy, and Germany, hobnobbing with various personalities of the time. Quite incidentally, Marie bore three children, the middle of whom, Cosima, was born at Lake Como in 1837.

Liszt needed money for this life style, and began giving concerts all over Europe. He basically invented the piano recital as we know it, but his concerts were much more than the genteel evenings we associate with that form of entertainment. Liszt's audiences cheered and screamed. Fatherhood had done nothing to diminish his attractiveness to women, and it was fashionable for them to pass out when he walked onstage. Liszt may have been the world's first great pop star. Marie and the children were left at home, wherever home happened to be, during these tours, and the tours grew longer and longer.

By 1842, the two acknowledged that their liaison was finished, and Marie returned to Paris with the children. It didn't take long for the separation to become bitter, and the hapless children became emotional footballs for their two self-consumed, larger-than-life parents. Liszt, who held all parental rights by French law of that time, sent his antique country mother to Paris to keep house for the children, away from Marie. Meanwhile, he gave concerts, traveling by coach to every two-mule town in Europe. By 1847, he was worn out, and wanted to devote more time to composing. He decided that a few concerts in the Ukraine would be his last. There, he met the woman who would dominate the rest of his life.

The two towering passions in the life of Princess Carolyne von Sayn-Wittgenstein are best illustrated by the story that she first bedded Liszt under a ten-foot-high crucifix. Liszt was still trying to balance his Catholic mysticism with his active libido. They were made for each other. The princess also owned a hefty chunk of the Ukraine. The only minor inconvenience was her husband, an advisor to the czar. Certain a divorce was around the corner, she persuaded Liszt to take a full-time position as a sort of music director at the small but refined court of Weimar, in Germany, where he was "guesting" for a few months every year. The princess met up with him in Weimar to await the divorce papers. The papers never came.

On February 26, 1849, Liszt successfully produced *Tannhäuser* at Weimar, despite the pitifully small orchestra. Wagner was extremely grateful for this token of favor from one of the world's most famous musicians; although they had met in Paris years before, this production sealed their friendship. Liszt wrote Wagner, expressing his admiration for the music and telling Wagner to count on him if he needed any favors in the future.

## A MEETING IN WEIMAR

Wagner needed plenty of favors in 1849. As soon as he showed up in Weimar, in flight from the arrest warrant in Dresden, he turned to Liszt. "Admit it," said the pianist. "You've done something very foolish." Wagner asked for money to escape to Switzerland, which Liszt gave him even though he wasn't very flush at the moment. The czar had declared Princess Carolyne AWOL and confiscated her lands, including her 30,000 or so serfs. Wagner called on the princess before leaving Weimar: they were unimpressed with each other, remaining so for the rest of their lives. Four days later, Wagner was in Switzerland, banished from Germany for the next eleven years.

## FUGITIVE PATHS

Liszt kept urging Wagner to go to Paris, and Minna, who joined him in Switzerland in September, supported this idea. Wagner duly went there in January 1850, but once again got nowhere. Meyerbeer still reigned supreme in the French capital. Wagner was miserable and unable to work on music. Instead, he got involved in a complicated love affair with a married lady in Bordeaux whose potty English mother was willing to support Wagner until the *scandale* erupted in public. After many tawdry scenes worthy of the Italian operas he claimed to dislike, Wagner rejoined Minna in Zurich in July. He was broke, as usual, and had no prospects. Germany and France were both closed to him. He reacted to his situation by venting bitterness in a pamphlet, "Judaism in Music," which he finished in August. The world had failed him, and he blamed the Jews.

It would strike a sane person as an irrational leap from resenting Meyerbeer's success to writing "Judaism in Music," but Wagner was not, conventionally speaking, sane. The logical processes of cause and effect were entirely absent in his thinking. Wagner was perfectly capable of tasting a rotten apple, or even hearing about one, and developing a creed around the notion that apples, all being rotten, are the cause of the world's problems. Furthermore, he could add without compunction, no one could claim any appreciation for the score of, say, *Tristan und Isolde* until they rid their lives of the pernicious influence of apples. The reader is advised to sample some of Wagner's theoretical writings before rejecting the previous sentences as frivolous.

Meanwhile, he had more success sorting out his thoughts in other essays. In January 1851 he published *Opera and Drama*, in which he laid out his ideas of a new direction for "music drama," and was then able to complete the outline for the four-part *Ring of the Nibelung*. He wrote *A Communication to My Friends*, which was a combination of autobiography, introduction to his existing operas, and statement of purpose for future works. After a grueling "water cure" at a Swiss spa, he returned to Zurich, where Minna once again joined him. Wagner organized a series of concerts, mainly because he had written much music he hadn't yet heard played by an orchestra. (He was already exiled from Germany when Liszt gave the only moderately successful premiere of *Lohengrin* at Weimar in 1850.)

These "cures" we always read about in the nineteenth century, and the "spas" everyone is always running off to, were the era's combination of resort, rehab, and fashion show. Here they addressed the health issues unique to their time, since nobody of the artistic or upper classes ever seemed to have a normal disease. They suffered from "nervous collapse," "total exhaustion," "the vapours," and the scariest malaise of the times, "brain fever." It was very fashionable to be in a moribund state. Chopin was said to be dying his whole life. Wagner was a man of his times in this respect. When a letter of his ends by saying, "Am near death—don't expect to survive," it was the equivalent of today's "Best regards." Biographers have often missed these conventions of the 1850s, and assure us that Wagner's life was sheer hell throughout this time. Apparently, it never got so bad that he considered getting a job.

In Zurich Wagner met Otto Wesendonck, a prosperous merchant who helped him out financially. Wagner almost immediately ran up debts beyond even Wesendonck's means, and further complicated the matter by becoming infatuated with Frau Mathilde Wesendonck. (Wagner was never interested in virgins, only in women who "belonged" to other men. Even Minna only got a proposal out of Wagner when she started receiving attentions from other suitors. Psychologists explain this as a by-product of an Oedipal complex. Later, Wagner was tasteless enough to speak of this quirk of his to Cosima.) Wagner relieved the tension by traveling to Italy (Wesendonck paid), where he later claimed that the sight of the sea off La Spezia inspired the opening measures of *Das Rheingold*, the first part of the *Ring*. He began composing without the slightest possibility of getting the *Ring* performed anywhere. He also became engrossed in philosophy. Schopenhauer's book *The World as Will and Idea*, with its stunning opening line "The world is my idea," blew Wagner away. It has traditionally been maintained that Wagner's world outlook changed as a result of this book, but recent scholarship prefers to see Schopenhauer as coincidentally giving voice to nebulous ideas Wagner already had. In any case, the "vision" off La Spezia sounds suspiciously like certain passages in Schopenhauer.

Wagner went to London to conduct a series of concerts, including extracts from his own operas, which bombed with the critics. (He almost always had more success with general audiences than with critics and, to a certain extent, still does.) He met Queen Victoria, who, like any other good German of the time, was addicted to Italian opera. She declared herself intrigued by Wagner's music, and asked if there were any possibility of translating his operas into Italian so they could be performed in London! It may have been the only time in his life when Wagner was speechless.

## LOVE MUSIC

The weight of the *Ring* was becoming unbearable, and Wagner's mind was busy elsewhere. Sometime in 1854 he became intrigued with the medieval legend of Tristan and Isolde. This seemed like a good idea to Minna, since a love-triangle opera would at least be performable and might produce some income. Wagner put aside *Siegfried*, the third part of the *Ring*, and devoted himself to composing *Tristan und Isolde*. As inspiration for this love story, he and Mathilde Wesendonck exchanged passionate letters and carried on an affair whose exact nature remains a mystery. We don't even know if they ever actually had sex. We do know that they were in love with the drama of a torrid *affaire*. Wagner was also steeping himself in Buddhist literature at this time. Clearly, *Tristan* would not be the simple, performable work for which Minna hoped in vain.

Wesendonck built a stately villa outside of Zurich with a guest house on the grounds, which the Wagners moved into. (What *was* Otto thinking?) Wagner's mind was alive in this time, sketching the outline for *Parsifal* while composing *Tristan*. Visitors came to the cozy, if irregular, love nest, perhaps none more interesting than those who arrived in September 1857.

Back in Weimar, Liszt was taking on music students. The most brilliant was a nervous young minor nobleman from nearby Berlin named Hans von Bülow, whose piano playing rivaled Liszt's and who showed great promise in the then-emerging art of conducting. Liszt transferred his three children from glittering Paris to live with Bülow's shrew-mother in dreary Berlin at the instigation of Princess Carolyne, who never missed a chance to shaft Marie d'Agoult. Young Hans was taken by Cosima's grace, aristocratic bearing, and striking, if not beautiful, looks (she inherited her father's large nose). Not seeing any other future, Cosima accepted the proposal from the twitchy Hans. For their honeymoon, they went to stay with, of all people, the Wagners and Wesendoncks. Cosima had met Wagner in Paris years before, but now she was overwhelmed beyond speech. While Bülow picked through the orchestral sketches of *Siegfried* at the piano (a feat Wagner himself could not manage), Cosima realized what a mistake she had made by marrying Bülow. She thought of suicide.

When the Bülows left, there was still Mathilde, but Minna was not having any fun. She taught the pet parrot to say "Wagner is a bad husband," and began to confront Frau Wesendonck. It didn't help when Wagner set some of Mathilde's love poetry to beautiful music in what would be known as the *Wesendonck Lieder*. Minna and Otto finally rebelled, and the little love nest was finished. Minna retired to a spa cure, while Wagner was packed off to that ultimate destination of failed lovers, Venice. Again, Wesendonck paid the bills. Codependency had not yet been identified as an illness.

Wagner rented a floor of the otherwise empty Palazzo Giustinian on the Grand Canal, and kept a highly dramatic journal (near death every day) for Mathilde's benefit. In fact, it was the perfect mood and setting to work on the fatally erotic *Tristan*, which was completed in March 1859. Mathilde proved more useful to him as a distant muse than as a next-door neighbor. Venice at that time was ruled by Austria, whose reactionary officials were less than thrilled with the presence of the fugitive revolutionary. Fortunately, the Venetian chief of police was a music lover named Crespi, who fudged reports to Vienna. But Venice was becoming too small for Wagner. He returned to Switzerland without a prospect in the world. The Wesendoncks welcomed him back and helped him out financially, but did not invite him to live with them. It was time to try Paris again.

Wagner did periodically write to Dresden, hoping for amnesty, saying how badly he wanted to return and promising never again to interfere in politics. The authorities wanted him to admit his revolutionary error and return to face trial, which, they hinted, was a formality and at which he would no doubt be acquitted. Wagner refused to do this. He never saw that he had done anything wrong. Minna urged him to comply, but he never did. Wagner, who is reputed to have had no ethics whatsoever, should instead be credited with an extremely selective and randomly evoked sense of ethics.

## DISASTER IN PARIS

The next Paris episode may be the most oft-told chapter in Wagner's life. The net result was the spectacularly disastrous production of *Tannhäuser* at the Opéra, which left Wagner more bitter than ever—ten years later he publicly called for the destruction of the city after it fell to German troops in 1871. What is less emphasized is how many admirers his several concerts won him. Charles Baudelaire, Catulle Mendès, Camille Saint-Saëns, Charles Gounod, and many other prominent artists and writers became Wagnerians at this time. His failure at the Opéra, where *Tannhäuser* was booed off the stage on three separate nights in a demonstration rooted in complicated causes, only confirmed their adoration for Wagner as a force against the establishment. Also at this time, Wagner's banishment from Germany was finally lifted. He made some excursions to Rhineland towns, noting that he felt "absolutely nothing" in setting foot on his native soil again. Yet there was no point in remaining in Paris, which he left once and for all in January 1862.

## ADRIFT

Minna was thoroughly sick of Wagner. After Paris, there were a few more cures, then the Wagners finally decided to live apart. Minna was set up in a modest apartment in Dresden, which was where she had always wanted to be anyway. Wagner criss-crossed Germany several times, trying to scare up new friends and benefactors, but even the most ardent fans had been warned against making any definite financial commitments to this human fortune-vacuum. He conducted lucrative concerts in Russia, spent the money, and set sights on Vienna.

In Vienna, Wagner finally heard *Lohengrin* for the first time. A successful production of *Dutchman* followed, and there was every reason to believe *Tristan* would be produced there. With his usual overoptimism, Wagner rented an expensive apartment and furnished it sumptuously. He wanted a comfortable home to work on his next opera, *Die Meistersinger von Nürnberg*. This new project, a comic opera full of easy melody, had been well received by friends who heard readings of the libretto. It would surely take Germany by storm. Wagner thought prosperity was right around the corner. It wasn't. Rehearsals for *Tristan* were falling apart. The tenor couldn't remember any of the role from one day to the next, and finally lost his voice completely. People said Wagner had "really gone too far this time," and that *Tristan*, whatever its musical merits, was absolutely unperformable. It was finally canceled by the Vienna company in

March 1864. Wagner was worse than broke. He had borrowed heavily against projected income from *Tristan* and even *Meistersinger,* which wasn't yet composed. Austrian law severely penalized late debt payments, and Wagner had to borrow at high interest to avoid prison. His attorney (Liszt's uncle, incidentally) told him bluntly to split town — fast. This he did on March 23.

In Switzerland again, no one was willing or able to put him up. He thought of marrying rich, and asked his sister Luise in Dresden to sound out Minna about a divorce. To her credit, Luise refused, and advised her errant brother to apply for a vacant job in Darmstadt. Instead, Wagner went to Stuttgart, for lack of anyplace else to go, and checked into a modest hotel. Even this was beyond his present means, but luckily there were some well-off music lovers in town who opened their dining room to him. On Monday, May 2, while he was at their house eating, he was handed a card and was told that the "Aulic Secretary of His Majesty the King of Bavaria" desired a word with him. Suspecting some debt collector of a cheap trick, Wagner sent word that he was not there. Back at his hotel the next morning, he was handed a bundle of "urgent" letters from Vienna (more bills), and told that Minister Pfistermeister of Munich was waiting to see him. Resigned, he agreed to see this man he still assumed to be a creative debt collector.

## TURNABOUT

No librettist, least of all Wagner, could have invented what ensued. The king had ordered Pfistermeister, who was his cabinet secretary (a uniquely Bavarian office, being both a personal royal advisor and a state minister), to track down Richard Wagner personally. Wagner was informed that the young king was a fervent admirer of his, and proposed to settle his debts, provide for his welfare, and give him anything he needed to accomplish his work. Pfistermeister invited Wagner to go with him to Munich and meet his number one fan. Wagner wrote a passionate letter of thanks to the king and hopped on the next train. Pfistermeister bought the tickets.

## LUDWIG AND MUNICH

King Ludwig II had assumed the throne of Bavaria in February. He was only eighteen years old at the time, devilishly good-looking, and a bit eccentric. Most short bios of Ludwig say he was already exhibiting signs of the insanity that would prove his downfall, but this is only benefit of hindsight. Insane, perhaps—but compared to which other European monarchs of the time? Ludwig's dynasty, the Wittelsbachs, had ruled Bavaria for eight hundred years, and a special bond was considered to exist between the family and the Bavarian people. Nor was Ludwig particularly strange by dynastic standards. His poor brother Otto had been committed to a locked cell at a young age. His aunt was functional but insisted that she had once swallowed a glass piano. His cousin Elizabeth, who became empress of Austria, was intelligent but preferred the company of horses and gymnastic equipment to people. And the infatuation of his grandfather, Ludwig I, with the hip-swinging adventuress Lola Montez finally cost him his throne.

Ludwig grew up in the castle of Hohenschwangau, whose walls were painted with medieval legends of Lohengrin. He developed a passion for Wagner's works before he ever heard one. When he finally attended a performance of *Lohengrin* in Munich at the age of fifteen, he knew his life mission was to cultivate its genius creator. Ludwig was homosexual, but in 1865 he was exceptionally naive even by the standards of the time. Once, he was moved to tears by the sight of a muscular, shirtless woodcutter he saw in the mountains. He confessed he had absolutely no idea why the sight upset him so. Loneliness remained the great leitmotiv of his life.

With his typical inability to restrain himself, Wagner moved into an ostentatious mansion in the best part of Munich. He immediately tricked out the interiors in a manner that made his Vienna excesses seem monastic by comparison. Expensive drapes, upholstery, and hangings of all kinds found their way into his house, causing comment from visitors who were quite accustomed to the heavy tastes of the times. Pink satin was everywhere, and one small room boasted a ceiling covered in rosettes of that same material. One of Wagner's many quirks was an addiction to fripperies of this kind, also including heavy French perfumes, which were at odds with the heroic virtues of his operas, but which he felt he needed around him to work. Tongues wagged.

Everybody presumes that artists are weird, and Wagner might have become popular in Munich if he had stopped at feminine frills. But that was only the start. He told King Ludwig he needed a new theater built in which his operas could be properly performed, and his old friend from revolutionary days in Dresden, the architect Gottfried Semper, was summoned to design a Festival House whose plan amounted to a reconfiguration of the city of Munich. A new school had to be established, where singers would be taught new techniques (to sing Wagner, of course). To head all these musical endeavors while Wagner composed new masterpieces in pink satin peace and quiet, there was no other choice than Hans von Bülow.

Getting Bülow to Munich was the easiest part, since he had made nothing but enemies in his native Berlin. Bülow came and was named "Performer to the King," with a mandate to develop the royal musical knowledge. Cosima came with him. Life was about to get very interesting in Munich.

## INTRIGUES IN MUNICH

Wagner and Cosima moved toward their fateful union by degrees. On November 28, 1863, they rode in a carriage together in Berlin while Hans rehearsed for a concert. They came to some sort of an agreement then and there. The problem was that Wagner, not Cosima, needed Bülow. In June 1864, when Wagner was installed as the debt-free composer to the king of Bavaria in a country villa, Cosima joined him with her two daughters and they consummated their relationship. Bülow showed up a week later and probably sensed something, since he timed one of his famous nervous fits for the occasion. Subsequently, there were furtive visits and letters from all three to Liszt, whose role in the imbroglio becomes almost comic in retrospect.

Liszt was living in Rome with Princess Carolyne, who was raising hell trying to squeeze an anullment of her marriage out of the pope. Finally, it appeared to be approved, and she and Liszt set a marriage date. On the eve of that date, a papal emissary called on the princess to inform her that, for reasons never revealed to history, the anullment was denied. One can almost hear Liszt sighing in relief. Just to set matters in stone, he suddenly took holy orders, becoming an abbé and looking terribly chic in his clerical collar. Now this curious man, who managed to escape marriage his entire life, descended on his daughter, her husband, and her lover, preaching the sanctity of wedlock. This caused a rift with Cosima and Wagner that would take many years to heal. In the meantime, he proclaimed sympathy for Bülow—at least publicly. When a friend of Cosima's rebuked Liszt for censuring his daughter, he confided, "I agree with you, but I cannot say so in my position."

Meanwhile, there was music to make . . .

Wagner insisted on bypassing regular channels at the Munich Opera—only Bülow could rehearse and conduct *Tristan*. No doubt he was right from a purely musical point of view, but Wagner now held an inherently political position as the king's favorite, and the combined tactlessness of Wagner and Bülow could have offended a room full of marble statues. In one famous episode, the Munich theater manager complained that the enlarged orchestra would mean losing valuable seats in the auditorium, to which Bülow responded, "What does it matter if the stalls seat a couple of dozen *Schweinehunde* more or less?" The remark was overheard and circulated, and the press went bonkers. Bülow, everyone felt, had to go. One paper carried a headline "Bülow is still here!" for four days in a row, the size of the type increasing each day. Wagner had to issue a public statement advising commitment to art over personalities. The fact that Wagner was playing the diplomat shows the desperation of the situation.

A week before this, on April 10, the day of the first orchestral rehearsal of *Tristan*, Cosima gave birth to her third daughter, named Isolde. The child was widely rumored to be Wagner's, which, in fact, she was.

## TRIUMPHS AND TRAUMAS

Cosima maintained the veneer of a marriage while pretending to be merely Wagner's assistant. One is tempted to ask, in the manner of congressional inquiries, how much Bülow knew and when he knew it. We'll never know for sure. Many of the letters that passed between Wagner and Cosima in this period were later destroyed by their daughter Eva for twisted reasons of her own. Judging from the timing of various visits among the parties concerned, including Liszt, and the dates of Bülow's various fits, it would appear that he knew plenty the whole time. The more he knew, the worse his role in this masquerade became. And yet a miracle was achieved: *Tristan* was produced against all odds. After all, history records many legitimate fathers, but only one musician who gave life to *Tristan*.

May 15, the day appointed for the premiere of *Tristan*, was a mess. Malvina Schnorr, the Isolde, caught a chill in her bath and lost her voice. The performance was postponed, causing many to speculate that the music really was unsingable after all. Friends and fans who had converged on Munich from all over Europe now had to return home un-*Tristan*ed. Then some creditors from a half-forgotten Paris debt of 1860 descended on Wagner's mansion demanding full payment. They held all the legal papers necessary to impound Wagner's furniture if the money were not readily handed over. Wagner had an attack, but Cosima calmly wrote the king, and the State Treasury was ordered to make the funds available. She went down to the Treasury building with one friend and two small daughters in tow, only to be told, in an effort to humiliate her publicly, that the large amount of money was only available in small change. Undaunted, Cosima hailed a cab and personally heaved sacks of silver coins into it until the impressed Treasury officials sheepishly offered help. Say what you want about Cosima; she was what a later generation would call a "tough cookie."

The curtain finally rose on *Tristan* the night of June 10, 1865, before a glittering audience. King Ludwig appeared in civilian clothes, hardly acknowledging his cheering subjects. Ludwig Schnorr von Carolsfeld, the tenor, and his wife Malvina surpassed all expectation.

Bülow was brilliant. The night was a triumph. The impossible had happened. Later, Wagner commented that future generations would be impressed by an era in which such a work was possible. The following few performances were even more successful—perfect, in Wagner's estimation.

Then things unraveled quickly. Schnorr went to Dresden after the last performance, and died of one of his era's undefinable illnesses (brain fever) on June 21. No one could believe the big, healthy twenty-nine-year-old was dead. His last word was "Tristan!" Everyone assumed the role had killed him.

That was only the start. A certain von der Pfordten, an old-line bureaucrat who hated Wagner from Dresden days, became prime minister of Bavaria. Pfistermeister also became a bitter enemy. Wagner could not resist advising Ludwig to dismiss Pfo and Pfi, as he called them. Ludwig humored Wagner but did nothing. Other factions angled around Wagner, playing him like a card. He was out of his league, but was constitutionally incapable of remaining aloof. In November, he and Cosima wrote an "anonymous" letter to a newspaper calling for the dismissal of the two cabinet ministers. It was a big mistake. Pfordten went to the king, telling him the real state of things. The people would sweep Ludwig from the throne, as they had done to his grandfather, if the composer were not sent out of the country immediately. Ludwig, for the first time in his reign, took serious counsel with his ministers and everybody else. Wagner had offended everyone by appearing to have total control over the king. Leaders of the church, business and industry, academics, bureaucrats, the queen mother, and virtually all factions were united, perhaps for the first time in the country's history, in their verdict: Wagner must go. Even the butchers and bakers who supplied the court signed a petition to this effect. Wagner, as always, had done a thorough job of it.

On the evening of December 6, 1865, Ludwig's second secretary was sent to Wagner's mansion to tell him that he had to leave the country. Wagner lost his head, heaping abuse in language so plain the secretary had to tell him to get hold of himself, since he was a royal representative on official business. The next morning, Ludwig

wrote him a note confirming this message, saying it was only tempo-
rary and expressing his undying devotion in the usual purple phrases.
Wagner spent two days writing frantic notes to the king, but finally
decided to heel and not jeopardize his cushy annual salary. He took
the 5 a.m. train to Switzerland on December 10.

## UNOFFICIAL EXILE, OR, THANK GOD
## FOR SWITZERLAND

In the calm of the mountains, Wagner reflected that things weren't
really so bad after all. He was never at his best in cities, where there
were so very many people to annoy. He had *Meistersinger* to complete, which Munich was still waiting to produce. While in the south
of France, on the lookout for a possible new residence, Wagner
received a telegram that Minna had died. He calmly wired back to a
friend in Dresden, instructing him to make arrangements for the
funeral.

Wagner found a house he liked on the shores of Lake Lucerne in
Switzerland, which he named Tribschen and where he determined
to settle "for good." King Ludwig paid the rent, and Wagner wrote to
*both* Bülows to join him there. Hans was sent off to concertize, while
Cosima and her three daughters moved in on May 12. Wagner
worked on completing *Meistersinger*.

Bavarian life did not stop when Wagner left, except perhaps for the
king. Isolated in his beloved mountains, writing passionate letters to
"the Friend" while his country teetered on the brink of war with powerful Prussia, Ludwig was discovering that reality was disappointing.
On May 22, Wagner's fifty-third birthday, while the cabinet debated
war, the king secretly left the capital. He appeared at Tribschen and
had himself announced as Walther von Stolzing, the hero of *Meistersinger*. If he was surprised to see Cosima there, he kept it to himself, and stayed for two days.

Munich was in no mood for such silliness. A scathing article
appeared in the press, bluntly accusing Wagner of a greed that
extended beyond the Treasury and into his conductor's marriage.

Cosima begged the king to save her reputation, sending a draft of a rebuttal letter for him to sign. Ludwig complied.

Who was the guiltiest party in this scam? Wagner, of course, saw sacrifice in others as a sign of devotion, and allowed the three people whose honor he should have defended the most to perjure themselves publicly. Bülow, who resigned his post in June, was bent on self-destruction. It is always easiest to blame Cosima for this letter episode, but she, at least, was fully aware of what she was doing. Her diaries are full of oblique yet clear references to the guilt she bore to her grave for leaving Bülow, but her mind was made up. She understood her remorse as the cross she had to bear on her sacred mission, which was to nurture the person and genius of Richard Wagner. This, we would say today, was dirty work, but somebody had to do it, and there's no arguing that she did it splendidly.

Ludwig must also be called to account, since after a certain point one must ask how much of naiveté is voluntary. The king began to realize that there was a great gulf between the concept of Wagner and the man, and began treating him a touch more distantly even while continuing the charade of love letters. Meanwhile, Bavaria utterly lost the six-week war, which left Prussia solely in charge of central Europe.

Ludwig kept seeking Wagner's "permission" to abdicate, but the last thing Wagner needed around his house was a spaced-out boy with no access to the Treasury. Instead, the country sighed with relief when Bismarck and the Prussians displayed great leniency with the defeated Bavarians, sensing they would be needed later. Ludwig stayed on his throne.

## HIGHLIGHTS AND LOW POINTS

Wagner sought to have Bülow reinstated in Munich, if only to conduct *Meistersinger*, which was taking shape. Cosima apparently resolved to refrain from discussing a divorce until after the *Meistersinger* premiere, which took place on June 21, 1868. It was probably the biggest opening night success of Wagner's career. Despite its unprecedented length, audiences went into raptures, and theaters all over Germany jockeyed to perform it. Performance royalties had also become standard by this time, guaranteeing additional income. Things were looking up for Wagner. Cosima chose this moment to confront Bülow, who agreed to a divorce, had a nervous malaise, and sought consolation from Liszt, who had broken off relations with Wagner and Cosima.

Although *Meistersinger* was a bona fide hit, Wagner was still regarded suspiciously by many different factions. Just when he most needed to proceed diplomatically, he reissued "Judaism in Music" in an expanded form, this time signing his name to it. Many of his fans, especially the Jewish ones, had forgiven the 1850 edition as a youthful aberration (much had been said carelessly in those revolutionary years, and even Karl Marx's writings were thought to have much in common with certain of Wagner's sentiments), but now all the ugliness was out in the open. *Meistersinger* was booed in Mannheim. Liszt clucked in disapproval. The crown princess of Prussia recommended the pamphlet to her mother, Queen Victoria of Britain, if she desired to read something "really cracked," and noisily endowed a Jewish orphanage in Berlin. Ludwig criticized Wagner obliquely, saying that people must come to realize that "all men are brothers, whatever their religion." (Insane? Ludwig may have been the only sane person in nineteenth-century Europe.) Of course, not everyone in Germany had a negative reaction to this pamphlet, and the German anti-Semitic movement took a great leap forward thanks to Wagner.

Home life proceeded heedless of the world. Their daughter Eva was born in 1868. Wagner picked up the unfinished score of the *Ring* where he had left off twelve years before (Act II of *Siegfried*), and a long-awaited son arrived in June 1869. He was named Siegfried. Life was now extremely pleasant at Tribschen, whose rent Ludwig continued to pay. Whatever Wagner's worth as a human being, he was a good father, including to Cosima's two daughters by Bülow, and the house was filled with music and pets. On Christmas Day, 1870 (also Cosima's birthday), she arose to the ravishing sounds of a new piece of music. Wagner had assembled a small orchestra in the vestibule of the house to play the first performance of the *Siegfried Idyll,* one of his few mature nonvocal compositions and a stunningly sumptuous piece of music still adored today. It may have been the most elegant gift in history.

It also meant Wagner was serious about completing and producing the *Ring.* There was a slight problem in that King Ludwig owned the *Ring,* including the portions of it not yet composed (Act III of *Siegfried* and all of *Götterdämmerung*). Wagner had no intention of producing the *Ring* in Munich—it needed to be in an ideal theater and meticulously supervised by him, and it was clear by this point that the Semper theater would never be built. Ludwig ordered *Das Rheingold* to be performed in Munich in September 1869. Wagner begged, pleaded, screamed, and abused everybody, but to no avail. Ludwig let it be known that Wagner's income would be cut off and all his works banned in Munich if he didn't shut up. That did the trick. *Rheingold* was premiered on September 22 while Wagner sulked in Switzerland. Actually, the Munich *Rheingold* came off rather well, even if the scenery and stage action were not what Wagner had intended. Wagner wrote Ludwig morbid letters, and Ludwig pretended to be contrite, assuring Wagner that he couldn't help himself but would abide by his idol's wishes on behalf of their shared vision. Meanwhile, he quietly ordered the production of *Die Walküre* for the following year.

The premiere of *Die Walküre* took place in Munich on June 26, 1870. Wagner, predictably, stayed home in Switzerland, and even Ludwig, who was getting increasingly unpredictable, did not attend until the third performance. Among those who did attend were the still-incommunicado Liszt, who was moved to tears, Brahms, Camille Saint-Saëns, and a great many other luminaries, including a large number of French devotees. *Walküre* was a great success. The king now asked for the completed score of *Siegfried.* Wagner said he couldn't quite manage to finish it, but would send it along as soon as it was done. He kept this fiction up for years after he had finished the entire *Ring,* and Ludwig stopped nagging him after awhile. He had other problems.

Bismarck and the Prussians were angling for war against the

French. Not really having any option, Ludwig, between repertory performances of *Rheingold* and *Walküre*, ordered Bavaria to mobilize on July 16, 1870. (He gave the mobilization order in French. Whether this was an elegant protest against the war or a lapse of judgment remains debated to this day.) On July 18, Cosima was informed that her marriage to Hans von Bülow had been dissolved by the civil authorities in Berlin. On July 19, the French declared war. The declaration was made by Emile Ollivier, who happened to be Cosima's brother-in-law and an old friend of Wagner's in Paris. On August 25 (Ludwig's birthday), Cosima and Richard were finally married in the Protestant church at Lucerne. It was a hell of a summer.

If Ludwig was no longer showing up at their doorstep, the Wagners now had a new wide-eyed groupie to idolize them. Friedrich Nietzsche had met Wagner in October 1868. Wagner was instantly impressed with the young man's intelligence, conversation, and knowledge of Wagner's work. When Nietzsche took a chair of philology at Basel in 1869, he became a frequent visitor to Tribschen—so frequent that he was regarded as one of the household. Wagner would be the obsession of his life; idol for now, later, in one of those about-faces that characterize Nietzsche's life and thought, his bitter enemy.

## CREATING BAYREUTH

Meanwhile, what to do with the *Ring?* Wagner remembered the pretty town of Bayreuth from a visit in 1836, and was delighted to learn that it had a baroque opera house with a relatively huge stage. In April 1871, the Wagners visited the town. The lovely old opera house turned out to be unsuitable, but the town impressed them. It was in Bavaria, but remote from Munich and very close to the center of Germany. There was no existing opera company or musical establishment to contend with. The mayor and townspeople were eager to help. The Wagners decided to settle there and build a theater especially for the *Ring*, which they would stage in a national festival. "So much the better," wrote Cosima. Once again, all that was needed was a fortune.

Europe had changed by 1871. The Germans defeated the French, toppled their government, and laid siege to Paris. Wagner and his Parisian wife laughed publicly when they heard the Parisians were eating rats. After the surrender, Wagner penned an embarrassing farce, *Eine Kapitulation*, which even the smaller theaters in Berlin politely declined to produce. Cosima thought it was charming. Meanwhile, Bismarck pressured Ludwig, as the most historically legitimate German monarch, to write a letter "inviting" the king of Prussia to assume the title of Emperor and legitimize the new order. Ludwig dithered but finally complied, and the letter was read at Versailles, where the German Empire, the Second Reich, was born. Although some facts are missing, it appears that Bismarck paid Ludwig handsomely for that letter.

Ludwig didn't like the Bayreuth idea at all, and said so. He knew Wagner would be hitting him up for cash, and Ludwig had projects of his own. Being little more than a puppet monarch in the new Reich, and with a mysteriously bulging bank account, the king had discovered the joys of building castles, if not in the air, then at least in the Alps. On a rocky crag across from Hohenschwangau arose Schloss Neuschwannstein, now perhaps the most recognizable castle in the world, designed, significantly, by the scenic designer of the royal theater. There, in a courtyard based on Act II of *Lohengrin* and with a Song Hall based on Act II of *Tannhäuser*, Ludwig could revel in Wagnerian imagery without the pesky reality of the man. He also built Linderhof, a neobaroque tribute to Louis XIV (a new obsession of his) that boasted a Venusberg Grotto, à la *Tannhäuser*, and a "Hunding's Hut," as in *Walküre*, on its grounds. These indulgences were seen as signs of impending insanity. Today we would allow this in the sort of pop stars who build private amusement parks.

Wagner applied to the kaiser for support for the Bayreuth plan, and was told to make a proposal to the Reichstag, or Imperial Parliament, which he refused to do. If the new emperor couldn't see what a boon the *Ring* would be to the new Germany, then there was no use begging. Wagner societies were formed all over Germany and in other countries to raise funds for the festival. The idea was that patrons would donate money and be guaranteed seats. If there were enough of a groundswell of enthusiasm, the festival would be held according to the original intention, that is, a true folk celebration.

The patrons plan did not work. Out of an original 1,300 patrons' certificates, only around four hundred were ever sold. Nietzsche wrote pamphlets urging the people to support the venture and implying, in his usual endearing style, that they were cultureless slobs if they didn't send money right away. Shockingly, this tactic failed to produce an avalanche of cash, and Wagner and Nietzsche decided the German people were as worthless as their new empire, since they so steadfastly refused to honor art and genius.

Actually, many were willing to help, but they naturally required concessions from Wagner, and he was well beyond granting any. Friends in Berlin offered him everything—a new theater, whatever artists he desired, unlimited budget—if he would hold his festival in the now-imperial capital. Wagner refused. If the festival were held in a large city it would become something else entirely, with court and society vultures stopping by the theater on their way to smart parties, tired businessmen falling asleep, and no end of nonsense. No. The German Reich had to come to Bayreuth to glorify Wagner, not the other way around. The Berlin festival option should be borne in mind when people say, as they often do, that Wagner was capable of doing anything for money. He certainly compromised his honor in quest of financing, but he never once compromised his art.

Meanwhile, Bayreuth was taking shape and running up debts. The Festival House was being constructed atop a hill just outside of the town according to Wagner's wishes. A ceremony was held in August 1873 to mark the reaching of the construction's high point, at which Wagner praised the king but said nothing about the kaiser. Using ideas Semper had incorporated into the planned theater in Munich, the structure was to be all of wood, with a sloped auditorium and, most radically, an entirely submerged orchestra pit. There was no horseshoe of boxes for society types to admire themselves—one either looked at the stage or at nothing at all. In any case, Wagner proposed to dim the lighting as much as possible in the auditorium itself.

Ludwig began to vacillate. He made Wagner an outright gift of cash to build a suitable new home in Bayreuth just off the grounds of the rarely used Royal Palace. Wagner and Cosima built Villa Wahnfried, a large house in the heavy style of the times, but they were starting to worry about the king. He never saw anyone any more and stayed isolated in the mountains. What would become of him? Finally, Ludwig wrote a passionate letter on January 25, 1874, declaring that the dream must not end in infamy, and promising the necessary funds for the festival. Although there were a few more fits and starts from the king and the Treasury, it appeared that the festival would indeed happen. Time was taken out to visit Liszt in Weimar. Relations were improving in that direction.

Rehearsals and production meetings began. Every singer and instrumentalist was individually "invited" to participate at less than their standard fees and, in some cases, for mere travel expenses. Machinists, designers, and costumers arrived. Cosima drew on her aristocratic education to juggle everything and everyone. Finally, the summer of 1876 arrived.

## THE BIG MOMENT

Ludwig couldn't wait to see the *Ring* at last, but let it be known that he would see nobody at Bayreuth, neither the kaiser nor cheering peasants nor anyone else in between. Wagner met his railroad carriage at a preappointed spot in the countryside, and accompanied the king to the local palace, where they talked late into the night. It was the first time they had seen each other in eight years. The dress rehearsals were to be given as "private performances" for Ludwig, with only Wagner in the secluded royal box and Cosima hidden underneath. After *Rheingold*, it was discovered that the acoustics were faulty in the empty theater, and people were allowed in to fill up the seats for the subsequent three performances, with strict orders not to look at the king.

When the actual festival arrived, it was an "event." Journalists from all over Europe and America wrote reports, and *The New York Times* carried reviews on the front page. Some were disappointed, others were in raptures, but everyone agreed that something major had happened in the realm of music and theater.

Villa Wahnfried's gardens were open every night. Artists hobnobbed with composers. Literati and glitterati brushed with royalty and nobility. Cosima handled artistic and aristocratic egos with an aplomb appropriate to her heritage, while Liszt charmed everyone in sight. His Roman collar only increased his appeal to the ladies. At one banquet, Wagner gestured toward his father-in-law, saying they all had him to thank, since without him no one would have ever heard a note of his music.

## AFTER THE PARTY

When it was over, Wagner was left with a sense of post-partum depression and a mountain of debt. The festival had been a disappointment in many ways. The *Ring* looked a whole lot like opera after all, and, for all its originality, was not immune to the screw-ups that accompany any production. Wagner went to wealthy London to conduct a series of concerts, but they were badly planned on the English side and failed to produce much net income. It was during this trip that the novelist George Eliot cornered Cosima at a party and said bluntly, "I hear your husband doesn't like Jews. Well, my husband is a Jew!" Unfortunately, we don't know how or if Cosima responded to this.

Wagner complained of illness and talked incessantly about emigrating to America, where, indeed, there were plenty of people willing to throw piles of money at him. Instead, he went to Italy, that time-honored destination of Germans-in-crisis. Naples cheered him up considerably, and he worked on *Parsifal*, the poem of which he had been reading to friends for years. It was on one of these trips that Wagner and Nietzsche broke relations for good.

Angelo Neumann, a former singer turned manager, paid a nice fee to Wagner and successfully produced the *Ring* at Leipzig in 1878 and triumphantly in Berlin in 1881. Wagner's other operas, especially *Tannhäuser* and *Lohengrin*, were being performed everywhere, including Italy, Britain, and the United States. Wagner could concentrate on *Parsifal*, which would constitute the entire next Bayreuth festival. It was six years in the making.

## THE LATE YEARS

Wagner's output of essays reached staggering proportions in these years, as he tried to clarify his philosophy. Every essay found him "more misunderstood than ever," and he would write another. He founded the *Bayreuther Blätter*, a newspaper to propogate his confusing ideas, and issued proclamations on vegetarianism and antivivisectionism. He also continued to plead for a Germany without Jews, or, at least, without Judaism. At the same time, he was distancing himself from the anti-Semitic movement, which had become a significant political faction in national politics, and relied more than ever on the talents of individual Jews. (Bülow, in perhaps his lowest moment, complained to a friend at this time that he should have had himself circumcised if he had wanted to be successful in Wagner's circle.) Amidst all this, Wagner worked on *Parsifal*.

From the start, *Parsifal* was meant to be something entirely unique. Wagner wrote the music specifically for the miraculous acoustics of the Bayreuth Festival House, and insisted this work never be performed anywhere else. He worked at great leisure, which is apparent in the score, reflecting his new life style. Ludwig paid off the debts from the first festival, and Wagner spent comfortable time in Italy with Cosima and the children. The king also placed the personnel of the Munich Opera at Wagner's disposal for the next festival, including the brilliant conductor Hermann Levi. The fact that Levi was Jewish was the ultimate irony for this final chapter of Wagner's artistic life.

Sixteen performances of *Parsifal* were given in the summer of 1882. King Ludwig did not attend, even though Wagner had constructed a special private entrance to the Festival House for him. Bülow intended to go, but never made it. Otherwise, almost everybody else from musical Europe was there. The audiences were struck dumb by this masterpiece, and the whole festival was more like a strange religious rite than anything else. One devotee shocked his friends at a dinner party by declaring that Wagner would surely be dead soon. After *Parsifal*, there was nothing left to say. Wagner may have agreed with this sentiment. He and the family went to Venice and moved into the Palazzo Vendramin (the present Winter Casino) in September. There they received visitors, including Liszt and Levi, and people noted that Wagner talked more and more of the past. On February 13, 1883, he died of heart failure.

Cosima appeared to die with him. She would not leave the body and refused to eat or drink. Bülow sent a telegram that may have been that pathetic man's finest moment. It read simply, *"Soeur, il faut vivre."* She cut off her hair, placed it in the casket, and began the journey to Bayreuth with the body.

Wagner was buried in the garden at Wahnfried while Cosima watched from the upstairs bedroom. Later, she spent a few hours at the gravesite, returning to total seclusion in her room. Her grieving exceeded the already heavy standards of the time. What outsiders couldn't see, however, was that she was already planning the next festival. The continuation of Wagner's life work was soon firmly under her own control.

# Richard Wagner, Superstar

◆

By the time Wagner died in 1883, he was the most talked-about composer in the world. Everybody had an opinion about him, either extremely positive or just the opposite. *Plus ça change* . . . He *stood for something* to almost everybody.

To German nationalists, he was the culmination of the cultural spirit of the people, a crystallization of all German aspiration. The extremists claimed Wagner as their own, the bulwark of Aryan defiance against Jewish intrigue, American materialism, French decadence, and Catholic despotism (in roughly that order). The paper Wagner founded, the *Bayreuther Blätter*, became the main perpetrator of this line of thought for several decades after Wagner's death under the leadership of Hans von Wolzogen, to whom Hitler himself acknowledged a great debt. The faction that grew around this paper was far-right even by Second Reich standards, and they thought the foreign-born Cosima, with her Jewish and American musicians, was far too cosmopolitan.

Thus the serpent's egg was laid right from the start, but it would be a mistake to think of Wagner as the exclusive property of the far right at any point in history. In fact, Wagner's art was also claimed by much of the left, which is at least equally logical. Wagner himself had once been a revolutionary, and his art certainly fit in that category. Many of his French fans preferred to see him in this way. His failure in Paris had been largely caused by the old aristocracy (i.e., the Jockey Club), to whom many French Wagnerites were automatically opposed, both politically and culturally.

In America, Wagner's popularity started in the large German immigrant community, but quickly spread far and wide. Americans were able to look at the operas from a slightly more removed vantage point than their European counterparts. As Dr. Joseph Horowitz has pointed out, the "newness" of Wagner's music won thousands of fans from surprising segments of society. The women of the suffragette movement, particularly, were devoted Wagnerians in America.

In Russia, too, Wagner's music found a home among the educated of the left. Italians approached Wagner cautiously but respectfully (as they still do); Verdi, for one, was extremely careful in his public statements about this composer whom he so clearly respected, if never actually adored. Legend has it that the score of *Parsifal* was on Verdi's piano when he died. The English reaction to Wagner was varied, though generally enthusiastic.

If critics were often hostile to Wagner early on, musicians tended to worship his music beyond the bounds of reason. Many took it on faith that this music really was "of the future," and had little patience for those who had trouble following the new sounds. This worshipful wave, in which Wagner's devotees regarded his music as more like a crusade, became known as *Wagnerismus* ("Wagnerism," but everyone used the German word to describe the phenomenon), and peaked around the turn of the century. The fanaticism of the Wagnerites and their condescension toward the less illuminated did much to alienate the general public in these years. Thus Mark Twain's brilliant deflation of *Wagnerismus*, "I'm told Wagner's music is better than it sounds." In fact, *Wagnerismus* played a large role in developing the gap between "high" and "low" culture, a problem that continues to plague the arts today worse than ever before.

Reaction, of a sort, set in. The early decades of the twentieth century saw people striving to lighten the burden of the Victorian years. This was also evident in clothes and interior design, and, for many people, works like *Meistersinger* went out of style along with bustles and velvet drapes. Nietzsche, one of the first to rebel against the "disease" of Wagner, called for more "light and air" (quoting Isolde, no less). The philosopher recommended the opera *Carmen*, with its vitality, as the real music of the future.

Whatever Nietzsche's qualifications as a music critic (and it's a murky subject), many agreed with his call for more light and air. Even musically sophisticated people found themselves able to enjoy Bizet's *Carmen* and newer works like Debussy's *Pelléas et Mélisande*, without necessarily having to swear off Wagner. Composers took note. They learned their lessons from Wagner, but wrote as they saw fit. Mahler conducted Wagner everywhere (except Bayreuth, where he was not welcome—one Jewish conductor was quite enough for that crew), but wrote symphonies. Richard Strauss, who also conducted Wagner all over, responded with *Salome* and *Elektra*, two of the *shortest* operas ever written. Stravinsky hit the world like a tornado with his *Rite of Spring*, and spent much of his career trying to write distinctly unlike Wagner.

Brevity was not the only reaction. People had come to see Wagner as heavy in every sense of the word. To some extent, this impression still holds true in the popular vocabulary. When the adjective "Wagnerian" is used in any context, it means plodding, overlong, and ham-fisted, at best. Strauss responded yet again with a "chamber opera," *Ariadne auf Naxos*, which calls for an orchestra of merely thirty-six members. (*Ariadne* also quotes *Rheingold* to take a dig at a plodding, ham-fisted character in its story.)

People still appreciated Wagner's music, but it was clear that he would not be imitated directly in the future. While composers were and are quite willing to use effects and discoveries from Wagner's scores, nobody outside of the asylums has attempted to write their own *Ring* or *Parsifal*. And no one worried about the issue of opera versus music drama anymore. A newer generation took this another step away from what Wagner had envisioned. Arnold Schoenberg and his students Anton Webern and Alban Berg moved toward atonality and the twelve-tone system. Many scholars can determine the points of origin of this development in the scores of *Tristan* and *Parsifal*, which is clear enough. But the spirit of the modernists was entirely different from Wagner—except in one important respect.

The gap between "music experts" and "normal people" became wider than ever. Suddenly, with "serious" music being seriously beyond most people, Wagner was starting to look relatively easy, and conservative, to most people.

Meanwhile, weird things were happening in Bayreuth. Cosima retired in favor of her son Siegfried, who enjoyed moderate success from 1906 until his death, a few months after Cosima, in 1930. (There had been no festival from 1914 until 1924.) Siegfried married a young Englishwoman named Winifred, who had grown up in Germany since she was nine years old. They promptly had four children, which was something of a duty for the predominantly gay Siegfried. In the uncertain postwar years, when nobody knew if there would ever be another Bayreuth festival, Winifred met a young misfit named Adolf Hitler—and promptly flipped over him. Their friendship would never fail, and Hitler was treated as a member of the family. Winifred took the reins of the Bayreuth festival in 1930. She counted on her friend Hitler for support, and he, in turn, took a keen interest in the festival after he became chancellor in 1933.

One thing everybody can tell you about Adolf Hitler is that his favorite composer was Wagner. Actually, Anton Bruckner, the benign Austrian of childlike faith, whose music offends no one except by its length, was Hitler's favorite composer. (Hitler's favorite movie was *King Kong,* by the way.) The Führer, whose title may well have been suggested by the libretto of *Lohengrin,* was certainly a Wagner devotee, but there is some question about how much of the music actually interested him. (His favorite opera was Wagner's early success *Rienzi,* never produced at Bayreuth.)

The relationship between Winifred Wagner and the festival on the one hand and Hitler and the Nazi Party on the other side is complex and full of paradoxes. In a way, the personal friendship between Winifred and Hitler saved the festival from the direct party control imposed on every other theater in Germany. There were no Nazi banners in the Festival House, nor were party songs sung at performances. A few Jews and other political undesirables even continued to perform at Bayreuth for a while. Yet there can be no question of one irreducible fact: Bayreuth was entirely compromised by its Third Reich associations. Thomas Mann, in exile, called it "Hitler's Court Theater."

Hitler worked hard to subsume Wagner into his own world vision, and co-opted the composer into his culture war. The choice of Wagner was not random, whatever Hitler's musical acumen—the basic material for a Nazi icon was there. The anti-Semitism, the disparaging of all cultures and races beyond the largely imaginary Aryans, and the desperate nationalism were fixed features of Wagner's thought. Even Wagner's support of vegetarianism fit in nicely with Hitler's world view. It didn't matter that Wagner contradicted almost every pronouncement he ever made with an equal and opposite pronouncement elsewhere; the Nazi mind was incapable of grasping such complexities. Hitler famously said that whoever "wishes to understand National Socialism must first understand Wagner."

This had two long-lasting results for the world outside of Germany. First, Wagner has become permanently associated with fascism in the popular imagination. In 1990, the architectural writer Alan Balfour could blithely call the buildings of Third Reich architect Albert Speer "Wagnerian," and not give it a second thought. Nothing could be farther from the cold, neoclassical, inhumane rigidity of Speer's designs for the Reich Chancellery in Berlin or the Nazi Party rally grounds at Nuremberg than the form-defying "infinite melody" of *Tristan,* to cite just one obvious example. But there's no arguing this sort of thing. It is convenient to understand Wagner as aesthetically fascist because of his own revolting politics and because of his association with Hitler's Germany.

However, Hitler's advent had another, quite opposite, effect on the world's view of Wagner, particularly in America. The cream of Germany's intelligentsia and many of the best artists in Germany fled that country around 1933, most arriving in the United States. Among many others, Mann, Schoenberg, and Theodor Adorno brought with them the debate about Wagner, while Bruno Walter, Otto Klemperer, Lauritz Melchior, Lotte Lehmann, and many others brought the music alive. Toscanini blew invective at the fascists, and stayed in

America. American musicians who might have spent more time in Europe stayed home. Wagner's art reached people in America and Britain in a new way.

Winifred was interrogated by American forces after the war. It would have been lovely to arrest her, but she was in fact able to show that she had helped Jewish and homosexual artists who would have otherwise been killed. This was sufficient, under occupation law, to get her off the hook, but she was given to understand that she should retire and keep her mouth shut. (She did retire, but she didn't always manage to keep her mouth shut.) Her sons Wieland and Wolfgang worked to resurrect the festival, and New Bayreuth opened in 1951.

The productions of this era, especially those by Wieland, are legends among opera fans and theater connoisseurs. Wieland, needing to disassociate the works of his grandfather from the ideology and trappings of the Third Reich, basically dismantled the operas to their barest components in order to reexamine them, free of baggage. The minimalist stage results, relying heavily on lighting and impression, were cleansed of nationalistic specificity and looked at as universal dramas. There were never any apologies out of Bayreuth during these years, merely an intense desire to forget the past and move on from it.

For the subsequent generation of Germans, forgetting the past and moving on was insufficient. The whole wartime generation has come under closer scrutiny along with all their institutions. Bayreuth has been the focus of impassioned debate, including from members of the Wagner family. Wolfgang Wagner assumed control of the operation after Wieland's death in 1966, and, for many, Wolfgang is inextricably linked to the Third Reich experience. The operas of Richard Wagner are now examined in Germany for their inherent complicity in the disaster of the Nazi experience. These productions often look strange to non-Germans, but Wieland's ideal of art disconnected from reality is not good enough for many contemporary Germans.

The phenomenon of Wagner, however, is no longer limited to the pretty streets of Bayreuth or the lecture halls of German academia. The complete *Ring* was first recorded under the direction of Sir Georg Solti and released between 1958 and 1966. Recordings by Herbert von Karajan and Karl Böhm followed between 1966 and 1970.

The famous Chéreau *Ring* was telecast in several countries in 1983. Meanwhile, opera companies proliferated in America, Britain, France, and elsewhere, and smaller companies experimented with all of Wagner's operas in a way that would have been unthinkable to earlier generations. Videos became available, and suddenly people who lived away from the major opera centers were able to watch these works at home, if they were so inclined. The Internet is becoming available all over the world, and Wagner is not absent from it.

Wagner's art can no longer be spoon-fed to the public by ideologues, be they political, literary, musical, or otherwise. It is too readily available to too many people. The debate has passed beyond the polemicists, and has finally arrived where it should have been all along—with the international public.

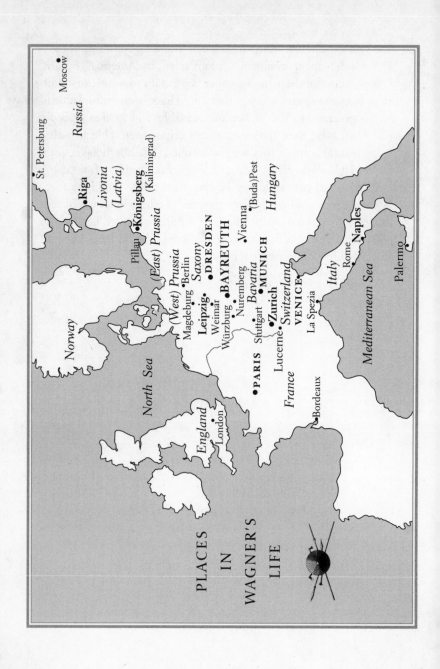

PLACES IN WAGNER'S LIFE

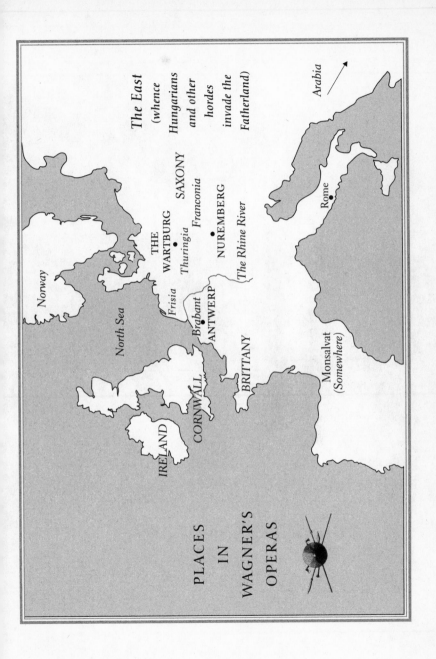

PLACES IN WAGNER'S OPERAS

Norway

North Sea

IRELAND

CORNWALL

BRITTANY

Frisia

Brabant
ANTWERP

THE WARTBURG
Thuringia

SAXONY
Franconia

NUREMBERG

The Rhine River

Monsalvat
(Somewhere)

Rome

Arabia

The East
(whence
Hungarians
and other
hordes
invade the
Fatherland)

# PART TWO

# THE
# OPERAS

◆

# THE FLYING DUTCHMAN

PREMIERE: DRESDEN, 1843.

## THE NAME

*What to call it* Tradition dictates that certain operas are known by their original-language titles only, while an English equivalent is used for others. We say, for example, *The Marriage of Figaro* and *The Abduction from the Seraglio*, but then *Così fan tutte*. Strange, but it sounds just as affected to translate certain foreign titles into English as it does to quote the original for other titles. *Nobody* says *The Rhine Gold* anymore, for example. This must be accepted as a quirk of the opera world, where reason and common sense rarely apply. *The Flying Dutchman* falls somewhere in the middle. It is usually called by its English name, and even a simple *Dutchman* will let everybody know what you're talking about.

*What it means* The word "Dutchman" refers to the main character, a sea captain from Holland. The word "Flying" has the sense of "rushing," rather than any airborne quality. "The Flying Dutchman," confusingly enough, seems to refer to the captain's ship as well.

*How to pronounce it* The English title is no problem, but you may have to attempt the German, *Der fliegende Holländer*, at some point. "Dare FLEE-gen-duh HOLE-end-dare" is close enough.

## WHAT IS *THE FLYING DUTCHMAN?*

This is the earliest of Wagner's operas to remain in the repertory, an opera prized for its uninhibited passion, eerie atmosphere, and brevity. The supernatural plays a central role in all of Wagner's subsequent operas, and nowhere is it depicted with such gusto as in *Dutchman*. The title role is a man condemned to roam the seas forever unless he can find a woman whose love will relieve his curse.

The sea itself plays a large role in this opera, inspiring Wagner to some of the most stirringly descriptive music he ever wrote. His own adventures on his hair-raising North Sea voyage in 1839 gave him the opportunity to apply his own experience to his music. The role of the redeeming woman also struck a deep chord with him, as it would in all his subsequent works. Although the legend of the Flying Dutchman existed in many written forms, several of which Wagner was familiar with, in this opera we see Wagner beginning to abandon external models and reaching into himself as an artist.

*Dutchman* enjoyed only a moderate success at its premiere and for the following several years. In the early twentieth century, it steadily grew in popularity, largely due to compelling characterizations of the two lead roles by great artists. The role of the Dutchman, in particular, is a career goal of bass-baritones, who revel in this rare opportunity to be the star and portray a multifaceted, riveting character. Audiences have taken to *Dutchman* ever since, perhaps more than experts and scholars, who have a tendency to speak of this opera in patronizing terms. They are always pointing to "youthful errors" and "operatic conventions" in the score, and look at the music as little more than the promising seed from which Wagner's later, revolutionary music dramas would spring. They are not entirely wrong— *Dutchman* has more in common with the other Romantic operas one sees than with any of the other of Wagner's later works, including recitatives, duets, trios, love arias, and so on. No matter how innovative it sounded in 1843, most of the score was written in accordance with the rules of the time, with evenly measured lines and stresses and climaxes falling in all the "right" places. However, scholars will never understand that opera audiences don't care a damn about music theories. People go to see the *Ring* or *Parsifal* for the same reason they enjoy *Dutchman* or, for that matter, any other so-called conventional opera: because it speaks to them on an emotional level. *Dutchman*, therefore, is best looked at on its own considerable merits rather than as a blueprint for later Wagnerian music theory. If Wagner had stopped composing after this opera, we would still be able to be thrilled by it.

## CAST OF CHARACTERS

THE DUTCHMAN *(bass-baritone)* The quintessential loner who fought with hell and lost, for now. In several of the source legends, he is named Vanderdencken, but he is never called anything but the Dutchman in this opera. This is one of the all-time plum roles for the rare voice type known as bass-baritone, which ideally encompasses anything a bass or a baritone can sing.

SENTA *(soprano)* Woman as Redeemer, through the power of love, constancy, and self-sacrifice. Wagner's original sketch named this character Minna (after his wife), but he later invented the name Senta for her. In Norway, household maids were called "Tjenta," and Wagner may have heard this word when his storm-tossed ship took refuge in a coastal village there. In any case, this role is prized by divas for its otherworldly character and its ample opportunities for gripping vocalism.

DALAND *(bass)* Senta's father, the captain of a smaller sailing craft. Daland is a basically agreeable man who is perhaps a bit too impressed by money. His music ranges from lyrical and inoffensive to rather bouncy, and lies fairly low in the voice.

ERIK *(tenor)* Senta's unofficial fiancé, a hunter. His occupation tells us that he is manly in a traditional way, and entirely earthy, contrasting with the Dutchman. He sings lovely solo music of the lyric Italian style, but must be able to hold his own in a fierce duet and trio.

MARY *(mezzo-soprano)* One of the standard mezzo mother figures who infest operatic stages, fussing around and saying things like "Upon my word!" and "What will the neighbors say?" The true purpose of these pestiferous types is to provide a low female voice against which the heroine's soaring notes may be favorably compared.

THE STEERSMAN *(tenor)* This one sings a pretty song at the beginning, and that's about it. Watch for up-and-coming tenors to milk this brief role for all it's worth, and then some.

## THE OPERA

### Overture

**Comment:** *Almost everyone on the planet knows the main theme of this Overture, whether they realize it or not. You've heard it everywhere, including several television commercials. It represents the Dutchman, and will be played throughout the opera any time your attention needs to be drawn to him or his ship. After this theme is repeated, and "echoed" in the French horns, as if off the cliffs of the Norwegian fjords, we hear themes associated with the sea, Senta's longing, the sea, sailors, redemption, and the sea. There's no need to study these themes ahead of time since there's nothing elusive about their meanings. All these representations are depicted in broad musical statements, obvious to every member of the audience.*

*Redemption is referred to with a theme of its own, and also in the final harp-accompanied chords that resolve the Overture. You don't really need to know ahead of time that the harps signify salvation; this seems to be a part of the collective unconscious. Hear harp, think salvation.*

*One early conductor spoke of the "wind that blows out at you wherever you open the score." Whether he was complaining or praising, you will agree with his observation after one hearing of the Overture.*

## Act I

Setting: A steep, rocky coastline in Norway. Daland's ship has just cast anchor, amidst a raging storm.

Daland has just gone ashore, climbing a cliff and looking around to see where he is. The sailors are at work, furling sails and generally cleaning up after their storm-tossed voyage. They sing as they work, and the cliffs echo their calls. Daland perceives that the haven he has moored in is no more than seven miles from his home port. The Steersman shouts from the ship that all is well despite the storm. Daland complains that he had seen his house on the shore and had hoped to be home that night, embracing his daughter Senta. Ah well! To have faith in the wind is to believe in Satan's mercy! He consoles himself that the storm will not last, and they will all soon be home. He reboards the ship and orders the sailors to sleep below. The Steersman is to keep watch.

**Comment:** *The sailor's songs are "echoed" off the steep cliffs of the fjords; actually played by the brass. The effect is slightly eerie, suggesting that the very human sailors are surrounded by fearful powers. Daland, an affable old salt, corroborates this, speaking gruffly about the powers of the winds and Satan, whose works he will shortly encounter.*

The Steersman yawns and stretches out by the helm as the storm abates. He sings about his loving lass in a vain effort to stay awake. As he is dozing off, the Flying Dutchman's large ship appears in the distance. It is an ominous vision, with black masts and "blood-red" sails. It approaches Daland's ship, casting anchor with a loud crash. The Steersman looks up, but somehow does not see the huge ship alongside. He sings another line of his ditty, and falls into a sound sleep. Without any sound, the ghostly crew of the Dutchman's ship furl their sails. The Dutchman steps ashore.

*Comment: Whatever directorial concept you are being tortured with at the performance you attend, one thing is absolutely crucial: the arrival of the Dutchman's ship must be a moment of drop-dead theatrical terror. It can be accomplished in any number of ways. Lighting, projections, or even moving flats can all work, since the bulk of the burden has been handled by Wagner and his shamelessly theatrical score for this moment.*

*It's hard to believe the Steersman doesn't see the ship alongside. The effect is slightly comical if played at face value, which is fine. There is always room for a touch of comedy in pseudo-Gothic horror. Other productions use the Steersman's cluelessness as a metaphor for the story. Most of us are too involved in our physical needs to notice evidence of the supernatural, even when it towers over us.*

It is time! Once every seven years, the sea casts the Dutchman ashore, letting him seek, in vain, for love, death, and redemption. How hard he has tried to die at sea, aiming for reefs, daring pirates with his treasure to attack his ship and kill him, all in vain! Even the pirates cross themselves and flee in terror. Nowhere a grave. Such is the terrible sentence of damnation. He addresses an angel of heaven. Was it mockery to tell the Dutchman to seek salvation on land once every seven years? Yet there is no other hope, unless it be to await the Day of Judgment and Doom, when the world will crack asunder and the dead will rise. Then everlasting oblivion may descend on the Dutchman and his crew. His ghostly crew repeat the prayer that everlasting oblivion may descend on them.

*Comment: If the ship must make an impression on its entrance, so must the Dutchman himself. Sad figures in the violas and cellos tell us right away that this man is, above all, weary. But what else is he? He is also strong and defiant. After all, he's in his present predicament because he once took on Satan himself. And of course he is a compelling presence. He has caused a woman to fall in love with him sight unseen, on reputation alone. This is a lot for a bass-baritone to convey. The recitative is stately and expressive, allowing for a great deal of* nuance. The subsequent aria, which begins where the Dutchman sings about how hard he has tried to die, is a more bravura piece, showing the stronger sides of his character. The emotional range necessary to play the Dutchman is huge.

Wagner specifically directed that the Dutchman wear "Spanish costume," and this is often followed in spirit if not to the letter. One commentator assumed this costume to refer to the Dutchman's origins in the "Spanish Netherlands," but that seems like a stretch. The fact is a Spanish outfit looks great, with the large black hat and black cloak emphasizing his mysteriousness.

Daland appears on the deck of his ship and is startled by the Dutchman's ship. He calls to the Steersman, berating him for falling asleep. The Steersman wakes up confused, singing again, then begging forgiveness. He picks up a speaking trumpet and calls out twice to the Dutchman's ship, receiving nothing in reply but long silences. The third time he asks the ship's name and nationality. Daland notices the Dutchman, standing motionless on shore with his arms crossed, and calls to him. What is your name and country? Without moving, the Dutchman replies that he sought shelter from the storm. Will he be denied? God forbid! exclaims Daland. But what is your name? "A Dutchman," is the only reply.

Daland greets the mysterious captain and asks if his ship is damaged. The Dutchman replies that his ship is safe, though it's been blown by storms for more years than he can count. He has been to too many countries to remember their names, but can never find his homeland. He asks to stay in Daland's house, saying he is rich and Daland will not regret offering him hospitality. Daland pities the Dutchman's bad luck and gladly offers him hospitality. He asks, as if it were an afterthought, what sort of cargo the Dutchman carries. The Dutchman makes a sign to two of his crew, who produce a treasure chest full of gems and pearls. Daland gasps. Who is rich enough to offer a price for such treasure? The Dutchman replies that he already quoted the price—hospitality for a single night. This chest is only a fraction of what the ship bears. What need has he for wealth, being without wife or family? But he would gladly trade all his wealth to be a part of Daland's home. Daland is stunned. What is the Dutchman saying?

The Dutchman bluntly asks Daland if he has a daughter. Indeed yes, a lovely child. "Let her be my wife!" exclaims the Dutchman. Daland expresses joy at this good luck, while the Dutchman urges him to accept the terms. Daland says he has prayed for just such a son-in-law, and would accept no other man, even if the Dutchman were slightly less wealthy. The two men praise this turn of events.

*Comment: Daland, of course, is all about money, and commentators must always do a little moral finger-wagging over this. Yet there is a certain gruff humor to the man as well, as seen in his "slightly less wealthy" comment. It is too simpleminded to portray Daland as a mere bad guy. Some productions take this cop-out route, and miss the humor entirely. (Don't be surprised, if you attend a "conceptual" production, to see Daland done up as a banker or something of that sort, thus making yet another searing criticism of capitalist society.) Daland, eager as he is to sell his daughter to the highest bidder, is also a hard worker, rather than someone who lives off other people's work. Being a Norwegian sailor is hardly the same as being a venture capitalist.*

The Steersman calls out. A prosperous south wind is blowing! Let the sailors man their stations, and soon they will be home. The Dutchman advises Daland to sail ahead, since his crew is weary and needs rest; his ship is swift, and will arrive soon. Daland boards his ship, where the sailors are lustily singing of their homecoming and preparing the ship to heave anchor. Daland gives the signal with a whistle, and they sail away, singing. The Dutchman pensively boards his ship.

*Comment: Another lusty chorus brings this act to a vocal end, but the last word is the orchestra's. We hear themes associated with ocean life, which the Norwegian sailors are now plying but the Dutchman is merely contemplating. There's no good dramatic reason to have the Dutchman remain behind while Daland sets sail—indeed, he never even asked directions, so to speak, to Daland's village. (The great Wag-*

ner scholar Ernest Newman [1868–1959], who will be referred to frequently throughout this book, suggests Wagner had the Dutchman remain so he could make an impressive solo entrance in Act II. Was Newman on drugs when he wrote this? The Dutchman makes his entrance with Daland!) Still, the effect in performance is subtle and excellent. The Norwegians are singing as they set sail, but the Dutchman seems to have the sea, and all its music, inside of himself at this point.

## Act II

Setting: A large room in Daland's house. On the wall hangs a portrait of a mysterious, pale man in a black Spanish outfit—the legendary Flying Dutchman.

The maidens of the village are gathered, spinning at their wheels. Mary urges them on their work, that they may get gifts from their boyfriends when they return from the sea. Senta does not spin with the others, but sits in a chair with her arms folded, gazing pensively at the portrait of the Dutchman. Mary, a somewhat older maid who seems to be in charge, tells Senta to sing and spin with the others. The girls tease Senta: she has no need to work, since her boyfriend is Erik the poor hunter, who will only bring her game instead of the baubles they hope to get from their sailors.

**Comment:** *This is irreverently known in opera circles as the Forty Fat Fräuleins scene, and can easily descend into parody.*

*Spinning songs were a standard of bygone days, since the work was dreadfully dull, and the whirr and clanks of the spinning wheel lent themselves well to musical accompaniment. Liszt made a brilliant piano transcription of this chorus, which was, for a while, considerably more popular than this opera.*

*While the music comes across well if there are actual spinning wheels on stage, some productions do not trust Wagner's orchestra to re-create the sounds of the wheels, and put so many of the contraptions on stage that it sounds like a small industrial plant.*

Senta sings a snippet of ballad to herself while staring at the portrait, making Mary complain that Senta is dreaming her youth away
staring at that image. Senta sighs. The Dutchman's story is so sad.
Why did Mary ever tell it to her? The girls tease her more. She'd better be careful! Erik is hot-blooded, and may get jealous of the picture!
Senta angrily tells them to be quiet, but they just laugh and spin
faster, as if to drown her out. She jumps out of her chair and tells the
girls to quit their dumb song. If they want her to join them, they'll
have to sing something better. She asks Mary to sing the Ballad of the
Flying Dutchman, but when Mary declines, she says she will sing it
herself. Let the girls listen carefully to the words! Mary defiantly
declares that she will continue to spin while the others listen.

*Comment: This is what's called a set-up, saying "I'm now going to
sing an important song and everybody had better listen!" In later years,
when Wagner had learned to make set arias look more like an organic
part of the whole, he was slightly embarrassed by this sort of thing in
the Dutchman.*

Senta, still in the armchair, sings sea calls, as if to herself. Have you
seen the ship on the ocean with black masts and blood red sails? The
ship's master, a pale man, keeps watch without a break, through the
howling wind whistling in the rigging, flying like an arrow without
aim, end, or rest! Yet he could be saved if he finds a woman who will
be true to him until death. Pray to heaven that he find her!

Senta turns toward the portrait. Once, the captain tried to round a
cape during a violent storm. In madness he swore to round it if it took
all eternity! Ho! And Satan heard him, Hoi-ho! And held him to his
word! Now he roams eternally. Yet he could be saved, if he finds the
path that God's angel once showed him. Pray to heaven that he find
the true woman!

The other girls are now listening in rapt attention, repeating the
prayer. Senta, who has risen from her chair, becomes more excited as
she approaches the picture. Every seven years the captain goes
ashore, and every seven years he has been foiled by faithlessness. Ho!
Off to sea, Hoi-ho! Heave anchor, no end, no rest! Senta collapses in

her chair. The girls continue the song. Where will he find the true woman?

*Comment: Wagner wrote that Senta's ballad was the germ from which he developed the entire opera. It is a strange and wonderful piece. Senta sings most of it not in the typical diva fashion, full voice with arms flailing, but in a sort of repressed intensity. It sounds somehow far away. The sea calls, especially, make her sound as if she is some kind of echo of the sailors we heard in the first act.*

*Like the Dutchman, she has a lot of character to establish in her first big vocal moment. Most of the time, Senta is played as a garden variety wide-eyed nut-case. The great Sentas have done more with the role, making her a sensitive woman in a claustrophobic society who connects with the sea as the one limitless feature of her life. For another girl in her position, the father would be an obvious object of nautical fantasy projections, but we've already met Senta's father, and he's simply not the kind of guy any imaginative person could project fantasies onto.*

As if possessed, Senta leaps up from the chair, saying she is the one who will save the Dutchman! The girls cry out for help, for just then Erik has entered the room and heard Senta's insane plea. "Senta," he cries, "will you destroy me?" Mary exclaims that the picture will go right out the door as soon as Daland returns. Erik says gloomily that Daland is coming; Senta, who has been motionless, starts at the news. The girls are thrilled to see their boyfriends again, and Mary, fussing as always, tells them their work isn't done. There's food to be cooked, and a hundred details to attend to. She and the other girls run out of the house.

*Comment: Well, Wagner had to get everybody out of the house somehow, didn't he?*

Senta is eager to run down to the dock, but Erik detains her. What is she doing to him? He has offered her father his faithful heart, his small possessions, and his hunter's skill for Senta's hand. Will she accept that? She begs to leave. Does Erik doubt her heart? Why such distrust? Erik says Daland only wants money. Can Erik trust Senta to plead for him, when her heart seems infatuated with the portrait on the wall, and consumed with the ballad she has just sung again? Senta evades him. She's but a child; she doesn't know what she sings. Does Erik fear a portrait and a song? He asks if she hasn't given him good reason to fear them. But shouldn't the poor Dutchman's fate move her? asks Senta. Shouldn't my own fate move you? counters Erik. She leads him to the picture, chiding him for comparing himself to the Dutchman. See the deep grief that looks down on her from the portrait. Alas! cries Erik. Satan has trapped Senta! Deeply troubled, Erik must now confide his dream to her. As Senta, exhausted, falls back into the armchair in a trance, Erik tells her he was lying dreaming on a cliff over the sea when he suddenly saw a strange ship approach. As he relates his vision, Senta, in her trance, appears to be having the dream herself. Two men came on shore. One was Daland. The other? asks Senta, with eyes closed. Erik recognized the other from his pale face and black outfit. He points to the portrait. Then Senta came and clasped the stranger's knees. He raised me up, interjects Senta, and then? Then, Erik says, he saw Senta and the stranger go out to sea. Senta suddenly awakes from her trance. *She must see him!* Erik exclaims that Senta is lost to him, and runs out of the room in despair.

**Comment:** *Erik, more than anyone else in this opera, actually develops as a character, and this is reflected, albeit subtly, in his music. He begins with a standard love song, saying "I still want to marry you and have a nice home," and so on. His second verse, where he voices his concerns about Daland and even Senta, is sung to the same melody, but there is opportunity to let the voice show that doubt has crept in. When he relates his vision, his music wanders a bit beyond the standard form of equal measures with stresses in the same place. By Act III, he will be clearly seen as almost beyond self-control. This development often goes unnoticed in productions, in which Erik is seldom taken seriously.*

After her excitement, Senta stares at the portrait and sings the prayer refrain of her ballad. Pray heaven, that soon a true wife . . . Suddenly, the door opens. It is her father . . . with the Dutchman! The pale captain enters the room. He and Senta stare at each other, transfixed and silent.

**Comment:** *This is one of opera's all-time great "boy-meets-girl" moments, although the effect should really be of two people who already know each other in some sense. They remain motionless and completely lost in each other, except when Senta briefly greets her father, through the rest of the scene until Daland leaves and they begin their duet.*

Daland carefully approaches Senta. Is she not happy to see him? Finally she greets her father. But who is the stranger? He explains the stranger is a seaman like himself, who has been away from home for a long time, traveling to many lands, where he has amassed great wealth. The stranger will pay handsomely for hospitality. Would it displease Senta to have him stay with them? She barely nods her approval, unable to speak.

Daland asks the Dutchman if he has overpraised his daughter, or is she not an ornament to her sex? The Dutchman, also unable to speak, nods in assent. Daland continues that the guest has also asked to marry Senta. If she likes him, he will marry her the next day. He shows his daughter some jewelry, assuring her that the Dutchman has plenty more. She can have it all if she marries him. But Senta has no eye for the jewelry; she hardly even notices her father. She and the Dutchman remain with gazes locked on each other. Daland finally begins to understand that he is not particularly wanted in the room, and says goodbye for the moment. He walks to the door slowly, watching the pair, very pleased by their attraction, and more than a little pleased with himself as well.

**Comment:** *Daland's aria here is a lovely, soaring number typical of the German Romantics, such as Weber or even Beethoven. Daland's*

*nature is utterly and fundamentally at odds with the two people on
either side of him. When he poses his questions to them, he is musically
answered only by soft taps of the kettledrum. Senta and the Dutchman
are little else than human heartbeats at this point.*

The Dutchman and Senta continue to stare at each other for some
time without speaking.

*Comment: Musical commentators don't have a very high opinion of
this moment. Newman, for one, complains that the youthful Wagner
could think of no other way to portray the underlying tensions of these
two than continuing the soft kettledrum beats, peppered with soft recollections of the Dutchman's theme and the redemption theme. Perhaps
this is not on the same musical plane as, say, the analogous scene in*
Tristan und Isolde, *but it works in the theater, especially if the two performers are capable of creating tension without moving a muscle. The
audience tends to remember this moment. It is impressive, in a Zen sort
of way, for its near-nothingness.*

The Dutchman softly breathes his thoughts. Is this love? Did
Satan leave him a heart just to torture him? Or is it a longing for
release from his curse, a longing for salvation? Senta tries to understand if she is dreaming or waking. Can she really be this
man's instrument of salvation? The Dutchman asks if Senta is not
opposed to her father's choice. Can she be true forever? She insists
she can. They both pray this may be so. The Dutchman says that
if she knew the fate that awaits her if she joins him, she would
flee. Senta staunchly replies that she knows a woman's sacred
duty, and swears fidelity to the Dutchman unto death with all
her heart. The two exclaim joy at this, he at last beginning to feel the
possibility of redemption, she feeling a new empowerment through
her vow.

*Comment: This is the time for our two lead singers to "give voice,"
and they must do so in a number of different ways. When they begin,
they rhapsodize about each other in the same sort of quietly intense*

measures Senta had used at the beginning of her ballad. When the Dutchman speaks of the fate that awaits Senta, we hear full-blooded sea music. The last part of the duet is a rush of passion, with all the vocalizing operagoers can expect from such a set-up. It can be orgasmically cathartic.

Daland walks in, saying that the villagers are gathering for a feast to celebrate the sailors' return. May he tell them there is a wedding to be celebrated as well? The Dutchman and Senta each nod, and the three rejoice. Senta solemnly gives her hand, the Dutchman defies all hell now that a woman loves him, and Daland urges them to the feast.

**Comment:** *Daland's reentrance here really is a bit much, with its "So, tell me, what have you two decided?" air, but we need him in order to have a rousing bass/bass-baritone/soprano trio. Senta's voice soars over the men's, creating a sympathy for this woman who is bursting loose at last.*

### Act III

Setting: The harbor, with the houses of the village in the background. Daland's ship is at the dock, with sailors aboard drinking. The Dutchman's ship is next to it, enveloped in eerie gloom.

The sailors aboard Daland's ship are drinking and dancing, celebrating their return home.

**Comment:** *The Sailors' Chorus is a straightforward, fun, and entirely hummable piece of music, snippets of which we have heard in the Overture and in Act I. The stage directions indicate that the sailors are to be dancing clumsily, stamping their feet at the stresses of each measure. It's hard to know exactly what effect Wagner was intending, because in actual performance the good gentlemen of the chorus invariably look like idiots and sound like a cattle stampede.*

The girls of the village arrive at the dockside with baskets of food and drink. They comment that the sailors seem to be having a good party without their help, but the sailors call for them to stay. The girls offer refreshment, saying they should send some over to their neighbors, the Dutchmen's crew. Daland's crew say the Dutch are still sleeping, exhausted from their voyage, but the girls are curious, and call to the Dutch. They are answered by total silence. The Norwegian sailors joke that the Dutch, apparently, are dead, and don't need food and drink. The girls try again. Don't the Dutch boys have girlfriends on shore? Aren't they hungry or thirsty? The Norwegian sailors join forces with the girls, calling for the Dutch to wake up. Silence again. The girls grow fearful: these sailors truly are dead! Daland's crew joke that this ship must be the legendary Flying Dutchman. Indeed, it looks just like it! Then let them be, advise the girls. There's no need to wake the dead. The Norwegians taunt the Dutch. How many years have they been afloat? The girls back away from the dock, afraid. They hand their baskets to Daland's crew, saying they'll return later, and run off. Daland's crew descend on the baskets, eating, drinking, and singing their song.

As they sing, there are stirrings aboard the Dutchman's ship. A blue light glows out of it. Although remaining calm elsewhere, the sea begins to churn just around the Dutchman's ship, and a wind blows through its rigging. The ghost crew becomes visible, and they sing about their captain. He is on land again, hoi-ho! The blonde maiden swears to him, hoi-ho! But she will leave him. Captain, you are not lucky in love! Their ship tosses about, though Daland's is calm. Daland's crew are frightened at the ghost chorus, and try to drown them out with their own song, but they cannot conquer the Dutch. Terrified, the Norwegians flee below deck, crossing themselves as they run. The Dutch ghost marks this with a shrill, mocking laugh, and a deathly calm descends on the scene as before.

*Comment: The double chorus is pure gangbuster opera at its best, and justification, if any were necessary, for the unaffected simplicity of the Sailors' Chorus. The ghost chorus has an airy quality, blowing over and right through the coarser Norwegians' simple tune.*

*This scene also provides the production team a good opportunity to pull out all the necessary stops to portray the point of conflict between the worlds of the living and the dead.*

Senta runs out of her house, pursued by Erik. He asks what evil power has led her astray. Daland's betrayal he could understand, but Senta's? Conflicted, she says she must do her sacred duty, but Erik asks what of her duty to him, when she led him to believe she would marry him? She asks, in her confusion, if she had sworn eternal faith to Erik, and he asks how she can deny it. He speaks lovingly of happier days they shared. When she put her arms around his neck and clasped his hand, wasn't that a promise?

*Comment: Poor Erik. Everybody complains about his lovely aria here. Indeed, he shuts down the action pretty effectively with his old-fashioned cavatina, but that's the point exactly. Without Erik's aria, all the action in Act III would be in the realm of the supernatural, and this story is about the clash of this world and the next. The real problem is that Wagner had not yet become as deft at this balancing act as he would in later years, and Erik's aria does strike us as a bit of a comedown.*

The Dutchman has appeared unnoticed and has heard the end of Erik's declaration of love. "Lost," cries the Dutchman. "Salvation is lost forever!" Senta tries to stop him, but the Dutchman boards his ship and orders the crew to put out to sea. Despite Senta's protests, he gives a loud whistle and takes his leave of the land forever. Senta insists she will keep her vow, the Dutchman declares he no longer believes in her or in God, while Erik begs Senta to save herself, since she is clearly possessed by Satan.

*Comment: Since many operas are based on love triangles, the final trio is a logical and exciting way to wrap things up. Wagner later discarded this practice as too traditional, but here he shows us what he could do with the genre when he put his mind to it. Although very brief, this trio provides both a climax and an emotional catharsis.*

The Dutchman turns to accuse Senta. She had sworn her fidelity only to him, and not before God. If she had, she would be eternally damned as well, like so many other women before her. He bids farewell to her and to hope. Erik calls for help. Senta tells the Dutchman she knows who he is and accepts the fate of loving him unto death. Daland, Mary, and others rush down to try to help her. The Dutchman denies that Senta knows who he is. He points to the red sails of his ship as they unfurl, and declares he is the Flying Dutchman, whom all sailors know. His crew begins their ghostly sea song. Daland and Erik hold the struggling Senta as the Dutchman bounds aboard his ship like lightning and instantly puts to sea. The villagers beg Senta to get hold of herself, but she struggles free and climbs up a cliff overlooking the sea. She calls after the Dutchman, telling him to praise his guardian angel, for she has remained true! She flings herself into the sea.

The Dutchman's ship sinks and instantly disappears. In the distance, the villagers see the Dutchman and Senta, embracing, soaring to heaven. They are transfigured. The curse is ended.

**Comment:** *Such an ending compensates with excitement for what it lacks in subtlety. The Dutchman's farewell address is stirring, and Senta gets to cast off some soaring phrases as her answer to a "suicide aria." No wonder the greats jostle to play the Dutchman and Senta.*

*As difficult as Senta's leap into the sea may be to pull off on stage, it's nothing compared to what Wagner has ordered up to follow that. Sinking a ship on stage and depicting the lovers' transfiguration is a tall order for any house, and few productions attempt it at face value. (Any that did would look downright ridiculous.) Expect a great deal of lighting effects and abstract expressionism instead. Small matter. After the Dutchman's theme sounds for the last time (read: "He's sinking"), the redemption theme, which has been prepared throughout the course of the evening, soars through the strings, well ornamented with harps. As we have already noted, no one in the audience will be able to misconstrue the harped-out salvific message, no matter what grotesqueries are happening on stage.*

## BASICS: WHEN TO EAT, DRINK, AND VISIT THE RESTROOM

One of the reasons for *Dutchman*'s continuing popularity with audiences could be that it is short. Unless the one-act version is used, this is your only opportunity to enjoy a Wagner opera without preparing your body as if for a triathlon. Act I is under an hour, Act II just about an hour, and Act III a scandalously short half hour. You can attend a performance of *Dutchman*, eat, drink, visit the restroom as your body dictates, return home with a head full of glorious music, and probably still catch the late news before bed.

But you may not always be so lucky with this opera. The one-act, no-intermissions edition is often used these days. The rationale for this is that Wagner originally wanted it done in this manner, and the one-act version was used when *Dutchman* finally arrived at Bayreuth in 1901. This is all true, but Wagner wanted many things done that we conveniently find easy to ignore (like most of his stage directions, for example). The fact of the matter is that hard-core Wagnerians don't feel like they've had an authentic experience unless they've suffered at least a little. Sitting through two and a half hours without appearing to have a thought for any carnal needs is considered a sign of devotion.

Perhaps. In any case, *Dutchman* still represents a laughably minor challenge to your constitution, and the one-act version is good, manageable practice for the real marathons, like *Götterdämmerung* and *Meistersinger*. Just approach it as you would a long movie that begins at eight o'clock, minus the popcorn and trips to the restroom.

## ROUGH SPOTS AND HOW TO GET THROUGH THEM

If you have major trouble staying attentive in this one, you're dead meat for any other Wagner opera. Still, it is an opera, and some moments will interest you less than others. *The Flying Dutchman* uses much of the classic operatic form of recitative, aria, ensemble,

chorus, et cetera, and Wagner never really mastered recitative until
he rethought it all on his own terms. (These are the "talky" sections
in between the showstoppers.)

Daland and the Dutchman engage in a bit of less-than-thrilling
recitative in Act I before they settle into a duet. Watch the performers
carefully. Even if their voices are similar in tone, are they convincing
you of the completely alien natures of these two archetypes? Act II
has no real lags unless the Erik is a clod. Even so, it's often as interesting to watch Senta reacting to Erik's words as it is to focus on Erik.
And there's no need to worry about Act III. Even though some see
Erik's intrusion as a wet blanket, his cavatina is very brief and quite
lovely. Although it sounds supremely oxymoronic, just remind yourself that any *longueurs* (see the Glossary) in this opera will be very
short.

## PRODUCTIONS: WHAT YOU MIGHT EXPECT TO SEE

First of all, you're lucky if you see anything at all, since everybody
likes to produce *Dutchman* pretty much in the dark. (You know, it's
supposed to be, like, spooky.)

If you can see the stage, there's no telling what will be there. Every
production likes to play games with this old favorite. Updating the
action to the twentieth century is one of the most common practices.
(Updating is what directors do when they have run out of other ideas.
It's all the rage at the moment.) There's no real reason why *Dutchman* shouldn't be updated—Wagner's setting the story in the eighteenth century was a rather random choice—except the Dutchman's
ship as oil tanker might lose a little of the romance that's so crucial to
the tale. On the other hand, you won't have to listen to the nautical
types in the audience carry on about errors in the rigging and sails.

The supernatural element of the story presents a challenge. *Dutchman* does not take place in an entirely supernatural space, like, it
could be argued, *Parsifal*. The supernatural is always framed within
the here and now. Witness the ghost chorus scene in Act III. Only the
Dutchman's ship tosses in the storm, while the rest of the stage is

calm. The score makes this as clear as the stage directions. Capturing the contrast of the two worlds is a lot harder than staging an infernal dance of death.

A controversial production by Jean-Pierre Ponelle (San Francisco, 1975, later seen also at the Metropolitan in New York) circumvented this by casting the whole story into the realm of the unreal. The story was presented as a dream of the Steersman, which would certainly explain his dozing off while the Dutchman's ship parks noisily next to him. The balance of the action took place on Daland's ship, with random details representing other places, in the manner of dreams. The Forty Fat Fräuleins had helms for spinning wheels. God knows what that was meant to signify, but it looked cool. Audiences had strong reactions to this production, pro and con, and it is still fiercely debated by partisans. The same year also saw an important production by Harry Kupfer at Bayreuth, where the drama was presented as Senta's hallucination. This is quite credible. Mary even warns Senta that bad things will happen if she continues to stare at the Dutchman's picture.

Whatever other concepts are paraded across the stage, a *Dutchman* production is successful if it (1) allows the characters of the two leads to come through, (2) creates a genuinely compelling weirdness around the Dutchman and his world, (3) can be convincingly moving, rather than kitschy, at the end, and (4) is sung gloriously.

## PERFORMANCE HISTORY AND ESSENTIAL LORE OF *DUTCHMAN*

*The Flying Wagners (1839)* How much of the *Dutchman* is a direct result of the Wagners' own harrowing voyage to London in 1839? All of it, if you believe the mythographers, and almost none, if you prefer the dry-as-dust scholars. The truth is probably in between. Wagner had already conceived of the *Dutchman* from various sources before leaving Riga, originally setting the action in Scotland. When the ship *Thetis* (whose dimensions match those Wagner indicated for Daland's ship) sought shelter in the fjord of Sandvigen, Wagner remembered the place and set the first act of the opera there. (It's called Sandwike in German.) He records in his autobiography that he made note of the sailors' song and its echo from the cliffs of the fjord, and there's no reason to doubt this. Also, anyone who has crossed the North Sea can attest to its inherently menacing feel. A calm, midday sky can turn pitch black in an instant when a sudden storm arrives, or forms out of nowhere (as in Act III). Either Wagner took this from firsthand experience or his powers of imagination should be more celebrated than they are.

*Minna's metamorphosis (1840)* In his first drafts of *Dutchman*, Wagner had named the heroine "Minna." Whether this was a tribute to his long-suffering wife or a suggestion that she throw herself off a cliff as a sign of devotion, we'll never know. In any case, he decided to name the heroine "Senta" when he moved the action to Norway. (Is Wagner lying again here? How many Scottish lasses are named Minna? What difference did the locale make?) As we have already seen, Wagner had been impressed by the sound of the word "Tjenta!" which is a Norwegian name for a housemaid, and came up with Senta. Interestingly, "Chencha" is the common Mexican name for a housemaid as well. Perhaps there really was more pre-Columbian transatlantic traffic than we usually assume after all!

*A low-budget debut (1843)* Opening night in Dresden was less than Wagner hoped for, despite the presence of his favorite soprano, Wilhelmine Schröder-Devrient, as Senta. The production was dreadful, with sets borrowed from the theater's other productions. There were no "cliffs" available for Act I, which must have made the "echo" seem rather gratuitous. Wagner complained bitterly about this, and his mania for being personally in charge of all aspects of production really started with this experience, culminating at Bayreuth toward the end of his life. The audience was pleased anyway but somehow bewildered by the musical difference between *Dutchman* and the previous season's *Rienzi*. In any case, Wagner's early biographers, who saw their idol as even more of a victim than he saw himself, maintained the premiere was a fiasco. This was not the case, although it was less of a success than *Rienzi*.

*Revisions (1850–64)* In later years (in Zurich in the 1850s and particularly at Munich in 1864, when King Ludwig gave Wagner the means to present "model" performances), Wagner changed a few details of the score of *Dutchman*. The Overture and the finale now ended with Senta's themes rather than the Dutchman's, and the noisiest passages were toned down, the mature Wagner having learned to create effects with fewer such tricks as cymbal crashes. Occasionally, a new production today will use the original 1843 score in some search for authenticity on the assumption that any revisions a composer makes are concessions to bourgeois-pig audiences (as if Wagner ever made any concessions to anyone!).

*Very foreign productions (1870s)* *Dutchman* cruised across Germany in a stately fashion in the 1860s and finally made it overseas, although in a slightly altered form. Its London debut was at Drury Lane in 1870, given in Italian as *L'Olandese dannato*, or, quaintly translated, "The Damned Dutchman." This was the first production of a Wagner opera in Britain. It must have worked on some level, since in 1877 it was staged again at London's grand Covent Garden (then called the Royal Italian Opera House) in Italian, which was the language of all productions there at that time. The prevailing theory was that singers had to sing in their native languages or risk sounding "false," a theory that Wagner had once propounded. The American premiere was in Philadelphia in 1876, in (you guessed it) Italian. No wonder people still refer to *Dutchman* as Wagner's most "Italian" opera.

*Cosima's Bayreuth production (1901)* Wagner's intention was that all of his works from *Dutchman* to *Parsifal* should be performed in his private shrine at Bayreuth. To complete the canon, Cosima presented *Dutchman* as the final new production of her "reign," having already done each of the others.

The 1901 Bayreuth production, presented in one act, as Wagner had originally wanted, was widely praised by critics. Another reason for the success that year was the Dutchman of Anton van Rooy, who was a real live Dutchman himself. Rooy was later "banished" from Bayreuth for participating in the unsanctioned 1903 Metropolitan Opera *Parsifal*. Destroyed he wasn't, staying on in New York and making a good deal more money there than he would have earned in Germany. His performances of the Dutchman at the Met through the first decade and a half of the century have become legendary, and solidified this opera's status as a star vehicle.

*Longest ovations at the Met (1959–60)*  In case there are any doubts about this opera as a star vehicle, let it be noted that the record for the longest ovations at the Metropolitan belongs to George London and Leonie Rysanek for their performances of the Dutchman and Senta during the 1959–60 season. Of course no one can say exactly how long the applause ran (even accounts among those who were supposedly there vary), but most agree on about thirty minutes.

# TANNHÄUSER
# UND DER SÄNGERKRIEG
# AUF WARTBURG

Premiere: Dresden, 1845; revised version, Paris, 1861.

## THE NAME

*What to call it* The official name of this opera, as written above, means "Tannhäuser and the Singing Contest on the Wartburg." Never attempt to call it that, in English or German. A simple *Tannhäuser* will do.

*How to pronounce it* The *umlaut* (those two little dots above the second *a* in *Tannhäuser*) is a distinctly German pronunciation indicator. You will sometimes see it spelled *Tannhaeuser*, which is the correct way to spell it if your typewriter or computer has no umlaut (see also *Götterdämmerung*). This is not a problem for English-speakers. The sound of *äu* is the same as our *oy*. Pronounce *Tannhäuser* to rhyme with "John Hoyzer." The *s* is voiced, like our *z*. Linger over the double *n* for full effect.

## WHAT IS *TANNHÄUSER*?

*Tannhäuser* shows us a romantic look back to an idealized Middle Ages, complete with castles, lusty troubadours, saintly ladies, and pious pilgrims who sing superbly. This cultural nostalgia pervaded Wagner's era as the Industrial Revolution rolled across Europe. It expressed itself in such diverse places as the popular novels of Sir

Walter Scott (*Ivanhoe* and others) and King Ludwig of Bavaria's proto-Disneyland castle, Schloss Neuschwannstein.

The story of *Tannhäuser* bounces between the reckless sensuality of the Grotto of Venus and the refined Christian court of the Wartburg Castle atop a hill. Allegorical interpreters and Jungian analysts are permitted a field day with this one. The net result is a tale of a man caught between his conflicting ideals of women—saintly virgin and seductive whore. This being a mid-nineteenth-century work, the outcome is a foregone conclusion.

For this libretto, Wagner blithely plundered medieval mythology, conflating several different legends and gaily mixing historical and fictional characters. Literary scholars of the time were appalled, but the quiltwork nature of *Tannhäuser* gives the audience a wide selection to enjoy, including earthy sex, sacred love, court formality, despair, and redemption, all painted in the broadest possible strokes. It is one of Wagner's most approachable creations.

It is also one of his most uneven. This is the opera Rossini had in mind when he supposedly made the famous observation that "Wagner has great moments and lousy quarter hours." On first hearing, there are undeniable *longueurs*. But the flip side is that the *longueurs* are never too *longue*—the dullest spectator can count on being woken up with a brisk tune every several minutes. *Tannhäuser* does not present any musical difficulties to the novice Wagnerite. There is no need to study harmony or leitmotivs ahead of time in the way one prepares for *Tristan* or the *Ring*. The contrast of moods in this piece is depicted in such a clear and broad manner that the most unmusical member of the audience will be able to follow. Other delights making *Tannhäuser* ever popular are an unforgettable chorus, which pops up whenever the action gets too slow, a rip-roaring soprano aria, a great baritone aria (for which baritones are truly grateful; much of Wagner's music for them in other operas is demanding and thankless), a thrilling "narrative" for the tenor, Wagner's only real ballet scene as curtain raiser, and some excellent ensembles.

## CAST OF CHARACTERS

TANNHÄUSER *(tenor)* A knight whose real name is Heinrich von Ofterdingen. Tannhäuser is a troubadour, which in Germany was called a Minnesinger. These knights were noble, unlike minstrels, and were expected to be equally at home in battle or composing verses and music.

ELISABETH *(soprano)* The lady of the Wartburg Castle, virgin niece of the Landgrave Hermann. This character is history's Saint Elizabeth of Hungary. While the historical Saint Elizabeth wore clothes of the poor and avoided court ceremony, our diva is invariably clad in high-medieval kitsch and seems quite at home presiding over court functions.

HERMANN, LANDGRAVE OF THURINGIA *(bass)* The lord of the Wartburg Castle and uncle of Elisabeth. Under the historical Hermann, the Thuringian court became famous for its refinement and piety. The Wartburg Castle exists to this day, near the city of Eisenach, and can be clearly seen from the Munich–Berlin train.

WOLFRAM VON ESCHENBACH *(baritone)* A troubadour at the Wartburg Castle and (a rarity in Wagner's works) a rather nice guy. The historical Wolfram wrote a medieval epic called *Parzival*, which Wagner would later plunder as a source for his final opera.

WALTHER VON DER VOGELWEIDE *(tenor)*, BITEROLF *(bass)*, HEINRICH DER SCHREIBER *(tenor)*, REINMAR VON ZWETER *(bass)* All troubadours at the Wartburg Castle. Although they have interesting legendary and historical sources, all we really need to know about these guys with confusing names is that they are always there together and they always burst into song.

VENUS *(soprano or mezzo-soprano)* Yes, *that* Venus. The all-purpose pre-Christian goddess of love. While this role is a brief one in terms of actual time on stage, it's considered a plum and is always performed by a major star.

A Young Shepherd (*soprano*) A brief role, but one everybody remembers. The music is agreeable to the voice. This is a "trouser role," that is, a man or boy in the story performed by a woman. Sopranos who like to be thought of as serious artistes are often found in this part, and it is a definitive debut role with a large company.

## THE OPERA

### Overture

The Overture opens with the opera's most famous tune, the celebrated Pilgrims' Chorus, which we will hear sung at several points later. It is first stated quietly (read "far away") by the horns, growing in the orchestra until it is thundered out by the trombones to a frenetic string accompaniment. It then fades away.

**Comment:** *The conductor Herbert von Karajan once explained that one should imagine an old lady stuck in a burning building while the fire trucks rushed to the scene, with the trombones being the sound of the sirens and the strings representing the old lady's heart palpitations. Whatever. This overture is frequently heard in the concert hall, and even shows up in church sometimes in organ transcriptions by Liszt and others. It is one of Wagner's "hits."*

### Act I, Scene 1

Setting: In the Grotto of Venus, the Venusberg.

The curtain rises on a ballet depicting a bacchanale, or orgy, in full swing. Nymphs and satyrs frolic about in an excess of sexual abandon. The music of the Bacchanale fades as the various nymphs and satyrs exhaust themselves. When there is total silence we notice Venus herself reposing on her couch, with the knight Tannhäuser out of it at her feet.

**Comment:** *Wagner's libretto summary of the ballet is extended, detailed—and hilarious. Apparently, a thorough knowledge of classical mythology was considered a prerequisite to attending an orgy in his day. Most modern productions try to go the other way and outdo each other in sheer raunch. In any case, there are many dancers chasing each other around the stage to very frenzied music for ten minutes. Even castanets are heard in the orchestra, which must have signified utter depravity to northern European audiences.*

Tannhäuser awakes as if from a dream. Venus makes the fatal lover's error of asking what's on his mind. He has lost track of time in her grotto, where he fled after rejecting the human world at the Wartburg. She is shocked that he should get tired of her charms and be nostalgic for the cold world above, and commands him to sing her praises. Picking up his portable harp, he strums and sings dutifully. (We have heard this tune during the ballet. It is a forthright, upbeat song that sounds more like a call to arms than a paean to the Queen of Love.) Three times he sings her praises, but at the end of each he adds that no mortal could endure such changeless ecstasy, and begs to be released. Venus is not accustomed to such treatment, and becomes increasingly annoyed with Tannhäuser. Go, she tells him, adding that he will never find happiness outside of her cave. It is almost a curse. As a parting shot, he says that he never did find fulfillment with her, and now will seek it from the Virgin Mary. Venus and her grotto disappear at the mention of the holy name.

### Act I, Scene 2

Setting: A valley. The Wartburg Castle is visible in the background atop a hill. There is a road or path meandering through the scene, with a roadside shrine to the Virgin near the center. Blue skies.

Tannhäuser hasn't moved, but the scene has changed around him. Sheep bells are heard, and the young shepherd approaches accompanying himself on his pipes. The Shepherd, a lyric soprano, sings gaily but hauntingly about merry May. From afar, we hear the approaching chorus of pilgrims, gathering for their journey to Rome. They arrive on stage, singing only snippets of their full chorus. As they mention sin and shame, the Shepherd asks them to remember him at their destination, while Tannhäuser wails of his own wretchedness. The pilgrims pass off stage.

The horns of a hunting party are heard in the distance. The knights of the Wartburg, Hermann, Wolfram, Biterolf, Walther, and Heinrich, arrive to find Tannhäuser prostrate with shame at the Virgin's statue. "Where have you been?" they ask him. "Don't ask," he replies. They entreat him to return to the Wartburg with them, although Biterolf is noticeably less enthusiastic than the others. Tannhäuser begs off. Wolfram insists, reminding him of Elisabeth. At her name, Tannhäuser suddenly comes to life—further evidence of the power of mentioning a woman's name in this opera. Wolfram adds that she's been pining away in Tannhäuser's absence and may even be in love. That's all Tannhäuser has to hear. "To her!" he cries. The rest of the hunting party arrives on stage in time to blow a fanfare for the finale.

**Comment**: *If you'll notice, everybody in Act I comes to, or goes away from, Tannhäuser, while he stands more or less still in the center of the stage. The sudden scene change in the middle, when Venus's world disappears, is a chance for the production team to show their stuff. The music shifts suddenly from erotic frenzy to the calmness of the Shepherd's pipes and clear voice. The effect is stunning and cleansing, like a good bath after too much sex. The passage of the pilgrims across the stage seems rather random at first, but it gives us a visual reference for later. It is what we would call a "tease." When they sing offstage in Act II, we, like Tannhäuser, can say, "Oh, there go the pilgrims on their way to Rome!"*

*When the hunting party arrives on stage right after the pilgrims' departure, we must begin to wonder if we are in a pleasant valley or a transit center. Here Wagner, the master of theater, distracts us by making the music and the action quite involved, compared to the previous scene-painting. I have seen productions in which these knights carry their lyres even in this scene, presumably to show their equal comfort with weapons and instruments. It means that every single person in this scene carries a musical instrument, making this valley look like Manhattan's Upper West Side on rehearsal day. When the knights sing to welcome Tannhäuser back to their company, we have a lush ensemble for male voices. Scholars sniff at this as melodic and traditional compared to the later Wagner, but we who are less concerned with theory can appreciate the sheer beauty of the music. The upbeat ending to the act makes us aware of the possibility of salvation for the hero.*

## Act II

Setting: The Hall of Song in the Wartburg Castle, a big, important room.

Elisabeth enters alone, greeting the noble hall she has not entered since Tannhäuser's departure.

**Comment:** *The act opens with this opera's great diva moment, Elisabeth's aria "Dich, teure Halle." It appears frequently on recital programs, even by many sopranos who shouldn't be singing it.*

Wolfram leads Tannhäuser in and discreetly withdraws backstage. Elisabeth welcomes her lost knight, pouring her feelings out to him quite indiscreetly. From Wolfram's asides we learn that he, too, has been chastely in love with Elisabeth. The men leave. The Landgrave Hermann, Elisabeth's uncle, enters and tells her of the song tournament about to take place in the hall. He suspects her love for Tannhäuser. Horns announce the approach of the guests. The long parade of knights and nobles, each accompanied by ladies and retinues, enter, singing praises to the hall and the Landgrave, while trumpeters blare fanfares. The competing knights, including Tannhäuser, Wolfram, and our other friends, enter with harps, and are ceremoniously seated before the assembly. In excruciating detail, Hermann announces the theme of the contest: the nature of love. Elisabeth herself will preside and award the prize. The pages command Wolfram to begin.

Wolfram sings a nice song about the purity of true love, embodied by Elisabeth, and prays that he may never "sully that clear fountain with impure thoughts." Tannhäuser jumps up out of turn and sings that Wolfram's sort of love is weak, while he himself has known the pleasures of the flesh. The assembly is astonished. Biterolf draws his sword, challenging Tannhäuser, in song, for insulting the honor of women. Tannhäuser retorts that Biterolf knows nothing of sexual love and should shut up. The crowd rises in agitation. Wolfram prays that the pure thoughts of his song may quiet the situation. Tannhäuser forgets himself completely, and grabs his harp to sing a lusty paean—to Venus! Elisabeth staggers as the other ladies run shrieking from the hall. The men surround Tannhäuser with swords drawn, but Elisabeth quells them. He has sinned, and wounded her heart gravely, but they are not the judges of the world. Tannhäuser must live and seek salvation. It is God's will. Tannhäuser is contrite again, the men insult him, Elisabeth prays. When the pilgrims are heard off stage, Tannhäuser runs off to join them with the cry "To Rome!"

**Comment:** *The famous Entrance of the Guests is Wagner in the tradition of grand opera: nine minutes of lush orchestra, horn fanfares onstage, offstage, and in the pit, and a procession that amounts to a medieval fashion show. While the contest itself is dull in comparison, Tannhäuser and his dirty ditties waste little time in spicing things up. The final ensemble is more elaborate and detailed than the one that ended Act I. It becomes a rich juxtaposition of human and divine justice, with Elisabeth's soaring voice (on a good night) providing the lattice around which the male voices intertwine.*

## Act III

An orchestral introduction describes Tannhäuser's pilgrimage to Rome. We hear themes associated with the pilgrims, Elisabeth's prayers, Venus's delights, and the jubilee at Rome. We then hear a good deal of angst. The curtain opens.

Setting: The valley, as in Act I, Scene 2, but in somber colors of autumn. It is dusk.

Elisabeth is at prayer before the statue of the Virgin. Wolfram appears and sings in admiration. The pilgrims come on stage slowly and a few at a time, singing of their absolutions received in Rome. Elisabeth combs the crowd for Tannhäuser, but he is not among them. They depart, she despairs. Quietly, she prays to the Virgin for death, so that her heavenly intercessions for her knight may be more effective than earthly ones had been. She leaves and Wolfram, who fears the worst, sings a song to the Evening Star, commending it to guard her in her journey, wherever it may lead.

*Comment: Elisabeth's prayerful aria opening Act III uses all the colors left unexplored in Act II to express solemnity and pious resignation. Wolfram's subsequent aria is the famous "Evening Star" ("O du mein holde Abendstern"), which has grown as hackneyed as anything else in Wagner. In the hands of an artist, it can be quite beautiful in a very sedate and haunting way. It is, in effect, the "eleven o'clock ballad."*

Tannhäuser staggers on stage. He's a mess. He tells Wolfram he's seeking the Grotto of Venus again since there's nowhere else for him to go. Wolfram presses him for information about his pilgrimage to Rome. Tannhäuser begins what is known as the "Rome Narrative." He walked penitently to Rome, refusing all comfort. Once there, thousands were granted pardons, but not him. When he told the pope of his stay at the Venusberg, the pope answered that he could forget about being saved until the wooden staff in the pope's hand blossomed forth in greenery ("until hell freezes over," we might say).

*Comment: Musicians like to praise the "Rome Narrative" to the skies; if you want to impress the experts, rave about it. The symphonic interweaving of themes foreshadows later Wagner, sometimes eclipsing the tenor. Various themes are laid out in the sequence of the music. It is quite possible to follow the story of Tannhäuser's pilgrimage to Rome without paying attention to a word and merely listening to the orchestra. Trudging lower strings moan out a theme we have heard in the introduction to Act III, a theme one might call "Tannhäuser's misery." When he gets to Rome, he hears bells and choirs from "on high," depicted in silvery tones by flutes and woodwinds. As he approaches the pope, these tones are repeated more menacingly by the brass. The pope's pronouncement of damnation (quoted by Tannhäuser, of course) is masterly. The first two and a half lines are on one note, in the style of a medieval chant. On the word "Venusberg" he starts to sing in minor intervals; that is, "off-key." The quoted pontiff continues to chant, but quite diabolically. He is as evil as Tannhäuser's sin. (This whole episode, as indeed the entire opera, is a less-than-subtle dig at the papacy by Wagner, who was as anti-Catholic as he was anti–everything else.) When Tannhäuser revives and hears the bells and choirs again (more flutes), he claims that they sickened him, and our ears agree that they sound a bit finicky after what we have heard. It is almost a relief when he calls on Frau Venus, and the orchestra instantly breaks into frenzied figures from the Venusberg scene.*

*Following the musical developments of the "Rome Narrative" is not only interesting for its own sake, but excellent practice of the theme identification skills you'll want for performances of the Ring.*

Tannhäuser calls out to Venus, who appears, gloating and singing. Wolfram prays ineffectively, finally crying out, "Elisabeth!" Tannhäuser does another about-face, and Venus vanishes. From the Wartburg a funeral procession approaches. Elisabeth's body is carried forward. Tannhäuser cries, "Saint Elisabeth, pray for me!" and dies under her bier. From the other side of the stage pilgrims appear singing of a miracle. A priest's wooden staff has blossomed in greenery. Tannhäuser is saved. The full ensemble sings praise to God while the Pilgrims' Chorus, the first theme of the opera, fully elaborated through the chorus and orchestra, rings forth.

**Comment:** *There are basically three musical archetypes around which the score is built: the pilgrims' music, representing salvation;*

*Elisabeth's prayers, representing piety; and the Venusberg music, representing fleshly sensuality. These overlap and clash here in Act III, but the music coming from the orchestra is usually matched directly to the action on stage, so there is little chance for confusion, which is not always the case in Wagner's later works. In fact, it wasn't always the case in* Tannhäuser. *In the original Dresden production, Wagner "signified" Venus's return only in the orchestra. Nobody understood what was happening. When he revised the opera for Paris, he put Venus back on stage and singing to make sure everybody comprehended the conflict of the two female archetypes.*

*Elisabeth's death is a bit "convenient," dramatically speaking. Indeed, it is astounding how often Wagner's heroines just seem to expire for no real reason beyond plot resolution or misogyny. Elsa in* Lohengrin, *Isolde, and Kundry in* Parsifal *all just sort of drop dead at the end of their respective operas. At least the hero does the same in this opera—the only instance in Wagner's work where the tenor-hero shares a psychospiritual death with the diva-heroine. Hearing the full Pilgrims' Chorus at the end wraps things up nicely. Just try not to whistle it on your way out of the opera house.*

## BASICS: WHEN TO EAT, DRINK, AND VISIT THE RESTROOM

*Tannhäuser* is a fairly short opera by Wagnerian standards, and presents no particular challenges to the average person's constitution. In most of the editions used, Act I and Act II are each about an hour and a quarter long, while Act III is about an hour. Some drowsiness may occur at the beginning of the third act. There is a long (eight-minute) orchestral introduction, Wolfram sings for a bit, the pilgrims make one of their endless treks across the stage, and we settle down for a long and lovely, but rather sedate, prayer from Elisabeth. This is followed by Wolfram's very meditative "Evening Star" song, until Tannhäuser returns and all hell (literally) breaks loose again. You may want to avoid eating heavily, having that extra cocktail, or taking cold medicine during the second intermission, or you'll risk dozing through some of the opera's nicest moments in the first part of Act III.

## ROUGH SPOTS AND HOW TO GET THROUGH THEM

*The Ballet* Most people can enjoy dance, at least for a few minutes. If you detest ballet, or if the production you're seeing is either too effete or too pornographic for your taste, just close your eyes and listen to the orchestra. While some of the Venusberg music may strike you as obvious, much of it is bizarre and quite radical.

*Act I* It's hard to get too bored in Act I—the scenery changes too often!

*Act II* The start of the act will grip you. Elisabeth's aria *"Dich, teure Halle"* is a big moment, and her duet with Tannhäuser is loaded with nuance. If the Elisabeth is a good actress, watch her carefully in this scene for indications of her complex nature; if she's not, the orchestra will give you the same information. Her uncle the Landgrave Hermann, however, is a different story. After the musical and visual spectacle of the Entrance of the Guests has caught the attention of even the dullest members of the audience, Wagner capitalizes on the moment to torture everyone to death with a boring speech by Hermann devoid of any interest. Later in his career, Wagner would learn to add very subtle touches to such moments, giving us the illusion that they must be at least deep if not thrilling, but this one is a wash any way you look at it. Take this time (seven minutes) to inspect the lovely medieval costumes of the chorus. If you are at a postmodern production where the chorus is attired in T-shirts and jeans (very unlikely outside of Germany), calculate your taxes or plan your next party.

The actual Song Contest begins with a less-than-exciting offering by Wolfram. This is deliberate, I think, on the part of Wagner the dramatist. Pure love is less dramatic than the earthy love Tannhäuser sings of directly after. Wolfram's song is not long. Watch Tannhäuser and see how well he convinces you that he is "dreaming of Venus" while Wolfram is singing about the other end of the love spectrum.

The rest of the act is a breeze.

*Act III* The first part of Act III is very mellow, but not boring. It is the contemplative part of the opera. Just get comfortable and listen closely.

In Tannhäuser's "Rome Narrative," there is much to hear in the orchestra even if (as often happens) the tenor's voice is wearing thin.

## PERFORMANCE HISTORY AND ESSENTIAL LORE OF *TANNHÄUSER*

*Rough beginnings* (1845–60) Wagner started making revisions to the score of *Tannhäuser* after its first performance. Part of the problem was that many of his ideas were unclear in performance, and everyone was dissatisfied with the tenor. Thus, the great tradition of complaining about the incapacity of the tenor singing Tannhäuser began on opening night, and continues unabated to the present day.

Public reaction to *Tannhäuser* was, predictably, varied. Some swooned in rapture, others retched, while most were plain confused. Jury-rigged performances appeared around Germany, prompting Wagner to write a pamphlet titled *On Performing Tannhäuser* in 1852. Excerpts were played at concerts and recitals all over Europe and, eventually, the New World. Full productions were rare and generally unsatisfying, although an important production of it in New York in 1859 did much to further the Wagner "cause" in the States. Finally, Wagner set his sights on the Paris Opéra as the best place for his *Tannhäuser* to conquer the world. He set about revising it again, cutting the Overture and expanding the Venusberg scene for the ballet junkies of Paris.

*Tannhäuser at the Paris Opéra* (1861) What followed was one of the most famous episodes in the history of opera. It was better than a fiasco, it was a genuine riot.

France has a long history of direct government involvement in the performing arts. To this day, managerial issues at the Opéra are cabinet-level issues. To get an opera produced there was, and remains, akin to passing a bill through a legislature. But the Paris Opéra was the apex at the time, and Wagner set his sights on it. His chief advocate with the French government was the wife of the Austrian ambassador, a Princess Metternich, who was unpopular both personally and as a representative of France's frequent enemy. So right away there was controversy among people who had never even heard Wagner's music. And then, of course, there was the music, always guaranteed to start a controversy.

And finally there was a certain group of gentlemen, you should pardon the expression, known as the Jockey Club. They were members of Paris's financial and aristocratic elite, notorious *bon vivants*, and a powerful bloc of boxholders at the Opéra (one can sense trouble already). The story ("legend" might be a better term) goes that they were accustomed to linger over their dinner, miss the first act of the opera entirely, and arrive for the second act. The ballet was always given during a later act of the opera so the good old boys of the Jockey Club could drool over their mistresses or prospective mistresses in the dance corps. The management tried hard to persuade Wagner to have the ballet in the second act. Since the Entrance of the Guests in Act II is something of a production number anyway, the idea was not absolutely unthinkable, but Wagner would not hear of it. In this instance, who can blame him?

The Jockeys geared for war, uniting all the various anti-Wagner (and anti-Austrian, anti-Imperial, anti-everything) factions. The first performance was greeted with whistles, catcalls, and noisemakers of all kinds. Though much of the audience was genuinely supportive of the work, it was only with difficulty that the performance managed to stumble to its conclusion. Even the presence of the Emperor Napoleon III and his Empress Eugénie did not quell the disturbance — indeed, their presence may have even been another cause of the riot. After the demonstrations grew over the second and third performances, with fights in the audience forcing the singers to sit down on the stage for up to fifteen minutes at a time while order was restored, the work was permitted to be withdrawn.

What exactly happened on those nights in Paris in 1861? Was it a clash of musical ideals, an antiforeign, anti-imperial expression, an assertion of power by a small faction, or a combination of all these causes? The matter remains debated to this day. Oddly, many Parisians became ardent Wagnerites as a reaction to the *affaire*, including such influential arbiters of the period as Baudelaire, Catulle Mendès, and Gustave Doré. We know that Wagner left Paris as soon as he could. His dislike of the French capital grew into one of his insane hatreds, and he was known to gloat gleefully and publicly when he heard the Parisians were reduced to eating rats in the siege of 1870–71. The Paris debacle was also one more clear indication that Wagner could not expect to gain fame and fortune by conventional commercial means, bringing him one step closer to creating his own universe in Bayreuth.

This story is sure to be brought up or referred to at any performance or discussion of *Tannhäuser*.

*Standardizing and Mainstreaming* Tannhäuser (1860–90) Meanwhile, the popularity of the opera grew, mostly through tidbits in the concert hall. Wagner himself supervised an important production in Vienna in 1875, and this is the edition we most often are presented with today. Confusingly enough, everyone persists in calling this the Paris version, but it is not. For one thing, it's in German, whereas the Paris version was in French. The important thing is that there was, at long last, an edition of the opera that pleased Wagner, and the number of productions in Europe and America rose sharply. In the 1880s, *Tannhäuser* was Wagner's most performed opera.

Tannhäuser *is "Canonized" at Bayreuth* (1891) After Wagner's death in 1883, his wife Cosima took the reins at the all-important Bayreuth festival. Her first new production, after a safe presentation of *Tristan* in 1886, was of *Tannhäuser* in 1891. This shocked many hard-core Wagnerites, who felt this opera was too traditional and conventionally operatic for Bayreuth, which should be reserved for the later "music dramas" such as the *Ring*. But Wagner had clearly instructed that all his works, whatever one wants to call them, from *Dutchman* to *Parsifal*, were to be duly presented at Bayreuth. He emphasized the point by telling Cosima, shortly before his death, that he "still owed the world *Tannhäuser*." The 1891 production was a great success with audiences and a sort of personal vindication for Cosima. It was in this production that Cosima, who did not like the "arms out" gesture the prima donna had found so "effective" for her entrance, secretly had the sleeves of the singer's gown sewn to the sides of her dress, thus eliminating any conventionally operatic gestures from her performance.

*Toscanini and* Tannhäuser (1930–33) In 1930, Arturo Toscanini was invited to conduct the first new production of *Tannhäuser* at Bayreuth since 1891. The first foreigner to conduct at Bayreuth, and an Italian at that, raised some nationalist hackles, but his *Tannhäuser* created such a sensation that one Nazi musicologist was moved to find evidence of Aryan ancestry in Toscanini's background. The success was repeated in 1931.

By 1933, what was once the Nazi threat had become the German Third Reich, and Toscanini, an uncompromising antifascist, quit Bayreuth. Hitler himself wrote an extremely polite letter to Toscanini, then in New York. Toscanini's reply (in English, no less) is priceless. He wrote what a "bitter disappointment" it would be to him if circumstances would not change sufficiently for him to return to Bayreuth. Since it was clear to all that the only change in circumstance that could mollify him would be Hitler's abdication, the matter was dropped and Toscanini spent the war years in America. Unfortunately, this stab at the Nazi co-opting of German cultural icons was softened when the great German composer Richard Strauss agreed to take over the conductor's podium at Bayreuth.

*Die schwarze Venus* (1961) Bayreuth was the site of yet another *Tannhäuser scandale* in 1961, when the twenty-four-year-old American Grace Bumbry took the role of Venus for the new production. Although her performance was, by all accounts, a triumph, the sight of a black person on Wagner's own stage was too much for certain elements of the audience to bear. Before we get too righteous about lingering effects of Nazi racial theory in modern Germany, we must remember that the Metropolitan Opera of New York only breached the color line in 1955.

## PRODUCTIONS: WHAT YOU MIGHT EXPECT TO SEE

Although directors with whacked-out ideas are eventually all drawn to Wagner, the general rule is that they leave *Tannhäuser* alone. The work is too firmly rooted in its medieval historical setting to make a lot of sense in, say, outer space or a suburban shopping mall. It does not take place in a sealed, inner psychological world, as do *Dutchman* and *Tristan*, nor in its own mythic space, like the *Ring* and *Parsifal*. A rarity like the successful Peter Sellars production for the Chicago Lyric Opera in 1988, with Tannhäuser portrayed as a televangelist and other postmodern touches, was actually attempting to look at the same issues as the standard productions, but in a more in-your-face sort of way. Productions that aim for a completely new reassessment of the basic issues of *Tannhäuser* have a hard time being anything other than parody, and that gets old pretty fast. Also, this is a relatively expensive opera to produce, and there are very few opera companies that can afford to mount a new production of it for such a brief term of service.

This still leaves a great deal of room for interpretation. For example, the Wartburg clearly stands for civilized society, with all its rules and confinements. How to represent that on stage? You can be very blunt about it, with the heralds and other lackeys in jackboots and armbands, as was trendy in Communist countries for a while, or you can drown the stage in medieval glitz and let the audience draw its own conclusions.

For the Venusberg scene, anything goes, scenically speaking.

There is one other aspect you may see emphasized. For some time, it has been popular to see Tannhäuser as the archetypal artist, misunderstood in all spheres of society. If the production stresses his physical isolation in respect to those around him, it may be in an attempt to follow this way of understanding the character.

The only other issue you should be aware of in different productions is (here we go again) which edition of the work is being presented. Almost all modern productions will follow the latest edition approved by Wagner (Vienna, 1875), or one so similar that only a Doctor of Music would notice, or care about, the difference. Occasionally, the so-called Dresden version pops up (as it did in London, for example, in 1984). If so, expect a truncated and less exciting Venusberg scene with little or no ballet, a longer Song Contest, and an overall harsher and less refined score.

## LOBBY TALK FOR *TANNHÄUSER* (IMPOSSIBLE LOVE — SOUND FAMILIAR?)

In many ways, *Tannhäuser* is Wagner's most dated tale. There is no getting around the fact that this is Romantic in every sense of the word, and the best productions are the ones that accept this fact at face value. The portrayals of sin and salvation are laid on with a trowel, and we moderns tend to look at that in a condescending way. Yet opera is often the science of saying the subtlest things in the biggest possible way, and *Tannhäuser* is not so remote from us as we would like to think. There are just a couple of hurdles to get past before we can see ourselves in this story.

The single most alienating element in the opera is the character of Tannhäuser himself. He is absolutely insufferable by any standards. Many of Wagner's characters are difficult to warm up to (Siegfried comes to mind), but they all have their reasons to be antisocial — except this one. The great tenor Jon Vickers even avoided singing this role because of Tannhäuser's total immorality. That's a hard one to fathom, considering that the other Wagner roles Vickers sang are hardly moral paragons. But the fact remains that nothing a tenor can do on stage is going to make the audience like Tannhäuser as a person.

Part of the problem in sympathizing with Tannhäuser as a person is that Wagner puts unrealistic demands on him. He must convince us that he is attractive enough to capture the hearts of both Venus and Saint Elizabeth of Hungary, which is a tall order for any man. And all this while meeting some of the hardest vocal demands ever asked of a tenor.

And yet as a type of person he is not so distant as we may imagine. Many men *suspect* themselves of being so attractive, despite any external evidence, that both Venus and Saint Elizabeth *would* fall in love with them if they happened to meet them. This secret, inner male ego is much more at the core of the story than any specific obnoxious medieval yodeler. The question is which of these two feminine ideals a man would choose if he could, and the answer is that the choice is not easy.

Tannhäuser is the sort of person for whom the grass is always greener elsewhere. Really, he sounds a lot like Franz Liszt, and it's surprising that no production has yet taken this tack. But we don't need to look so far back into history to find analogues of Tannhäuser. Don't we all have someone in our lives who is never happy where they are? How about that cousin of yours who yearned for a family and a house in the suburbs, only to complain of the boredom and confinement once married and mortgaged? Isn't the longing for/fear of commitment a common theme in our time? Being torn between two ideals of a perfect life is a fate that has clobbered many people.

Elisabeth is certainly familiar to all of us once we look past her pious proclamations. All of Wagner's heroines are interesting, and Elisabeth is no exception. Like the others, she is engaging because of her ambiguities. It is a mistake to take the connection between our heroine and the historical Saint Elizabeth too literally. This one is very earthy and full of chutzpah, a fact she establishes musically as soon as she enters and sings her rip-snorting aria *"Dich, teure Halle."* Although she is a model of purity, she has some very human longings. When Tannhäuser sings his first offensive song at the contest, Wagner's instructions for her in the libretto describe her as torn between rapture and shock. In other words, she's quite aroused in spite of herself. And notice that Wolfram's kind words and deeds don't do a thing for her. She never seems to notice he's there. Indeed, she never once addresses a single word to Wolfram, even when only the two of them are on stage. So much for her interest in what we would call "husband material." Even though she is wiser, Elisabeth is quite analogous to Tannhäuser. The difference is that she wants both saint and profligate, so to speak, in the same person, whom she will then rescue from his lower self. We have new words for this sort of impulse today, but the dilemma is as old as people.

Elisabeth's piety, however, is not a facade. Her lecture to the knights at the end of Act II shows an evolved, and strikingly modern, understanding of religious principles. Elisabeth is best seen as an idealist trying to function in an imperfect world.

The conflicted desires of Tannhäuser and Elisabeth have much to say to us. At the very least, we learn, yet again, that love (mutual admiration and attraction) is the easy part on the conceptual plane, while finding common ground for coexistence is the goal that eludes most people.

# LOHENGRIN

PREMIERE: WEIMAR, 1850 (UNDER THE DIRECTION OF FRANZ LISZT).

## THE NAME AND HOW TO PRONOUNCE IT

This is one of Wagner's simplest titles, and its pronunciation has no hazards for the English-speaker. The accent is on the first syllable, and the *h* is barely audible. The title is the name of the opera's hero, which, in spite of seeing this name plastered all over billboards, programs, and newspaper articles, we must make believe we do not know until the very end of the story. This is a prime example of opera's request that we suspend belief beyond all reasonable bounds.

## WHAT IS *LOHENGRIN?*

Lohengrin is an opera about an archetypal myth presented as a medieval fairy tale. At first glance, it is almost comical in its commonplaces of this genre, containing, as it does, a knight in shining armor, a damsel in distress, an evil witch, a magic swan, a good king, and no shortage of knights, soldiers, and fair ladies. All program notes will refer to this opera as the apex and grand finale of German Romantic opera. Wagner rooted his story firmly in a historical moment, A.D. 933, when King Henry the Fowler of Saxony was uniting various German states to fight against Hungarian invaders. This gives the opera fanfares, choruses, and thrilling orchestral passages, as well as a not-always-welcome militaristic aspect. *Lohengrin*, however, is more than all that. The knight appears and saves the lady on the sole condition that he never has to tell his name or his story. The issue, then, becomes the nature of love and its limits. After a performance of *Lohengrin*, audiences can be heard discussing the politics of relationships as much as the music or the performance.

To explore this subject, Wagner uses some very subtle techniques that were revolutionary in their time and that were to find a fuller expression in his next opera, *Tristan und Isolde*. In fact, many experts find more interest in *Lohengrin* as a transitional piece from his earlier, traditional operas to his later unique music dramas. This is a great mistake. *Lohengrin* has long been a favorite of audiences (perhaps Wagner's most popular work), and few people would sit in a theater for five hours merely to study background information on *Tristan*. This opera, obviously, can stand on its own merits. In fact, the relative traditionalism and naiveté that many critics find in *Lohengrin* may account for much of its popularity with audiences. The ensembles, duets, and other features of standard opera that Wagner decided had no place in his later music dramas abound in *Lohengrin*, giving sheer listening pleasure to us who are less concerned with the musical controversies of the mid–nineteenth century.

The musical vocabulary Wagner uses to express the mysticism of the story is beautiful, well constructed, and easy to love. The ritual and fanfare that punctuate the opera serve primarily as a framework for the human story. Elsa, the heroine, has a mystical side to her, allowing for much sublime music, while the role of Lohengrin, the otherworldly knight, is lyrical in the extreme and easily the least "barkable" part Wagner ever wrote for a tenor. Program notes never tire of calling the work "Italianate," whatever that's supposed to tell us. Lest the opera get too ethereal between calls to arms, Wagner also gives us the character of Ortrud, who chews up the scenery whenever she gets a chance. Small wonder that *Lohengrin* remains popular.

## CAST OF CHARACTERS

LOHENGRIN *(tenor)* The definitive knight in shining armor, the mysterious stranger who arrives to save the day on the condition that he never reveal his name or origin. We find out later that he is a knight of the Holy Grail and therefore a "higher being" (Wagner's words). It is possible that we are meant to understand him, like Tannhäuser before him, as an artist, somewhat above the world but not above needing love.

ELSA VON BRABANT *(soprano)* A strange but not unsympathetic woman who is given to trances and unusual dreams, some of which turn out to be prophetic. She is the Princess of Brabant (coastal Belgium) rather by default, since she has sort of misplaced her brother Gottfried, the rightful prince. The role is challenging to sopranos since they must portray a wide range of emotions while retaining an air of innocence, from misunderstood dreamer at the beginning to a real and earthy woman wanting to know who her husband is in Act III.

ORTRUD *(soprano or mezzo-soprano)* A major diva role, and one of the truly great bitches of opera. The historical moment of *Lohengrin* looks at the Christianization process of Germany along with its nascent nationalism. Ortrud, who is a pagan, is seen as an opponent of both. She is relatively quiet and sneaky in the first act, conniving and ballistic in the second, and basically silent in the third until she lets out with some peel-the-wallpaper screams at the end. No peasant herself, she is a princess of the House of Frisia, which has claims on Brabant. Wagner never entirely reconciled himself to Christianity and always had a soft spot for pagans.

COUNT FRIEDRICH VON TELRAMUND *(baritone)* Ortrud's easily manipulated husband, and the one who accuses Elsa of murdering her brother and harboring a secret lover. He had, not incidentally, once asked Elsa to marry him. Telramund, as he is usually called, is generally thought of as weak rather than downright wicked, a distinction reserved for his pagan wife. The role contains much punishing music for relatively little reward, and it is hard to feel strongly about poor Friedrich one way or the other.

KING HENRY THE FOWLER *(bass)* Borrowed from history, Henry the Fowler was the king of Saxony, a state in eastern Germany, from A.D. 919 to 936. Having negotiated a nine-year truce with invading Hungarians in 924, Henry set about training soldiers and fortifying the land. At the beginning of *Lohengrin*, he has come to Brabant to rally support for his cause. Although he is sympathetic to Elsa in our story, this role is more a symbol than a full human. The historical Henry was elected Holy Roman Emperor (Kaiser). The *Encyclopaedia Brittanica* informs us straightfacedly, "the story that he is called the Fowler because he was laying bird snares when informed of his election as Emperor may be regarded more as legend than fact." We are very grateful for this information.

THE HERALD *(bass)* A kind of narrator with a booming bass voice, usually accompanied by trumpets. The Herald stands in the center of the stage in the first two acts making heavy-sounding official pronouncements. The Herald was a standard feature of Romantic opera, serving to grab the audience's attention at crucial points with lines like "Hear ye!" and "Mark well, O good people!" Although this device was eventually discarded by Wagner and others, it was an effective method of creating a certain formal structure for operas in which it was appropriate, such as *Lohengrin*.

## THE OPERA

### *Prelude*

Beginning very softly in the strings and woodwinds, this famous prelude describes a vision of the Holy Grail, whose significance is not explained until the end of the opera, as it emerges from the heavens. The climax, at exactly two-thirds of the way through, uses the same theme, thundered out with horns and cymbals, signifying the Grail in full revelation. The music dies away to describe the Grail returning to the upper heavens after having bestowed its blessings on the people and the land.

**Comment:** *This is always called a prelude rather than an overture. since it does not rely on melodies from the opera itself in the manner of most overtures, including those of* Tannhäuser *and the* Dutchman. *Although there are thematic connections to the rest of the work, the Prelude aims to set a tone of reverence and holiness appropriate to a vision of the Grail without actually representing any of the subsequent story. Wagner scholars have made much of the revolutionary achievement of this independent prelude. Actually, Mozart and even Rossini might be said to have done the same in several of their operas. Furthermore, the Prelude really is quite narrative in that it is analogous to the story of Lohengrin, who comes from a heavenly place, does his magic, and leaves. The great achievement of the Prelude is in its sheer beauty, but don't say that around any scholars. To call the Prelude "ethereal" is cliché but inevitable. In case we are too dull to appreciate its message, Wagner has left us detailed program notes explaining what we should do if we happen to have a vision of the Holy Grail, including the priceless instruction that "the beholder falls on his knees in adoring self-annihilation." The blessings of salvation pouring forth from the Grail are a theme that would be explored by Wagner in greater depth, and much greater length, in* Parsifal. *This prelude has been famously described as "two squeakinesses with a brassiness between them."*

## Act I

Setting: The banks of the River Scheldt (properly pronounced "Skelt," but no one does) in Brabant, with Antwerp in the background.

King Henry the Fowler has arrived from Saxony to rally support among the Brabantines for his upcoming war against invading Hungarians. While there, he has agreed, as king, to judge Count von Telramund's suit against Elsa, the Princess of Brabant. Telramund explains that he had been made guardian of Elsa and her brother

Gottfried by their dying father. One day, Elsa took Gottfried for a walk in the woods. She returned alone, asking Gottfried's whereabouts with, as he says, "feigned concern." Convinced of her guilt by her trembling, Telramund was seized with disgust at this maiden whom he had intended, by right, to marry. Instead he married Ortrud, from the line of Radbod. He now formally accuses Elsa of fratricide, and claims Brabant for himself and his heathen but noble wife. He adds that Elsa is delusional and, if all this isn't enough, appears to have a secret lover.

*Comment: This long, formal trial sequence packs in a lot of information. Wagner intended to portray the medieval system of the liege lord (King Henry, in this case) traveling about to hear law cases. The stage instructions call for Henry to stand beneath a massive "Tree of Judgment," as was the custom. Large trees are not currently fashionable for this scene.*

*Telramund's reference to Ortrud as a "child of Radbod" is gratuitous for the present story, but tells us something about Wagner and his sympathies. Radbod was a pagan lord of Frisia (northern coastal Holland), who at first said he would accept Christian baptism, but then jumped out of the baptismal font when it was explained to him that he wouldn't meet his pagan father in Christian heaven. Wagner admired this story greatly. It appears in another form in Act II of Die Walküre.*

The shocked king calls for Elsa to be brought forth, and the herald issues the summons. Elsa enters, attended by her many ladies. The king asks her if she accepts him as her judge. She nods, but does not speak. When he repeats the accusation, she only replies, "My poor brother!" The onlookers comment on her pure expression, but wonder if she is entranced. Bidden by the king, she says she turned to God in her gloom, who granted her sleep. Then she saw a knight in "shining armor" come to her from heaven. "He shall be my champion!" she says twice.

*Comment: Elsa's entrance and her "dream" narrative pose a chal-*
*lenge to the soprano. She must project innocence, piety, and a certain*
*dreaminess without coming off like a total space case. It is best accom-*
*plished vocally, with as little attempt at acting, if we can call it that, as*
*possible. The "dream" itself is often heard in recitals, where sopranos*
*can revel in its otherworldliness without having to consider the operatic*
*context.*

Telramund says he is not deterred by a maiden's dreams. He is willing to put his just cause to the test of combat. Elsa agrees, saying her
champion will be the knight whom heaven sends, who will receive
her hand and her kingdom in gratitude. With much formality, the
king proclaims a trial by combat, and the herald calls Elsa's champion forth. No one approaches. A second call goes unanswered until
Elsa and her ladies fall to their knees in prayer. The men declare a
strange marvel appearing on the river. A boat drawn by a swan is
approaching. In the boat stands a knight in glistening armor whose
radiance is dazzling. The women thank God. Elsa dares not open her
eyes. The knight disembarks, Elsa looks and cries out in ecstasy.

*Comment: If Elsa's entrance is tricky, Lohengrin's is near-impossible*
*for a mere mortal tenor to pull off. He must convince the audience,*
*through his looks and demeanor, that he is literally God's gift to*
*women. Small wonder that King Ludwig once took a fit at the sight of*
*a dumpy tenor Wagner had chosen for the role, and commanded his*
*immediate replacement.*

The knight (whose name is Lohengrin, but—remember?—we
must pretend we don't know that) sings a sweet farewell to his
beloved swan who had drawn his boat across the waters. The onlookers comment on his noble magnificence, which holds them spell-
bound. He salutes the king, who asks if he was sent by God, as he
appears to be. Not denying it, he explains that he was sent to defend a
falsely accused maid, and asks Elsa (by name—how does he know
it?) if she accepts him as her champion. She immediately offers him

everything she has, agreeing to be his wife. He says Elsa must promise him one thing: that she will never ask him his name, his lineage, or where he comes from. She says she will never ask. He asks if she has understood him well, and repeats the question. She insists she will never ask. He immediately exclaims, "Elsa, I love you!" and formally accuses Telramund of false charges.

The knights of Brabant urge Telramund in vain to recant, since his sword will be useless against this Godsend. The Herald announces the combat, which is arranged with much brass fanfare while the various factions pray. The king commences the combat with three strikes of his sword against his shield. Lohengrin effortlessly vanquishes Telramund, granting him his life and commending him to penance. All express joy and wonder except the dejected Ortrud and Telramund.

**Comment:** *The entire first act has the pace and feel of a formal court function, complete with trumpet fanfares and heraldic pronouncements. This is relieved only by Elsa's dreaminess and Lohengrin's otherworldliness, which seem to suspend the action. The combat itself is usually anticlimactic. Either we are treated to the spectacle of a tenor and a baritone duking it out with the huge swords typical of the early Middle Ages, or the whole affair is carried out in the symbolic realm (for example, the old stage trick of turning the sword upside down to form a cross, causing the evil Telramund to shrink in terror). Either way, it's all merely a set-up for the elaborate ensemble that ends the act.*

## Act II

Setting: The courtyard of Antwerp Castle, with the knights' abode in the background, the Kemenate (the women's hall) on one side, and the Münster, or church, on the other.

Telramund and Ortrud, dejected and alone, slink about the shadows of the courtyard, while sounds of revelry are heard from inside the knights' hall. Telramund blames Ortrud for dishonoring him, since she told him she had actually seen Elsa kill her brother. Now he is a victim of God's judgment. Ortrud cries out "God?" and laughs horribly. Her husband notes that His name sounds horrible on her lips. Ortrud questions whether "God" is Telramund's name for his own cowardice. He could have vanquished the mysterious knight. Even if he had succeeded in only severing a piece of the knight's finger, he would have lost his power. But there is yet hope for them. In her witchy way, she has learned that the Godsent knight would lose his power if he revealed his name. She herself will vanquish the stranger through Elsa. The two sing of vengeance.

*Comment: The scene between the bad guys Ortrud and Telramund is painted in the darkest orchestral tones and is quite effective after the pomp of the first act, although their little "oath duet," rounded off by bass clarinet and trombone chords, borders on the corny. George Martin's* Opera Companion *says it could come from any Italian opera— "even a bad one."*

Elsa appears at the window, ecstatic in her new happiness. Telramund hides. Ortrud smarmily calls up to her, blaming the debacle on Telramund and asking Elsa (four times) what had she ever done to offend Elsa. The supremely gullible Elsa falls for it, and leaves the window to come down and comfort the supposed penitent. This leaves Ortrud momentarily alone on stage, and she calls upon her pagan gods Wodan and Freia to aid her trickery. Elsa appears, forgiving Ortrud and generally being chummy. Ortrud uses the opportunity to plant the first doubts in her, saying she is concerned that Elsa might be too trusting of this stranger knight. Elsa laughs off Ortrud's warnings. What could this unfortunate woman know about such a creature as the knight? Elsa and Ortrud enter the Kemenate together.

*Comment: High woodwinds accompany Elsa's appearance on the balcony above, driving home the contrast to the previous "evil doings" scene. Ortrud's invocation of the pagan gods Wodan and Freia is the mezzo's first opportunity to chew up the scenery. Do not expect subtlety.*

Morning. People gather in the courtyard. The ubiquitous herald appears, full of news. Telramund is banished, King Henry confers the crown of Brabant on the stranger knight (who refuses all titles but Protector), the knight will marry Elsa that day, and the next day he shall lead the Brabantines in the king's campaign against the Hungarians in the East. The people cheer and disperse, except for four grumbling nobles who gather and mutter. Who is this unknown knight to embroil Brabant in a distant war? Is their own land threatened? But who will stop these events? Telramund, who apparently has been hiding in the bushes all night, steps forward, shocking the nobles. He says the knight is a sorcerer, bent on ruining the land. He will set things right. The nobles follow him away.

**Comment:** *This short scene is more important for plot development than for any inherent musical interest. The four kvetchy nobles are important. Apparently, doubts about Lohengrin are latent among the Brabantines amidst all the cheering, depicting a macroscopic projection of Elsa's dilemma. The personal and the political overlap throughout this opera.*

The courtyard fills with people, while Elsa's elaborate bridal procession makes its way from the Kemenate. Just as she is about to enter the Münster, Ortrud jumps out of line and screams bloody murder, insisting she will not defer to Elsa. Elsa realizes she has been duped. How could Ortrud have changed so completely from the contrite woman she had been the night before? Ortrud replies that for one brief hour she had forgotten her noble blood, but now she demands to know the name and lineage of the stranger knight who claims leadership of the country. The king and the knight appear from the rear, magnificently attended. The knight comforts Elsa, and contemptuously dismisses Ortrud's ravings. Suddenly, Telramund appears. The crowd is shocked to see the banished count, but before he can be apprehended, he charges the knight with sorcery. He, too, demands to know the knight's name and lineage to make sure he is worthy to be Protector of Brabant. If he won't tell the disgraced Telramund, he must tell the king. "Not even the king may know," replies the knight, ordering Telramund and Ortrud back. The knight asks Elsa if she demands to know. Elsa says she does not, but before they enter the Münster, she catches sight of Ortrud and momentarily hesitates. Rallying, she accompanies the knight and the procession into the church.

**Comment:** *This scene is not Wagner's most successful marriage, pardon the expression, of music and action. The action, such as it is, consists of Elsa taking forty minutes to cross from stage right to stage left. Smart productions incorporate the formality and stasis of the scene into a sort of ritual representation of the action. Attempts at realism here bog everything down. Wagner paints this scene in rich ensemble harmonies and choral intricacies, which went against his later theories of opera and are therefore a rare opportunity to hear what magnificent things he could do with the genre.*

*Whenever anybody mentions the idea of the knight's name, we hear an instantly recognizable theme in the orchestra. This was the music Lohengrin sang when he warned Elsa that she must never ask "the question." It thunders again in the orchestra at the end of Act II, when Elsa looks back at Ortrud and hesitates to enter the church. Clearly, she is beginning to have her doubts.*

## Act III

The joyous spirits of the wedding are depicted in an orchestral prelude. With no break in the music, the curtain rises on the bridal chamber of Elsa and the knight, who enter serenaded by their numerous attendants.

**Comment:** *The thrilling Prelude to Act III, with its shimmering strings supporting a thundering brass and cello melody, sounds to the modern ear more martial than marital. It is familiar from the concert stage, where it generally uses the "Name" motif as a makeshift ending. It is also familiar from movies, where it inevitably accompanies scenes of war and destruction (cf. "HELP!"). Most people who could whistle the tune would be shocked to know this is a wedding theme. Of course,*

*Lohengrin is very much about the intersection of love and war, with some God and some Deutschland thrown in, so perhaps once again the music makes more sense than the program notes.*

*As for the subsequent Bridal Chorus, yes, it is that Bridal Chorus, as in "Here Comes the Bride." All that need be said about this most hackneyed piece of music in history is that it sounds better sung here in soft choral harmonies than it does in the local church, endlessly repeated on the reedy organ while the bride tries to disentangle the train of her gown from the door jamb. Wagner would have agreed that it has absolutely no place in a church.*

Left alone at last, Elsa and the knight express their love. She confesses how unequal she feels to him, unworthy even to know his name! He clumsily tries to comfort her, assuring her that she need not worry about him having base origins. In fact, he has left behind great splendor and joy to be with her. This really sets her off. Were his origins really all that glorious? What could she offer to such a creature, other than the simple love of a pure maiden, to keep him happy? How long before he will want to return to such splendor and joy? "Stop torturing yourself so!" he tells her, but she responds, "Yet how you torture me!" She imagines the swan returning to carry him away. He will leave some day—she is sure of it! Unable to contain herself, Elsa demands his name and his origin.

Just then, Telramund and the four grumbling nobles rush in to kill the knight. Elsa hands the knight his sword, with which he kills Telramund in one blow. The others drop their weapons. Sadly, the knight orders the corpse brought before the king. There he will give a full account of the death, and tell his name and his story.

*Comment: Wagner achieves great psychological perception with the words and music of this superb scene, the only truly intimate one in the whole opera. While Elsa's about-face reads with laughable suddenness in the synopsis, the gradations of her unraveling are quite believable and even inevitable on stage. Lovers often turn hostile for no better reason than fear that they are not good enough for the beloved, who will certainly leave one day. The most pathetic character here is not Elsa,* whose insecurities are perfectly human and understandable, given the circumstances, but Lohengrin, who has lived his life on a separate plane. Now that it is time for him to comfort another human being with justifiable concerns, he simply cannot do it. Throughout the scene, he tends to say little more than "Oh, Elsa, please don't!" The truly great tenors manage to convey a palpable sense of guilt over their inability to console Elsa.

## Act III, Scene 2

Setting: On the banks of the River Scheldt. Dawn.

Distant trumpet calls are heard, separately at first, then in response. The armies assemble, region by region, on the stage. All greet the king as he appears, declaring his pride at the unity of the German lands.

*Comment: Wagner intended this to be a scene of chest-swelling magnificence, even advising smaller theaters that could not stage it appropriately to cut it altogether. The various trumpet fanfares from onstage, backstage, the orchestra pit, and even, sometimes, from different places within the auditorium, are undeniably thrilling. The union of different German armies, represented by Saxons, Brabantines, and others, under one leader, was little more than a dream when Wagner wrote it, but has come to mean something very different in our century. Most productions settle for the pageantry while eliminating the nationalism. Besides, does anybody really know, or care, about differences in costume and armor among various Germanic knights of the tenth century?*

Elsa enters, dejected and silent, with her ladies. The knight appears to the cheering crowd, but he tells them he cannot lead them into battle. Producing Telramund's body, he explains that he was attacked in his chamber, and asks the king to judge him. He is declared innocent. He then accuses his bride of being lured into betraying him, demanding to know his name contrary to her oath. Let everyone hear his story.

In a distant land stands the castle of Monsalvat, in whose midst is the most glorious shining temple in the world, containing a vessel of wondrous power. The purest men take care of it, and once a year a dove descends from heaven to renew its power. It's called the Grail, and those who serve it have supernatural power. When a knight of the Grail is sent into the world to defend the right, he remains all-powerful as long as he is unknown, but must flee when he is revealed. "The Grail sent me to you," he declares. "My father Parzival wears its crown. I am its knight—and Lohengrin my name."

Elsa stumbles, Lohengrin catches her, sadly reproving her. She begs him to stay. He cannot. He prophesies victory for the king, and eternal safety for Germany from the Eastern hordes. Suddenly, the swan returns to the shore still towing the boat in its beak. Lohengrin says farewell to Elsa, leaving his sword, horn, and ring to give to her brother when he returns. Ortrud bursts on the scene, screaming that the swan is Gottfried, who will never be transformed now. Thus do the gods punish those who abandon them! Lohengrin falls in prayer, and the swan transforms into Gottfried, causing Ortrud to drop dead. Lohengrin proclaims the young duke as the leader of Brabant, and departs on the boat. Elsa falls lifeless.

*Comment: In the hands of an able cast, Lohengrin and Elsa's separation can be devastatingly sad on a human level, despite all the hocus-pocus surrounding the situation. Ortrud's brief but intense scene is generally played to the hilt. The music is loud and shrill, she curses, fumes, and usually does everything but bite the head off a bat. It can be shocking and disconcerting or campy and hilarious. Gottfried sometimes appears, but often is merely "indicated" by some stage technique.*

## BASICS: WHEN TO EAT, DRINK, AND VISIT THE RESTROOM

*Lohengrin* is medium-long by Wagnerian standards. It's shorter than the major workouts like *Götterdämmerung* and *Meistersinger*, but longer than *Tannhäuser* or most standard operas. Performances of *Lohengrin* usually begin at 7:00 p.m.

The first act of *Lohengrin* lasts about an hour, the second is close to an hour and a half, and the third is just over an hour. This means that people who have rushed from home or work to make the seven o'clock curtain will invariably eat at the first intermission, gulp a cocktail with their sandwich, and sleep blissfully through the longish last scene of Act II, with its lack of action and narcotic choral ensembles.

Be smarter than they are. Eat a reasonable meal before getting to the opera house, save the first intermission for a trip to the restroom, and then eat again and have that drink at the second intermission. Horns and sopranos blare through Act III, so none but the narcoleptic will fall asleep there.

## ROUGH SPOTS AND HOW TO GET THROUGH THEM

The painfully beautiful Prelude may lead you to believe the first act will remain on the same ethereal plane throughout. This is not the case. The first scene is all about heraldic proclamations, Telramund stating his case, and King Henry directing traffic. It's less than thrilling to most people. Try to focus on Telramund. He gets to display his voice best in this scene, even if he isn't singing any "arias," so to speak. See what he is conveying by his gestures or, if you're lucky, vocal nuances. Is this a weak man or an evil one? Telramund can be played either way. If the baritone is conveying nothing at all, get comfortable and wait (about eleven minutes) for Elsa to appear, after which everything will be fine until the curtain comes down.

The first scene of Act II may not be the best music Wagner ever wrote, but it's good operatic fun, with its two evil plotters contrasted with Elsa's little ditty. Ortrud, of course, will wake the dead before she leaves the stage, so no problems here. The next little episode, with Telramund and the four Brabantine knights, is very brief and shows that Wagner could move characters quickly when he was so inclined.

There are some *longueurs* in the final scene of the act. Do not, under any circumstances, expect anything in particular to *happen* on stage. The action is interior here, not exterior. We are witnessing the beginnings of doubt and faithlessness in Elsa. If she manages to convey this with her voice or in some other manner, the first scene of Act III will be very powerful and convincing. If she does not, then just prepare yourself for a *tableau vivant* with sumptuous choral accompaniment rather than the usual operatic confrontation, and you'll be fine.

As is usually the case with Wagner, the third act is bang-'em-up from start to finish. Laugh at those wimps who left the theater after Act II, and enjoy yourself.

## PERFORMANCE HISTORY AND ESSENTIAL LORE OF *LOHENGRIN*

*First performance (1850)* Franz Liszt had found himself a cushy position at the court of Weimar, a pleasantly small town in Germany, which happened to have been the home of the great German poets Goethe and Schiller. Liszt was hired to reignite Weimar as a cultural gem, and he set about his task diligently. As part of this project, he introduced *Lohengrin* to the world in 1850. The resources at hand were painfully small; the orchestra consisted of thirty-eight musicians.

*Cygnophilia (1858)* Prince (later King) Ludwig of Bavaria had a "thing" for swans from earliest childhood. Much of his youth was spent in the castle of Hohenschwangau, whose lake was teeming with the graceful birds and whose walls were covered with depictions of swans and the various medieval legends of Lohengrin. When his nurse attended a performance of Wagner's opera at Munich in 1858, he was transported by her description of the evening and fell in love with the work before he ever heard a note of it. He badgered his father, the very undreamy King Maximilian, into ordering a performance of *Lohengrin* at the Court Opera so he could attend, and the rest is history. After he came to the throne in 1864, he indulged this love even further: one evening he posted bands in the hills around the lake at Hohenschwangau to play themes from the opera while his trusty aide, Prince Paul von Thurn und Taxis, was tarted up as the Swan Knight and floated about the lake in a swan boat. King Ludwig

was so pleased by this little *divertissement* that it was repeated the following night.

At least Ludwig kept his *Lohengrin* escapades in the private sphere.
Kaiser Wilhelm II had himself photographed in full Swan Knight
drag, and circulated this grotesque image all around Germany. He
then made an official entrance into Hamburg in a boat drawn by
swans. Unfortunately, the kaiser was never reviewed by the same
board of experts that declared Ludwig insane.

*The Unheard Opera* Wagner, having been exiled from Germany in
1849, was not present at the Weimar premiere of *Lohengrin*, despite
Liszt's best diplomatic efforts to find a way for him to attend. In fact,
Wagner did not hear the work played by an orchestra (except for a
few concerts of excerpts he, Liszt, and Bülow gave in Switzerland in
the 1850s) until he attended a performance at Vienna in 1862. In
1875, he conducted a single performance, also at Vienna, marking
the one time in his life he conducted the piece himself.

*"The next swan . . ."* (1922) It's hard to believe now, but people once
took Wagner's stage instructions very seriously. This meant, among
other things, that Lohengrin was expected to make his entrance on
an actual little boat drawn by a cut-out, papier maché swan. It always
presented a problem. The great tenor Leo Slezak (father of the Hollywood actor Walter) once missed his cue, only to see his swan boat
"sail away" without him. Unperturbed, he asked the stage crew,
"When does the next swan depart?"

I'm not sure why, but this pleasant little story has achieved the status of the Funniest Thing That Has Ever Happened among opera
fans, and even among some normal people. It is a universal rule that
someone will tell this story if you mention *Lohengrin*. Endure it, and
don't admit you already know the punchline.

*The Millennial* Lohengrin (1936) The year 1936 marked the
thousand-year anniversary of the death of King Henry the Fowler.
Hitler wanted a particularly monumental production of *Lohengrin*,
and Bayreuth complied. Also, this was the year of the Berlin
Olympics, and all the foreigners who had avoided the festival since
1933 were expected to return (fewer than one hundred of them did).

Although the 1936 production by director Tietjen and designer Preetorius looked like typical Third Reich monumentalism, everybody,
including a few bona fide anti-Nazis who were there, agreed that it
was one of the finest Wagner performances in history. Hitler was said
to be moved to tears, and offered to send the production to London as
a gift for the projected coronation of Edward VIII. It would be nice to
record that Edward rejected the offer out of a sense of ethics, but, in
fact, his only reservation was that all opera bored him, and he hoped
he wouldn't have to attend himself. Fortunately, the coronation
never took place.

*"Revenge of the Chinamen"* (1950)  The Chinese language and musical idiom have served European critics as an instance of incompre-
hensibility often employed against new music. The following is
quoted from Nicolas Slonimsky's *Lexicon of Musical Invective: Critical Assaults on Composers since Beethoven's Time* (Seattle: University
of Washington, 1969):

> The *Musical World* of June 30, 1855 gives this account of the music
> of *Lohengrin:* "It has no more real pretension to be called music
> than the jangling and clashing of gongs and other uneuphonious
> instruments with which the Chinamen, on the brow of a hill,
> fondly thought to scare away our English blue-jackets." Ninety-five
> years later, by an ironic turn of history, the Chinese actually played
> *Lohengrin* music to British and American soldiers in Korea, to scare
> them away! An International News Service dispatch from the north-
> west Korean front, dated December 5, 1950, quotes Henry Roose,
> twenty-year-old private from Lima, Ohio, as saying: "I was one of
> five hundred men who fought their way out of a Chinese Commu-
> nist trap. . . . Around 9 p.m., an eerie sound sent shivers along my
> spine. A lone bugler on a ridge one hundred yards away was playing
> Lohengrin's Funeral March.* A Chinese voice speaking English
> floated across the valley, saying: 'That's for you, boys—you won't
> ever hear it again.'"

*There is no funeral march in *Lohengrin*—presumably it was the introduction
to the third act of the opera, the melody of which can be played by a single
bugler. N.S.

## PRODUCTIONS: WHAT YOU MIGHT EXPECT TO SEE

*Lohengrin*, as we have seen, is a fairy tale. That can mean several different things to people, but what you will probably see on stage is someone's idea of what a fairy tale is. For the past several years, fairy tales have been understood as myths explaining developmental phenomena of the subconscious—which means, for staging purposes, that you can expect to see Elsa and Lohengrin deployed more as psychic symbols than flesh-and-blood types. The score backs this up with a great deal of stasis. A lot of the time, Elsa and Lohengrin don't really move—even their bedroom scene calls for little physical action! A production that moves in this direction will probably also have the chorus standing still most of the time. The result will look like Greek drama, which works well.

Sometimes, although less frequently with this opera than other Wagner works, someone will have a dreaded political concept to put forth here. The inherent nationalism in the work demands some response in German productions, if not in others. There has been no single towering success of this type that has earned an important place in *Lohengrin* annals.

Details of decoration tend to take precedence over political theory with this opera. In years gone by, audiences liked to think of the Middle Ages in terms of high romance, like *Robin Hood*, and productions went in for high (anachronistic) kitsch. Then everyone thought of the Middle Ages more in terms of Monty Python, and we were presented with a generation of grim, drab, "bring out your dead!" impressions of the Dark Ages. We await the next wave.

Lighting always plays a primary role in a production of *Lohengrin*, showing the intrusion of Lohengrin's celestial world on the gritty reality of Ortrud and Brabant. Thomas Mann once called the score of *Lohengrin* "silver and blue," which is a lovely metaphor, but it's surprising how many designers have taken Mann at his word. Nine productions of *Lohengrin* out of ten are studies in silver and blue.

In March 1998, the Met unveiled a much-anticipated production of *Lohengrin* by director Robert Wilson, famous for his work with such contemporary composers as Philip Glass, David Byrne, and

Tom Waits, as well as for some interesting takes on Romantic opera in Europe. A brouhaha occurred on opening night, where opponents booed the production lustily while supporters railed against those they perceived as stuck in "traditional" productions. Indeed, except for a few interesting *Dutchmans*, the Met had never presented any very daring productions of Wagner operas. Oddly, the Wilson production was quite traditional in its own way: the director used Wagner's own sketches for blocking and stage deployment, and Wilson's "Blank stage" was positively baroque compared with Wieland Wagner's early productions. Even the color scheme of the Wilson production was—what else—blue with silvery-white fluorescent highlights! Hardly a complete reassessment of the work in question. Unfortunately, debate devolved to the reductive all-pro or all-con level one hears in German theaters (where their historical legacy demands such a politicized approach), and the final word on this production is yet to be written. The good news is that New York was abuzz with Wagner controversy for a while, and even the *New York Post*, of all papers, got its licks in with the priceless front-page headline "Bronx Cheers at the Met!" (March 11, 1998).

One last note: Do not, at this point in history, expect to see the tenor hauled on stage by a mechanical swan unless the production is being *very* sarcastic.


## LOBBY TALK FOR *LOHENGRIN* (WHAT'S IN A NAME?)

A surprising number of people find the basic premise of *Lohengrin* to be contrived and alienating; that is, who would marry a man without even knowing his name? We have looked at the psychological considerations. Do we ever really know the people we love? How much of ourselves should we reveal if we want to retain "power" with people? In this light, the issues of *Lohengrin* appear very modern indeed, but there is no doubt that the emphasis on the name itself as the key to the hero's identity strikes many as little more than a gimmick.

Actually, the idea that power is connected to a person's name is common to all cultures. It is something of a fetish among primitive peoples, and persists in civilized cultures. Saint Augustine taught that "names are the consequences of things," implying a direct causal relationship between an object and its name. Most of the medieval legends of Lohengrin use the central idea of his namelessness. We all know the fairy tale of Rumpelstiltskin, whose "guess my name" and missing child motifs are strikingly close to *Lohengrin*'s. Carlo Gozzi's "Chinese" fairy tale *Turandote*, with its hero-suitor with a secret name, became the other famous "name" opera, *Turandot*, by Giacomo Puccini. Another of Puccini's operas employs a subtler, more "realistic" use of the name game. In *La fanciulla del West*, the characters must decide whether the hero is Dick Johnson, in which case he is a fine gentleman from Sacramento, or Ramirez the Bandit, in which case he is all bad. In fact he is the latter, and is only saved from "himself" and from the ire of the chorus by the redeeming love of a pure woman. She is aided in her task by a striking and heavily orchestrated "redemption theme" in the orchestra. The psychological and musical handling of the situation is extremely Wagnerian.

Not that the typical Wagner scholar would appreciate the comparison to Puccini any more than to Rumpelstiltskin. They traditionally prefer to think that all of the master's ideas were, in some sense, entirely original. Wagner himself clouded the issue, saying his actual model for *Lohengrin* was the story of Zeus and Semele as told in Ovid's *Metamorphoses*. In that myth, the earthly Semele is not satisfied with her divine lover Zeus in human disguise, and insists he reveal himself to her in his full glorious essence. When he does, she is consumed. Readers sensitive to feminist issues will sniff out a theme here. Notice, in these examples, that it is the male lover whose nature is too magnificently powerful in its fullness to coexist with the woman's in society.

The Ovidian source of the story is very interesting, of course, but it does not explain the centrality of the name as the key to the hero's identity. The following possibility of a source is sure to rankle some traditional Wagnerians. Some of the most striking examples of name power come to us from Jewish traditions, of all interesting places. God Himself has a name too sacred to be uttered by the pious — indeed, most Christians today probably don't know it. God gave

Adam power over the creatures by granting him the right to name them (Genesis 2:19–20), which is strange, since Adam was still the only person on earth. To this day, Jewish families name newborns after deceased relatives, since to name them after a live one might in some sense take life away from that person.

One Jewish legend that particularly resonates in *Lohengrin* is that of the thirty-six *tzaddikim*. These are living saints who are so righteous in their lives and deeds that they are the sole reason God allows the world to continue. No one knows who the *tzaddikim* are — the man across the street or the neighborhood shoemaker might be one. (They are always men.) In some versions, they themselves do not know that they are *tzaddikim* until they are suddenly sent on a magical rescue mission revealed as a vision from God. In either case, they must always vanish after their deed is done. If ever they reveal their identities, their magical power disappears.

This is a great deal more like the story of *Lohengrin* than anything in Ovid. The nineteenth century marked the first great interaction of Jews and Gentiles in central Europe, a process Wagner was vociferously and disastrously involved in, so there is no question that he could have been familiar with this story. He, of course, would never have admitted such a thing, but is it not plausible? What was his anti-Semitism but a perverted obsession and something of an inferiority complex? Bearing this in mind, Wagner's claim of inspiration from Ovid, while revealing of male sexual megalomania, seems like a deliberate obfuscation of a possible closer source.

Wagner's original production of *Parsifal* at Bayreuth called for a chorus of thirty-one knights of the Holy Grail. By adding the characters of Gurnemanz and the Four Pages, and not counting the disgraced Amfortas and Titurel, this would bring the number of those initiated into the community to thirty-six.

# TRISTAN UND ISOLDE

PREMIERE: MUNICH, 1865.

## THE NAME

This opera is usually just called *Tristan*, but people also speak of *Tristan and Isolde*, the two protagonists of the story. If you attempt it in German, besides saying *und* (pronounced "oont"), remember to use the back-of-the-throat German *r* sound in *Tristan*. The heroine's name is pronounced "ih-ZOL-duh."

## WHAT IS *TRISTAN*?

In its barest form, the legend tells of the knight Tristan (or Tristram), who was the son (or stepson, or nephew, or other) of King Mark of Cornwall, and who was in love with Mark's wife (or fiancée) Isolde (or Iseult). In most versions, Tristan and Isolde are caught making love, and subsequently die in one way or other.

The legends behind this framework of a story are very old and diverge from each other frequently. The geographical places of Cornwall, Ireland, and Brittany recur in the several versions, telling us of a probable Celtic origin. The first written versions of the story came from France and Norway in the twelfth and thirteenth centuries, but the tale had long been popular among storytellers and balladeers and continued to be so long afterward.

Europe in the Middle Ages was in many ways a more coherent unit than it is today, and popular tales made their way across the continent with amazing rapidity. People all over Europe sang and told stories of this love triangle, each time adding details or making changes to render the tale true for themselves. The interpretations ranged from the highly symbolic to the downright raunchy. In that way, Tristan and Isolde were more like symbols than actual people with biographical facts. The closest modern analogue of this phenomenon might well be the comic book hero, who maintains a few defining characteristics while performing an impossible number of deeds.

Tristan and Isolde were the archetypes of illicit lovers, two people for whom love was a greater motivation than law, custom, or duty. Most versions of the story use the device of the love potion, but that is almost superfluous. Dante lists Tristan among the souls in hell who have been conquered by lust. The name is only mentioned, not explained, showing how well Dante's audience knew this figure. The visual arts were no less committed to the story. Any museum that has medieval artifacts is sure to have at least one representation of it.

A favorite image from the tale depicted in art is the graves of the two lovers, usually showing vines from each grave growing up and intertwining. This is a significant aspect. The intertwined vines symbolize a sort of grace conferred on the couple, an acknowledgment of a love too great even to be subject to the immutable laws of certain death and divine judgment. The lovers are not really responsible for their love. Is anybody?

The issue is, at face value, love between a man and a woman, but most people in the audience might find their own memories or dreams of romantic love better resonated in, say, *La bohème*. Tristan and Isolde are no less archetypal in Wagner than they were in the medieval legends, and the real issue here is the terrifying, compelling nexus of love and death.

It is well known, even among Americans who have little regard for foreign languages, that the French call an orgasm *une petite mort*, "a little death." The overly amorous have always been seen as self-destructive and inclined to suicide. This has been true for Pyramus and Thisbe, for Dido, for Don Juan, for Romeo and Juliet, as well as for Bonnie and Clyde and Thelma and Louise and the doomed lovers who form the human aspect of *Titanic*. There are probably a thousand other well-known examples. In literary analysis it is called Eros/Thanatos, from Greek words referring to love and death. We say it in Greek because it is an important feature of Greek mythology, and so people don't think we're just talking about Woody Allen movies.

Regarding Wagner's other operas, this book has not concerned itself in any detail with the complicated, if fascinating, sources of their stories. *Tristan*, however, must be considered in a different way in this and other aspects. The basis of this story is the notion of a love so great that it transforms all existence, including death itself. To look at this subject, Wagner created a psychomusical vocabulary that still makes heads spin a century and a half later. People call the music of this opera "infinite melody." It keeps propelling itself forward (like love), but has no definite starting or stopping points (such as birth and death). From literally the first bar of the score, Wagner reinvented the art of music.

There has always been a mystique surrounding this opera. While people may jump up and down praising or deploring Wagner's other works, they generally just get a glazed, ethereal look on their faces when *Tristan* is mentioned. This is partly due to the score, partly to the symbolism of the story, and partly to the history of the opera itself.

*Tristan*'s libretto is perhaps as radical as the score. At the time of its premiere, it was bluntly denounced as bad poetry. Perhaps it is that, but at least it's not conventional poetry. Short verse phrases of a word or two or three compose most of the vocal lines. The characters often speak symbolically rather than in complete sentences, suggesting rather than telling. Tristan himself is particularly given to freakish modes of expression. Knowledge of German is only a partial help, while translations are, at best, approximations, and often equally nonsensical in English. Good luck to those who think they don't need to read up a bit before the performance because modern opera houses provide simultaneous translations. They won't get very far with this one! That's the bad news. The good news is that we in the modern era should be quite accustomed to theatrical performances where symbol is valued more highly than cohesion. Many of today's more avant-garde works for the theater and what we call performance art owe an unacknowledged debt to the libretto of *Tristan*.

In terms of actual performance, the roles of Tristan and Isolde may well be considered the two most difficult in all opera. Merely surviving these roles guarantees the singer a place in musical history. The very few who have mastered the roles have become legends in their own right.

In fact, this means that you are less likely to attend a live performance of *Tristan* at this point in history than any other Wagner opera, including the entire *Ring*. There are remarkably few people who can sing the title roles, but that's only part of the problem. In the early part of the twentieth century, performances of *Tristan* were fairly common. Any jaded opera fan will tell you this is because there used to be real Wagnerian singers, and such creatures simply don't exist any more. Whether or not this is true (and don't ever argue the point with those people, nor do you need to mention that those Golden Age performances were invariably cut to shreds), modern audiences have been spoiled by recordings of this opera in a way that our predecessors were not. It's true that the vocalism you are likely to hear in the house will probably not match that on one of the famous recordings of the 1950s or 1960s (some would push it back to the 1930s), and you will have to endure old-timers comparing today's "paltry imitations" with the titans they claim to have heard forty years ago. That's just part of the game. If you have the opportunity to attend a performance of *Tristan*, you do it. Period.

Wagner, it cannot be stressed enough, wrote *living theater*. There is a direct, physical connection between a singer and a listener in a live performance, from the vibrations in the singer's throat through the medium of air into your ears and, perhaps, gut, without the intercessions of any mechanism. Such a connection cannot be reproduced but only represented on a recording. It is a sexual as well as mystical connection, and that's exactly what *Tristan und Isolde* is all about. Let the experts debate the singers until the end of time; there never has been, and there never will be, a perfect Tristan or a definitive Isolde. That's no reason to miss out on the live experience of this masterpiece. You never tasted Escoffier's cooking either, but that's no reason to starve to death.

Wagner follows an unusual format in unfolding the story. It is almost nonchronological (not in the sense of the action itself, which is chronological, but in unveiling the motivations). Most synopses begin with a paragraph explaining what happened before the opera starts. This synopsis attempts to unfold events as Wagner wanted them told in the opera house—it's not always easy to follow, but will eventually become clear by the end.

## CAST OF CHARACTERS

TRISTAN *(tenor)* A hero-knight of Cornwall (southwestern England). Tristan is an orphan, which is why he has the "sad" name, but is the nephew and favorite of King Marke. By the time we meet him, Tristan is melancholy and world-weary in the extreme.

ISOLDE *(soprano)* Princess of Ireland, onetime fiancée of Morold, whom Tristan killed in combat. Isolde is skilled in magic arts, especially healing.

BRANGÄNE *(mezzo-soprano)* Isolde's maid, confidante, and mother figure. Her name is pronounced "Brawn-gay-nah."

KING MARKE *(bass-baritone or bass)* The king of Cornwall, and Tristan's uncle. Marke has never married, since he wants to leave his kingdom to Tristan. But jealous knights persuade him to take a wife, and Tristan concurs with this to prove that he is not manipulating the king for his own benefit.

KURVENAL *(baritone)* Tristan's trusty buddy, a straightforward type of man utterly devoted to Tristan.

MELOT *(baritone)* The bad guy. Melot is a knight of Cornwall, jealous of Tristan's favor with the king. This is a thankless role even by Wagner-baritone standards, consisting of a grand total of fifteen lines.

A YOUNG SAILOR *(tenor)* This is another case of a striking solo for tenor to raise the curtain, as in *Dutchman.* Once again, count on this worthy soloist to try to make an impression with his brief moment. The Young Sailor should sing offstage.

A SHEPHERD *(tenor)* An odd role, consisting of poking his head over the wall periodically in Act III to ask Kurvenal how Tristan is doing. In theory, this is the guy playing the "shepherd's pipe," so he has to be offstage while the "pipe" is playing.

## THE OPERA

### Prelude

**Comment:** *The Prelude to* Tristan *is well known from the radio, concert hall, and several movie soundtracks. It is usually connected with a nonvocal arrangement of the* Liebestod *that ends the opera. In the theater, there are always some who are surprised not to hear the one after the other.*

*The Prelude begins pianissimo in the highest reaches of the cellos. At the beginning of the second complete measure the oboes, supported by bassoons and English horn, join in to make a strange harmony. This is the celebrated* Tristan *chord, about which tomes have been written. Wagner fans nod in ecstatic comprehension at the mere mention of "The Chord." It is Western music's most noted example of "unresolved dissonance," which is just a fancy way to say it sounds incomplete in some sense. It struck many of its original listeners as being as shocking as a bomb blast, and it still sounds strange today. (The notes are F, B, D♯, and G♯, if you want to know.) Musicologists name these four notes as the basis of all twentieth-century explorations of atonality (see Glossary). Dramatically, it depicts the self-perpetuating nature of desire, which is what we'll be dealing with for the next few hours. The chord is eventually resolved, but not until the very last measure of the score. This, too, is part of the "story" of the opera.*

*The Prelude continues to build throughout the orchestra, always propelled forward even after the climax (which is, as in the Prelude to Lohengrin, about two-thirds of the way through), like a love that continues after death. One reviewer called Karajan's 1972 recording of this piece "the soundtrack to* The Joy of Sex."

*The Prelude was the first part of the score to be composed, and, while there are motifs in it that will be heard again in the opera, one shouldn't expect depictions of subsequent events or characters in the music. It is a symphonic representation of the issues at stake.*

## Act I

Setting: A pavilion on the deck of Tristan's ship, which is sailing from Ireland to Cornwall. Isolde is sitting on a couch, lost in thought. Brangäne is looking out at the sea through an opening in the draped walls.

An unseen Young Sailor sings of his sweetheart, an Irish maid he has left behind. Isolde, roused out of her trance, asks who dares to mock her, hearing the sailor's reference to an Irish maid as a dig at herself. Brangäne says the coast is in sight. They will reach Cornwall's shore by night. Never! exclaims Isolde, who denounces herself as a degenerate member of her race, unworthy of her sorcerer mother. She cannot even summon the winds and the waves to smash this defiant ship, claiming the lives of all aboard as a prize. Brangäne tenderly tries to console her, asking Isolde what has been troubling her and what she has been hiding since they began the journey. Isolde only cries, "Air! My heart is choking! Open wide!" Brangäne parts the curtains forming the pavilion, and the rest of the ship's deck appears as the Young Sailor sings his song again.

Sailors perform their tasks, while Tristan, standing apart, stares out to sea. Kurvenal is relaxing at Tristan's feet. Isolde glares at Tristan, muttering the strange words, "Chosen for me and lost to me . . . death-destined head! Death-destined heart!" She points to Tristan and asks Brangäne what she thinks of "that lackey" over there, the one who does not dare to look at her. Brangäne is shocked. Surely Isolde cannot mean Tristan, the supreme and peerless hero. The timid one, says Isolde sarcastically, who flees the blow (of her words and glance) because he has won a corpse as bride for his master. Go, she tells Brangäne, ask him yourself why he avoids talking to Isolde, even looking at her! Only he knows why. Isolde commands Brangäne to order Tristan into her presence.

Brangäne approaches Tristan at the helm. Kurvenal gets Tristan's attention, telling him to be careful. Isolde's envoy approaches. Tristan starts at the sound of the name Isolde, and Brangäne tells Tristan her lady wishes to see him. Tristan bids Brangäne tell Isolde that the long voyage will be over soon. Brangäne repeats the request. Tristan points to the shore, and says he will escort the radiant lady to his king when they land. Brangäne says Isolde commands his presence without further delays, but Tristan claims to serve the lady by remaining at the helm and delivering her and the ship safely to King Marke. Brangäne loses patience, telling Tristan to obey the lady's command.

Kurvenal intercedes for him. Tell the Lady Isolde, he says, that it's Tristan's duty, as the man who won her for the crown of Cornwall and the realm of England, to conduct her to his uncle the king, and not to attend on her. Tristan the hero is famed throughout the world! Kurvenal goes on to sing the story of Cornwall's triumph at Ireland's expense. Tristan tactfully tries to quell him, but Kurvenal sings, while the crew listens, of Lord Morold, Isolde's onetime fiancé, who came to Cornwall demanding tribute, but Tristan killed him in single combat. Morold's body lies buried on a floating island, but his head was sent back to Ireland as mock tribute. Tristan the hero sure knows how to pay tribute!

Brangäne rushes back to Isolde, who has been watching this exchange and who seethes as the crew repeat Kurvenal's offending song. Isolde, mastering her fury, asks Brangäne what Tristan said, but cuts her off, saying she heard every word herself. So Brangäne has heard about Isolde's disgrace: let her now hear how it came about.

Isolde could tell the sailors a different story from the one they were singing, about a small boat that drifted along Ireland's coast with a dying man in it. She nursed him with her healing arts. He called himself "Tantris," but she figured out he was the famous Tristan who slew her beloved Morold and sent her the head, himself wounded in the combat by Morold's poisoned sword and then suffering from a festering wound. When "Tantris" lay recovering, thanks to her care, she noticed a notch missing out of his sword. It fit perfectly with a splinter that was embedded in Morold's skull. She swore revenge, but as she lifted the sword to kill Tristan, his eyes met hers, and her resolve failed. Brangäne wonders how she didn't recognize Tristan as the same "Tantris" she helped to nurse.

**Comment:** *Tristan calling himself "Tantris" so he could seek the healing of Isolde, who would crave his death as the murderer of her fiancé, was a goofy and possibly intentionally amusing gimmick of the medieval Tristan legends. Newman compares this with Winston Churchill sneaking into the Nazi cabinet by using the alias Chinston Wurchill. Wagner may well have been attracted to the sound of the name (he emphasizes this detail sufficiently) because it connects Tristan to the Tantra, the mystical writings of Hindu and Buddhist tradition. In his private correspondence at the time of this opera's composition, Wagner frequently wrote of the beauty of Nirvana. He saw Tristan and Isolde as headed toward Nirvana, although only Wagner could have called it that. These lovers are not exactly achieving bliss by relinquishing desire!*

"Tantris" left Ireland in good health, continues Isolde, but Tristan returned to demand the Irish princess as a bride for his weak uncle Marke, Cornwall's king. Would Ireland have suffered the insult of this vassal suing for Isolde if Morold had lived? And yet, Isolde realizes, it was she who brought this shame upon herself by failing to kill Tristan when she had the chance! Now she must serve him. Brangäne recalls only the happiness when peace was concluded between the two countries. Who knew then that there would be such grief? Isolde remembers how boastful Tristan was when he returned to Ireland—comparing this to how he had to be concealed the first time—and how he pointed to her and bragged what a treasure she was for his lord and uncle. The adventure was but a lark for him! She

curses Tristan, and calls for vengeance, death—and death for both
him and her!

*Comment: This famous episode, beginning when Isolde tells Bran-
gäne to hear her side of the story, often shows up at recitals as "Isolde's
Narrative and Curse." It is one of Wagner's many great examples of an
arching crescendo of emotion, depicting the character's state becoming
more and more frenzied the more they think about it. Clearly,
although she does not say it in so many words, Isolde is in love with
Tristan in a big way. This is why she didn't kill him when she had
him at her mercy in Ireland. The narrative climaxes in a state bordering on hysteria. When Isolde imagines Tristan's carefree manner in
fetching her for the king, the original German reads "Mir lacht das
Abenteuer," or "The adventure laughs at (for) me." At the word "lacht,"
she hits one of the two high B's in this narrative. "Lacht" is also the
word to which Wagner assigns Kundry's unforgettable high B in Parsifal. Isolde, we should understand, does not like being laughed at. The
other high B is at the word "preis," referring to herself as Tristan's
"prize." These two notes can be good indicators of what sort of an evening lies ahead.*

Brangäne calls this anger madness. What else could Isolde hope
for? What better way for Tristan to repay his debt to her than by
arranging a royal marriage? And what a king to wed, who has such
noble knights as Tristan to serve him! Isolde gazes ahead wildly, saying she could not bear the torment of staying by that splendid man
and remaining unloved. Brangäne asks where is the man who would
not love and be consumed by Isolde? She confides that she would
know how to keep any man attentive to Isolde. Does the princess not
know of her mother's arts of sorcery? Does she imagine her mother
would have sent Isolde to a foreign land without any means of help?
Isolde praises her mother's wisdom and powers, crying again for
vengeance and an end to her heart's distress. Brangäne opens a small
chest, containing different potions. She sorts through them—antidotes, balms—finally producing a flask she calls the noblest of all (it
is the love potion). Isolde corrects her; she knows of a better one. She

shows it to Brangäne, who recoils in terror. "The death potion!" Isolde cries.

Kurvenal enters, urging the ladies, in his gruff and familiar manner, to get ready and look lively. More formally, he addresses Isolde, saying Tristan the hero bids the lady to prepare for landing, that he may escort her to the royal castle. Isolde masters her emotions, and replies grandly that Lord Tristan must come and attend her to seek her grace and make amends for an unatoned offense. Only then may he escort her properly. Isolde repeats the words pointedly to Kurvenal, making sure he gets the message and will deliver it to Tristan. Kurvenal goes to Tristan, and Isolde impulsively flings herself on Brangäne, crying farewell to her and the world and her mother and father.

Brangäne does not understand. Isolde composes herself, telling Brangäne to prepare the potion of reconciliation. Isolde hands her a flask, but Brangäne concludes that it is the death potion. She begs for pity, but Isolde says it is she who should be pitied. Repeating Brangäne's words mockingly, she says her mother would not have cast her away without some means of help. For sharpest pain, her mother gave her this, the death potion. Brangäne must obey her. Just then, Kurvenal announces Tristan, who enters. Brangäne and Kurvenal withdraw. Tristan and Isolde stare at each other in the most terrible silence.

*Comment: So there you have it—love and death in nearly identical bottles, with the concept of reconciliation floating about between them. This scene can get pretty confusing, with Isolde and Brangäne fussing around the medicine chest like two old ladies looking for the right cold remedy. Many directors nowadays follow Wieland Wagner's lead and dispense with the dumb little props, presenting this as a debate about the relative powers of love and death.*

Tristan and Isolde engage in guarded repartee, she accusing him of disobeying her commands and avoiding her, he excusing himself on grounds of loyalty to King Marke. Isolde reminds him that a blood debt exists between them. Tristan insists that was settled at the peace negotiations, but Isolde claims she now speaks on behalf of her own person, not her nation. She must fulfill her oath—vengeance for Morold! Why did she not kill Tristan when she had the chance? Gloomily, he draws his sword, offering her his life. Isolde balks, saying King Marke would not appreciate her killing his favorite vassal. They must drink reconciliation instead. She motions to Brangäne to bring her the flask. Brangäne hesitates, but then complies.

From outside, the ship's crew is heard singing. They are close to landing. Tristan remains still. Isolde takes the prepared cup and approaches him, telling him how he could be absolved of all guilt by drinking. Tristan starts up wildly, grabbing the cup from Isolde and ranting incomprehensibly about his honor, loyalty, defiance, and heart dreams. "Everlasting mourning the sole consolation!" he exclaims, drinking the potion. Isolde seizes the cup from him and finishes off the contents, toasting Tristan as "traitor," and thrusting the cup aside.

Tristan and Isolde gaze at each other, waiting for some effect. Their agitation grows. Some miraculous change is occurring. Is it death? They murmur each other's names—and fall into a passionate embrace. They have drunk the love potion! Trumpets are heard in the distance announcing King Marke.

*Comment: Talk about the magic of love! This powerful moment uses themes we have heard in the Prelude and other places to depict repressed desire as Tristan and Isolde gaze at each other. At the moment of an unforgettable "pluck" from the orchestra, they cast off inhibitions and land in each other's arms. Later, it becomes clear that we are not to understand this as the effect of the love potion itself as much as a mutual decision to cast off appearances and proprieties, and admit the love that already exists between them. It is because they assume they are about to die that they are able to express the truth of their love. Death/night strips away the lies (as in social customs and laws) of life/day. For two singers to be able to project the proper nuances in this nonvocal moment is a major accomplishment.*

Brangäne enters, wringing her hands and wondering what will happen next. Tristan and Isolde slowly emerge from their embrace, he wondering if he had been dreaming about honor and she about shame. Could they each have thought for a moment the other did not love them? Together they sing of their rapture. They are lost to the world, but won for each other. Brangäne beckons the ladies from below deck to come up and help prepare Isolde, while the sailors hail King Marke. Kurvenal enters the pavilion and tells the two that the king is approaching. Neither Tristan nor Isolde can follow what is happening. She asks Brangäne, and the unhappy servant confesses she gave the love potion. Tristan and Isolde exclaim each other's names in horror, realizing they must live. The king's retinue boards the ship.

**Comment:** *Brangäne's entrance sometimes gets a howl out of the audience, since the mezzo often puts her hands to her cheeks at the sight of the lovers' embrace and does everything but shriek "Oy, vey!" This leads many to leave the theater believing, incorrectly, that Brangäne had switched the potions by accident rather than by design. When Kurvenal enters, there is much scurrying on stage and in the orchestra, as the horns blare out thrilling fanfares to announce the king. These are in sharp contrast to the intensely interior music we had been hearing. It is the real world crashing in on the dream world of the lovers, something we will see again in a more developed form in Act II.*

## Act II

Setting: After a prelude, the curtain rises on a garden of King Marke's castle. Night. Isolde is anxiously waiting for Tristan to come to her. Horns of the royal hunting party are heard in the distance.

Isolde asks Brangäne if she can still hear the horns. Brangäne assures her the hunters are still near, but Isolde does not believe her. She hears the wind in the trees and the waves of the stream, but cannot hear the horns. Why does Brangäne insist the hunters are still near? Does she want Isolde to suffer more in anticipation? Brangäne senses Isolde's mad anxiety, and warns her to keep her head. Caution must be observed. Tristan has an enemy at court—the knight Melot. She saw how he looked at Tristan when they arrived from Ireland. Melot hastily arranged this night hunt to trap not beasts, but Tristan with Isolde, so he could denounce them to the king. Isolde thinks Melot planned the hunt out of love for Tristan, to give him time to be alone with her. Why is Brangäne delaying giving the signal? Why does she not extinguish her torch, the last light of the evening, so the darkness of night will be complete and Tristan will know to come?

Brangäne pleads to leave the torch burning; let it show Isolde what dangers are present. Isolde will not heed her. Brangäne curses herself for substituting the potions, but Isolde assures her they are all pawns of a greater mistress, the Queen of Love. All are subject to Her; even Death, whom Isolde had vainly sought to control until Love took over the matter. Isolde must display her obedience to the Love Spirit, whatever She may command. Brangäne asks one thing only, that the torch be left burning. Isolde sends Brangäne to keep watch on the tower, and grasps the torch. The light prevents night, so let it perish, though the light were her own life! She throws the torch to the ground, where it slowly dies. Brangäne ascends the tower as Isolde sees Tristan approach.

**Comment:** *The torch business (representing light/safety/reality) is effective in the theater, but don't expect to see an actual torch, modern fire laws being what they are.*

Tristan and Isolde embrace madly, wildly addressing each other's hands, eyes, hearts. They praise the night, where their love lives, and denounce the day, which separates them. They compare who suffers most from daylight. Tristan blames day for making him obey honor and loyalty, while Isolde counters that daylight made her beloved look like a traitor whom she should hate. He tells her he recognized sweet death in the cup she offered him, which would end day and open his breast to the power of night. They praise the love potion, which did not cause their love but merely dispelled the illusions of daylight and consecrated them both to night. Yet spiteful day still has the power to separate them, though they no longer believe its illusions.

*Comment: Scholars and "serious" Wagnerians twitch if you call this and the subsequent sections the "love duet." Indeed, it doesn't seem like the right thing to call this massive event which, except for Brangäne's torch business at the beginning and Marke's long address at the end, basically forms the entire Act II. Some call it the* Liebesnacht, *or "Night of Love," but that sometimes refers only to the next, more subdued phase of the scene. If we can't call it a love duet, what can we call it?*

*The problem is that it's not exactly a duet, nor is it really love as we usually understand it. The first part of this scene, when the two lovers meet and embrace, is famously intense and, in a word, loud. This part contains Isolde's two high C's that come out of nowhere, and either get lost in the shuffle or can kill a bowl of goldfish, while the tenor is right there with her in terms of sheer hysteria. Many first-timers get the feeling that this is not romance but rather a battle to the death, and, in a sense, they are not wrong. Tristan is something of a superman and Isolde is certainly meant to be understood as a superwoman, and their coming together is the encounter of powerful attractive and antagonistic charges. It is like thunder. The two are pushing each other toward death. Later, this will be handled more in the manner of a seduction. In this first part, it is a challenge.*

*So much for love, but what about "duet"? Certainly this scene differs from most love duets in opera. Generally, love duets express sentiments along the lines of "You are so beautiful and I love you!" Those sentiments are remarkably absent here, where the lovers engage in a sort of extremely passionate philosophical debate. Also, most love duets begin tenderly and build to a climax, whereas this one starts full throttle and settles into a sort of quiet bliss. Yet this is more of a duet than Wagner usually wrote, simply by virtue of the fact that the lovers actually do sing together at various points here. Up until this point in his career, Wagner was careful not to let this happen (cf.* Die Walküre, *where*

*Siegmund and Sieglinde hand off the vocal line to each other like a hot potato). Wagner's theory was that people don't talk at the same time, and therefore shouldn't sing at the same time.*

*Some of the credit for relaxing this dogma in* Tristan *may go to the composer Rossini, of all people. Legend has it that Wagner called on the genial old man at his country home in France, partially to pay respects after the journalists wrote lies about Wagner badmouthing the popular, retired Rossini. While Wagner was expounding his theory, Rossini interrupted him to mention that the point, really, was moot, since people don't sing at each other in the first place! Wagner thought it over and realized that realism was not his goal for* Tristan und Isolde, *and a bit of artistic license was acceptable. One hopes this story is true. (See* Richard Wagner's Visit to Rossini *in Part Three, "Wagner in Print.")*

Tristan and Isolde ask the Night of Love to descend on them, that they may live released from the world. World-redeeming night extinguishes the last glimmers of their former thoughts and beliefs, memories and fears. They each declare they are the world in themselves, floating in sublime ecstasy. Their only wish now is never to waken. Brangäne is heard from the tower: Let the lovers beware, night is ending.

**Comment:** *Brangäne's call of warning is, for many, the greatest masterstroke of the whole opera. It floats majestically (one hopes) over the lovers and the theater. Brangäne is a sort of intermediary between the two worlds (for example, she's up in the tower—get it?). The song of the watchman, a friend or well-wisher who guards the lovers and warns of the coming dawn, was a conventional form of the Middle Ages. This form, known as* aubade *in Provence and* alba *in Italy ("morning song"), is based on sadness as the night ends and the lovers part. Brangäne's call, and the very short one after the next section, inherit this tradition.*

*The beautiful* Liebesnacht, *or "Night of Love," section of this scene relies on exceptional sweetness. The orchestra shimmers with muted*

*strings, while the lovers' singing is more like sighing than the blaring of
the first section. Don't berate yourself if you fall asleep in this part. It
isn't boredom, it's a reverse shock to your body, like lying down directly
after a thirty-minute aerobic workout. You are being seduced into the
dream world, as the lovers are. They will build up again in pace and
volume before their love scene concludes.*

They wonder if death can reach their love. Tristan doubts it, while
Isolde notes that their love no longer resides in Tristan nor in Isolde
but in the little word "and" that connects them. If that little word
were destroyed, then they would die together, endlessly, namelessly,
without fearing, living on only as love. The voice of Brangäne repeats
"Beware! Beware!" from the tower. Daytime approaches. The lovers'
rapture builds in waves as they welcome the unending night of death,
where they can be united in a new consciousness, the self-knowing
highest joy of love!

The now-menacing trumpets of the hunting party are heard, and
Brangäne utters a shrill cry. Kurvenal rushes in, begging Tristan to
save himself, but it is too late. King Marke, Melot, and the other
hunters enter to find Tristan and Isolde still embracing. Tristan, after
a long and heavy silence, notes that "dreary day" now dawns, "for the
last time." Melot cruelly points out the lovers to King Marke, brag-
ging that he has preserved loyalty and honor.

**Comment:** *Law, duty, other people, and daylight all come crashing
in on Tristan and Isolde. Reality, in a word, has shattered the love
experience, if only temporarily. The lovers could have run, hidden,
eloped, or used any number of ruses, but presumably they have been
playing this game for a while by now, and their words just before
Marke's arrival make it clear that the time for compromises is over.
Their love requires the final fulfillment. They are accepting and inviting death.*

Has Melot really preserved love and honor? asks Marke, whose
slow and measured phrases tell of his utter shock at the discovery. If

Tristan is capable of betrayal, should Marke hope to find loyalty in Melot or anyone else? Is there such a thing as truth, if Tristan can be false? Why did Tristan serve Marke for so long, increasing the glory of his crown? When Marke's wife died childless, he swore not to remarry, that Tristan might inherit the kingdom, but Tristan joined the other vassals in requesting a queen, and promised the fairest maid of all for Cornwall. It was not Marke's idea, it was Tristan's. Was it only to open Marke's heart to the maid in order to poison it better? Why should Marke, who has not earned hell, be condemned to suffer it?

**Comment:** *Poor Marke has the worst reputation of any of Wagner's long-winded bass-baritones, including Wotan and Hans Sachs. His address here lasts a full fifteen minutes, all of it sung in exceedingly plodding phrases depicting Marke's stunned condition. Actually, he's not as bad as people make him out to be, and his address improves considerably with repeated listenings. He is, in many ways, the most pathetic character in the drama, and his words are clear and heartfelt. His tragedy lies entirely in Tristan's betrayal rather than Isolde's. He praises Isolde, but was never led to expect love from her, while Tristan has been his one friend and heir, more son than nephew. This also increases our sympathy for him at the end of the opera. Marke's sadness is a convincing and radically daring way to bring the stratospheric tone of the* Liebesnacht *back down to earth.*

Tristan, in sympathy with Marke, says he cannot answer these questions. He turns to Isolde, asking if she will accompany him to the land where he must now go, the dark land of night from which his mother sent him when she died giving birth to him. Isolde replies that she has followed Tristan to one strange land and will follow him to the next. Tristan kisses her on the forehead. Melot draws his sword in a rage, challenging Tristan as a traitor. Tristan asks who calls him. He sees Melot, once his friend, saying Melot was blinded by jealousy at the sight of Isolde. Tristan lets his sword drop, and Melot wounds him deeply, prevented from dealing a death blow only by the intercession of Marke.

**Comment:** *Tristan's inability to answer Marke's sensible questions is sad and beautiful. He is confessing that he can no longer answer for his actions, and accepts whatever consequences this implies. Some tenors go an extra step with this, and plunge themselves headlong onto Melot's sword, which is perhaps overdoing it. We already know from his entrance in Act I that Tristan is a bit morbid.*

### Act III

Setting: A ruined castle along the rocky and barren coast of Brittany. Tristan lies as if dead under a lime tree. Kurvenal is nearby.

A Shepherd plays a sad song on a pipe.

**Comment:** *The* pianissimo *strings paint a picture of unrelieved desolation. They give way to the Shepherd's pipe, actually an English horn, which plays unaccompanied. It is an unparalleled portrayal of a spiritual wasteland. Those who say Wagner was only good for ear-splitting climaxes and ham-fisted crescendos should spend a lifetime or two listening to this four-minute segment.*

The Shepherd peers over the wall, asking how Tristan fares. Kurvenal answers that he sleeps. Does the Shepherd not see any ship approaching? No. He will play his sad song until he sees a ship on the horizon, and then he will play a happy tune. He leaves.

Tristan revives enough to ask, "Where am I?" Kurvenal is thrilled to see him restored to life, telling him excitedly that he lies in his own castle of Kareol in Brittany. The song Tristan half-heard was the Shepherd tending Tristan's flocks, but the hero only partly comprehends. Kurvenal must explain to him that he is in the castle he grew up in before he went to Cornwall. Now Kurvenal has carried him off the boat from Cornwall on his own strong shoulders to his ancestral home, where the light of his homeland sun will heal his wounds.

Tristan sees it differently, but cannot explain it to Kurvenal. He had recently been to where he was "before he was" and to where he is destined to return—the wide realm of night. One thing is certain there: divine, everlasting, total oblivion. The light of day called him back, that same light that still shines around Isolde. The sun's bright rays have burst open death's door, and to expire with Isolde and in her has been granted to him. Alas, all the deceits and madness have reawakened in his heart. The day and its light are cursed! Will it burn forever to witness his pain? Will this light burn forever to keep him parted from Isolde, even at night? When will this light be extinguished?

**Comment:** *Tristan's monologue (or monologues, since there are two more of them directly following) are famous, but are rarely heard in recital programs. The theory is that you can sing the whole role if you can sing this part, and if any tenor can sing the role, he does. These monologues are ballbusters! Nowhere are Wagner's words of advice to his singers more important than here, when he told them to pay attention to the small notes and let the "big" notes take care of themselves (see "Sound Advice," p. 312). He also neglected to add that the tenor here must find some orifice other than the mouth through which to breathe, since the score offers no possibilities to inhale through the mouth. There is no need for nuance or what some singers call "artistry" in this scene. All the nuance is written into the score. What the tenor must do is hit each of the many notes at the dynamic Wagner has indicated—nothing more! Above all, no barking! Perhaps three men in the twentieth century have managed this.*

Kurvenal is shocked at what Tristan says, and tries to encourage him. He will see Isolde that very day. So Isolde still lives, mutters Tristan faintly. It was she who called him back from the night. Kurvenal tells him to be happy Isolde lives. She cured him of the wound he received from Morold. She can cure him of Melot's wound. She is coming now from Cornwall.

Tristan is beside himself at the news of Isolde's pending arrival. He praises his friend Kurvenal, who has shared his every adventure and misfortune, but his present anguish Kurvenal cannot share. If Kurvenal understood it, he would run to the lookout and see if the ship is approaching. He hallucinates that the ship is approaching, with billowing sails and fluttering flags. Can Kurvenal not see it? The same sad tune of the Shepherd is heard, and Kurvenal must admit the ship is not yet in sight.

Tristan grows melancholy. The sad tune is an old theme of his life. It once brought the tragic news of his father, killed in battle just as Tristan was born, and told him about his mother, who died of grief as she bore him. For what fate was he born? The sad tune reminds him—to desire, and to die! No, oh no! It's not that. Longing, longing, dying to desire, but not to die of longing! Never dying, yearning, crying for death's rest! Once, he lay dying in the small boat. He heard the sad tune as the wind blew him toward Ireland's maid. She cured his wound but opened it up again. She gave him the poisoned cup. He hoped to find the final healing there, but it only brought everlasting torment! The drink, the drink, the fearful drink! Now there is no healing for his longing, not even death! Night casts him out into day. The sun burns. Is there no release? But he realizes he prepared the poison himself, from his parents' distress. Curse him who prepared that poison! He collapses.

**Comment:** *If you think these paragraphs are confusing, you should read the libretto. Tristan is beginning to unravel at this point, and his words get confusing as the music varies between frenzy and near stasis. As in Isolde's "Narrative and Curse" in Act I, this part of Tristan's monologue climaxes around his curse.*

*Although Tristan has a good opportunity to depict the unraveling of a human being here, the role never does really reveal its motivations. Isolde explains herself well, but why is Tristan so death-obsessed? This murkiness is central to his character. It recalls Lancelot in the medieval legends, who is never explored as deeply as Arthur and Guinevere.*

Kurvenal tries to calm Tristan. With a choking voice, he asks if Tristan is still alive, joyous when he sees him move his lips. Slowly coming to his senses, Tristan asks if Kurvenal can see the ship yet. Kurvenal assures him it is coming today.

Tristan is transported into a ravishing ecstasy at the thought of Isolde waving from the ship. Can Kurvenal not see her yet? She brings comfort and peace and his final refreshment. Oh, Isolde, how beautiful she is! Can't Kurvenal see her yet? He must go where he can see. He becomes frenzied. Is the ship coming? Kurvenal restrains Tristan; at the same moment he hears the Shepherd, now playing a happy tune on his pipe.

Kurvenal cries out. The ship is in sight! Tristan's excitement grows yet more. Didn't he know she would come? Of course Isolde is alive and on her way, or why else would Tristan still live? Kurvenal calls out to the approaching ship. It bears a bright flag, a sign that Isolde is on board. The ship passes out of sight, behind rocks. Tristan worries about the danger of the reef. Are Melot and his men aboard? Surely all is lost. Kurvenal sees the ship pass and arrive safely in harbor. He hurries down to meet it and to carry Isolde back up to the castle.

Tristan excitedly praises this beautiful day, which races his blood and rejoices his spirit. Delirious, he raises himself up. Bleeding, he once battled Morold. Now bleeding, he will pursue Isolde. Insanely, he tears the bandages from his wound, ecstatic as it gushes blood. Isolde is coming!

*Comment: Tristan rants as he writhes in frenzy at the news that Isolde is coming. If he was unraveling in the preceding sections, he has pretty much flipped out by this point. The orchestra echoes this. It plays recognizable music from the love scene in Act II, but in broken phrases. Love has snapped him.*

*As for the bandage and blood business, yes, it is written in the actual stage instructions, and one gets the feeling that Wagner wanted everybody to see the blood flow—lots of it. It is ghastly as well as grotesquely orgasmic.*

Isolde calls Tristan from afar. He lurches to her, saying the torch is extinguished. She rushes in breathless and they embrace. Barely able to exclaim her name, Tristan dies in her arms.

*Comment: They call out each other's names as they had after drinking the potion in Act I, when they were united in love, but this time very faintly, since they are now uniting in death.*

She begs him to rise, just one more time, just for an hour, that she may die with him. She calls him spiteful, punishing her thus. Can she not tell her sorrows to him just one more time, not even once? She imagines he is waking, and collapses unconscious on his body.

Commotion is heard from afar. The Shepherd climbs over the wall to tell Kurvenal a second ship has arrived. Kurvenal calls for weapons. The helmsman of Isolde's ship rushes in, confirming that Marke has arrived with soldiers. Brangäne's voice is heard from afar, calling for Isolde. Kurvenal asks what she wants, and Brangäne tells him to open the gate. Kurvenal calls her a traitor. Melot is heard outside, and Kurvenal laughs heartily, challenging him. Melot rushes in with soldiers, and Kurvenal strikes him dead. Brangäne tries to calm Kurvenal, but he calls his men and a fight ensues. Marke is the next to call Kurvenal, but he replies to the king that there is nothing but death to be found within. The king may enter if that's what he wants. Marke enters with Brangäne, who runs joyfully to Isolde. Marke asks for Tristan. Kurvenal, who is now wounded, points out the dead body to the king and, calling Tristan's name, dies grasping the hero's hand.

Marke surveys the death and addresses Tristan, his dearest friend. Brangäne brings Isolde to her senses and explains that she told the king about the love potion. In haste he put to sea to find Isolde, to release her from her marriage vows and allow her to be with Tristan. Marke asks Isolde why she had not told him of the potion, and how relieved he was to find that Tristan did not willingly betray him. He flew full sail to give her to this glorious man in marriage, but with these peaceful intentions, he caused nothing but death. Isolde cannot hear him. She is already senseless to this world.

*Comment: They're dropping like flies at Castle Kareol! Kurvenal and Melot die matter-of-factly, befitting their entirely unimaginative existences, and contrasting with the prolonged death throes of Tristan and Isolde. Marke's forgiving of the lovers is a splendid touch, showing that nobody really needs to die, at least not because of law or vengeance or any earthly reason. Tristan and Isolde must die to fulfill their inner destinies. If every creature's goal is self-actualization, these two can only actualize themselves in death. It's really not about who's sleeping with whose wife anymore.*

Isolde gazes ecstatically upon Tristan's corpse. Look how gently and mildly he smiles. Don't the others see this too? How he shines ever lighter, borne amid the stars. Don't they see it? Isolde hears wonderful music that knows, explains, and reconciles everything. The waves of sound are like perfumed clouds around her. Shall she listen? Shall she breathe them and plunge into them? To drown in that ocean of sound, infinite Everything, World Spirit, unknowing, descending—highest bliss!

**Comment:** *This is the moment half the audience has been waiting for, the celebrated* Liebestod, *or "Love-death." It is familiar from concert programs, in which sopranos who would never sing Isolde work wonders with this distinct piece. The* Liebestod *is different from the rest of the role, requiring not only different demands on the voice but a certain something from deep inside the woman who sings it as well.*

*Almost all the commentaries call the poetry of the* Liebestod *untranslatable, which would imply that the meaning is perfectly clear in German but doesn't carry across to English. This is not the case. If Tristan was twisted and snapped, so to speak, in his scene, Isolde, by contrast, is now cut loose and soaring. The meter of the poetry is extremely basic: ONE-two-THREE-four. This is misleading, however, since the music uses this metric structure merely as a framework for a pattern of seamless waves. These waves build upon each other in a great sweep, and suggestive words, such as "radiance," "soaring," and "breathing," ride on the crest of sound. The soprano needs more than the legato line of the bel canto singer to give the whole an inherent unity; she needs an inner cohesion—what we might call a mega-legato. Seamlessness is one of the goals in singing the* Liebestod. *Her singing ends with an octave leap at "highest bliss," from F-sharp to F-sharp. If she can carry this smoothly, she will take the audience with her.*

*This transformation is the central idea of the* Liebestod, *and it's the reason the soprano must rely on something inside herself to make it come alive. The entire life experience of a woman goes into achieving this metamorphosis for the audience. This is why the* Liebestod *cannot be faked. Dramatics won't carry it, and neither will personality in the outward sense. The inner woman must come across the footlights and hold a sort of mirror to the audience. Clearly, narrative poetry would have no place here.*

## BASICS: WHEN TO EAT, DRINK, AND VISIT THE RESTROOM

*Tristan* is one of Wagner's most evenly balanced operas in terms of times of the respective acts. Each act is about one and a half hours long, with the first and third being just under and the second being just over. No one intermission of this opera is the "go to the rest room or die" intermission. Nor does any single act as a whole offer any particular challenges by being the "mellow" part, where those who have overindulged at the bar or cafe are sure to pass out. Standard theater strategies will be fine here.

## ROUGH SPOTS AND HOW TO GET THROUGH THEM

As a rule, *Tristan* will either capture your imagination or it won't. That said, there are a few moments that even seasoned Wagnerites find more challenging, let's say, than others. In Act I, Brangäne and Isolde take some time saying little until they get down to what's really going on. Listen to the orchestra here, if the soprano and the mezzo aren't holding you. You will recognize distorted and repressed love and longing everywhere. Also, people tend to expect more action the first time Isolde and Tristan come face to face in the opera. This misses the point entirely. Be patient—sparks will fly soon enough, sufficient to blow your wig off. This initial encounter shows them attempting to comply with the world's expectations of them, and they're not having an easy time of it. If you are familiar with the singers' voices from recordings or other performances, listen to see how well they are persuading you that they are not quite themselves in this scene. Some performers convey this with acting instead, which is almost as good.

In Act II, we have already seen that the quiet, central part of the love scene is not boring, but people tend to snooze here anyway. Forgive yourself and move on. The end of the act is, of course, everyone's chief gripe about this opera. Marke is the human element of the story; he is deeply hurt, and people who are deeply hurt do not tend to express themselves in florid phrases. Of course he's anticlimactic. That's the whole point. Try to follow his words and gestures, and see if he can arouse enough sympathy to persuade you of his humanity. He is the closest thing to you in this drama, whatever your actual life experience has been. If that doesn't work, just bide your time and be assured that an intermission is coming after he stops singing.

Even if the tenor and the soprano have lost their voices for Act III, there is always the orchestra. Your attention cannot wander during this awesome act.

## PRODUCTIONS: WHAT YOU MIGHT EXPECT TO SEE

Every decent production of *Tristan* attempts to show the same thing: the gradual separation of the lovers from our world and their increasing isolation in their own. There are a great many ways to portray this.

The original Munich production in 1865 stressed motifs of ancient Celtic decoration. This looks rather quaint to our eyes, but the point was to achieve a sort of exoticism, and old Ireland was as exotic to those Bavarians as outer space is to us.

*Tristan* was perhaps the first Wagner opera to excite really new ideas in reforming stage designers. Adolphe Appia was a twenty-year-old Swiss music student who made the trek to Bayreuth for the premiere of *Parsifal* in 1882. He immediately grasped that the visuals were lagging behind the audios, so to speak. Over the next few years, he came to see the electric light as the medium that would make the difference in stage design. He published a book called *Music and Stage Production* in 1899 which contained a final chapter on his ideas for a production of *Tristan*. Here Appia tackled the problem head on. Since *Tristan* is an internal, spiritual journey, representing the outer, material world is inherently at odds with the score. Lighting should be used in new ways to signify the sensations of the basically unseeable world in which this drama unfolds.

Wild stuff for 1899! So wild that Appia didn't get a chance to work on an actual *Tristan* until Toscanini invited him to design a new production at Milan's La Scala in 1923. Appia cleared the stage of everything unessential: the ship's mast, the trees, and, for Act II, *everything* except the lovers surrounded by torchlight. It *bombed!* The audience had no clue what they were seeing, and no patience to find out. The production was withdrawn, and opera houses around the world showed *Tristan* more or less at face value for the next thirty years.

When Wieland Wagner turned the opera world on its head with historic productions of *Parsifal* and the *Ring* in 1951, he, like his grandfather Richard, acted as if all his ideas sprang fully grown out of his own head, with no debt to those who went before. Naturally, anybody who knew about Appia saw the influence right away. Since *Tristan* was the work most ripe for Appia's theories, it was also a clear choice for Wieland's next production. The 1952 *Tristan* at Bayreuth was the ultimate in the Wieland technique that came to be known as *Entrümpelung*, or "cleaning out attics." The stage was basically blank, there were no props and no sailors, courtiers, or extras on stage. In short, just the essentials. Wieland's infallible sense of light and color told the story, and he was well aided by great singers, without whom none of this would have mattered. Thus his famous remark "Why do I need a tree on stage when I have an Astrid Varnay?"

*Tristan* production fashions paralleled those of the *Ring* for many years, at Bayreuth and elsewhere. Profound blankness gave way to ritualistic totemism and Jungian reference. After the Stonehenge craze, productions in the 1970s and 1980s tended to be abstract but cautious. For example, if you see one of these productions hauled out of mothballs, expect Act I to be represented by a *really* big sail. (Karajan was addicted to big sails in his *Tristan* productions, and others followed.) While stylistic experimentation for the *Ring* was meeting with success all over the world, many way-out stagings of *Tristan* were not well received. A 1980 Munich production populated Act III with steel objects looking like discarded war matériel, rushing water, and, in a real stretch, sheep. The audience genuinely hated it.

Recently, the artist David Hockney designed a very successful production in Los Angeles stressing, of all things, ancient Celtic motifs! The important point to make is that the world of Tristan and Isolde is not the same world we live in. Once that point is made, the details of their world are quite irrelevant. Apparently, there is no social or political critique, if that's what Munich was attempting in 1980, quite as powerful as Wagner's rejection of the entire physical world in the myth of *Tristan*. It is a different experience from the *Ring*.

Details of staging vary considerably. Must Isolde really "switch" the potion flasks on Brangäne, that Brangäne may switch them back? Will a torch be extinguished? Today's directors will vacillate between Wagner's original, literal instructions and Wieland's commitment to nothingness, sometimes adding new or bizarre touches of their own. You will hardly ever see Isolde crumble on top of Tristan at the end. It just doesn't work any more. Isolde understands that Tristan is not embodied in his corpse, so her union with him need not be a literal union on the floorboards. Expect to see her with arms outstretched, probably in a spotlight, attempting, with gestures, voice, and soul, to portray transformation.

## PERFORMANCE HISTORY AND ESSENTIAL LORE OF *TRISTAN*

*The puzzling score* (1860)  Wagner gave a series of orchestral concerts in the winter of 1860 to introduce his music to the Parisians. He rented the Théâtre Italien at his own expense, and, of course, ended up losing money. But the concerts were a success among audiences, which were attended by most of the musical luminaries of the time, including Meyerbeer. The *Tristan* Prelude, however, presented some problems. At the first rehearsal, the musicians freely confessed themselves clueless as to what was intended. Much yelling and bossing by

Wagner and Bülow, who had come to assist, caused resentment among the French players, but eventually accomplished the task. The concert audiences were hardly less puzzled. At the third concert, someone actually hissed the Prelude, but this made the rest of the audience cheer so lustily that Wagner was moved to tears. Wagner's French fans, who included so much of the progressive intelligentsia, were mostly won over by these concerts, since nobody could hear a single note of the *Tannhäuser* performances at the Opéra.

*Yes, but can anyone sing it?* (1864–65) The good French musicians of 1860 were not the last to throw their hands up over this one. The prominent tenor Alois Ander was engaged to sing Tristan at a projected Vienna production of 1861. Ander, apparently, did not rise above the usual stereotypes of tenors, and had great trouble remembering his music from one day to the next. When he asked the soprano how she managed to remember her music for the no-less-demanding role of Isolde, she replied that she hadn't the faintest idea. Ander never did master the music, and he complained to anyone who would listen that it wasn't his fault. The music was downright unsingable—especially the monumental Act III monologue. One day in October, Ander was touring the chilly crypt of an old cathedral, and his voice vanished. Experts examined him and found nothing at all wrong with his vocal cords, but no one could squeeze a note out of him. The fact that Ander had lost his voice in a crypt did nothing to dispel the aura of fatality that was accumulating around this opera.

Ander finally regained his voice the following September, but by then the Isolde was starting to have troubles. The Vienna *Tristan* was doomed.

*So it can be sung, but it can kill you* (1865) The story of the premiere of *Tristan*, with all its attendant backstage drama, has already been recounted as an inherent part of the Wagner biography. Ludwig Schnorr von Carolsfeld sang the role, blew everybody away, and died within a week of the final performance.

Whatever the reasons for Schnorr's death, it has remained a part of the mythos surrounding this opera. It was probably all just an unfor-

tunate coincidence, but that doesn't make good copy. His wife, Malvina, who was equally impressive as Isolde, didn't escape easily either.
She fell under the influence of a Fräulein von Reutter, a medium
who received messages from the departed Schnorr. The gist of these
communications was that Wagner should marry Malvina, should
encourage King Ludwig to marry von Reutter, and, most significantly, should write easier music for the voice! Malvina was sent away
empty-handed on all counts from Wagner's house, and descended on
the king telling tales of the adulterous affair with Cosima. Ludwig
told his secretary he was fed up with Wagnerian intrigues, but
humored the composer enough to send Malvina out of Bavaria.

*Defining the style* (1886)  The first new production at Bayreuth after
the death of Wagner was *Tristan* in 1886, chosen because its small
cast made it the most practical of all the operas. Much was at stake.
Cosima needed to prove that she was the right person for the job—
there was no shortage of candidates for the position of festival chief.
Many objected to Cosima's lack of professional experience, while
another faction was appalled that this half-French, half-Hungarian
woman, who even went so far as to employ Jews, should run what was
becoming perceived as the shrine of German culture. (Bayreuth
has always attracted a lunatic set who make even the Wagners look
normal.)

Cosima, apparently, thrived on confrontations, and she had no
intention of letting go. She consolidated her legal position (Wagner
had died without a will), and meticulously eliminated everyone who
stood in her way. She personally directed every detail of the new production, including the music, whose tempi she dictated from the
piano. Her mania for micromanagement was legendary—every
move, gesture, and sound had to be as she saw fit.

The new production was a critical, if not financial, success. The
minimal movements, the hushed orchestra, and the supremacy of
the text all became hallmarks of her somewhat stifling directing style.
Many were unimpressed. The great soprano Lilli Lehmann said
those who worked under Cosima developed a grotesque mannerism,
while Shaw rightly complained of the lack of spontaneity from such

techniques. The declamatory style that Cosima insisted on, emphasizing every word, devolved into what would be called the Bayreuth bark. And yet subsequent generations are indebted to Cosima in many ways. Although photographs of the 1886 production look typical enough, she had greatly simplified sets and costumes by the standards of her times. This, combined with the economy of expression she demanded, was very much at odds with the florid, to-hell-with-the-drama opera of that period. Although few now believe it, the process of clearing out the stage, which culminated in Wieland Wagner's productions seventy years later, actually began with Cosima, and she was a major force in subjecting vocal histrionics to dramatic unity.

*Vocal exercises* (1900–13) Olive Fremsted, a great Isolde of the first decade of the twentieth century, believed in getting in shape for Isolde in a literal way. When in New York, she would run through Riverside Park—holding her breath! Fremsted measured her breath control by counting how many lampposts she could run past on a single breath.

*What does it really take?* (1930s) Kirsten Flagstad may have been the Isolde of the century. Her Metropolitan and Covent Garden appearances in the late 1930s are legendary. No discussion of Wagner performances can fail to mention her, or her classic secret to singing the Wagnerian heroines, particularly Isolde: "A comfortable pair of shoes."

# DIE MEISTERSINGER VON NÜRNBERG

PREMIERE: MUNICH, 1868.

## THE NAME

The name means "The Mastersingers of Nuremberg." It is generally just called *Meistersinger* by English-speakers. Pronouncing this is easy: MICE-ter-ZING-er. If you want to try the whole thing in German, just remember to say FUN for *von*, and good luck with *Nürnberg*.

## WHAT IS *MEISTERSINGER*?

This is the only comic opera Wagner ever wrote, and its fans have heaped extravagant praise on it since its premiere. It has been called a masterpiece of lightness and human warmth, "the greatest smile in the German language," and inevitably earns references to "midsummer sunshine."

All of which is true, but this avoids a more obvious adjective you'd better know right from the start. *Meistersinger* is, more than anything else, *long*. It is the longest opera ever written, at least among those performed more than once or twice before disappearing, and has even earned a place in the *Guinness Book of World Records*. And only nineteenth-century Germans and their fans could have found this work light and airy. To our ears it sounds, in its texture and overall feel, as light and airy as a supper of beer and sausages.

A Mastersinger was a member of a guild who wrote poetry and songs according to a codified set of rules and standards. They were artistic descendants of the Minnesingers we met in *Tannhäuser*, whose art flourished in late medieval and Renaissance Germany, particularly in Nuremberg. This opera is, among many other things, a great comment on the creative process of music.

Of course, no comment on creative process could possibly last for six hours, and there are other issues at stake here as well. None of Wagner's operas is as compromised by politics as this one. Wagner sought to identify and glorify a certain spirit, artistic and otherwise, in the very heart of the German people, creating a potential powderkeg for generations to follow. The Third Reich chose the city of Nuremberg for its rallies and congresses based largely on the mythos created by Wagner, and the Bayreuth festivals during the Second World War consisted solely of performances of *Meistersinger*, given for soldiers and workers on leave as invited "Guests of the Führer." As Frederic Spotts says in his riveting history of the Bayreuth festival, the basic message was "Kill for Wagner and the Fatherland." It has also proven the hardest Wagner opera to separate from its politicized past. Whereas *Lohengrin* and the *Ring*, for example, are easily recast within nonspecific psychological or mythological spaces, *Meistersinger* is ontologically rooted in questions of German identity. When Wieland Wagner was successfully and brilliantly universalizing these operas in the 1950s and 1960s, *Meistersinger* tripped him up on more than one occasion.

Nor did we need the Third Reich to invent problems in this opera for us. Some were there right from the start. Wagner was unable to celebrate a German national spirit without the marks of xenophobia and paranoia that have disgraced German patriotism time and again through history. Another problem is the character of Beckmesser. This role has long been identified as a caricature of the Viennese music critic Eduard Hanslick, who frequently wrote against Wagner in articles that could be lucid and insightful in one moment and prejudiced and foolish in another. Hanslick was of Jewish descent, and early listeners to this opera heard, in Beckmesser's serenade, a satire of synagogue singing. Wagner insisted that Beckmesser was not about any one individual, but represented artistic reaction and pedantry. While one wants to believe Wagner in this case, we must bear in mind that his original name for the character of Beckmesser was Hanslick.

The political issues in *Meistersinger* are important and complicated, but the opera remains in the repertory, ironically, because of its fundamental humanity, expressed in an easy-to-appreciate musical idiom.

## CAST OF CHARACTERS

HANS SACHS *(bass)* Mastersinger and shoemaker. The historical Hans Sachs wrote scores of mastersongs, many of which survive. He also married four times, and his last wife was forty-four years younger than he. At the time of the opera, our Sachs is about sixty-six years old, talented as a songwriter and shoemaker, and terribly wise.

VEIT POGNER *(bass)* Mastersinger and goldsmith, Sachs's rich neighbor and fellow Mastersinger. Pogner has only one daughter and heiress, Eva. He is a typical good fellow, hard-working, neither too bright nor too dull.

SIXTUS BECKMESSER *(bass-baritone)* Mastersinger and town clerk, a pedant who believes in rules above spirit in art and life, although he is perfectly capable of deceit. Also referred to as the Marker, Beckmesser is the official in the guild of Mastersingers who "marks" errors in singing and composing.

WALTHER VON STOLZING *(tenor)* A young knight of Franconia. Walther is an orphaned country squire looking for love and adventure in Nuremberg. As a member of the minor aristocracy (called *Junkers* in German), he is already held with a bit of suspicion by the middle-class Mastersingers.

DAVID *(tenor)* Apprentice to Hans Sachs, a bumptious young man somewhere between puberty and adulthood. David is a double apprentice to Sachs, since he is apprenticing as both a shoemaker and a Mastersinger.

EVA *(soprano)* Pogner's daughter. Eva is a pretty maiden and heiress with a filial affection for her neighbor Sachs that keeps threatening to overflow into something more.

MAGDALENA *(soprano)* Eva's nurse. Another operatic nonbiological mother, Magdalena, called Lena or Leni for short, is a bit older than Eva, and has a "thing" for David.

A NIGHT WATCHMAN *(bass)* One of the great walk-on, walk-off roles in opera. Although there's no shortage of basses in this work, the Night Watchman should have an instantly discernible voice. Newman points out that these night watchmen were a standard feature of the smaller, more old-fashioned towns of Germany in the time of Wagner's youth, their chief purpose being to wake people up in the middle of the night to tell them it was all right to go back to sleep.

*Other Mastersingers*

KUNZ VOGELGESANG *(tenor)* Furrier; KONRAD NACHTIGALL *(bass)* Buckle-maker; FRITZ KOTHNER *(bass)* Baker; BALTHASAR ZORN *(tenor)* Pewterer; ULRICH EISSLINGER *(tenor)* Grocer; AUGUSTIN MOSER *(tenor)* Tailor; HERMANN ORTEL *(bass)* Soap-boiler; HANS SCHWARZ *(bass)* Stocking-weaver; HANS FOLTZ *(bass)* Coppersmith.

# THE OPERA

## Prelude

**Comment:** *This is perhaps the most frequently played of Wagner's opera preludes on the radio and in the concert hall, although it has not yet made a big splash on the television and movie circuit. It draws a very detailed picture of the drama about to unfold, contrasting themes of the self-assured, affable burghers of the proud town with light love music and a stirring if slightly pompous march associated with Mastersingers themselves.*

*In the opera house, the Prelude leads directly into the opening act, with no break.*

## Act I

Setting: The nave of Saint Catherine's Church in Nuremberg, around the year 1550. Services are in progress.

Eva, daughter of the wealthy Mastersinger Veit Pogner, is at services with her nurse Magdalena. The congregation is singing a chorale. Walther von Stolzing, a young knight recently arrived in Nuremberg, is standing in the back of the church apart from the congregation, trying to get Eva's attention. When the chorale is finished, the members of the congregation leave, and Walther pushes his way through them to approach Eva.

**Comment:** *The boisterous Prelude contrasts sharply with the very serious chorale directly following it. Chorales are relatively simple hymns meant to be sung in the vernacular by the congregation, often using familiar tunes as their basis. Martin Luther's "A Mighty Fortress is Our God" is probably the most famous example. Wagner composed an excellent one for this opening moment of the opera, and softens the chorale's necessary severity by scoring sweet love music in the orchestra between verses, depicting Walther panting on the sidelines.*

Walther gets close enough to Eva to ask her to stop and hear just a word from him. Eva gets rid of her nurse Magdalena by sending her back to find a missing kerchief. Walther floridly begins begging pardon for breaching etiquette, but before he can get to the point, Magdalena returns with the kerchief. Eva tells her to go back and find her brooch, but Magdalena again returns before Walther can get to the point. Eva now sends her back for her prayerbook, and Walther manages to spit out his question: Is Eva betrothed? The young knight was not quick enough, for Magdalena returns in time to hear the question, and begins to fuss. The nurse thanks Walther for the attention. May they expect him at Herr Pogner's house again? Walther says he wishes he never saw Pogner's house, upsetting Magdalena. Pogner had brought the stranger home and offered him hospitality the night before, and this is how it is repaid? They certainly cannot discuss such delicate matters here. What will people say? Eva points out that the church is now empty, but that worries Magdalena all the more. Walther demands an answer to his question, and, just then, Magdalena sees David, Hans Sachs's young apprentice, whom she fancies. The sight of David melts her propriety a bit, and she explains to Walther that Eva is, in a sense, betrothed, though no one knows who the bridegroom is. The judges will name the bridegroom tomorrow, when they award the prize—Eva—to a Mastersinger after a song contest. Does the bride choose? asks Walther. Forgetting herself, Eva cries, "You, or no one!," almost causing Magdalena to faint on the spot.

Walther paces, and the ladies size him up. Does he not look like David? asks Eva. Magdalena thinks she is referring to her sweetheart, or at least to Saint David, a patron of poets, but Eva means the David who slew Goliath, the handsome one in the painting by Dürer. Magdalena sighs, "Ah, David!" and David, the apprentice, appears.

**Comment:** *Eva must send Magdalena out of the room to look for small personal items not once, not twice, but three times. This sets the tone for the whole opera: understatement is not to be expected.*

*This scene has Wagner incapable of resisting another name game, as in almost all his operas. Who wouldn't think Eva is speaking of Magdalena's boyfriend? The Saint David they refer to is the patron of lyric poets and is also the patron saint of Wales, that nation of poetry and song competitions, and his emblem is the harp. Some commentators refer to this Saint David as the patron of the Mastersingers, but Act III makes it clear that King David, who is credited with the Psalms, is their patron. The subsequent emphasis on King David is a curious choice for the anti-Semitic Wagner, but he probably found a way to convince himself that David wasn't really Jewish. The reference to "the painting" is a nice way to remind the audience that Albrecht Dürer worked in Nuremberg—further proof of the artistic distinction of that city.*

Magdalena flirts briefly with David, who presently must return to work. He is setting up a platform for a meeting of the Mastersingers, who are having trials in a little while. Anyone can be declared a Mastersinger who passes the test, and then may compete for Eva's hand on the next day. Magdalena tells Walther to wait there and learn the rules of the contest from David. Herr Pogner will be there shortly, and good luck may side with Walther. The young knight tells Eva he will see her that evening. He will win her, whether with his sword or by singing a mastersong! The two ladies hurry away.

**Comment:** *David is usually portrayed by an up-and-coming tenor who invariably feels he really should be singing Walther. Count on David to jump around onstage in some fortyish tenor's vain attempt to portray adolescence. If, in the following scene, you feel like strangling this overaged brat, forbear. A good, if not star, second tenor is necessary for the superb quintet in this opera's Act III.*

*Magdalena is Eva's nurse, which is a theatrical way to say "female companion" or "mother figure," rather than today's meaning of "medical attendant." In a nice touch indicative of the humanity for which this opera is praised, Wagner hints that Magdalena is slightly older than David. The other apprentices give David some good-natured ribbing about this. Since today's directors are usually incapable of grasp-*

*ing the notion of "slightly," one often sees David and Magdalena por-*
*trayed as a Renaissance Harold and Maude.*

Apprentices arrive, moving furniture and setting up for the meeting of the Mastersingers. They tell David to help them and stop chattering, but he dismisses them and speaks to Walther instead. "Begin!"
he says, mysteriously. That's what the Marker will say, and then one
must start singing. When Walther asks who the Marker is, David
wonders if the knight has ever been to a song contest before. "Not
one with judges," answers Walther. David is perplexed. Walther has
never studied, yet he wants to become a Mastersinger that very day.
David himself has been studying for a year with the greatest of them
all, Hans Sachs, learning both the art of the mastersong and the trade
of cobbling from his learned hands. Walther interjects that David
must know how to make a good pair of shoes by now.

Yes, that takes time, says David, who is anxious to show off how
much he has learned. He rattles off the curious names of the different
tones and melodies used in mastersongs: the "red," the "blue," the
"fennel," the "cinnamon-stick," the "snail," and thirty-one others.
Walther cries to heaven for help with this endless list of tones and
melodies! But those are just their names! says David. One must know
how to sing them according to the rules. Plenty of breath, no cracking, no humming before or after the word, and every ornament just
as the Masters require them. Any stray variation of detail could disqualify the contender, even if everything else were well sung. David
himself has worked hard, but hasn't gotten very far. When he errs, he
gets the "knee-strap stroke" melody from his Master Sachs. Let this
be a warning to Walther: first he must be a singer and a poet, then
learn to combine the arts to become a Mastersinger. The other
apprentices berate David for talking rather than helping them to set
up the room for the Mastersingers.

Walther exclaims the Master's honor will be his. He must only find
the right tone for his verse. David tells the apprentices they are setting
up the room wrong. Only the small box must be used, as this is a trial
day rather than a full competition or a song school. The apprentices
erect a small stage in the middle of the room, with a stool and a table

on it. They also hang a chalkboard by the table, which will be used by the Marker to record errors. They rib David as they work. He bosses the others as if he were already a Mastersinger, but has earned no laurels from the Masters except kicks and cuffs on the head. David laughs them off, and tells them to arrange the chalkboard so the Marker can reach it easily. The Marker—doesn't this make Walther nervous? The Marker faithfully records any departure from form, and seven errors disqualify the aspirant. But if the singer succeeds, he will wear the flower garland of the guild! The apprentices dance around the trial stage, scattering in alarm as Pogner and Beckmesser arrive.

*Comment: If David is eager to show off his knowledge, Wagner is right there with him, detailing the minutiae of the art of mastersinging to an excruciating degree. David's list of thirty-six exemplary tones is sadistic overkill. That, of course, is merely one opinion. Some commentators, including Newman, point to this scene as the acme of Wagner's warm sense of humor, with Walther's subsequent cry of "Heaven help me! What a lot of tones there are!" being the funniest thing since the world's first pie fight. You decide.*

Beckmesser is needling Pogner: What use is the mastersong contest if Eva, the prize, still has the right to refuse the winner? Pogner counters that a suitor who cannot command Eva's affections shouldn't be wooing her at all. Beckmesser agrees wholeheartedly; he only wants Pogner to put in a good word for him with Eva. Pogner says he will, but Beckmesser isn't convinced. Walther greets Pogner, who asks the knight what brings him to their guild meeting. Walther boldly states he wishes to be admitted as a Mastersinger. He meant to say something to Herr Pogner about it at dinner the night before, but forgot. Two more of the guild, Nachtigall and Vogelgesang, enter and are introduced. Beckmesser asks Pogner who the young man is. Pogner says he is an aspirant to the guild. Beckmesser mutters to himself. He does not like this young knight. But Pogner has proposed his membership; he must be allowed to try out.

The rest of the Mastersingers have arrived one by one, with Hans

Sachs being the last. Kothner produces a list. All the Masters were called to this trial and guild meeting. Who has arrived? He takes the roll call. Each answers in turn and takes his seat. All are present except Vogel, who is ill. Kothner notes that there is a quorum. Let them elect a new Marker. Pogner says to let that wait; he has important business to propose.

The next day is Saint John's Day (June 24), when the Mastersingers leave their religious songs for love songs, and go out into the meadow. There the people can listen to their art with laymen's ears, and prizes are awarded to the best. Pogner has thought about what prize he can offer, since God has made him rich. Wherever he has traveled in Germany, he has found that burghers like himself have the reputation of caring only for money and nothing for art. To show that this is not the case, and for his own honor and that of his town and way of life, he offers as a prize the hand of his only child and heiress, Eva, to the Mastersinger who wins the contest.

*Comment: Pogner's address is long and full of the excruciating detail typical of this opera, but it is melodic and a great chance for this bass to sing beautifully. Many are surprised to discover that Wagner put this on the program as a set aria at several concerts he gave to raise enthusiasm for this opera before its premiere.*

The Masters and apprentices praise Pogner. Vogelgesang says he wishes he were single, and Sachs notes that many would gladly give up their wives for a chance. Kothner urges the unmarried men to get to work. Pogner adds that Eva must agree to the match. Kothner questions this, and Beckmesser says they might as well just let her choose a husband, and leave mastersongs out of it altogether, but Pogner protests. Eva can choose her husband, as reason demands, but he must be an award-winning Mastersinger!

Sachs points out that a girl's heart and the art of mastersinging do not always burn with the same fire. If Pogner really wanted to honor art, he would let the people decide the winner of the contest. The others, led by Kothner, protest this. What do the people know about the rules of mastersinging? Sachs quiets the fuss. He knows the rules of the art form as well as anybody, but thinks it wise to let the people judge once a year to make sure the life of the form has not been killed by dull habit. Only people who are not familiar with the details of the rules could judge that! Beckmesser notices nervously how the apprentices are delighted by Sachs's anarchic idea. Sachs says the guild should come down from the clouds and let the people tell them what they like for a change, so that the people and art may thrive together.

Vogelgesang praises Sachs's intentions, but the others are opposed. Nachtigall says he holds his tongue when the people speak, and Kothner pronounces running after popular favor to be the disgrace and downfall of art. Pogner suggests Sachs's idea may be going too far too soon, but will the guild accept the rules for the contest as he has proposed them? They agree, with Sachs saying that the provision of Eva's consent satisfies him. Kothner calls for any who wish to be enrolled in the contest, and Pogner introduces Walther von Stolzing as a knight of his acquaintance who recently left his castle in the country to come to town and who wishes to be accepted as a Mastersinger. The youth's nobility concerns some of the stodgy burghers, but Sachs reminds them of their founding principles: lord or peasant may become a Mastersinger. What matters here is art.

Kothner asks Walther the name of the Master with whom he studied, and Walther names the great medieval Minnesinger Walther von der Vogelweide, whose work he studied from an old book during the long winter nights in his castle. Sachs praises this Master as an excellent teacher, but Beckmesser grumbles that he's been dead too long to teach the rules. Kothner asks where, then, did Stolzing learn the art of singing? The young man answers that he learned to sing in the meadows, when summer returned. He took what the book had taught him all winter, and heard his voice resound in the splendor of the summer forest. Vogelgesang praises the answers as poetic and artistic, but Beckmesser is having none of it. Naturally, he says, Vogelgesang ("Birdsong") likes the idea of finches and titmice for teachers! Kothner asks the Masters' opinion—he thinks the young man is in the wrong place. Sachs clamors to let Walther sing for them.

**Comment:** *Amidst all this, Walther sings what we might call the first "aria" of the opera, "Am stillen Herd," describing his study of Vogelweide and his lonely development as a poet and singer. This piece actually reflects the form of the mastersong (verse/verse/aftersong) rather well, and certainly better than the Trial Song Walther is about to sing.*

*Some readers will already have met the great lyric poet Walther von der Vogelweide in the* Tannhäuser *chapter, where he appears as one of the noble singers. Wagner is describing a "trickle-down" artistic process, from the aristocracy in the Middle Ages to the middle class in the time of the guilds and finally to the people, as we'll see in this opera's final scene.*

Kothner asks Walther if he's ready to sing, and Walther answers grandiloquently that he will take what he has learned in books and study, field and forest, and all his noble studies of arms and chivalry and courtly arts, and let it flow into a mastersong for their judgment. Beckmesser is already confused. Can any of them make sense out of this torrent of words? Walther has the choice of a sacred or profane theme—naturally, he chooses love, which Kothner says qualifies as profane. He directs Beckmesser the Marker to his booth and explains his function to Walther. A curtain is pulled across the Marker's booth, to help the singer concentrate. Kothner takes the large rulebook and reads Walther the rules of the mastersong.

A mastersong must have two stanzas of equal length, with rhyme at the end of the line, sung to the same melody. After these comes the aftersong, or third stanza, with a separate melody. If no more than four syllables of this song are to be found in any other mastersong, this song may be considered for the contest. He directs Walther to sit in the chair, as is the custom. Walther says he will comply for the sake of his beloved, and sits. From inside the box, unseen, Beckmesser loudly shouts "Begin!"

**Comment:** *The form of a mastersong, as delineated by Kothner, is the form of this opera as a whole. Each of the first two acts is about the same length, and each ends with an elaborate ensemble. The third act*

*has a long developmental detour, and finally ends in another ensem-*
*ble, which subsumes the first two while superseding them. Funny, but*
*this arcane little fact seems to appeal most to the sort of pedants this*
*opera purports to caricature.*

"Begin!" sings Walther, taking this phrase as the departure point
for his song. So said the spring to the forest, calling it to life in a
resounding swell of joyous voice! Walther's song grows in youthful
ardor, somewhat wild and hard to follow, but resonant with passion.
However, it is clearly offending the sensibilities of the Marker, whose
many loud chalk marks counting the singer's errors are heard coming
from the curtained booth. After several chalk marks accompany a single line, Walther becomes agitated and rises from his seat, a major
offense against custom. Composing himself, he manages to continue
with his second verse.

"Yet, begin!" he continues. So spoke a voice from his breast when
he was still ignorant of love, making his heart pound, his blood swell!
How soon the breast answers this call that brings new life! Let the
noble song of love now resound!

Beckmesser parts the curtains of his booth, asking Walther if he is
finished yet. There is no more room on the chalkboard to record
errors! He shows this to the Masters, who laugh. Walther protests that
he is only now reaching the point where his song praises his lady, but
Beckmesser tells him to sing elsewhere, since he is finished here.
Walther pleads with the other Masters, and Pogner advises the
Marker to be calm, but Beckmesser will not back down. This knight
has failed, and the Marker does not even know where to begin counting the errors, since the song had no beginning and no clear ending.
And talk about obscure meaning (one of the chief errors for a Mastersinger), did the song have any meaning at all? And where was the
melody? The Marker counted at least four approved tones within the
mess. Several other Masters admit they couldn't make anything out
of the song, some adding it made them a bit nervous, one calling it
"ear-splitting noise." Kothner notes that Walther even jumped up
from the singer's chair!

**Comment:** *It's not hard to see Wagner speaking of himself in this scene, whose music was described by critics as either impossible to follow melodically or "ear-splitting noise." Walther's Trial Song itself, or what can be heard of it through the ruckus, is all youthful ardor. The "murmur of spring" is represented in the horns and lower strings. The orchestra will recall this in Act II, when Sachs sits under the elder tree and ruminates about love and life.*

Sachs, who listened to Walther with interest, says he, for one, found the melody new. If it didn't follow their rules, then they should listen more carefully to the song, and try to follow its rules. Beckmesser calls this frivolous. Let Sachs sing to the common people in the marketplace; one becomes a Mastersinger through rules! Sachs begs the Marker's indulgence to hear the song out, but Beckmesser wonders why the opinions and rules of all the Masters should bow before Sachs's alone. God forbid going outside the rules! responds Sachs, slyly adding that another rule requires the Marker to be impartial toward singers. Is Beckmesser not competing in the contest as well? How could he judge a rival impartially? The Masters accuse Sachs of going too far in personal attacks, and Pogner pleads for calm. Beckmesser says Sachs should mind his own business, which is cobbling, and adds that the new pair of shoes he ordered is late. The Masters call for an end to the bickering, but Sachs orders Walther to sing, if only in defiance of the Marker!

Walther's third stanza sings of the black ravens and crows that screeched at the sound of his voice, but a bright bird soared into the air, bidding him follow into the heavens where his love song would honor his lady. Hardly any of this can be heard. Beckmesser is splitting a gut counting errors of misplaced rhymes, obscure meanings, wrong breathings, and so on. The Masters laugh and jibe, Pogner sadly wonders if this whole idea is any good in the first place, while Sachs muses on the hopelessness of hearing this new voice, who is clearly a poet-hero. While the frenzy continues, Beckmesser calls for a vote. Most of the Masters vote to reject Walther. The apprentices gleefully begin to dismantle the Marker's box and other furniture, while all exit in great confusion. Only Sachs remains there alone, a theme from Walther's song nagging in his head.

**Comment:** *The various comments of the Masters while Walther continues to sing form a stunning ensemble. It's truly a sort of battle. Ensembles are rare enough in Wagner's later works. The tonal balance here is remarkable, especially considering the exclusively male voices.*

### Act II

Setting: A street scene in Nuremberg. Pogner's grand house is on the right, with a lime tree and a stone bench in front of it. Sachs's more modest house, with its street-level storefront and workshop, is on the left. There is an elder tree in front of it. An alley runs between the two houses, winding up a hill. Many other gabled houses are visible.

Apprentices from the various stores and houses are closing shop, singing about Saint John's Day as they work. David, closing the shutters of Sachs's house, is dreaming about Mastersinger honors. The apprentices tease David for his airs. Magdalena appears with a basket of treats, trying to find out from David how Walther fared at the song trial. David tells her the knight failed entirely. This upsets Magdalena, who snatches the basket of treats away from David's hand and runs into Pogner's house, where she lives. This astounds David, who is perhaps wondering why Magdalena is showing such an interest in the knight.

The apprentices dance around David, singing of the love that's everywhere in midsummer. An old man courts a young maid, while a young apprentice courts an old maid! David is about to attack the brats when Sachs appears, reproving him for not rising above the situation. Sachs sends his apprentice to bed without a singing lesson. They both withdraw into Sachs's house.

Pogner and Eva come walking pensively up the alley. Pogner thinks about calling on Sachs. There's a thing or two he'd like to discuss with the shoemaker. He debates with himself, deciding not to. And Eva—what does she have to say? Eva replies that an obedient child only speaks when spoken to, and Pogner praises her goodness, asking her to sit on the stone bench with him. She joins him nervously, seeing he is determined. What a beautiful evening! Isn't Eva excited about the next day, when she will win a husband before the whole town? She asks if it must be a Mastersinger, and he reiterates that it must be—but one of her own choosing. Magdalena signals that dinner is almost ready. Eva asks if there is no guest for dinner, and it begins to dawn on Pogner that there is something between Eva and the knight who was suddenly inspired to try to become a Mastersinger. Pogner enters the house, while Magdalena and Eva exchange secrets at the doorway. Is all hope lost? Eva agrees to try to sound out Sachs, who is fond of her. Magdalena says she has another message for Eva—from Beckmesser. Eva has no interest in it. They enter the house.

**Comment:** *This scene should let us know that Eva is slyer than she lets on. Note how she avoids answering her father, saying an obedient child doesn't speak unless spoken to. Well, Pogner is in fact speaking to her, but she clearly has learned how to work him on matters other than matrimony. This is important, because if we think Eva is nothing but a bimbo, her intimate scenes with Sachs will make no sense.*

Sachs and David emerge from the shop. Sachs tells David to set up his bench and worktable under the elder tree. David stands still after setting up, wondering what is happening on this strange night. Why is Lena acting funny? Why is the Master working late? Sachs sends him to bed.

Sachs arranges his tools on the table, but leans back pensively. The smell of the elder tree intoxicates him, inviting reflection. But what does a poor old shoemaker have to say? Better he should stretch leather and forget poetry!

He works, but stops after a while and gives himself up to reflection. It (the young knight's song) was so new! He can't quite hold on to it, but he can't forget it either! Like birdsong, everyone would assume you were crazy if you tried to sing it yourself. It had all the urgency of spring. If it upset the Masters, it certainly pleased Hans Sachs!

*Comment*: *This mini-monologue is Sachs in a nutshell—amused, philosophical, industrious, yet prone to reveries. His little rhymed couplet including his own name is typical of the historical Sachs, who was addicted to the habit of rhyming his own name in his ditties.*

Eva timidly leaves her house and walks to Sachs's worktable. He asks why the dear child is up so late. Is something wrong with her new shoes? No, answers Eva. She hasn't worn those yet—they are being saved for the next day, when she will wear them as a bride. Sachs and Eva enter into a long and cagey conversation, each one trying to get information out of the other while covering their own intentions. Who will the groom be? Who knows that? Sachs lets slip that he is currently working on Beckmesser's shoes, and Eva tells him what she thinks of the Marker by advising Sachs to use plenty of pitch on the soles—so Beckmesser will get stuck in one place and leave her alone! But there are so few bachelors available. Perhaps Eva should reconsider. But, she responds, would not a widower (meaning Sachs) do? He excuses himself from consideration. He's too old. She does not let him off the hook, saying she always thought he liked her. He carried her as a child, but now she sees his affections were fickle. Sachs muses that he once had a wife and enough children. Eva says she thought Sachs might take her as both wife and child into his house. The closeness of the conversation addles them. Are they toying with each other? Sachs confesses he is confused. He has had a rough and disorienting day.

Eva uses Sachs's confusion as her opportunity to speak up. What was rough about his day? Was it the singing school? Yes, answers Sachs. A young nobleman caused a big stir. He sang his chances away without any hope for a reprieve. Magdalena calls Eva from the window of Pogner's house. No reprieve? presses Eva. Did he sing so badly that nothing could help him become a Master? My child, answers Sachs, there's no hope for him, because a natural-born Master stands last among Masters. Magdalena calls again: Pogner is asking for Eva. But didn't the knight win any friends among the Masters? Sachs would like to be his friend, but adds that the knight's proud manner did not make it easy. He should fight his battles elsewhere, and let the quiet Nurembergers enjoy the fruits of their labor in peace! Eva leaps up at this comment. Fortune will smile upon the knight elsewhere, away from all these rotten little envious burghers and Master Hanses! She crosses the alley and meets Magdalena at her own door. Sachs nods his head. "Just as I thought," he says to himself. "Now to find a way!"

**Comment:** *What, exactly, is Eva up to here? On the one hand, she is sorting out her several feelings, including a filial affection for Sachs. On the other hand, she is wisely hedging her bets. She really wants Walther, but could accept Sachs as a husband too. Anyone but Beckmesser!*

The women exchange information by Pogner's door. Magdalena tells Eva that Beckmesser will be coming by to serenade her. How will they get rid of him? Eva knows: Magdalena must disguise herself as Eva and stand at the window, while Eva will wait under the lime tree and hope to see Walther. Magdalena is hesitant at first. David might see her at the window and get jealous. On second thought— that's not such a bad idea! Pogner calls from within. Eva sees Walther approaching and sends Magdalena inside.

Walther and Eva throw themselves into each other's arms in a frenzy of passion. He bewails his failure at the song school. Now he can't compete for her hand. He's wrong, Eva tells him. He is her only choice. "You're wrong," counters Walther. Her father said it must be a Mastersinger, and everybody heard him say it. No there's no going back, even if Pogner wanted to. He complains about the Masters and their dead rules, their moribund conventions. Walther imagines them staring covetously at Eva. Should he endure this from these Masters? Walther is Master in the freedom of his own home. The only hope is for Eva to follow him there!

The loud call of the Night Watchman's horn is heard. Walther grabs the hilt of his sword, preparing for battle, but Eva advises calm and tells him to hide under the lime tree until the Watchman passes. Magdalena pulls Eva inside the house.

The Night Watchman comes ambling down the alley, singing out the hour of ten. Let the people guard their fires and lamps, that no accidents happen. Praise God the Lord! He goes off down the street singing.

Comment: *The Night Watchman's call and song slice through the action like a knife through butter. The horn call sounds "off-key" in the context of the score—an excellent touch instantly recognizable as "intrusion."*

Sachs, meanwhile, has been eavesdropping the whole time. An elopement! he exclaims, opening the top half of his shop door a bit. That can't happen!

Walther paces nervously. Eva appears at the door in Magdalena's dress, making Walther mistake her for "the old one." Eva clarifies this by throwing herself back in his arms, and they aim for escape through the alley, where Walther assures her that his servant and horses are waiting. At just the right moment, Sachs opens his door and shines his lamp down the alley. "Alas! The shoemaker!" cries Eva, cowering in the shadows. Walther tries to head for the street, but Eva complains that it's winding and unfamiliar to her, and the Night Watchman went that way. They can't continue up the alley until the shoemaker leaves—it's Sachs, and he knows Walther. Hans Sachs is my friend! protests Walther. Don't believe it, cautions Eva, since he spoke only ill of you. Sachs too? wonders Walther, getting angry.

Beckmesser comes slinking up the alley, carrying a lute and looking around to avoid the Night Watchman. Walther is all for getting even with the Marker then and there, but Eva warns him against waking her father. Let Beckmesser sing his wretched song and leave, and then they can elope. Sachs, who has been struck with a good idea, sets up his worktable outside of his shop and settles down to work. Eva and Walther hide in the bushes at the base of the lime tree, and Beckmesser tunes his lute under Eva's window.

Sachs starts hammering loudly at a pair of shoes and singing a full-voice verse of "Tra-la-las." Beckmesser complains about the noise. Sachs sings a lusty song about how God took pity on Adam and Eve after He cast them out of the garden and told an angel to make them each a pair of shoes. Beckmesser complains. Walther asks why the song is about Eva, who responds that she's heard the song before, and it's not exactly about her, but surely Sachs is up to something. Beckmesser finally gets the attention of Sachs, who asks the Marker why he's up so late. Not worrying about the shoes he's working on now, he hopes. Beckmesser pleads for quiet, but Sachs returns to his song. "Eva, Eva, doesn't it bother your conscience that angels like me must work late making shoes on account of human feet?" Walther doesn't know if Sachs is toying with them or the Marker, and Eva explains the song is meant for all of them. It makes her sad, but Walther is lost in Eva. Beckmesser tells Sachs to keep quiet, but Sachs says he must sit outside in the fresh air and sing if he's to stay awake and work this late, all to finish Herr Beckmesser's shoes. Now hear the third verse! He invokes mother Eve to feel for the lot of a shoemaker, whose work is always trampled on. He signs off with a couplet: "Hans Sachs is a shoemaker, and a poet too!"

Eva's window opens, and Beckmesser now worries that Eva will think Sachs's vulgar song is his own serenade! How to make him stop? He asks Sachs, as an esteemed colleague and Mastersinger, to listen to his serenade song and tell him his frank opinion of it. Sachs declines such an honor, using Beckmesser's insulting words from earlier in the day. What does he know of poetry? No, he must concentrate on the shoes. He sings again full throttle: "Eva, Eva, tra-la-la." Beckmesser peevishly assigns Sachs's attitude to the fact that he wasn't made Marker himself, and swears he never will be. Sachs hammers away at the shoes. They finally reach a compromise. Beckmesser will sing his serenade and Sachs will mark errors with whacks of his hammer. Beckmesser poses in front of the window. Sachs pronounces, "Begin!"

Beckmesser sings two lines of his serenade, and Sachs hits the shoe he is making with his hammer, indicating an error. Beckmesser shivers, but continues. Another line, another whack. After the third, he asks Sachs what the problem is, and Sachs suggests a better way to sing the attempted line, so the tone, rhyme, and stresses will fit. Beckmesser mutters, but continues, getting out a line here and a line there in between Sachs's hammer strokes. They bicker, Sachs clearly relishing this opportunity to mark the Marker. Beckmesser becomes more agitated as he realizes his maiden love (actually Magdalena in the window) is growing weary of this unserene serenade. After a second verse of singing and hammering, Sachs asks if Beckmesser has finished his song, because he has finished his shoes!

*Comment: Beckmesser's serenade is a great opportunity for some good comedy, requiring sound theatrical instinct and, above all, a sense of timing. The role of Beckmesser is traditionally taken by a veteran baritone—one whose voice itself may have seen better days, but whose lifetime of work can make his scenes in the opera a master class in stagecraft.*

*The actual words and music of his serenade are deliberately hard to follow. The words themselves are almost impossible to translate, although some very clever translations have been made that carry the spirit, if not the exact wording, of what is happening. Beckmesser uses the most tortured phrases to describe the most commonplace things, such as the sunrise, the beautiful blue day, and so on. The stresses fall in all the "wrong" places. The effect is roughly that of "My old KEN-TUCK-ee home in THE sun so BRIGHT basks!"*

David, awakened by the noise, pokes his head out of his window and sees, to his consternation, Lena at the window being serenaded by Beckmesser. He vows to make the singer pay for this outrage, whoever he is. One by one the neighbors along the alley open their windows, peering out and asking what all the fuss is about, of course greatly adding to the confusion. Some appear on the street in their nightclothes and carrying lamps. David, now armed with a billyclub, jumps out of his window and starts whaling away at Beckmesser, despite Magdalena's helpless protestations from the window. The neighbors on the street throw first insults and then punches at each other as years of smoldering resentments large and small erupt into a full-fledged riot. The young journeymen appear, all armed with clubs, and join in the brawl, which now seems to include the entire population of Nuremberg. The butchers are causing it! No, the tanners are to blame! Look at those stupid weavers! The Masters appear at the side alleys and scream for calm. The women yell for help and egg on the men from the upper windows, dousing everyone with buckets of water and God knows what. Pogner manages to pull Lena, who he thinks is Eva, away from the window.

When the riot reaches its peak, Walther moves to cut his way through the crowd, with Eva on his arm. Sachs leaps out from his door and grabs Walther by the arm, simultaneously shoving Eva into the arms of Pogner, who has appeared at his door calling for Magdalena.

*Comment: The riot scene is written with dozens of choral parts going in all directions—too many to make coherent sense, which must have been Wagner's intention. Vocally, it's almost a free-for-all; the unity comes through the orchestra, with fuguelike themes weaving through the score. It's like the spirit or glowworm snaking through the people, which Sachs will speak of later when he is reflecting on the riot. The scene can be genuinely funny in the hands of a good director, with shutters and doors opening and closing and all manner of things flying out windows. The best productions let it go a little wild. If it's too controlled or "conducted," it tends to look like the local choral society having a genteel pillow fight after a rough rehearsal.*

Suddenly, the Night Watchman's horn cuts through the noise of the crowd. The people flee in panic and vanish in an instant, all doors and windows shutting. Sachs, who still holds Walther in one arm, kicks David into the shop and pulls Walther along inside. Beckmesser tries to gather himself, and limps away. The Night Watchman turns the corner and walks into a scene of perfect calm and peace. He sings that the hour of eleven has struck. Let the people take care that no ghost ensnare their soul, praise God the Lord. He walks off alone, bathed in peaceful moonlight.

*Comment: We know what the horn call means when we hear it, since it's already been "set up" for us. It's a great way to get everybody back indoors and end the riot. Many see great significance in the Night Watchman, particularly as an emblem of the state, which bumbles along oblivious of the true activities of the people.*

## Act III, Scene 1

Setting: The interior of Sachs's ground floor workshop. The following morning.

Sachs, alone, is at his table, poring over a large volume. David sheepishly enters, hoping Sachs won't see him and scold him for his behavior the night before. The apprentice is dressed nicely and wearing ribbons for the festival, and carries a basket of food and flowers. He stammers some lame apologies. If only Sachs knew Lena as David does, he'd understand that David just couldn't help himself when he saw her serenaded by a stranger. Sachs remains engrossed in his book. David assumes the silence means the Master is even madder at him than he thought. Sachs closes the book with a thud, instinctively making David drop to his knees. Sachs finally looks up. What lovely flowers and ribbons! he says, to David's surprise.

Sachs makes reference to the night before — perhaps it was Polterabend, the noisy celebrations before a wedding. David begs forgiveness again. Today is Saint John's Day. Yes, says Sachs, hazily. He tells David to recite the poem he has been working on. David begins singing, but in his agitation, he is singing the tune that Beckmesser had sung the night before. He starts again, singing about Saint John on the banks of the Jordan, baptizing babies from all the nations. A German lady brought her child, and the saint named him Johannes, after himself, but back in Nuremberg, on the banks of the River Pegnitz, they called him plain old Hans.

Hans! exclaims the none-too-bright David. This is Sachs's name day too! He offers Sachs treats from his basket, but Sachs sends him along, bidding him to dress well as befits a Mastersinger's herald and not to disturb the sleeping knight. David kisses Sachs's hand, and leaves, much relieved.

**Comment:** *So David, who aspires to be a Master Poet of the German language, has just figured out that Hans is short for Johannes. Yet the libretto purports that this dim bulb recognized Magdalena in disguise across the alley, even though Pogner thought she was his own daughter* *when he stood close enough to pull her into the room. In fact, it is apparent that David did not recognize Beckmesser, whom he was thrashing, but still made out Lena's form. Such, perhaps we are asked to believe, is the power of love on Midsummer's Eve.*

Sachs leans back, deep in thought. Madness! Madness everywhere! He has looked everywhere, has studied histories of the city and the world to find the reason why people tear at each other till they draw blood. What can it be but the same old insanity, without which nothing—nothing!—happens. Someone ignites it, then no one can stop it. Even in good old hardworking Nuremberg, in the heart of Germany, with a bit of young love, the madness soon spreads through the streets and alleys. Then everyone is going at it, with clubs, fists, beatings, unable to quench the fire of insanity. What caused it? A goblin? A glowworm that couldn't find its mate? The elder tree? Or Midsummer's Eve? But now it is Midsummer's Day, and let's see how Hans Sachs can finesse the madness and accomplish a noble work! Because if madness won't leave people alone even in peaceful Nuremberg, then let it serve those common endeavors that can't come out right without a touch of lunacy.

**Comment:** *This famous* Wahn *monologue delves into Sachs's humanity, which dominates the massive Act III. The word* Wahn *has many meanings, including madness, illusion, folly, and dream. It's rather like the Italian word* follia, *if that's any help.*

*So what are we to make of Sachs's ontological change from bemused instigator in Act II to philosopher of despair in this monologue? Today, he would be diagnosed as having bipolar disorder, but these shifting moods are central to the character of Hans Sachs. Actually, the cynicism of the philosopher is a far cry from genuine despair, as we see from the chipper finale of the monologue. It is the melancholia of the poet, which is only superficially at odds with the popular man of the people. Sachs is a man of broad outlook. This explains his role as intermediary between the tradition-bound rules of the guild and the free spirit of Walther, as well as his own position of shoemaker and artist.*

*The long first scene of Act III is where we look at the people involved in the story in an intimate way. Besides the insights into Sachs's character, the latent love triangle (Sachs/Eva/Walther), which has only been hinted at, comes out in the open.*

Walther comes out from the inner room. He is oddly transfixed, having had a dream so beautiful and delicate he hardly dares to recount it. Sachs informs him that the very art of the poet is the ability to recall a dream, since dreams are where all madness (*Wahn*) is revealed. The art of poetry is nothing but true dream interpretation. And did the dream perhaps tell Walther how he might become a Master today?

Walther balks. He doesn't want Masters' honors, and besides, there's no hope of achieving anything from that quarter. Sachs assures him there is hope, or he would have aided rather than stopped the attempted elopement of the night before. The Mastersingers are an honorable lot, despite their shortcomings. It's easy to see why Walther's beautiful song upset them with its passion. Walther questions the difference between a beautiful song and a mastersong. Sachs responds that all songs are beautiful in the springtime of life, but when someone can recapture that beauty after the cares of life's later seasons have weighed him down, then he is a Master. Walther should learn the rules of the Masters, that they may help him in years to come. How can you recapture an image that has fled? Sachs picks up pen and paper and bids Walther recount his dream. Sachs will take care of the form.

**Comment:** *When Walther enters the room, the orchestra swells to music associated with Midsummer's Day. Not only has the knight arisen from sleep, but something in him has arisen as well.*

Walther sings a verse about a lovely garden that invited him in one rosy morning. Sachs is pleased, and directs him to sing another just like it. Walther asks why, and Sachs explains it is like a wife to the first verse. Walther sings of a tree with gloriously healing fruit that grew in the garden. Sachs comments that this verse is also good, though it didn't end in the same tone as the first, a detail that offends the Masters. But no matter. Such is the unpredictable nature of spring. He directs Walther to compose an aftersong, which is like a child of the first two verses. If the first two verses are a good match, it will show in the "children," or last verse. Walther sings of a beautiful woman he saw standing next to him in the garden, who entwined his body and pointed to the fruit of the Tree of Life. Sachs, moved, praises the aftersong, even with its rather loose melodic form. Sachs orders a second section repeating the first three stanzas, since the meaning and the rhyme schemes are still incomplete. Walther sings a song whose melody roughly repeats what he has sung, but whose words tell of the power that arose within him that evening after he drank from the woman's eyes. As he gazed into the sky, he beheld, instead of fruit, a host of stars clustering in the laurel tree.

Sachs is deeply moved, saying that a third section would tell the meaning of the dream beautifully, but Walther has grown impatient. Sachs wisely lets the matter drop, telling Walther just to remember the melody and hold fast to the vision when he sings it for a wider audience. Walther asks what he means, but Sachs informs him only that Walther's servant and baggage have arrived at the house, and Walther should dress himself splendidly for the stately adventures that await. They retire into the inner room.

**Comment:** *Many find this scene belabored, with its focus on the minutiae of the songwriter's art and its elaborate metaphor of two verses "mating" to produce a third verse. Actually, it is a key scene, and perhaps the most modern episode in the whole opera, emphasizing the internal process of the artist over the concept of absolute art. This has been a central feature of twentieth-century aesthetic theory, for better or worse. Nor is the biological conception of art such a stretch, either. Dante, interestingly, includes a digression on the science of embryology within a discussion of poetic process in the twenty-fourth canto of his* Purgatorio *(i.e., almost in the middle of the* Divine Comedy*).*

*The song in question, of course, will become, with new words and*

*some musical refinements, the famous Prize Song of the next scene.*
*There are echoes of Walther's Trial Song from Act I in it as well. The*
*whole opera, then, is concerned with the birth process of this love song.*

Beckmesser looks in at the window, and, seeing Sachs's shop
empty, walks in. Although silent, he is obviously reliving the scene
last night, where he got the bruises that now make him hobble
around. He imagines David whacking him some more, and makes
angry gestures toward Eva's window. After some time, he leans on
Sachs's workbench and notices the paper Sachs had written while
Walther was singing. So, he concludes, Sachs was writing a courting
song of his own! Now the town clerk understands everything. He
conceals the paper in his pocket when he hears footsteps approach.

*Comment: Wagner's stage instructions for this episode are elaborately*
*detailed, calling for an extended "dumb show." "Dumb" might indeed*
*be the operative word here, since all but the very greatest actors look*
*pathetic making "gesticulations of ire and jealousy." There's also more*
*than a touch of sadistic glee here. We already saw Beckmesser get*
*beaten—now Wagner adds insult to injury, literally, by making him*
*even more of an object of ridicule. It's not easy to credit the author of*
*the* Wahn *monologue with this cruel, and none-too-brief, bit of non-*
*sense. The subtle orchestral dexterity of this scene, however, is among*
*the best in the opera.*

Sachs enters, surprised at seeing Beckmesser. Sachs asks the clerk
if his shoes are satisfactory. Beckmesser complains that they are too
thin, and Sachs agrees they must be, with all the hammer strokes he
gave them while counting errors in Beckmesser's song. Beckmesser
loses his temper, accusing Sachs of starting the riot the night before
to further his own ends and steal the maiden for himself. But he's on
to Sachs now! Sachs says Beckmesser is deluded ("*Wahn*"); Sachs is
not in contention for a bride. Beckmesser calls him a liar, and produces the love song, in Sachs's handwriting, as proof. Sachs denies it
still, and tells Beckmesser to keep the poem as a gift, so no one can
call him a thief.

Beckmesser is thrilled to have a poem supposedly written by the popular Hans Sachs. He praises Sachs, and looks forward to a renewed friendship—as long as there are no tricks involved, and as long as Sachs never lays public claim to the poem. Sachs assures him on both counts, but warns Beckmesser to study the poem carefully. It is difficult and needs just the right tone and melody. Beckmesser has no qualms there. He is a master melodist. He praises Sachs again, laughing at the young adventurer (Walther) who upset everything so. He promises to vote for Sachs for Marker at the next guild election, and leaves full of confidence. Sachs smiles wistfully to himself and declares Beckmesser the most malicious person he's ever met—although the clerk's thievery fits in very well with his plan.

**Comment:** *The Beckmesser grotesquerie continues unabated in this confrontation, but the music is well scored for the orchestra. In this scene, Wagner uses many light and witty figures in the orchestra—the kind we expect from operas that call themselves comic, but a rarity here.*

Eva enters the shop, confused though beautifully decked out all in white. She complains about her new shoes, first saying they pinch and then that they fall off. Sachs goes along with her charade, bending over her foot. Walther appears at the door to the inner room, dazzlingly arrayed in his noble best. Eva sighs at the sight of him, and Sachs slyly says he now sees the problem. He slips off her shoe and pretends to work at it, endlessly chattering about shoemaking and adding that perhaps he should court Eva after all, while the lovers gaze transfixed at each other and hear nothing. Sachs says he heard a lovely song this morning—if only there were a third verse to complete it! On cue, Walther sings the completion of the Dream Song, whose form and melody are on the model of the first two sections, but whose poetry finishes the vision. The stars of his dream become a crown on the brow of his beloved, who then crowns the poet's head with a wreath, filling him with the rapture of Paradise. Sachs interjects to Eva, "This, my dear, is mastersong." Before Walther finishes, Sachs pretends to fuss some more with the shoe;

and Eva, overcome with several conflicting emotions, falls sobbing on his breast. Walther also grasps Sachs's hand in gratitude, and there is a long moment of silent bliss while the three embrace. Sachs manages to extricate himself and leave the two young lovers leaning on each other.

*Comment: Even though Sachs had already declared himself "too old" for Eva, we are meant to understand his gesture here as noble, self-sacrificing, and wise.*

Sachs sublimates his own desire for Eva and emotion for the situation by singing a long and grumbling song about the unhappy life of a shoemaker. Nobody talks to him unless their shoes hurt. Even the young maidens toy with him. At last he masters himself, and cheerfully goes looking for David, who thinks of nothing but food and Lena. Before he can get too far, Eva grabs him by the arm. "Sachs! My friend!" she exclaims in great emotion. How much she owes him! He made a woman of her, and if the choice were hers, she would offer him her hand in marriage. Sachs, quite overcome, reassures her that he knows the story of Tristan and Isolde, and has no desire to play King Marke. His mood lightens when David and Lena appear at the door in their holiday best.

*Comment: This is the climax of the human drama. Eva's cry of "Sachs! Mein Freund!" is as emotionally raw as anything in Wagner. It's hard to make exact sense of what she says, since she really could have "chosen" Sachs at any time, but the music and their interactions here and in Act II make clear the warm relationship between them. This warmth could have gone astray, as Sachs understands so well, and he is noted as a character who has achieved a sort of wisdom in resignation, to use a Wagnerian vocabulary.*

*The reference to Tristan is matched with an actual quotation of the beginning of that opera's Prelude. Scholars go into conniptions over the "warm wit" of the quotation, while others justifiably see it as an example of how even the greatest artists are susceptible to moments of puerile self-indulgence. In any case, you can count on the know-it-alls in the audience, and anyone else who's read the program notes, to jostle their neighbors and nod with the contentment of the Buddha when they hear the* Tristan *quote, just to let everyone around know that nothing's getting by them.*

Sachs announces that a child, the song, has been born in his house. Sir Walther is its parent, Sachs and Eva Pogner are the godparents, and Lena and David must be the witnesses. But since, by local custom, an apprentice may not be a legal witness to a christening, Sachs orders David to his knees and cuffs him on the ear, thus giving the time-honored sign that he has attained the rank of journeyman. Now the child must be named; it will be called the "Blessed Morning Dream Interpretation Melody." Let each of the party say a few words.

**Comment:** *It should be noted that, in nature, a live birth usually takes less time than this song's birthing process. Promoting David is a lovely sign of generosity on Sachs's part. The cuff on the ear was indeed the traditional ritual gesture accompanying promotion to journeyman, not unlike dubbing a knight, or, in another coming-of-age ceremony, the ritual slap given by a bishop to those receiving confirmation in Catholic tradition. Unfortunately, most people in the audience don't know anything about a journeyman's cuff on the ear, and assume it to be just another episode in Sachs's and David's ongoing S & M relationship.*

Eva praises the melody, and the prize (Walther) it will win for her; Sachs determines to subdue and use the yearnings that the song has stirred in him in his own love poetry; Walther asks that what the melody confides to his friends in the workshop may win him the prize in public contest; David and Magdalena express joy that David's new status permits them to marry. Sachs sends Eva and Lena to Pogner, and takes Walther to the festival meadow. David closes shop.

**Comment:** *This, my friends, is the moment you've all been waiting for, the celebrated Quintet. There is no better moment of vocal ensemble writing in all opera, and few equals. Even the great Trio toward the end of Richard Strauss's Der Rosenkavalier owes something to this, with its analogous contrast of young love and resignation. Although Wagner had certainly proven that he could write ensembles, with the first two acts of this opera being proof enough for anyone, perhaps he wanted to show that he could write a good old "line 'em up at the footlights and sing pretty" type of quintet. It's enough to make you want to scream (perhaps like Minna Wagner), "To hell with your theories, Richard! Write more beautiful music!"*

### Act III, Scene 2

Setting: A meadow on the banks of the River Pegnitz, with Nuremberg visible in the background. The people of the town have begun to gather and continue to arrive throughout the scene. There is a stage erected on one side of the meadow, festooned with banners and decorations. The people are dressed in holiday best, with ribbons, flowers, and all sorts of decorations.

The guild of shoemakers enter under their banner, singing of their art, followed by the tailors, who sing of a tailor who once sewed himself up in a goatskin during a siege of Nuremberg, danced on the ramparts like a crazy man, and frightened the enemy away. The bakers march, singing that they feed the world. The apprentices run to the riverbank to help a boatload of pretty young maidens ashore. David is among them, forgetting his new status, and the apprentices tease him that Lena is watching. When David realizes this is true, he bids farewell to the maidens and runs to Lena.

**Comment:** *This is meant to be a scene of joy and fun unparalleled in Wagner's works. Indeed, when the tailors "bleat" in imitation of the goat, it's rather a unique moment for Wagner. Productions today try to make this as much fun as possible, and as far as possible from the regimented pageants popular during the Third Reich.*

The Mastersingers, including Pogner with Eva, arrive in procession under their banner of King David, and the people cheer them. Sachs stands to address the crowd, and the people greet him almost reverently, singing a chorale to words written by their favorite Mastersinger, urging each to awake, and greet the new morning, which dispels the clouds of doom. Hail Hans Sachs!

**Comment:** *The entrance of the Mastersingers, with their familiar four-square music, shows them at their bourgeois best, proud and slightly smug. The people then sing "Wacht auf!," the poem the historical Sachs wrote honoring Luther and the "bright dawn" of the Reformation. Wagner's music is lyrical, swelling, and gorgeous. The assembled chorus chose this piece to sing at the ceremony marking the laying of the foundation stone for the Bayreuth Festival House in 1871. God did not cooperate that day, and sent a soaking and relentless rain, making everyone regroup in the old Opera House.*

*The tune named "Wacht auf!" was likewise written by Hans Sachs, and is still found in most hymnals (including some Catholic ones) under the name "Sleepers, Wake!" Ironically, it is usually sung at Advent (December, directly opposite Saint John's Day), the darkest time of year in the Northern Hemisphere. It was famously harmonized by J. S. Bach.*

Sachs is moved by the Nurembergers' greeting. He speaks humbly of himself, saying he is only worthy of praise because of what Nuremberg and its glorious traditions have made him. Sachs then praises Pogner, whose song contest for Eva's hand embodies the best of the Nuremberg spirit.

**Comment:** *Sachs has a tendency to go on, and this monologue is no exception. The orchestra provides much of the interest here, weaving themes associated with Sachs's resignation (both of Eva in particular and of the world and its follies in general). The emotion Sachs is meant to portray here is his private, melancholy reflection on life, though his words are standard grandstanding. This is the sort of character depth a singer must be able to portray in the role, and shows why younger* *basses almost never sing Hans Sachs. Life experience and a certain air of acceptance must be there, even if the voice is not in its first bloom.*

Pogner, very touched, thanks Sachs. Beckmesser, who has been nervously looking at the poem crumpled in his pocket, gripes and fusses and accuses Sachs of writing an incomprehensible poem. Kothner calls the contest to order, and Beckmesser, ordering the apprentices to secure the wobbly stage, prepares to sing. The crowd comments on him. This one's a good clerk, but rather old for Eva, isn't he? He can't even walk straight! Kothner orders "Begin!"

Beckmesser strums his lute and embarks. Using a tune much like his meandering serenade, he attempts to sing "Sachs's" poem. The words come out entirely wrong, despite his cribbing with the sheet. The Mastersingers and the crowd look at each other nervously. What is Beckmesser talking about? Is he losing his mind? The clerk continues, but it only gets worse. The crowd begins to laugh at him, repeating his bizarre words and adding meanings of their own. Beckmesser pulls himself together and makes one final sally, but the crowd cracks up as he finishes, unable to suppress their laughter when he sings *"Leberbaum"* (liver-tree) instead of *"Lebensbaum"* (Tree of Life).

*Comment: It's rather refreshing to see Wagner, of all people, engage in a little silliness this one time. He must have had a lot of fun composing this part of the poem and its atrocious puns. For example, Walther's "herrlich ein Baum" ("a glorious tree") becomes "häng ich am Baum" ("I'm hanging on a tree"), and so on. Beckmesser's arch little tune emphasizes each offense with many of the coloratura flourishes that the historical Mastersingers overused in their period of decadence. The effect can be hilarious in the hands of a capable singer-actor.*

Beckmesser quits the stage and runs to Sachs, accusing him, who is so highly regarded there, as the author of this drivel before he throws the poem at Sachs and runs off into the crowd. Everyone is perplexed. Hans Sachs wrote such nonsense? The Mastersingers smell a scandal. Sachs quietly picks up the crumpled paper and declares that modesty forbids him to lay claim to such a beautiful song. Everyone assumes he is joking, but he tells them he means what he said, provided the song be properly sung. Whoever could do that would be declared a Mastersinger on the spot. Let anyone who can prove him right enter the circle as his witness!

Walther approaches Sachs, causing a stir. The Masters laugh at Sachs's slyness, saying they'll suffer such irregularities just this day. Now, says Sachs, see if Lord Walther von Stolzing can pull this song off! The apprentices announce "Begin!"

Walther mounts the stage and commences his song as he had sung it that morning. Kothner, who holds the poem to check for errors, is so enraptured by the beauty of the song that he lets the paper slip from his hands. Walther notices this out of the corner of his eye, and allows himself to improvise the song as the spirit moves him. The woman in the garden of whom he sings is no less than Eve, and the garden is Paradise! The crowd approves. The song is not easy at first, yet it is undeniably beautiful and worth following when sung like this! Walther continues: in the evening, his poetic soul recognizes the lady of the laurel tree as the Muse of Parnassus! The people note the song's grace, faraway yet familiar. The Masters concede that it is well rhymed, if unusual. Walther sings of the woman of his dreams, who awoke both love and poetry in his heart. In winning her, he wins both Parnassus and Paradise! Before he can even finish, the people express their rapture at his song. How like a dream it is, beautiful, yet elusive. They call for the winner's garland, and the Masters rise, unanimously awarding the garland to Walther.

**Comment**: *Here we have all of Walther's dreams in their final form as the Prize Song. The gimmick of Kothner dropping the page, allowing Walther to vary the melody from what we have already heard more than once, is often cited as a great moment of stagecraft, letting story circumvent the problem of the Mastersingers' "marking" the performance. The stage instructions, which say that Walther sees this happen and responds accordingly, are often missed by directors, performers, and audiences alike.*

*Lest you think, from reading these pages, that the Prize Song will be old news by this point, minor variations notwithstanding, think again.*

*First of all, the comments of the crowd and the Masters form a beautiful ensemble frame around the song itself, gilding, if you'll pardon the pun, the song as we know it. The melody is deceptively elusive, introduced by two lovely and refreshing C major chords and beginning in an approachable form, but wandering all over the place according to its own internal logic before resolving. If people in the audience complain of its repetitiveness on the way out of the theater, challenge them to whistle it. Not one in a hundred will be able to.*

*As a piece of vocal music, the Prize Song lies high in the voice, with some dangerously exposed notes and a great deal of ornamentation. This is dramatically appropriate, since Walther would not be presenting his intimate thoughts of the morning quite the same way in front of all Nuremberg. Lighter, lyric tenors often like to take a whack at it in recitals, since Wagner didn't write much music for their type of voice and this is one of their few available choices. Sometimes it works, sometimes not, but the real danger lies in thinking that the entire role of Walther is a light, lyric, "Italianate" tenor role. So it is, compared to Tristan or Siegfried, but overly ambitious tenors take this a step further, and add Walther to their repertoires thinking it will be smooth sailing. This can be fatal: tenorial careers have crashed and burned in this role (no names, please). What they forget is that there's a good five hours (!) of singing before the Prize Song, most of it against a thick Wagnerian orchestra and chorus, the latter being something not even Tristan and Siegfried have to worry about. Walthers run out of voice even more often than Siegfrieds, and then, let me warn you, the audience is in for the most torturously long night imaginable.*

Walther kneels before the ecstatic Eva, who places the winner's garland around his neck. The people praise Sachs, whose sly plan has made everything right. Pogner approaches Walther with a gold chain and medallion of King David, thus accepting him into the guild of Mastersingers, but Walther rejects the honor bluntly. Everyone is shocked by this snub, and they turn instinctively to Sachs.

Sachs takes Walther by the hand, and gently but firmly tells him not to be so contemptuous of the Mastersingers. Walther owes his present happiness not to his rank or arms, but to the fact that he is a poet and has been accepted as such by the Masters, who have preserved what is best and most German in the old arts, bringing them from the confines of the aristocracy out to the people. Sachs warns the crowd to beware the evil tricks that await their nation. If the German people and realm should decay under false, foreign rule, no prince would understand his people any more, and who would know what is German and true unless it lived in the spirit of the Masters? Therefore, let them be honored! Then even if the Holy Roman Empire should one day vaporize, there would still be holy German art!

Walther accepts the chain of the Mastersingers, and all the people join the praise of holy German art, hailing Nuremberg and its dear Hans Sachs.

**Comment:** *Sachs's final monologue is a problem. The second half, with its warnings of foreign rule, is particularly objectionable. First he acts the skillful peacemaker, then tells the crowd never to forget their artistic heritage as represented by such guilds as the Mastersingers. The line reads "Honor your German Masters," and the sense is clearly "Honor the guildmasters of your country and the traditions they have preserved," which is actually quite a democratic sentiment for Wagner. No matter. Critics of this opera like to focus on this line, playing games with the translation. For example,* The New York Times *quoted the line, out of context, as "Obey your German Masters!" (the verb is* ehren, *"to honor"), as if Richard Wagner needed any help emphasizing his chauvinism!*

*In any case, nobody is imagining the xenophobia and paranoia in Sachs's warning about foreign rule and the degeneracy of the German* Volk—*it's right there plain as day. Even Newman takes exception to this monologue, but he and the others have found a way to praise the opera while decrying this speech. It's really very simple: blame it on Cosima.*

*Certainly, Cosima is a plausible culprit. She had the special brand of noxious, nationalistic prejudice reserved for the foreign-born (like Napoleon before her and Hitler after her). In a letter to King Ludwig, she boasted how her influence kept this speech in the libretto when Wagner wanted to edit it and end the opera with the Prize Song. Proof, say the scholars, that it's her fault, and that she was even worse on these issues than Wagner himself. Perhaps, but anybody who believes that Wagner needed his arm twisted by Cosima to keep from editing himself is delusional*

## BASICS: WHEN TO EAT, DRINK, AND VISIT THE RESTROOM

Pay close attention here, or you could risk serious trouble.

*Meistersinger* performances usually begin at 6 p.m. So do several other Wagner operas, including *Parsifal* and *Götterdämmerung*, but the rules are slightly different here since it's the third act of *Meistersinger* that's the killer. One advantage of the longer third act of this opera is that your body will be more accustomed to the sheer act of sitting by the time you are required to put it to the big test. The biggest problem here is planning your victual sustenance. Naturally, you will want to try to eat something before you arrive at the opera house, and perhaps have a booster snack from the overpriced cafe in the lobby at intermission. However, you will be ravenous by the time the performance ends! Most people never even notice the disturbing politics of Sachs's final monologue because they are too busy thinking about which pizza parlors might still be open on the way home.

Plan this out ahead. Inquire from friends or the ushers which restaurants are open late in the vicinity, and set your sights there.

Definitely show your opera savviness by visiting the restroom at the second intermission. Greenhorns may skip the opportunity, having just emerged from the riotous and relatively brief Act II wondering why everybody thinks *Meistersinger* is so long and expecting to hold out till they get home. Chances are they will be seen running up the aisle, accompanied by gestures of panic and despair, a mere hour and three-quarters into Act III.

You can also prove your wisdom by ordering that cocktail at the first intermission and allowing it to seep into your body during the fun second act. Anyone taking alcohol or other sedatives at the second intermission will be slabbed out five minutes into the third act.

## ROUGH SPOTS AND HOW TO GET THROUGH THEM

Basically, either you are going to enter the mind-set of *Meistersinger*, with all its length and detail, or you're not. If you're not, there's no guidebook in the world that can make this anything but the longest opera in history (which it is), peppered at widely spaced intervals with a riot scene, a quintet, some festival music, and a Prize Song.

Even if you are a potential fan of this opera, there will be some episodes where your attention wanders. If the veteran operagoers of your acquaintance scoff at this, remind them that in previous generations this opera, like *Tristan*, was invariably cut in performance everywhere but Bayreuth. Nowadays, cuts are fewer, if they exist at all.

You may also take encouragement from the fact that the score of *Meistersinger*, with all its subtleties, is the most accessible music Wagner ever wrote. You never need to feel like you're "missing" anything, or that there are deep musical truths being revealed that everybody is getting except you. It's all right there begging to be heard, if you're awake to hear it.

The opening of Act I is stunning, but matters soon unravel with David's fifteen-minute instruction in the art of mastersinging. The best idea for this section is to fall dead asleep or practice deep meditation. Pogner's entrance is also less than sensational. When he is talking to Beckmesser, the orchestra plays snippets of themes we have heard in connection with Walther's courtship of Eva. These snippets are subtle and fragmented, contrasting Beckmesser's attempts at courtship with Walther's. See if you can hear them and identify them, and then see if and how well the performers onstage are responding to them. Act I soars once Walther starts singing, and the rich, all-male ensemble that concludes the act is a time to sit back and let the Niagara of sound wash over you.

Act II is one of Wagner's greatest achievements in unflagging lyric theater. Eva and Sachs may seem long-winded to read about, but their repartee is swift. What we are hoping to see here is the attraction, latent and slightly dangerous, between the two. Can the performers convince you of this, or do they look like a young tart and an old lecher? Most often, they seem entirely uninterested in each other. If the bass and soprano at the performance you are attending can create an air of quiet fire in this scene, the dramatic depth will be greatly enhanced.

Act III, of course, is the Longest Thing in the History of Civilization. However, it is loaded with sublime music, even though Sachs shuts it down at every turn. He has five actual monologues in this act, two of which are about shoemaking and one about German racial destiny. He has a great deal else to say as well in between monologues. No one else in this act can be accused of understatement, either. Basically, you're in good hands in Act III if (1) the bass portraying Sachs can convince you of the warm and nuanced humanity beyond his politics, (2) the Beckmesser is a good actor who can "work" an audience, and (3) the tenor's voice holds out. Any of this can go wrong at any moment, but the first scene of the act, lasting almost an hour and a half, changes characters frequently. If the Beckmesser is a bore, Eva may save the day, and so on. The festival scene is not too long—less than an hour—and if Sachs is boring in his monologues, there are usually lots of pretty costumes on the choristers to help hold your attention.


## PRODUCTIONS: WHAT YOU MIGHT EXPECT TO SEE

If there is a successful way to present this opera separated from its specific historical context, no one has yet found it. Unlike *Lohengrin*, which is a fairy tale, and *Tristan*, which takes place in the psyche, *Meistersinger* is just too rooted in the sixteenth-century German milieu, and almost all American productions accept this fact. You will probably have to settle for something that looks like the Oktoberfest area of your local theme park re-created on stage, or, as Frederic Spotts put it, "ye gables of olde Nüremberg."

Even Wieland Wagner, whose brilliant and revolutionary productions in the 1950s and 1960s seemed capable of redefining every work in his grandfather's opus, had trouble with this one. In the first postwar season in 1951, while Wieland's *Parsifal* and *Ring* were turning the opera world on its head, Bayreuth presented a perfectly traditional *Meistersinger*. After all, as Wieland himself had written in the 1951 program, the nature of *Meistersinger* calls for naturalistic production. When Wieland finally tackled this opera himself in 1956, his de-Nazified production was something of a flop. Act II was basically blank: two benches and two abstract trees. Act III was a sort of lecture hall amphitheater, with the onlookers forming almost a Greek chorus.

This production had the honor of earning the first boos in the history of the Bayreuth Festival House, and Wieland was widely accused of using shock tactics merely for effect—a charge he loathed and denied to the end of his life in 1966. His second *Meistersinger*, in 1963, was considerably more traditional. The third act festival was recognizable as old Nuremberg, but Wieland added many classical Greek motifs, a reference that had served him well to internationalize Wagner's other operas. The muses were present on stage (albeit in bust-enhancing dirndls), and the people and guilds gathered, as if spontaneously, rather than marching in fine Teutonic order.

This touch proved to be influential. Productions today tend to stress the popular rather than the hierarchical aspects of the festival scene.

European productions twist themselves in all directions to relieve this opera of its Nazi-associated imagery. Karajan's Salzburg production of 1974 stressed the mythological rather than the historical past. The sets were poetic, pre-Raphaelite visions, in an attempt to gild the guilds, as it were. By all accounts, it was superbly beautiful, but whether it was politically convincing is still debated. Another important production in Buenos Aires in 1980 extended this idea by making the setting of the opera so richly gorgeous that nobody could think it was anywhere on planet earth, least of all late-medieval Germany.

If too *pretty* doesn't work, there's always too *ugly*, which is what Götz Friedrich tried in his recent Deutsche Oper production in Berlin. The time of the story was moved up to the mid-nineteenth century, Wagner's time. The burghers and peasants of Nuremberg were all recognizable, but there was no attempt to prettify them. In fact, everyone on stage looked a bit raunchy, sporting an abundance of eye patches, crutches, and bandages. The message, presumably, was that there was corruption in this society beneath the pretty veneer. We are grateful to Herr Friedrich for pointing this out—as if it weren't apparent enough in the libretto! One problem with that production's line of thought (besides the obvious problem that you had to look at ugly people for over five hours) is its implication that a well-scrubbed, well-dressed population is *not* corrupt. This notion fits in well with the aesthetic values of the Nazis themselves, who were always presentable no matter what atrocities they were committing.

This is always the problem in director-driven theater with a political agenda: the more the directors try to distance themselves from fascism, the more they reveal their own fascist-friendly thought processes. Still, Friedrich must be given credit for trying to do something with this cultural albatross. It's very fortunate that, in contemporary Germany, he hardly had any other choice.

Until some genius finds another, more convincing way to produce *Meistersinger,* it looks like we're stuck with "ye gables of olde Nuremberg," and must rely on ourselves (an option critics and directors rarely take seriously) to sort out the many contradictions of this problematic opera.

## PERFORMANCE HISTORY AND ESSENTIAL LORE OF *MEISTERSINGER*

*Work in progress (1860s)* Wagner's idea of a fun evening with friends consisted of him reading aloud from his dramas while they sat in rapt attention. As thunderously dull as this may sound to us, everybody who has left a memoir of such evenings attests that he was absolutely fascinating as a reader/armchair actor. It seems clear that Wagner could have had a successful career as a dramatic actor, and we should remember the theatrical home life of his formative years.

While *Tristan* made no sense when read without music, and the *Ring* simply took too long to be comprehensible in a single reading, *Meistersinger* wowed people in this fashion. We are told that Wagner's ability to recite lines was so good that he didn't have to say the name of the speaker before saying the line, modulating his voice to let his hearers know who was speaking. Considering the size of the *Meistersinger* cast, his range must have been incredible.

*Yet another faux pas in Munich (1868)* Although Wagner was *persona non grata* in Munich by 1868, Ludwig decided to show him great favor the night of the premiere of *Meistersinger,* and invited Wagner to sit with him in the royal box. With the audience cheering wildly after each act, Wagner had the unheard-of effrontery to take a bow from the royal box itself, as if he were a sovereign acknowledging his subjects. Trivial as this may sound to us, this act offended the etiquette-conscious Bavarians as much as anything else Wagner pulled while in Munich.

*The definitively German opera overseas (1880s)* No one had much hope for *Meistersinger* outside of Germany, but it proved successful in London (1882) and New York (1886). (The French and the Italians have never had any particular stomach for it.) One of the reasons for its popularity in the English-speaking opera centers is that it worked surprisingly well in English translations.

If we today think *Meistersinger* heavy in tone and proportion for a comic opera, apparently it wasn't thought so in the 1880s. No less an authority than Arthur Sullivan, whose frothiest tunes continue to delight people, publicly said *Meistersinger* was the best comic opera ever written. Perhaps we should remember that *Meistersinger* was invariably given with hefty cuts well into the 1970s everywhere but Bayreuth.

*The wartime opera (1943)* Wieland Wagner's famous, if not notorious, 1956 production of *Meistersinger* was not his first in Bayreuth. He rarely spoke of his first production of the opera, which was in 1943. It's not hard to see why. First of all, the production itself was entirely literal and representational, even though Wieland had already begun experimenting in pared-down productions at smaller opera houses. Second, the 1943 *Meistersinger* was an exercise in wartime propaganda. It was the only opera given at the 1943 and 1944 festivals, because Winifred Wagner and Hitler had decided the *Ring* might be too much for wounded soldiers (!) and *Meistersinger* would renew their sense of the holiness of German culture. The musical standards remained high, even though the large chorus had to be filled in with members of the SS on leave. A performance from 1943 is currently available on recording, but many, including Wagner enthusiasts, find the whole thing impossible to listen to.

*Making prime time (1980s)* And now for something completely different . . . *Meistersinger* earned a fleeting but amusing reference on the hit TV series *Cheers*. When Waldo, the "brainiest" of Carla's many children, wants to attend a performance of *Meistersinger*, he attempts a rough outline of the plot to Sam, the affable but not over-cultured bartender. After Waldo explains the conventions of the Song Contest, Sam exclaims, "I get it! Like *Star Search!*" The suddenly world-weary kid sighs, "Sort of!"


## LOBBY TALK FOR *MEISTERSINGER*: NUREMBERG AS CITY AND CONCEPT

If we had to choose a single theme underlying *Meistersinger*, it would be the combination of old and new in art, or, stated another way, looking at the best of art as coming from the intersection of free artistic creativity and disciplined methodology. Nietzsche wrote about these two approaches to the creative process in *The Birth of Tragedy*, where he contrasted the Dionysian and the Apollonian urges in people. That book concludes with an extravagant hymn of praise to Richard Wagner as the culmination of all artistic spirit, praise Nietzsche would spend the rest of his life choking back. Nevertheless, the Wagner who was writing the *Ring* inspired something in the young philosopher. It is now clear that the supposed classical models Nietzsche wrote about had very little to do with ancient Greece and a great deal to do with Richard Wagner. *Meistersinger*, even more than the *Ring*, addresses the issue of the Dionysian spirit (free artistic creativity and anarchic destruction) and the Apollonian spirit (disciplined methodology) in art, and manages it much more pleasantly and convincingly than Nietzsche did.

Nuremberg is not a random choice for the setting of a story looking at these issues, much less a merely quaint choice offering pretty settings. It is a city whose history and ethos are soaking in the same conflicts as this drama, in the area of aesthetics and in much else besides.

Nuremberg rose to prominence in the Middle Ages, largely on the prosperity created by its guild system. The guilds were part trade union, part fraternity, and part school. By the fifteenth century, the craftsmen and guilds of Nuremberg were famous throughout Europe and beyond for their excellence and ingenuity. The scientific arts, cartography, and metalwork particularly flourished. Timepieces of great accuracy were produced there, attesting to the technological knowledge in this city, which was, in a sense, the Silicon Valley of the late fifteenth century. The guilds that ran these and all industries in the city ensured excellent standards. The Mastersingers we meet in the opera, who identify themselves as furriers, soap-makers, and so on, were probably, in real life, heads of those guilds rather than actual workers. It may not be going too far to compare the idea of the sixty-six-year-old Hans Sachs making a pair of shoes to the picture of Jimmy Hoffa driving a truck.

The guilds also competed with the churches in matters of social welfare, instituting rudimentary plans for pensions, unemployment, and other matters of daily concern. Nuremberg boasted an evolved sense of social conscience. A "retirement home" was opened in the fourteenth century and is still functioning today.

Even mundane tasks reflected the values of the old Nurembergers. The famous doll houses of Nuremberg, built up to seven feet high, are prized by museums throughout the world. "Doll house" is misleading, since they were much more than mere toys. The doll houses were extraordinarily detailed models of the large abodes of the time, including all the various supplies and objects to be found in them. They were used for training young women who expected to become mistresses of their own houses in the future. A single glance at one of these doll houses shows us that the houses of the Nurembergers were much more than domestic dwellings. The ground floor was a warehouse, animal pen, and, often, a storefront, perhaps like Sachs's workshop. The rest of the house contained offices, nurseries, infirmaries, pantries, and kitchens as well as bedrooms and common areas. A housewife of Nuremberg was an office and warehouse manager, cook, teacher, seamstress, doctor, and nurse as well as wife and mother.

All the training and instruction for such a life could have been accomplished just as well with paper diagrams or, at most, plain boxes, without the fine detail and adornment typical of these models, but that was not the Nuremberg way. To be of real value to the Nurembergers, they had to be beautiful as well. The doll houses are perfect examples of the old Nuremberg ethic, wherein enterprise, craftsmanship, utility, and beauty were all valued as one and the same.

While the Holy Roman Empire did not have any single capital city, Nuremberg always held a special place of honor among the cities of the realm. It was known as the Treasure Chest of the Empire, and the crown jewels were kept there from 1424 to 1800. Beginning in 1356 and continuing for many centuries, the emperor traditionally convened the first Reichtag (as it was then spelled), or Imperial Parliament, in Nuremberg. For the symbolically minded, this implied that the wealth and glory of the Empire was based, in a sense, on the solid middle-class values of Nuremberg.

This special relationship between the city and the Empire even survived the Reformation for a while. Nuremberg, with its hardworking, no-nonsense aura, was prime ground for the Reformation and the self-sufficient industrial ethic that came to be associated with it. The city went Lutheran in a big way. The Catholic Emperor Charles V, famous in history and a figure not unknown on the operatic stage, could not afford to alienate the Protestants of Nuremberg. It remained a favored imperial city despite the religious breach. We can judge the Nurembergers' appreciation of the emperor by the fact that they sent 80,000 troops to fight with him against the Turkish invaders at the siege of Vienna in 1529 when the imperial requirement was only half that number.

Even the great upheaval of the Reformation itself was sustained by Nuremberg on its own terms. While the other Lutheran cities engaged in wholesale destruction of church art as a protest against the perceived idolatry of the Roman faith, Nuremberg was almost unique in preserving its priceless treasures. The local regard for beauty and craft was greater than the destructive passions of the moment. Like the Mastersingers at the end of the opera, the Nurembergers culled from the entire spectrum of possibilities, from traditional to progressive, without either becoming slaves to any one dogma or rejecting dogma altogether.

Eventually, Nuremberg declined, and by 1600 much of the leadership in technology had passed to the Lowlands and other places. The Thirty Years' War (1618–48), which wiped out so much of Germany, also debilitated Nuremberg's industry, since much of its market was gone. Politically, the peace treaty of 1648 recognized three hundred virtually independent small states and free cities in Germany, and the Empire gravitated toward Vienna and Austria. The city was a quiet place by 1700, already something of a museum piece and tourist destination. In 1806, the Holy Roman Emperor relinquished his title and became emperor of Austria in name as well as in fact, finally surrendering the pretense of having anything to do with Germany. Nuremberg's imperial days were over.

By the time of Wagner's visits in the 1830s, much of history had passed over Nuremberg. This, of course, made the old town the focus of much attention from the Romantics, who were addicted to looking into the past, real or imagined, to find their ideals for the future. The legends of the Reformation held a particular resonance for the Germans of the 1860s, looking for answers to the endless questions of national identity. Paradoxically, yet not without reason, Nuremberg represented links to the glories of both the Holy Roman Empire and the Reformation in the popular sensibility. In retrospect, it stood for everything "good" in Germany.

This is why *Meistersinger*, with its indirect but obvious praises of Luther and the Reformation, could be such a great success even in arch-Catholic Munich in 1868. Its symbols had lost their original referents and had become sentiments, easily manipulated by a master of theater. Unfortunately, Wagner was not the last master of theater to manipulate such sentiments.

Adolf Hitler knew what he was doing when he chose Nuremberg as the official city of Nazi Party rallies. He needed a centrally located German city that was not too rigorously associated in the public mind with any single one of the many factions of German history in order to subsume the powerful imagery of previous greatness and incorporate it into his Reich. A park outside of town was suddenly transformed into a sort of physical manifestation of Hitler's ideal—grounds and stadiums where hundreds of thousands of the German *Volk* could parade to receive the Will of the Führer. Architect Albert Speer and filmmaker Leni Riefenstahl were among the many who contributed brilliantly to this imagery, assuring that minds still reel, so many years later, at the mention of the word Nuremberg.

Nor was Richard Wagner forgotten in the Nazi *Kulturkampf*. Everything that made Nuremberg ripe for Wagner worked no less for Hitler. Endless performances of *Meistersinger* were part and parcel of the Nuremberg party rally experience. Even the fetishization of the words *Reich* and *Volk* has roots in the libretto of *Meistersinger*.

There is considerable evidence that the citizens of Nuremberg itself were less than enthusiastic about the honor Hitler had bestowed on them by choosing their city as the showplace of National Socialism. The City Council was controlled by Communists and Social Democrats until those parties were suppressed, and even after the fateful 1933 election of Hitler as chancellor of Germany, seventy thousand Nurembergers rallied in the streets against National Socialism. Many Nurembergers today are extremely resentful of the stigma they carry in the worldwide imagination as "hosts" of the Nazi gatherings. They quite rightly point out that other cities, most notably Stuttgart, actively lobbied Hitler to be chosen for the party rallies.

Nuremberg, however, was no oasis of sanity against the National Socialist onslaught. The Nazi agenda had been propagated there by the notorious Julius Streicher, one of the party's most virulent attack dogs. In 1923, before most people had ever heard of Adolf Hitler, Streicher began publishing *Der Stürmer*, a violently anti-Semitic weekly whose banner bore the headline "The Jews are our Problem!" on every issue. Streicher had support among the Nuremberg police force, and the Nazi Party held semiclandestine rallies in the city as early as 1927.

Nor had the Jews of Nuremberg enjoyed centuries of peace before Streicher. While some Catholics continued to live in the Protestant city, Jews did not always enjoy the same relative tolerance, and apparently never had. The Imperial Chapel on Nuremberg's main square, where the emperor worshiped when in residence, was built on the site of a synagogue that had been destroyed in a fourteenth-century pogrom. The plaque on the outside wall makes no mention of this. In 1938, a full month before *Kristallnacht* (the infamous night of November 9, when Jewish businesses and homes were destroyed throughout Germany), the main synagogue of Nuremberg was torn down by a state-supported mob. The synagogue was located on Hans Sachs Platz. (Wagner had complained of the "arrogance" of the flagrantly "Oriental" synagogue in the heart of Nuremberg.)

The party rally of 1935 proclaimed the Nuremberg Laws, which stripped Jews of German citizenship and basically legalized violence against them, further associating the city with Nazism. The Allies joined in the propaganda war by convening the Nuremberg Trials of Nazi crimes against humanity in November 1945. The tribunal met in a city that had been bombed out of existence in the last days of the war. With that sad logic of warfare, the beautiful old city was wiped out, while Speer's harrowing rally grounds were spared. Much of the old city has been painstakingly and beautifully reconstructed and continues to be. Saint Sebold's Church, the main repository of priceless church art, was only reopened in 1995.

However much we may wish all this history away, it is absurd to think we can approach the city of Nuremberg in the opera in question merely as a mythological space, independent of the actual place. The opera is too great to be consigned to the garbage heaps of history. It isn't going away. Even focusing exclusively on the positive human aspects it presents will not whitewash the facts; after all, the Nazis prized *Meistersinger* for those same innocent virtues. There must have been those who got teary-eyed at the *Wahn* monologue, bemoaning man's inhumanity to man, and who then left the theater and participated in murder. It makes one wonder if art has any redeeming power at all.

Nuremberg has seen the best and absolute worst of human capabilities. It is a mirror in which we might take a hard look at ourselves.

◆

# DER RING DES NIBELUNGEN

## THE NAME

It means "The Ring of the Nibelung." A Nibelung is a dwarf in the mythic world of this saga, and the particular dwarf in question is named Alberich, a character in this work. Today, one usually just says "the *Ring*," and people know what you mean. You can attempt it in German—it's basically pronounced as written. Whatever you do, don't call it "The Ring of the Nibelungen," as so many people do. The *-en* ending of *Nibelungen* here is the possessive case in German.

## WHAT IS THE *RING*?

The *Ring*, as it has come to be called, is a vast and unique masterpiece. It is a series of four operas, or one opera in four parts, meant to be performed on successive nights in an extraordinary "festival" atmosphere. Any way you look at it, the *Ring* is probably the longest chunk of music and/or drama ever put before an audience. It is certainly one of the best. There is nothing remotely like it.

So what is the *Ring*? In one sentence, it is a German Romantic view of Norse and Teutonic myth influenced by Greek tragedy and a Buddhistic sense of destiny told with a sociopolitical deconstruction of contemporary society, a psychological study of motivation and action, and a blueprint for a new approach to music and theater. Phew! It's a wonder it only lasts four days! Believe me, the preceding sentence is calm compared to most summaries of the *Ring*.

Everything that can be said about a work of art has been said about the *Ring*. This is because the *Ring* saga, like any truly great work of art, has as many meanings as there are people to interpret. It has been seen as a justification for governments and a condemnation of them. It speaks to traditionalists and forward-thinkers. It is distinctly German and profoundly pannational. It is the basis of most analyses of Wagner, and the most "conceptualized" theater piece in history. It provides a lifetime of study for musicologists and thrilling entertainment for the tone-deaf. It is an adventure for all who approach it.

In the last generation or so, people have also discovered that the *Ring* is not quite as scary as it was once thought to be. As recently as 1961, George Martin was able to say bluntly that the *Ring* was not for the casual operagoer. All this has changed. Perhaps television and in-house translations have helped. Perhaps it's because anybody with an interest in theater sooner or later hears about this piece as the ultimate goal of any director or designer. Perhaps we need fewer explanations about the famous leitmotivs that form the basis of the music, since we are well trained by our media to register a response to a snippet of music (think of the shark theme in *Jaws*). Or perhaps people are just less willing to believe that they're not "smart" enough to get it. For, while the *Ring* is an inexhaustible resource for inquiry into virtually every subject, there is nothing to "get" except awesome theater. George Bernard Shaw, a famous fan of this work, and one who had *plenty* to say about its deeper meanings, summed it up best. After freely confessing himself to be a "superior person" for whom the *Ring* "has a most urgent and searching philosophical and social significance," Shaw offers an encouragement to "modest citizens who may suppose themselves to be disqualified from enjoying the *Ring* by their technical ignorance of music. They may dismiss such misgivings speedily and confidently. There is not a single note of 'classical music' in the *Ring*—not a note of it has any other point than the single direct point of giving musical expression to the drama."

◆

# DAS RHEINGOLD

Premiere: Munich, 1869

## THE NAME

*What to call it*  Basically *Rheingold* will do, unless you're being quite formal, in which case you can add the *Das*. Calling it *The Rhinegold* went out of style fifty years ago.

*How to pronounce it*  This is a more delicate issue. If you are saying it in English, and spelling it "Rhinegold," there is no problem. If you are attempting German, make sure to give the first *R* a healthy glottal fricative, which is that back-of-the-throat sound Scots make with the word *loch* or French with the word *arriver*. Only then is it advisable to add the article *Das*.

## WHAT IS *DAS RHEINGOLD?*

*Das Rheingold* is the *Vorabend* ("fore-evening," or "prologue") to the *Ring*. It is by far the shortest of the four *Ring* operas, about two and a quarter hours long, but it was written to be performed without a break. Besides being the shortest, *Rheingold* is also in many ways the brainiest *Ring* opera, and also the chattiest. It sets forth the moral, philosophical, dramatic, and musical issues of the saga, and relies heavily on a sort of conversational tone to do so. In some ways, it is the least familiar part of the *Ring*. There are no "set pieces" in *Rheingold* that can be separated from the whole and played on the radio or in the concert hall, nothing akin to "The Ride of the Valkyries," the

"Forest Murmurs," or "Siegfried's Funeral," found in each of the subsequent works. Except for Loge's spiel about the value of love, there
are no real narrations or monologues such as those we find so frequently, and at such length, in the rest of the *Ring*.

*Rheingold* is primarily a series of dialogues and confrontations
interspersed with brief, shattering musical effects. The Prelude, the
first glow of the gold, Wotan's dreams of Valhalla, the descent into
Nibelheim, Alberich's call to the Nibelungs, and the finale are as
original and as easy to appreciate on first hearing as anything in
Wagner.

Which is not to suggest that the rest of *Rheingold* is dull. On the
contrary, a good performance of it will leave you almost breathless
with its magnificent sweep. Musicians particularly admire it, and
first-timers are usually surprised at how much they have enjoyed it. It
is quite easy to follow, since most of the leitmotivs, the much-
discussed themes of the *Ring*, are laid out in the course of this story.
In other words, we see the gold—we hear its "theme"; Alberich
curses the Ring using the Curse of the Ring theme, and so on. In the
subsequent operas, these themes will be used to refer to people,
things, and events that actually occur in this opera.

## CAST OF CHARACTERS

WOTAN *(bass-baritone or bass)*  The unofficial, but undisputed, chief
of the gods. The gods, as we find out, are neither all-powerful nor all-
knowing, though they can put on a good show when they want to.
Wotan is ambitious for power and not above compromising his own
high ethics to get it. His rule, precarious as it is, is based on law and
contracts, symbolized by carvings on the shaft of the Spear, which he
carries everywhere. He also wears an eye patch, and has several different stories to explain this.

FRICKA *(mezzo-soprano)*  Wotan's wife, and the goddess of marriage.
Poor Fricka basically just wants a nice home with a husband who
stays there. Did *she* ever marry the wrong guy! The prosaic wife who

cannot understand her husband's ideals (to say nothing of his affairs) is a theme from Greek and Roman mythology; it's also how Wagner liked to think of his own first wife.

FREIA *(soprano)* The goddess of flora, harvest, immortality, and other such stuff. Freia is ever-young, beautiful, desirable, and doesn't have a whole lot to say here other than "Help!" She is also known as Holda.

DONNER *(baritone)* The thunder god, who walks around with a large hammer, usually looking ridiculous.

FROH *(tenor)* The god of spring.

LOGE *(tenor)* The god of fire and trickery. Yes, you read that right. Every ancient culture has a sort of divine "trickster," and Loge is the slippery and wily one here. Loge is considered quite second-class by all the gods except Wotan, who needs his abilities. He dwells apart from the other gods.

ALBERICH *(bass)* A Nibelung, or dwarf, who lives primarily under the earth.

MIME *(tenor)* Another Nibelung, and Alberich's brother, although they are distinctly lacking in filial affection.

FAFNER *(bass)* A big, sweaty, coarse giant who fears Nibelungs and envies the gods.

FASOLT *(bass)* Fafner's brother giant, equally big, sweaty, and coarse, but with an odd romantic streak in him that proves his undoing.

ERDA *(contralto)* The all-knowing Earth Mother, also known as the Wala.

THE THREE RHINEMAIDENS Three water-nymph sisters who have one job in life, and can't do it. Their father is the River Rhine, in whose waters they live, play, and flirt.

WOGLINDE *(soprano)*, WELLGUNDE *(soprano)*, FLOSSHILDE *(mezzo-soprano)*.

## THE OPERA

### *Prelude and Scene* 1

Setting: The depths of the Rhine River.

Woglinde is swimming through the river, singing first nonsense words and then of the rollicking waves of water. She is joined by her sister Wellgunde, and they frolic together. Their sister, Flosshilde, joins them and gently chides them that they are guarding the gold poorly, and they'd be sorry if someone stole it.

Immediately there appears an ugly snarling dwarf named Alberich sliming around the riverbed. Flosshilde tells her sisters to be on guard. Father (the Rhine) has warned them of such an enemy. The three Rhinemaidens, as they are called, ask the dwarf what he wants. He says how he would love to enfold their little forms in his arms. Flosshilde laughs at her own fears. The enemy is in love! Woglinde, to teach him a lesson, beckons him, but the ooze of the riverbed makes him slip and sneeze. She darts up and down, always staying just out of his reach. Wellgunde advises the poor dwarf to forget the teasing Woglinde and come to her instead. He approaches her with expressions of love and lust. She has a look at him, and tells him in detail how ugly he is. Flosshilde reproaches her sisters for their frivolity. Isn't the dwarf handsome? She and Alberich exchange tender expressions from a distance until she, too, dismisses him as ugly and croaking. He wails of the pain the Rhinemaidens cause him with their deceptions, but they insist they are without any fraud at all. They would be true to any man who could catch and hold them! He chases them in vain around the river while they swim away and laugh at him.

A glow penetrates the waters, and there is a dazzling gleam of gold on the top of a rock. The sisters comment on its beauty, and sing of the magnificent Rhinegold. They joyfully invite the dwarf to join in its praise. Alberich cynically says their golden water toy would be of no use to him, but Woglinde says he'd be more in awe of it if he knew its wonders. Wellgunde explains that whoever would make a ring out of the Rhinegold would win all the world's wealth and power. Flosshilde advised caution, since they are to guard it against thieves, but Woglinde retorts that only he who would swear to forfeit love forever could fashion the gold into a ring. No one will give up love—least of all this horny little gnome! They insist he laugh and sing with them. He threatens them instead. They panic as they realize love has made him crazy. Alberich mounts the rock, declares to the waves that he curses love, and steals the gold. The Rhinemaidens wail and cry for help.

**Comment:** *The Prelude to* Rheingold *is one of the most celebrated "coups" in musical theater, and detailed analyses of it abound. Basically, it is 136 bars of E-flat "unpacked" into a swirl of life in a single crescendo. The mood shifts, as does the key, when the first voice is heard. Nonsense words begin the vocalizing, followed by alliterative speech and then dialogue. It is a musical depiction of creation, from formless void to humanoid interaction. This great sweep of music is not heard on the radio or in the concert hall, since it is part of a story rather than a story in itself.*

*Everybody loves the Rhinemaidens' scene and always has, despite the obvious difficulties in staging it. For one thing, it is supremely lyrical and lies pleasantly in the voice. Also, the Rhinemaidens are the only remotely fun creatures we are to meet in the* Ring, *even if they are rather ditzy. Commentators generally cite them as representing primal innocence. George Bernard Shaw saw them plainly as tarts. Wagner used the term "eternal feminine" to describe them, an important concept in Goethe and others. The beauty of this term is that it encompasses the entire spectrum of male projections of women.*

*Some critics have cited this scene as an example of Wagner at his most uneconomical. Alberich must be wooed and rejected first by one Rhinemaiden, then the next, and finally the last, repeating the process each time. He certainly could have made the same statement merely once and been done with it, but it seems clear that Wagner was enjoying the time spent with these three and their pretty music. Audiences enjoy it too, and no one ever complains that this scene is too long.*

*By the way, don't waste any time wondering how a dwarf is walking around the bottom of a river. This is myth, you see, and there will be far greater strains on your credulity as the cycle continues.*

### Scene 2

Setting: A mountaintop clearing.

Wotan, the king of the gods, and his consort Fricka lie sleeping. Fricka awakens and bids her husband wake up. He mutters in his sleep about power and glory. He declares the eternal work completed—the gods' superb mountaintop stronghold is built! Fricka asks if he has forgotten the price he agreed to pay for the new home— her beautiful sister Freia. He dismisses that as inconsequential, causing her to gasp at his loveless frivolity, and remind him that the women were kept away from the meeting when Wotan contracted with the giants to build the proud structure, for which he bartered away Freia. What, she asks pungently, is holy to you hard men when you go after power? Didn't Fricka herself beg me for this building? he retorts. Yes, she answers, she wanted a home, a lordly abode that might tempt her wandering, cheating husband to stay home, but all he could envision was a fortress to increase his power. Wotan says that no home can keep him from wandering in search of variety—he will not surrender that sport! Loveless man, she exclaims, who can so glibly gamble a woman's love and value for power! He responds that he values women too much for his wife's comfort rather than too little, and reminds her that he gave up one of his eyes to marry her. As for Freia, he has no intention of surrendering her to the giants, and never had.

Just then, Freia rushes on stage, begging protection from the giants who are even now chasing her to carry her away. Wotan distractedly asks her if she hasn't seen Loge, the trickster god of fire, who promised to find some loophole in the agreement. Fricka is annoyed that Wotan should have put so much trust in the mercurial Loge, who is nothing but a liar, but Wotan says the situation demanded cunning.

**Comment:** *Wotan's character is well defined by the stately and impressive music that accompanies his first appearance. His dreams of Valhalla, the yet-unnamed castle lurking in the foggy background, are beautiful but slightly pathetic. Wotan desperately wants to believe that his new home will give him everything he desires: security, status, and power. His wife sees things differently and perhaps more realistically. Fricka is often played as a nagging Hausfrau, which is reductive. She always makes a remarkable amount of sense, and it's pretty clear that life as Mrs. Wotan is not a breeze. The issue at stake in this part of Scene 2 is the balance of love and power, a theme that colors the whole of the Ring.*

The giants Fafner and Fasolt come lumbering on, demanding payment for the building of Wotan's fortress. Fine, says the king of the gods, name your price. Fasolt asks him if he has forgotten that he already pledged Freia as payment for the castle. Wotan replies that the giants must be off their heads. Freia is not for sale, and they should name another price. Fasolt bluntly accuses Wotan of treachery. The marks of solemn compact carved into Wotan's Spear—symbol and embodiment of his great but finite power—do they mean nothing to him? Fasolt warns Wotan to beware of breaking his agreement, since Wotan is only what he is by virtue of contracts. Wotan says that the giants should never have taken literally what was said only in jest. What use is the fair Freia to brutes like them? Fasolt, rather obviously love-struck, says they merely want what every male wants—a lovely woman to abide with them. Fafner, the more cynical of the two, says that he personally cares very little for owning Freia. The real pleasure comes in depriving the gods of her, for without the golden apples that she alone can produce in her garden, the gods' youth and beauty will fade. They will age and die, and the time of their power will pass, so let her be taken! He orders Freia to follow them. Her brothers Donner, god of thunder, and Froh, god of spring, arrive to defend her, but Wotan stops them from intervening, compelled by the contract-attesting marks on the shaft of the Spear. Just then, Loge appears.

*Comment:* Poor Freia doesn't get a whole lot to do in this opera. While the other "auxiliary" gods Donner and Froh each get some impressive music to sing toward the end of Scene 4, Freia doesn't even get to sing her own leitmotiv. Most of the time she runs around the stage like a bimbo crying "Help!" while chased by two hulking, sweaty giants (the opportunities for sarcastic humor here are sometimes too much for directors to resist). The clodding chords that accompany the entrance of the giants, which are quoted by Richard Strauss in his opera Ariadne auf Naxos to accompany the boneheaded Major-Domo, are impressive, but the real masterstroke is the touchingly lyrical music for Fasolt. Despite his gross appearance, the guy just wants a pretty bride. He is a sort of proto–King Kong.

Wotan is annoyed at Loge's tardiness, and asks him what he has found as a substitute for Freia. Loge defensively answers that he could not do the impossible. Fricka gets in a dig at Wotan for having trusted Loge, and Donner and Froh add their snide comments. But Wotan insists Loge's wiles are even better when he delays in revealing them. The giants demand immediate action without delays, and Wotan orders Loge to produce something.

Pretending to be hurt by Wotan's ingratitude, Loge tells all that he has searched on earth, in the water, and in the air, but nowhere has he found a power greater than woman's beauty. There was, however, a single exception. The Rhinemaidens told him how the Nibelung, "Night-Alberich," rejected in his advances, took revenge by stealing their gold, and now prizes it above all things, including love. The Rhinemaidens asked Loge to intercede with Wotan, that he might return their gold to them. Wotan calls Loge either mad or malicious. He is in trouble himself. How can he help the Rhinemaidens? The giants grudge Alberich the gold, since he has already caused them plenty of problems. But what power does this gold give him? Loge evasively says that a ring made of the gold would give its owner supreme power. Wotan has heard of this, and Fricka asks what power the Ring would give a woman. Loge explains that a woman who owned the Ring could keep her husband faithful. She and Wotan agree that the Ring would be good to have, but Loge tells them they'd have to renounce love to gain the power, and neither of them would do that. Besides, they're too late. Alberich didn't hesitate to curse love—the Ring and its power are already his!

Wotan exclaims bluntly that he himself must have the Ring. But how to get it? Easy, replies Loge. Steal it from the one who stole it. Then Wotan can return it to the Rhinemaidens, as they asked. Wotan is not interested in the Rhinemaidens, and Fricka adds that she has no desire to know about those three trashy marriage wreckers. Fafner deduces that the gold is worth more than Freia, since its commander also gains eternal youth. He announces to Wotan that Freia may stay with the gods in exchange for the Rhinegold. Let the god use his cunning, but get the gold by evening, or Freia will be the giants' forever. They drag her away as a hostage, while Loge comments on their journey across the Rhine. No one is listening to him. The gods are lurching to the ground, weary. Loge understands that they haven't eaten Freia's golden apples this day, and are aging already. He himself doesn't need to worry, only being a demigod, and Freia only grudgingly gave him the occasional apple anyway, but the others are in serious trouble. Wotan musters himself, telling Loge to accompany him to Alberich's home in Nibelheim, deep in the earth. They must get the gold! To return it to the Rhinemaidens? asks Loge teasingly. Never mind them, answers Wotan, Freia must be freed. We'll go there by way of the Rhine, says Loge provocatively, but Wotan insists they find another way. They disappear through a chasm in the rocks while Fricka, Donner, and Froh implore them to be quick about their business.

**Comment:** *Loge dominates this part of the scene. He is sarcastic, philosophical, and a bit long-winded if you don't know what he's saying. Lately, it's been the fashion to assign the role to lighter-voiced tenors who are good actors, and even good comedians, and they usually ham it up quite a bit.*

*When Loge tells of the Rhinegold, the Ring, and so on, the orchestra plays variations of the themes we have heard when these objects and situations were played out on the stage in the first scene. This is the beginning of the involved system of leitmotivs for which the* Ring *is so famous.*

## Scene 3

A musical interlude depicts Wotan and Loge's journey through the earth to Nibelheim.

**Comment:** *This interlude begins typically enough, with dark muddy tones suggesting both the physical journey into the earth and the questionable motives and consequences of the journey. Soon we hear the familiar Rhinegold theme, now sounding ominous played on the bass trumpet. This is followed by a sinister rhythmic theme in the orchestra, which had already been suggested in Loge's narration when he described the toiling servitude of the Nibelung slaves. It grows very loud, supported by percussion, until the orchestra fades out and all we hear is the cadence literally hammered out on twelve anvils. It is a striking effect that never fails to grab the attention of those who have drifted away during the longish previous scene.*

Setting: Nibelheim, the subterranean cavern home of the Nibelungs.

Alberich is harassing and beating his brother Mime, demanding the helmet he ordered him to make. Mime produces the helmet, which Alberich seizes, accusing Mime of plotting some use of it for himself. He puts on the helmet and instantly vanishes. Mime cannot see him, so Alberich tells him to feel him instead, delivering a series of invisible kicks to the howling dwarf. Now he, Alberich, will be everywhere at all times, unseen, coercing labor out of his wretched Nibelung slaves! They will mine the earth day and night for him, increasing his hoard of gold, not daring to linger. His voice trails off.

Loge and Wotan appear, asking Mime why he's whimpering. Mime explains to them that the Nibelungs were once a happy race, mining and smithing for the pleasure of it and to make ornaments for their women. Now they are slaves to Alberich because of the power he has gained through the Ring. He admits that he had planned to use the magic helmet, the Tarnhelm, himself to escape Alberich's tyranny, but now Alberich has that as well! Mime asks the intruders who they are, and Loge says they are friends who will free the Nibelungs. Alberich returns, visible now, fulminating at the Nibelungs, threatening all, flaunting his power. Almost as an afterthought, he asks Loge and Wotan what they want. Slyly, the two flatter him, saying they have come to see for themselves the one who is the envy of all, the all-powerful Alberich. Alberich recognizes them, taunting Loge for associating with the "Elves of Light," as he calls the gods. Wotan points out that power is useless in joyless Nibelheim, but Alberich discloses his plan to conquer the whole world with the wealth of Nibelheim. Then he will torture the fallen gods by raping their women out of sheer spite and lust, since he has no love. This provokes Wotan nearly to violence, but Loge calms him and continues his flattery of the dwarf. Truly Alberich is the envy of the world, but how will he guard against theft? Loge thinks himself so clever, remarks Alberich, that he assumes all others stupid. The Tarnhelm gives him the ability to assume shapes as well as become invisible. He can intimidate any foe with the magic helmet. Loge will not be convinced by words, and dares Alberich to prove it. Unable to resist, Alberich dons the Tarnhelm and instantly turns into a giant serpent, hissing and spitting.

Wotan laughs at the silliness of the trick, but Loge feigns terror and begs the hideous serpent for his life. Now do you believe me? asks Alberich, resuming his dwarf shape. I wouldn't have if I hadn't seen it, answers Loge, suggesting that Alberich might be wiser to turn himself into a tiny creature so that he couldn't be found, but, of course, that would probably be beyond Alberich's capability. Goaded, Alberich pits the Tarnhelm back on, and instantly becomes a small toad, "ribbeting" on the ground. Wotan immediately steps on the toad, Loge grabs the Tarnhelm, and Alberich, captured, resumes his form, cursing. Loge and Wotan drag their captive up the chasm of the rock, back to the mountaintop clearing.

**Comment:** *The Alberich of this scene is very different from the frustrated little gnome of Scene 1. Here he is frankly drunk with power, as is Wotan as well, but Alberich's reaction to it is coarser and louder. This is perhaps why he will fall from power faster than Wotan does—he lacks Wotan's veneer of civilization. Throughout his appearances in the Ring from this point onward, Alberich is very clear about his disdain for the gods' beauty and loftiness.*

*The production challenges of this scene are obvious. The serpent never fails to elicit laughter from the audience, so most productions accept the inevitable and play it for laughs. Wotan's reaction to the transformation provides some justification for this. The second transformation shows us some humor in the orchestra, with soft "ribbets" in the winds.*

### Scene 4

Setting: The mountaintop clearing, as in Scene 2.

Loge taunts the captured, raging Alberich, who asks what his ransom is. Wotan calmly demands his hoard of gold. The dwarf cries out against such a sacrifice, but considers that so long as he has the Ring he can always find another hoard of gold. Next time he won't fall for any tricks! The Gods loosen his hand and, whispering to the Ring, Alberich summons the Nibelungs with the hoard. The Nibelungs crawl out of clefts in the rocks, while Alberich, imperious even in his captivity, hurls abuse at them, ordering them not to dare look up at him in this state and to return to work immediately. The shrieking Nibelungs disappear, still terrified of Alberich. Loge tells the dwarf to remove the Tarnhelm from his belt—that, too, is part of the hoard. Alberich hands the helmet over, and demands to be let loose. Wotan says there is yet one last item: Alberich must surrender the Ring. Alberich pleads, threatens, and screams. "Take my life, but not the Ring!" Wotan does not care a whit about Alberich's life, but the Ring he must have! Alberich accuses the god of hypocrisy, vying for the power of the Ring without having paid the terrible price it cost to forge it. Yes, he admits, "I stole it. But if I sinned, I sinned only against myself. But you, eternal one, sin against all that was, is, and will ever be if you seize the Ring from me!" Unimpressed, Wotan tears the Ring off Alberich's hand and puts it on his own hand, entranced. Loge unties Alberich's hands and feet, telling him he is free. This gets a bitter laugh out of Alberich, and he greets his freedom with ominous words. Let the Ring be cursed. Let it bring death to whoever wears it, happiness to no one, and envy to all. The pathetic dwarf crawls away.

**Comment:** *Most people agree that the curse on the Ring is little more than a formulaic musical and dramatic gesture—obviously it will be bad news for everybody involved. But the terms of the curse are important as well. It will bring death to those who wear it, but all others who fall under its spell will live on in envy; that is, they cannot die. This detail will prove important later in the drama.*

Fricka, Donner, and Froh enter, eager for news. The giants with their captive Freia follow. Fasolt bemoans surrendering the lovely goddess. If he must accept the Nibelung's gold in lieu of her, let the gold be piled up high enough to block her entirely out of sight, because he can't bear to give her up if he can see any part of her. Wotan, impatient to conclude the business, agrees, and the giants plant their walking staffs in the ground. Freia is placed between the staffs and slightly behind, that the gold may be piled up to form a wall in front of her. Donner and Loge heave the gold into a pile, while Fafner keeps patting it down tight. At last the hoard is exhausted, but Fasolt can still see Freia through a gap in the pile of gold. Fafner demands the Tarnhelm, which Wotan disgustedly adds to the pile. But Fasolt is not yet out of his misery. Through the tiniest crack he can still see Freia's beautiful eye. No! He can't leave her while he can see her! Loge protests that the hoard is exhausted, but Fafner demands the Ring on Wotan's hand. Loge says the Ring is not part of the hoard, but will be returned to the Rhinemaidens, which prompts Wotan to inform all that he is not surrendering the Ring to anybody for any reason. The giants say the deal is broken, and grab Freia to drag her away again. Fricka, Donner, and Froh plead with Wotan to surrender the Ring, but Wotan is adamant. He will *not* relinquish the Ring.

**Comment:** *The piling of the gold to hide Freia from view is a rather contrived way to get Wotan to give up the Ring, but it is effective in showing the extent of the gods' humiliation at this point, that is, how Wotan has "prostituted" them for the trappings of power.*

*Helpful hint: The Rhinegold itself made the Ring. The rest of the gold is what the Nibelungs mined in servitude to Alberich as Master of the Ring.*

A mysterious form emerges from the ground, a woman who warns Wotan, in ominous tones, to yield. Wotan asks the identity of this woman who threatens him. She is Erda, the Earth Mother, proto-ancestress of the world, who sees all that was, is, and will be. Usually she sends her daughters, the three Norns, who spin the fabric of time and fate, to Wotan nightly in his dreams, but now she must speak in person. All that is shall come to an end. A dark day dawns for the gods. Give up the Ring! Wotan begs more information from the all-seeing Earth Mother, but she abruptly tells him he has received suffi-cient warning, and vanishes.

Wotan determines to know more from the Earth Mother, but the other gods counsel caution. To provoke Erda would be madness. Wotan delivers the Ring to Fasolt, welcoming Freia back home. Fafner immediately sets to packing up the gold, causing Fasolt to demand his fair half-share. Fafner points out that Fasolt was so obsessed with Freia that he doesn't deserve an even half. Fasolt calls on the gods to judge his case, but they say nothing. Only Loge advises him to allow Fafner the gold, but keep the Ring. Fafner demands the Ring, and Fasolt claims it by right, since he holds it. "Hold it tight, then, lest you drop it!" cries Fafner, who knocks his brother dead with one blow. He takes the Ring, throws it in his sack of gold, and leaves. Wotan is beginning to realize the power of the Ring's curse.

Loge points out how lucky Wotan is. He gained power with the Ring, and even more power when he lost it! Wotan ruminates Erda's dark warnings, while Fricka asks him why he is hesitating to enter his new fortress. As if conscious of it for the first time, Wotan remarks that he has paid for the fortress with bad wages.

Donner comments on the oppressive air that has been hanging about them for the whole of this difficult day. He commands the clouds to gather themselves to him, with all mists and vapors. Swinging his great hammer and gathering the gloom about it, with one great blow he causes a burst of lightning to clear the air. Froh commands a rainbow to arc from their clearing to the mountain summit, now plainly visible with its peerless castle glistening in the evening light. The gods stare entranced at its majesty, primarily Wotan, who is struck by a passing but unexplained idea. He salutes the castle, and grandly offers his arm to Fricka. "Follow me, wife," he says, "and live with me in Valhalla." She is a bit overwhelmed by the idea, asking what the name Valhalla means. He explains vaguely that it will become clear over time.

The gods approach the rainbow, while Loge remains behind, noting how the gods hurry to their own end. As the gods prepare to enter Valhalla, the Rhinemaidens are heard, as if from the river below, bewailing their lost gold. Wotan is annoyed with the reminder, and bids Loge silence them. Loge advises the Rhinemaidens to forget about their gold and bask instead in the shimmering glory of the gods. The sisters continue their lament, adding that everything high up is tainted, while only the depths remain pure. Wotan says nothing, but draws himself up proudly and leads the other gods across the rainbow to their new home in Valhalla. Loge remains behind.

**Comment:** *The entrance of the gods into Valhalla is meant to be a moment of pure magnificence, the panoply of power in its moment of full glory. Many people these days feel uncomfortable with such a pose, especially those who see the Wagner–Third Reich connection too directly. Directors are often found "hedging" this scene in some way. Worse yet are the occasional conductors who undercut the self-conscious grandeur of the music. This is a mistake. Loge's comments are explicit enough to let us know that we are not meant to be "rooting" for the gods, so to speak. Besides, the answers are in the score, as always. Wagner weaves together many leitmotivs at this point, includ-*

*ing music associated with the Rhinegold as a counterpoint to the Val-
halla music, so any flatliner can understand the corrupt center of the
gods' new grandeur. However, the overall feel must be one of splendor,
or else their eventual fall will not be sufficiently impressive. The finale
to* Rheingold *also happens to be the loudest part of the entire* Ring,
*which certainly says something. As Robert Donington so interestingly
points out in* Wagner's "Ring" and Its Symbols, *Valhalla not only
stands for hollow pomp and illusory power, it also signifies the transi-
tory nature of genuine worldly achievement.*

## BASICS: WHEN TO EAT, DRINK,
## AND VISIT THE RESTROOM

Well, this one's a no-brainer. Either you get your physical needs met
before the beginning of *Rheingold* or you just grit your teeth and
hang on. *Rheingold* was written without an intermission, and is
almost always performed that way. Most evening performances of
*Rheingold* start at 8:00 p.m., which is laughably audience-friendly by
Wagnerian standards.

## ROUGH SPOTS AND HOW TO GET THROUGH THEM

Many people will tell you that there are no *longueurs* in *Rheingold*.
This is true—if you know what's going on. If you don't, you will find
the two mountaintop scenes (Scenes 2 and 4) unnecessarily chatty.
You can always hope to rely on the in-house translations, but if you
do, you had better pay pretty close attention to every word. This will
mean your eyes won't be on the performers, and that's a particular
shame in this piece. Loge, especially, has important details to relate,
but they are better read ahead of time so you can enjoy the tenor's
characterization of the role. See if you find yourself attracted to
Loge's duplicitous character. Is the tenor "seducing" you, or is he just
prancing about the stage trying to convey some operatic equivalent of
slipperiness? And is there a real, qualitative difference between

Loge's flickering presence and the stalwart, glorious gods, or are they all just standing around looking statuesque? These are the details that make *Rheingold* such an enjoyable brain-tease in performance. If the production is sensitive to details of this nature, the two hours and twenty minutes of this work will fly by before you realize you forgot to stop at the bar or the restroom on the way to your seat.

# DIE WALKÜRE

PREMIERE: MUNICH, 1870.

## THE NAME

*What to call it* This one can be a bit confusing. The only English equivalent for *Walküre* is "Valkyrie," which means a kind of warrior goddess. In this case, it refers to Brünnhilde, the heroine of the *Ring*. Usually, one would just say *Walküre* in conversation, and leave off the *Die*, which means "the."

*How to pronounce it* If you are settling for English, it's pronounced "VAHL-keh-ree," or anything close to it. In German, there's that nasty *ü* to negotiate. There's no need to strain yourself on it, since you'll never get it exactly right anyway. It's basically "VAHL-keu-ruh." The important thing to remember is that the accent is on the first syllable, and the last vowel is "uh." The first word is pronounced "Dee."

## WHAT IS *DIE WALKÜRE*?

*Die Walküre* has almost from the beginning been the most popular of the *Ring* operas, and the one you are most likely to see outside of a full cycle of the *Ring*. It's not hard to see why. The situations in *Die Walküre* brought out some of the most frankly emotional music Wagner ever wrote. Siegmund's and Sieglinde's self-discovery in each other in Act I is thrilling; this is somehow Wagner's most convincing love scene in terms of sheer romantic passion. Wotan's dilemma is involving, and we meet Brünnhilde in this opera. She and her eight Valkyrie sisters make much unique music.

Not that one should expect a "hit parade" here. Fricka doesn't come up for air as she expounds her take on things, and Wotan's moral and philosophical problems concerning his abandonment of Seigmund and the punishment of Brünnhilde are spun out at some length. In order to appreciate *Die Walküre* as a whole, rather than languishing in anticipation of the big hits, one should give it the same attention and preparation given to, say, *Das Rheingold*.

Such work will not go unrewarded. *Die Walküre* makes a great first impression, and then keeps getting better with every hearing. Despite its mythical world of gods, Valkyries, and heroes, this opera has a good claim to be the most human one Wagner ever wrote.

## CAST OF CHARACTERS

WOTAN *(bass or bass-baritone)* Our chief god is somewhat wiser by *Walküre*, though no closer to serenity.

FRICKA *(mezzo-soprano)* The goddess of marriage is still trying to create a manageable home life, and farther than ever from her goal. In this opera, Fricka plays the role of a moral compass to Wotan, as well as a nagging wife.

SIEGMUND *(tenor)* One of the two twins Wotan fathered on a mortal woman while calling himself Wälse (the twins are thus known as the Wälsungs or Volsungs). Siegmund has grown up alone and at odds from the society of other men. This is one of Wagner's most sympathetic creations, though not through anything he actually says or does.

SIEGLINDE *(soprano)* Siegmund's twin sister, the other Volsung.

BRÜNNHILDE *(soprano)* Wotan's favorite among the Valkyries, the warrior maidens he fathered on Erda.

HUNDING *(bass)* A great big lout of a man who married Sieglinde after she was abducted by his kinsmen. Notwithstanding these unattractive qualities, Hunding is about the only character in the whole *Ring* who can keep his word of honor.

THE VALKYRIES *(sopranos and mezzo-sopranos)*

GERHILDE, ORTLINDE, WALTRAUTE, SCHWERTLEITE, HELMWIGE, SIEGRUNE, GRIMGERDE, ROSSWEISSE

## THE OPERA

### Act I

Setting: The interior of Hunding's large but primitive house, built around the trunk and branches of an ash tree. A fire is burning in the hearth. A large, rough door is upstage.

A brief prelude depicts a man running through a storm. Siegmund, exhausted, opens the door, exclaiming, "Whoever owns this house, I must rest here!" He collapses in front of the fireplace.

**Comment:** *The cellos and basses play a repeating rhythmic figure to portray Siegmund's flight. This is punctuated by the brass, which blares Donner's thunder motif from* Das Rheingold. *Commentators, who can be so dreadfully literal, inform us that this signifies the thunder of a storm through which Siegmund is running. Well, yes, of course it does, but there's more to it than that. We have, in theory, just heard* Das Rheingold *the night before we are hearing this, and our most recent memory is the magnificent entrance of the gods into Valhalla. The thunder motif is more a symbol and reminder of the gods' grandeur than a specific indicator of weather conditions. Siegmund is here associated with that godliness, but imperfectly, as befits his half-human nature. The thunder motif is unchanged in itself but its surrounding orchestration is entirely different. In* Das Rheingold, *it was stately, unadorned, regal, and imperious. Here it is supported by repeating rhythms impelling it forward. We have left the ethereal realm of the gods and arrived at the plane of humanity, with all its complications.*

*The Prelude and Siegmund's sudden entrance and collapse are a powerful and excellent opening for an opera that is both an entity in itself and one in a series. It is also one of theater's most successful expressions of that old idea "It was a dark and stormy night . . . "*

Sieglinde enters, wondering who the stranger is on her hearth. He tosses and turns and gasps for water, which she brings. They gaze at each other with sympathy, tenderness, and perhaps recognition. He drinks, his eyes never leaving hers, and asks who she is. She answers that both the house and its woman are Hunding's property. The guest may stay until Hunding returns. Siegmund agrees, saying that a wounded, weaponless guest will not give her husband any cause for alarm. Concerned, she asks to see his wounds, but he dismisses them as minor, further explaining that he never would have run away from battle except that his shield and his spear were smashed. She offers him a hornful of mead, which he refuses until she tastes it first. They drink, staring ever deeper into each other, until he gets up to leave. Misfortune always follows him, and he doesn't want to bring any on her. Then stop, she tells him. He cannot bring misfortune into the home of misfortune. "I call myself Sorrowful," he says. He will wait for Hunding. They continue to stare at each other with growing emotion.

**Comment:** *The immediate bond between Siegmund and Sieglinde is expressed superbly in the orchestra. Their words, throughout this act, sometimes make them difficult to love, but the gorgeous music while they gaze at each other puts us firmly on their side. The first theme, played by a solo cello, is particularly admired by experts and ordinary listeners alike. It will expand later in the act as their passion explodes.*

They hear Hunding approach. Sieglinde opens the door, and Hunding enters sternly. This stranger needed shelter, she says. "Did you provide for him?" he asks his wife. Yes. Siegmund says that Hunding wouldn't scold his wife for giving him shelter. Hunding impressively asserts that his hearth is sacred—let his home be sacred to the guest. He hands his armor to his wife, and orders her to serve supper, noting to himself how alike she and the stranger are. He asks the stranger where he comes from. Siegmund replies that he does not know where he is, much less where he was. Hunding tells his name, and explains that all the rich surrounding lands belong to his kinsmen, who protect his honor. Now, won't the stranger tell his story . . . if not to him, then at least to his wife, who is so obviously interested? Embarrassed, she admits that she would like to know more. Siegmund begins his story.

*Comment: Hunding's stentorian theme, blasted by the brass, is slightly reminiscent of the giants' in* Das Rheingold, *only rather more impressive. Hunding is not related to the giants, except perhaps spiritually and as an enemy of Wotan's world vision. The tension throughout this scene tells us the real conflict between Hunding and Siegmund is one of clashing natures.*

Siegmund says that he can call himself neither "Peaceful" nor "Joyful," but must call himself "Sorrowful." His father was called "Wolf," but he hardly knew his mother or his twin sister. One day, he was out hunting with his warlike father, and they returned home to find their house burned down, the mother slaughtered, and the sister vanished and presumably burned in the flames. He escaped the nameless enemies with his father. They lived for many years in the woods, always defending themselves and escaping their enemies. He became known as the "Wolf Cub."

Hunding comments that he has heard dark rumors of such a pair. Sieglinde presses for more of the story. During one such attack on the "Wolves," continues Siegmund, he lost his father. Alone, he had to leave the woods and enter the world of people, but there was no happiness for him there. Misfortune trailed him, and he was always at odds with all, no matter how helpful or friendly his intentions. Hunding drily observes that the Norn (Fate) who gave him his destiny did not love him, and no man could enjoy offering him hospitality. Sieglinde gamely asserts that only cowards fear lone, weaponless men, and asks for yet more of the story.

Siegmund recounts that a girl who was being forced into a loveless marriage called on him for help. He slew her brothers, but this courageous act turned the girl's anger to sorrow. She lamented their deaths. The kinsmen of the slain men fell upon him, and he defended himself and the girl until his weapons were shattered. He watched her die, and finally escaped. "You can see," he says to Sieglinde, "why I can't call myself 'Peaceful.'" Hunding stands. Those were his kinsmen the stranger fought, but he arrived too late at the battle. Now he returns to find the villain in his own home. He has promised hospitality for the night, and will keep his word, but in the morning they will fight to the death!

Hunding orders Sieglinde to take his nightly drink into the bedroom and to wait for him there. Sieglinde prepares the drink, silently, urgently trying to draw Siegmund's attention to something in the tree trunk in the center of the room. Hunding watches them carefully, until he and Sieglinde finally withdraw.

*Comment: It takes an extraordinary tenor and a subtle conductor to keep Siegmund's long narrative interesting. People who have read Wagner biographies or Cosima's Diaries will recognize the theme of "I don't know why nobody likes me when I'm really a nice guy" from Wagner's own life. This narrative is also complicated by another of Wagner's maddeningly pedantic name games, with "Peaceful"* (Friedmund) *and "Joyful"* (Frohwalt) *as well as "Sorrowful"* (Wehwalt) *and "Wolf-Cub"* (Wolfing). *Here again (as in* Lohengrin *and* Parsifal*) the name is the key to the character, and the game continues right through the end of the act, when Siegmund ("Victor") is given, and assumes, his rightful name (i.e., true nature). "Wolfe," obviously, is Wotan, although his "real" name in the human world is "Wälse." He will tell more about his reasons for wandering the earth and fathering twins on a human wife in his long monologue in Act II.*

*There is some mimed business at the end of this scene, as Sieglinde tries to make Siegmund see the hilt of a sword planted in the tree. We hear the still-unexplained sword motif played on a triumphant solo trumpet. We had heard this before in* Das Rheingold, *when Wotan was "struck by an idea." The tension at this point is superb, with tympani beating out the rhythmic outline of Hunding's ominous theme throughout.*

Alone, Siegmund gives vent to his feelings. His father Wälse promised him a sword in time of distress, and here he is, weaponless, waiting for vengeance on his head. He longs for this beautiful woman, but she too is a captive of the enemy. Wälse! Wälse! Where is your sword? A flame from the hearth jumps up, and Siegmund sees a glimmer in the tree trunk. What is it? It reminds him of the woman's eyes. glowing through the dark, hopeless night. The flame dies down, the room darkens, and Siegmund falls asleep on the ground.

**Comment:** *This is Siegmund's spotlight moment, the only real alone-on-stage segment of the opera, and it is awesome. The low-level fear of the preceding introduction explodes into voice, as he cries for his father who abandoned him. The two "Wälse!" exclamations, held for as long as the tenor can hold them, bespeak deep and total panic, while the balance of the narrative is a loving and tender reminiscence of Sieglinde, making demands on the tenor's expressivity as well as his lungs.*

Sieglinde enters and wakes him up, explaining that she has drugged Hunding's drink so that Siegmund can save himself. She shows him the sword and tells its story. At her wedding, when she was forced to marry against her will, the guests sat drinking. A stranger came in, an old man whose hat slouched below one eye, but whose single visible eye cowed all with its authority. She alone was filled with a sad longing by this stranger. He flashed a sword, and thrust it into the trunk up to the hilt, declaring it the property of whoever could pull it out. All tried, and all failed. Then she knew the identity of the stranger, and for whom the sword had been planted. It was for a friend who would rescue her! If only that friend were here now! Siegmund declares himself the hero who will win both the sword and woman.

A sudden gust of wind blows the door of the hut open; frightened, Sieglinde asks who came in or went out. No one left, but spring has burst into the house, explains Siegmund. Spring, in his glory, seeks the house of his sister Love, and Spring and Love are united. You are the spring, she declares joyfully, I longed for through the dead winter. "Let me look at you—where have I seen that noble face before?" She realizes that it is her own, which she has seen reflected in the stream. He answers that she is the image he has hidden within himself. "That voice!" she says. "I know it. I heard it as a child. But more recently too, when my own voice echoed in the forest!" Your eyes, she continues, are those of the stranger who came to my wedding, by which his child recognized him. Tell me, are you really named "Sorrowful?" Siegmund says she must name what she wishes, and he will take his name from her. And was his father really called "Wolfe"? Only to foxlike enemies, he explains, but he was named "Wälse." If Wälse was your father, then it was for you that he planted the sword, and I will call you by the name I love—Siegmund! Yes, he answers, I am Siegmund, and this sword will be your wedding gift, protecting you as I carry you away from here. He grasps the hilt of the sword, naming it "Notung," because he finds it in time of distress. Ecstatically, he draws the sword out of the tree, bidding this fairest of women to follow him out into the night. She stops him long enough to tell him that she is Sieglinde, his own sister who has longed for him, and whom he has won along with the sword. Then wife and sister she'll be to him, and let the blood of the Wälsungs flourish! Together, they flee, entirely consumed by their passion.

**Comment:** *From the word go, there have been those who cannot handle watching two twins make violent love to each other on stage. Actually, if one wants to get technical about it, it's really a triple case of incest, since each of the twins is also fondling the memory of their father at the same time. But those who are incapable of metaphor would do better not to attend a performance of the* Ring *in the first place, and much more is going on here than incest. Siegmund and Sieglinde are in the process of discovering their selves, which is as good* *as any other definition of love. His face is her reflection, his voice her own echo, to which he responds with the sublime notion that she is the image he has kept hidden within himself.*

*This celebrated duet is really not a duet at all, since the two lovers sing separately and never overlap each other. Wagner felt strongly about this as the proper way to depict the discovery of love, although he later modified this view somewhat for Tristan und Isolde. Wagner is at his heights as an opera composer in this scene, painstakingly building each of the details into a sweeping, and utterly believable, climax.*

*Siegmund's unabashedly lyrical Spring Song, for all that has been written about the unique nature of Wagnerian music drama, is a flat-out, bold-faced aria. "Notung," the name of the sword, is based on the German word Not, which is a handy word signifying "need," distress," and even "emergency."*

## Act II

Setting: A rocky mountain pass.

After a brief prelude, we see Wotan and his daughter Brünnhilde, the Valkyrie. He tells her that Siegmund and Hunding will fight. She must give her divine support to Siegmund. Hunding's spirit can go where it wishes after he is slain—he is not needed in Valhalla. Ecstatic, she gives her war cry of "*Hojotoho!*" She sees Fricka approaching in her chariot drawn by rams, and says she prefers combats of the battlefield to domestic ones. Repeating her war cry, she leaves.

*Comment: The swirling, rushing Prelude tells us we are in the middle of unfolding events. The repeated sword theme reminds us of Siegmund and heroism, we hear the twins running in their passion, and finally there is the charging theme everyone will recognize as "The Ride of the Valkyries." This is not the complete piece known by that name, which will raise the curtain on Act III, but just enough to introduce us to Brünnhilde. It's what we would call a tease. Commentators go through great exertions to demonstrate that it is played differently here than in*

Act III (since Wagner would never repeat himself, etc., etc.), but it's
pretty obvious that Wagner knew a hit tune when he heard one.

In Act III, the "Hojotohos" are sung by the other eight Valkyries, in
many cases by women whose entire careers are based on perfecting the
technique. This is the only place where Brünnhilde actually sings
them, and a little creative "fudging" is to be expected by the diva, since
she has so much else to sing besides. It's well worth a glance at the
printed music to understand why, even if you don't think you read
music. She is expected to traverse over an octave, from G below middle
C to high C, in forte voice, ending each phrase in a single upward
swoop, and then to hold on to the high Cs at the end. Do not try this at
home. Many sopranos turn this into an ascending whoop and hope
that it will conclude somewhere in the vicinity of high C. After that, the
two measures of trill followed by another high C sustained for a further
two measures might be regarded as a bonus prize. One can't help thinking that a certain amount of wildness on the part of the Brünnhilde
was anticipated by Wagner. The point here is to curdle the gastric
juices of the audience, not to pass a singing test at a baroque conserva-
tory. However she navigates it, it's clearly a hell of a way for a soprano
to make an entrance—or a living.

Alone, Wotan mutters that he must face the same conflicts as ever
with his wife. Fricka enters, purposeful but still calm. She has sought
out her husband in he wilds he loves so as to exact a promise from
him. Hunding has called on her as the goddess of marriage. She has
heard his prayers and sworn vengeance on the Volsung twins. What
wrongs have they committed by falling in love, asks Wotan. If anything is wrong, it's the bonds that keep people in loveless marriages.

Fricka slyly says she knows how little Wotan regards vows of marriage, but is he ready to bless the union of a brother and sister? When
was that ever done? It is done now, says Wotan, not without a bit of
condescension. He advises Fricka to accept the power of love and
bless the twins' union. This angers her. How little he has cared for the
gods' honor lately! And why should she plead the cause of wedlock to
him, of all husbands, who has betrayed their marriage so often! He
abandoned her while he flew about with the savage Valkyries he

fathered, and then he left her for years to live as Wälse with a common mortal, siring those twins who now mock her honor! Wotan is
frankly baffled that Fricka can only see an affront to her own honor in
his fathering of the Volsungs. She can only understand banal custom
and tradition, while his far-sighted goals are beyond her narrow
mind. The gods need a hero—one who is independent of the gods
and not bound by their restrictions—to do for the gods what they cannot do for themselves. This tack entirely fails to impress the goddess.
Independent of the gods? Who breathes life and light into men?
Who protects them? What would they aspire to without your prod-
ding? "In your Siegmund, I find only you, for only through you does
he stir." Not so, protests Wotan. Siegmund created himself, and owes
nothing to my protection. Then leave him on his own now, she adds
hastily. Take back the sword you gave him. He won the sword himself, says Wotan lamely, beginning to sense the flaws in his own case.
But who planned for him to need the sword? she presses. Didn't you
plant it in the tree? Didn't you lead him to find it? Hadn't you
promised it to him? Wotan stands up to answer her, but can say nothing. She continues. Against Wotan himself she would do battle, but
under the circumstances Siegmund is nothing but a slave and should
be punished as such. Or will a slave make a mockery of the queen of
the gods?

After a long silence, Wotan, defeated, asks, "What do you want?"
"Do not protect the Volsung," is the reply. He agrees, but she continues
her demands. The Valkyrie must not protect Siegmund either. Wotan
protests that he cannot forsake the man who found his sword, but
Fricka insists Wotan withdraw its magic. The sword must shatter, and
Siegmund be rendered helpless. Just then, Brünnhilde comes back,
beginning her war cry but stopping short as she sees Fricka. Fricka
imperiously demands Wotan's oath that the Valkyrie will aid Hunding
in the fight, and he helplessly gives it. Fricka tells Brünnhilde to heed
her new orders, and exits in triumph.

**Comment:** *In this scene we are back in the moral confrontation world
of* Das Rheingold. *Most people see Fricka as an archetypal nagging
wife, which is not really a fair description. Certainly Wotan is not the*

*all-time catch of a husband. His pomposity alone would make him insufferable. Indeed, a close look at Fricka's words reveals that his lust for power disturbs her even more than his philandering. One cannot help wondering how much of this scene was culled from Wagner's domestic life with Minna. In any case, the symbolically minded view Fricka as an embodiment of Wotan's conscience, which is plausible.*

*The libretto specifically dictates that Fricka make her entrance in this scene in a chariot drawn by rams. Even Wagner himself dispensed with this outrageous effect when he produced the* Ring *at Bayreuth. This scene is Fricka's last appearance in the* Ring. *Thus, however she makes her entrance (and few productions bother to rent a dainty pair of rams from the local zoo), bet on Fricka's exit to be very, very grand.*

Brünnhilde is aghast at Fricka's words, and asks Wotan to explain. How wretched he is, he exclaims, the saddest of all creatures! How he would love to unburden himself to her, but wouldn't he then be loosening his grip on his own will, in some sense, if he were to do so? No, she assures him, since she herself is the very embodiment of his will. He agrees that talking to Brünnhilde is much like conversing with himself, although he must still keep his thoughts secret from all others. He begins a long account of events as he has come to understand them.

When the first joys of love had passed, he thirsted for power, and won the world. He bound potential enemies with treaties and contracts, urged on by tricky Loge, who has since fled from him. Then Alberich cursed love and won the Rhinegold with all its power. He himself stole the Ring from Alberich and paid for Valhalla with it instead of returning it to the Rhine. Wise Erda advised him to get rid of the Ring or risk hastening the end of the gods, but she refused to tell him more. He followed her into the earth and literally raped her for more information, learning much. As a result of this encounter, Erda bore Brünnhilde, Wotan's "other self," and her eight Valkyrie sisters. They brought him the spirits of the bravest slain heroes from the battlefield to defend Valhalla from its many foes. Alberich still wanders, fueled only by vengeance and rage. If he should ever regain the Ring, he would muster all creation against the gods. Fafner now sleeps crouching on the Ring, but Wotan cannot take it from him since he gave it to him in good faith. Thus he who rules by treaties is a slave to them.

There is only one hope now for Wotan and all the gods—a hero who, of his own free will and without any help from the gods, against whom he would even fight, must do what the gods cannot do (i.e., secure the Ring). That is why he reared Siegmund and gave him the sword, but Fricka revealed the utter hollowness of that plan. Alberich's curse follows him. Now he must betray Siegmund, his heart's beloved. Bitterly, he cries out that all is in vain, and let the vain pomp of the gods pass away! There is only one thing he longs for now—the End! And Alberich is working relentlessly toward that End. Erda had told him that the time of the gods' passing would be near when the Dark One fathered a son, and Wotan has lately heard that Alberich had bought a woman's love with gold, and she now bears that child of hate. Let this child seek the prize he wants—he himself can fight no more. Brünnhilde must fight for Fricka's cause.

Brünnhilde declares that she will never fight against Wotan's beloved son. But instead of being comforted by her loyalty, he turns on her wrathfully. "Obey my command: Siegmund falls! This is the Valkyrie's task!" He leaves in fury.

*Comment: For a long time it has been fashionable to roll one's eyes at the mention of Wotan and his monologues, of which this is by far the longest. "We know all this," the jaded say. "We saw it on stage last night." Not true. Only a very small fraction of this monologue covers territory already seen on stage, and even then it is placed in a new context. The arrangement of musical themes, and the permutations in which they are presented here, as if subtly but significantly transformed by the magic and delusions of Wotan's memory, are of primary importance to the development of the story.*

*Much of the blame for the failure of this scene to ingratiate itself to the public must lie with the singers, many of whom have failed to grasp Wagner's intent here. Fortunately, some possess the artistry and intellect to reveal the power of this scene, because the power certainly is there. The narration begins quietly and shadily, one might say, grow-*

*ing as Wotan's thoughts emerge out of a dark pool of anxiety. His thoughts follow one upon the other, building to the conclusion that there is no answer but oblivion. It is one great arc, and the performer must be able to communicate all the subtle gradations along its sweep. If there is any part of the* Ring *that warrants studying up close, as by repeated listenings to a recording with libretto in hand, this is it. Or you could just fall asleep with the rest of the jaded.*

Brünnhilde, alone, is hurt and deeply puzzled by Wotan's fury. She has never seen him like this. She withdraws into a cave.

Siegmund and Sieglinde appear, running in their mad flight. Sieglinde, though exhausted, insists on pressing on, but Siegmund assures her that she can rest a while. She tells him to leave her—she will only bring disaster and shame on the friend who saved her. Horns announce that Hunding and his kinsmen are approaching, and she imagines the hunting dogs tearing at Siegmund's flesh. Hysterical, she seizes her brother, finally collapsing in exhaustion. He tenderly lays her down and guards over her in silence.

Brünnhilde emerges from her cave and regards Siegmund. After a long and poignant while, she calls his name and bids him look at her. Only those slated for heroic death on the battlefield see her face. Now she greets him whom she chooses for her own. Where am I going? he asks. To Valhalla, to join the fallen heroes in Wotan's hall. Will Wälse be there? Yes, she answers, he will. Are there women in Valhalla? Yes, she replies, beautiful handmaidens to grant his every wish. Will Sieglinde join me there? No, Brünnhilde answers, you will not see her there. With perfect calm, Siegmund caresses the sleeping Sieglinde and tells Brünnhilde to send his greetings to Valhalla, to Wotan, to Wälse, to the heroes and the maidens, for he will not follow her there.

Brünnhilde insists he will die—he has seen the Valkyrie's face. Hunding will kill him. Siegmund almost laughs in scorn. His sword will take care of Hunding, and she may take him to Valhalla instead if she is so thirsty for blood. Brünnhilde tells him the sword will fail. He who gave it its magic now takes it away. Siegmund quiets Brünnhilde, lest she wake Sieglinde and frighten her. He cries "shame" on his father Wälse for abandoning him yet again. If he must die, then let Hell take him—he will not go to Valhalla. Brünnhilde pleads that he let her protect Sieglinde—for the sake of his unborn child she now carries, but he replies that he alone will protect Sieglinde. If he must die, then he will kill her first himself. He raises his sword, but Brünnhilde, overcome by such devotion, stops him. She swears that Sieglinde will live, and Siegmund will prevail in combat. She runs off while Siegmund watches her. He returns to caress the sleeping Sieglinde until Hunding's approaching horns rouse him to draw the sword and enter battle.

*Comment: Leave it to an operatic genius like Wagner to make us fall utterly in love with the hero of the story just in time to kill him off. This scene, called the Annunciation of Death (Todverkundigen, if you want to get precise about it), is one of the most powerful in the Ring, drenched in mystery, ritual, and love. Our sympathy is with both characters. Brünnhilde meets her only brother to prepare him, against her instinct, for death, while he proves the depths of his love for Sieglinde by choosing union with her in Hell rather than separation from her in Heaven. The tenor must also convince us of Siegmund's tenderness with gesture and body language, since much of the lovemaking in this scene is left unsung.*

*Siegmund and Sieglinde have certainly been very busy between Acts I and II. Literal-minded directors, who are the curse of our times, sometimes feel they must represent the cause of Sieglinde's pregnancy onstage, as if we in the audience would have trouble believing it unless we saw proof. That is generally done at the end of Act I, where Wagner has obliged by providing several bars of frenzied orchestral music after Siegmund's final outburst. Lest we get bored listening to mere orchestral music (!), Siegmund is often obliged to toss Sieglinde on the ground and do what must be done for the sake of theatrical credibility. Consider the proportions of the average Wagnerian singer and judge for yourself what this accomplishes for the sake of credibility. Most people would rather just take the libretto's word for Sieglinde's pregnancy and leave it at that.*

A storm approaches, while Sieglinde, alone, writhes in agonizing nightmares, reliving the terrible night when her mother was killed and she herself was carried off. Lightning shows Hunding approaching on the ridge, calling "Wehwalt" to fight. Siegmund answers the challenge, charging him, while Sieglinde screams for the madmen to kill her instead. Brünnhilde emerges toward the fighting men, guarding Siegmund, but Wotan appears, making her shrink back. At Wotan's command, Siegmund's sword shatters, and Hunding stabs him with his spear. Sieglinde collapses. Wotan stares fixedly at Siegmund's lifeless body. Only Brünnhilde moves, gathering the pieces of the shattered sword and then carrying Sieglinde away. In a voice so choked with emotion it is barely a whisper, Wotan tells Hunding, Fricka's slave, to go tell his mistress that she is avenged. Wotan has kept his word. "Go!" he rasps, and Hunding falls dead on the spot. Wotan then remembers Brünnhilde's defiance of his orders, and storms off to find and punish her.

**Comment:** *This very long act (one hour and forty-five minutes) concludes rapidly with an abundance of action. For the last generation or so, directors have enjoyed keeping Siegmund alive long enough after his wound to see Wotan and recognize him as his father. This isn't in the libretto or the supplementary stage directions, but it's too poignant to resist. Wagner himself may have given the cue for this particular bit of business, since an early prose sketch of this scene had Wotan appear here as Wälse, that is, as the "old man in the slouched hat" Sieglinde mentioned in Act I. He clearly liked the idea of Siegmund recognizing his long-lost father, but apparently could not come up with any convincing reason for Wotan to don the outfit.*

### Act III

*Setting:* The Valkyries' rock in the mountains.

The Valkyries call to each other as they gather on their rock, reuniting after collecting slain heroes on the battlefield. They ask each other whom they are carrying to honor in Valhalla, and discover that the dead heroes' horses whinny and fight with each other as if possessed by their masters' hatred. This causes the Valkyries to laugh and shout with glee. The eight who have gathered wonder where Brünnhilde is, noting that "War-Father" would greet them coldly if she were not with them. They see Brünnhilde flying through the air on her horse Grane. Never have they seen Grane gallop so furiously. They greet her from afar, and notice, as she approaches, that Brünnhilde is carrying a woman rather than a customary slain hero.

*Comment: This, of course, is the "famous" scene from this opera, and many who are in the audience to experience a night of whooping Valkyries will be surprised by its relative briefness. Yet the point is made in a few minutes. The eight wild full-voiced women and the furious orchestra manage to make an unforgettable impact. The music is dizzying, intoxicating, and sinister—like war itself. Using women's voices to carry this message was perfect genius on Wagner's part. For more on this scene, see "Lobby Talk for* Walküre" *below.*

Brünnhilde approaches her sisters with Sieglinde, crying for help. Never before had she run from battle, but now she is pursued by the Battle-Father himself! The sisters notice storm clouds brewing in the north—Wotan is charging toward them on his sacred horse! Brünnhilde begs for help—a horse to carry Sieglinde away, but the Valkyries cannot join her rebellion. The wretched Sieglinde begs to be allowed to die, but Brünnhilde tells her she must live for the sake of her unborn child. A Volsung grows in her womb! Instantly transformed by the news, Sieglinde begs for help from the Valkyries, but they remain adamant. Brünnhilde gives her the shattered pieces of Notung and tells her to flee to the east. Three of the Valkyries have flown in that direction, and they tell how Fafner has transformed himself into a dragon and guards the Ring and the horde of gold. It isn't a safe place for a woman, but Wotan does not like to go there. Sieglinde can avoid his anger there. Brünnhilde will await Wotan on the rock and suffer his anger, delaying him while Sieglinde escapes. Now Sieglinde must bear the hero, who will reforge and wield the sword. His name will be "Siegfried." Sieglinde ecstatically blesses Brünnhilde and runs away.

*Comment: This frenzied scene introduces us to two important musical themes. The first is when Brünnhilde gives the name to the unborn child. This will be one of Siegfried's several leitmotivs, the one often referred to as Siegfried the Brave, and is played, transformed, and replayed throughout the saga. Directly after this, Sieglinde blesses Brünnhilde in a long, soaring musical phrase. This will only recur once, at the very end of* Götterdämmerung. *This leitmotiv is the punchline, so to speak, of the whole saga. For more information on it, see the comment at the end of* Götterdämmerung.

Wotan enters in fury. The Valkyries timidly try to hide Brünnhilde amongst themselves, further angering Wotan. Did they inherit such whining spirits from him? He lists Brünnhilde's wrongs: no one but she knew his thoughts and intentions, yet she took up arms against him. And now she dares to hide? Brünnhilde presents herself, ready for punishment, but Wotan pronounces that she herself has already made her own punishment. She was created by his will, and opposed his will. Therefore, she must cease to exist as she was. She is banished from his sight forever. The Valkyries wail, and Brünnhilde cannot believe what she hears, and yet there is more. She is confined to the mountaintop in sleep, defenseless against any man who takes her. The Valkyries scream out against this most unjust of punishments, but Wotan is hardened against them. Does such a fate terrify them? Then let them be gone, or they will each share the same punishment! They flee, while Brünnhilde lies prostrate in humiliation.

*Comment: This may rank as the vocally noisiest scene in the entire* Ring, *with the Valkyries vying with each other to display the most terror. It is absolutely unnerving.*

*Wotan spins out his accusation in a series of eight statements, each in the form of "I did X, but you denied X." It's all pretty convincing, within the convoluted reasoning of this saga.*

For a long while, Brünnhilde and Wotan are alone and silent together, while the storm that hailed the god's approach dies down. Timidly, Brünnhilde asks if her offense was so shameful as to warrant such a punishment. She begs her father to be calm and explain it to her. He instructs her to ask herself what she did. She replies that she carried out his true wishes—in siding with Siegmund she carried out the will of Wotan's heart. Exactly, he replies. She did what he longed to do. While he mastered his longing, and suffered for it, she allowed herself to swirl in the bliss of love. Then let her light and loving heart be her guide, for they too must be parted.

Brünnhilde pleads intellectual weakness. She cannot follow his subtle arguments, and only knows to love what he loves. So if you were happy to follow the guidance of love, he replies coldly, then let her love the one who will conquer her. She seizes this opportunity. At least let it be a hero, and not any coward who will take her in her sleep! Wotan says that she has rejected him, and he cannot help her. But the greatest hero will be born to Sieglinde! Although her deed has torn her away from Wotan, at least it ensured the birth of the Volsung hero. Please let her be taken by the greatest hero! Wotan does not want to hear of the Volsungs, but Brünnhilde is insistent. This one thing he must allow! she says bravely. Let the mountain be surrounded by fire, so only a fearless man may approach her! Crumbling under a wave of emotion, Wotan cries out "farewell!" to this brave, wonderful child. If she must be parted from him forever, then, yes, he will create such a fire around her as never blazed for any bride! Only one shall win the bride, one who is freer than he, the god. Tenderly he embraces her, drinking in the last look of her bright eyes. He then kisses her divinity away and lays her down to sleep under her breastplate and helmet.

Picking up the Spear, he strikes the ground and orders Loge to set the mountaintop ablaze. Flames soar up around the sleeping Brünnhilde, and soon the entire mountain is ablaze. Wotan, amid the flames, again lifts his Spear, and pronounces that "No one who fears the tip of my Spear shall ever cross the fire!" In absolute dejection, he walks away, twice looking back at Brünnhilde's recumbent figure.

**Comment:** *In this celebrated scene, Brünnhilde repeats the Siegfried the Brave motif when she is begging Wotan for a ring of fire to deter cowards. She knows who the hero will be, and Wotan must also get the reference. His pronouncement that the fire will keep out any who fear the tip of his Spear is also sung to the same theme. It is an imposing moment, requiring the bass to sing magisterially at the top of his range, and this at the end of a long evening of singing. Only the great basses can pull it off with conviction.*

*Wotan's pathetic situation is magnificently depicted in the orchestra. After he commends Brünnhilde to "One freer than I, the god," the orchestra picks up a sad strain, which has come to be called the motif of Wotan's dejection. It is a figure with no inherent logical musical resolution, played first by the woodwinds in a piano to fortissimo crescendo, and repeated to the accompaniment of swirling strings. The theme is then repeated two more times, now with the strings joining the woodwinds in carrying the theme to the point of unbearable tension. Just when you think the orchestra cannot get any louder, the horns, which have been playing long, low harmonies, "slice" the unending crescendo, so to speak, with a new theme. This is the slumber motif, which will be quietly repeated later as the curtain descends on the sleeping Brünnhilde amidst the magic fire. In other words, Wotan's dejection is so huge that it has no resolution except oblivion. Conductors often stretch this out to the limits of human endurance, and who can blame them? It's a moment to which everyone in the audience responds. It describes a predicament one can see, for instance, at any neighborhood bar, where the hard-cores greedily seek numbness from their problems. The slumber theme is later directly associated with Brünnhilde, but it is Wotan who passively walks through the balance of his role in the* Ring *as if drugged. In any case, emotional expression in the orchestra has never surpassed what Wagner achieved here. Composers of film music and Broadway musicals, with their one-after-another false climaxes, should be required to spend a few years studying these five pages of the score.*

*For all the extreme emotionality of opera, for all the piles of corpses and dead young lovers and sad people experiencing great crises, there are few scenes anywhere that affect people as powerfully as this one.*

*And yet what is there in this scene that is so devastating? What is the separation of two individuals compared to the cosmic cataclysm of the rest of the story?*

The tragedy is not yet Brünnhilde's, and no longer Siegmund's. This is about Wotan, but Wotan as Everyman rather than the imperious symbol of the Rheingold finale, crossing into Valhalla with Spear held high. He is experiencing the tragedy everyone must go through at some point or other—that of letting go because one has to, not because one wants to. On the most literal level he is leaving his favorite daughter forever, right after losing his only son. This is sad enough in itself. He is also clearly leaving the one person who understands him. Wotan has, to state it mildly, put some extreme expectations on his children. They were to defend the status quo, defend his own position, and right the wrongs he committed. They had to correct history. This is the moment in his life when Wotan realizes that his children are a disappointment to him—not because they have fallen short of his love (on the contrary, he has come to realize that he loves Siegmund and Brünnhilde more than he knew he could, and precisely because they have acted contrary to his plans), but because he himself has been living delusionally in regard to his children. If we are to understand Brünnhilde as the embodiment of Wotan's will, another tragic dimension is added. This is the moment in life when he gives up, period. Indeed, this moment, rather than the finale of Götterdämmerung, marks the end of the gods' reign. In Act II of this opera, Wotan said that he now waits for "the End," but it was clear from his music and his actions that he still cared a great deal, and would have loved, if there were a way, to retain his power. From here on, he has given up even wanting anything. This is the End. The rest, from his point of view, is epilogue.

## BASICS: WHEN TO EAT, DRINK, AND VISIT THE RESTROOM

Performances of *Die Walküre* usually begin early, at 6:00 or 6:30 p.m. It's impractical to eat before then, plus you'll be hungry again later in the evening, just in time for your stomach to growl with the Valkyries in Act III. Do whatever you need to do to be comfortable for the first act so you can completely give yourself over to the great love scene without bodily distractions.

Act II is long and tends to lose those who have come for the good tunes. On the one hand, you'll want to eat something at intermission, if Siegmund and Sieglinde haven't made you *too* excited (don't laugh—it happens). On the other hand, don't eat or drink too much or you're guaranteed to sleep through Wotan's monologue, which would be a shame. This will take a bit of foresight. Most of Wagner's long acts are the first or third, and one can plan accordingly, but this one is right in the middle.

The Metropolitan Opera opened the 1986 season with a gala performance of its new production of this opera, scaring many of the glitterati who attend opening nights more out of devotion to social success than for the German monologues. Several of these were seen solving the "when to eat and go to the restroom" problem by leaving the opera house after the exciting first act, going to nearby restaurants (dressed beyond all respectable bounds), and returning just in time for "The Ride of the Valkyries" in Act III. Unfortunately, there was no law in effect to prosecute these loathsome *poseurs* for their criminal actions.

The third act, like the first, is just over an hour, and makes no demands on your constitution.

## ROUGH SPOTS AND HOW TO GET THROUGH THEM

The popular Act I is often performed, unstaged, in the concert hall, so you can imagine that it won't be very hard to get through. Attention can wander during Siegmund's monologue, although it shouldn't. The monologue is divided into three parts, each separated by a set of interjections from Hunding and Sieglinde. Each of the three parts should have its own "tone" and "shape," and yet there should be a single overall structure to it as well. Watch how well the tenor is convincing you of this. Moreover, see if he can muster a level of sympathy in you in spite of Siegmund's naive victimology. If he can, he's an artist. If he can't, just hang on and mark time with Hund-ing's and Sieglinde's questions. The whole thing isn't all that long, and you will be rewarded for your patience with one of the all-time great love scenes afterward.

It's Act II that separates the art lovers from the dilettantes. The sec-ond act of *Walküre* is a workout. It's shorter than the long acts of *Par-sifal, Meistersinger,* and *Götterdämmerung,* but for whatever reason this opera has the reputation of being more "popular" than the oth-ers. Those who had hoped to breeze through a hit parade are then strained to and beyond their limits by this nearly two-hour segment.

Act II is best considered as a series of discrete, mostly one-on-one confrontations. These are (1) Wotan/Brünnhilde, (2) Wotan/Fricka, (3) Wotan/Brünnhilde, (4) Siegmund/Sieglinde, (5) Siegmund/Brünnhilde, and (6) everyone (except Fricka, although she's referred to). All of these dialogues, so to speak, are interesting in themselves, though the bulk of the act is composed of numbers 2, 3, and 5. Num-ber 2 (Wotan/Fricka) is a moral-philosophical argument, so naturally one is better off knowing what is being said. Fricka, however, comes at her husband with all guns blasting. This is reflected in the music, and only a narcoleptic could fall asleep here. Wotan's monologue, it cannot be stressed too often, really requires a bit of perusal ahead of time. Even if the performance you are attending will provide a simul-taneous translation, you'll want to give some attention to the singer and the nuances of characterization one is coming to expect from today's "smart" basses. Number 4, with Siegmund and Sieglinde, is another opportunity for you to fall in love with Siegmund. If the tenor is an oaf, don't worry. Just ignore him and listen to the orches-tra—there's plenty of lyricism there to get the point across. Everyone can appreciate the subsequent Annunciation of Death scene, and then the act concludes with surprising swiftness.

Act III—no problem. Wagner raises the curtain with one of the all-time great potboilers, as if to say, "All right, you've been good kids for the last couple of hours. Here! Have a tune!" He follows this up with an orgasmic outburst from Sieglinde and eight other howling sopra-nos. Having thus secured everybody's attention, he settles in for about thirty minutes of the most beautiful, moving, and human music ever written. If you have any problem getting through Act III of this opera, give up. There's no hope for you. Next time, stay home and watch music videos—the three-minute kind.

## LOBBY TALK FOR WALKÜRE:
## A NOTE ABOUT HORSES AND MUSIC

People all over the world have long responded to musical representations of horses. The easily imitated clip-clop of a walking or cantering horse is the very signature of American Western songs, for example. It is used in Ferde Grofé's *Grand Canyon Suite*, and is the main feature of the popular song "Desert Skies" by the Marshall Tucker Band, both pieces of music depicting a pleasant ride. In a slightly faster modulation, "clip-clop" is the basis of the spirited 6/8-meter folk tunes popular for dancing the world over.

A galloping or charging horse is a different matter altogether. The sound of a gallop, whose three beats any child can easily imitate by clapping the hands together and then slapping the thigh once with each hand, has an inherent sound of urgency and excitement. People were especially susceptible to this sound before there were automobiles. The very sound of a gallop produced a gut-level reaction to the effect that "something is happening." Perhaps we are conditioned the same way when we hear a siren, an effect that twentieth-century composers like Carlisle Floyd and Steve Reich have used to create the same sort of adrenaline rush in the audience. We do not respond quite the same way our ancestors did to the sound of a gallop, and yet it still holds some sway over us.

The gallop can be easily and effectively imitated in music. Two metric measures, such as those used in analyzing poetry, are useful here. The first is a dactyl, which is the name of a three-beat rhythm that has the stress on the first beat or syllable, as in the verse "HICK-o-ry DICK-o-ry DOCK." Dactyls in classical poetry sound heroic. The *Aeneid* is written in a dactylic meter because it is an epic. It is also chivalric, that is, about horses. (Actually it's about war and heroism, even though horses, and one horse in particular, figure prominently in it. The point is that charging horses, chivalry, and the excitement of war were the same thing to the premodern mind.) Dactyls are harder to pull off in English, but "The Charge of the Light Brigade" is written in them: "INto the VALley of DEATH. . . . " This is clearly about horses, and no other meter would do.

Some people hear the gallop in the opposite direction, "short-short-STRESS." This is called an anapest. It's the meter of the currently popular expression "bah-da-BING." Beat out this rhythm with your fingertips and eventually your inner musical ear cannot help but hear that celebrated musical depiction of charging horses, Rossini's *William Tell* Overture. Even in our somewhat post-equine era, such music never fails to produce a feeling of exhilaration, of urgency, of what we appropriately call a "rush." Could the creators of *The Lone Ranger* have chosen any other music for their theme? Even without the direct references to horses, we still get the "rush" message. Led Zeppelin must have known this when they chose a rapidly repeating anapestic riff (da-da-DUM) for the background of their "heroic" song "Achilles' Last Stand."

The Valkyries are clearly to be understood as riding flying horses; that's how they get to Valhalla. Even Wagner, who demanded the impossible out of stagings, understood that "flight" would have to be conveyed by the orchestra. However much he might have wanted the Valkyries actually to fly in his production, he occasionally accepted that there were limits to what could be done. Fortunately, he was able to use the orchestra effectively enough to convince people they were seeing flying horses.

The "Ride" begins with rapid upward figures in the strings, like whirlwinds. The next theme introduced is, predictably, a quick dactyl to represent galloping. However, these dactyls are not played by the strings or the brass, as in the *William Tell* Overture, but very delicately in the woodwinds. The theme is literally created out of air. Also, the first beat is only lightly stressed. The "hooves" portrayed never "land." The famous main theme is then introduced majestically in the brass.

The thunderous brass theme, used by thousands of producers for films, shows, and television commercials, beautifully represents the motion of large wings in flight—thrusting "down," gracefully returning "up." This theme was first sketched by Wagner in the margins of a notepad, and he originally intended it for the Norns in *Götterdämmerung*. In that incarnation, the theme had no stresses—that is, no one note was emphasized over any other. Wagner found it dull. When he applied the theme to the Valkyries, he found that stressing the first note of each measure created the aural analogue to the vision he was seeking. (Many renditions of "The Ride of the Valkyries" fail to stress the first note, but that's how it's written.)

So we can see that Wagner accomplished a great vision in musical terms, but why is this piece of music so ubiquitous? Who really cares about flying horses? In Renaissance epics, the flying horse was a metaphor for male sexuality. This is especially true in *Orlando Furioso* by Ariosto, an extremely influential work. One character in that epic can never "tame" the flying horse, and is carried by it all over the world, out of control. (Dante had described the lustful, including Tristan, as blown "here, there, up, down," by an infernal wind.) Meanwhile, another character in *Orlando Furioso* learns to tame the flying horse, and is able to retrieve long-lost items and secrets from the dark side of the moon.

We don't know how much of this Wagner consciously had in mind when he wrote *Walküre*, but it is surely apparent to everyone that Brünnhilde is a marvelously complicated, gender-bent character.

◆

# SIEGFRIED

PREMIERE: BAYREUTH, 1876.

## THE NAME

This one is pretty simple. The lead character of the opera gives his own name to the work, and there aren't any variations on it. But pronouncing it is trickier than you thought. The first *S* is voiced; thus, "ZEEG-freed."

## WHAT IS *SIEGFRIED*?

This is the opera veteran Wagnerites use to scare newcomers. "Heavy and dark," they say, not without reason, and "not a tune in the whole thing," which is patently untrue. "It's all about Siegfried, who's impossible to love, and the few other characters are familiar from the previous operas and they keep repeating themselves." Again, true and not true.

If the *Ring* has much in common with fairy tales, then *Siegfried* is surely the segment most emblematic of that genre. It is a classic coming-of-age drama, and the strong, young, naive hero must battle an evil dwarf and a dragon before he gets the girl. Wotan is here, no longer as the king of the gods but as a mere Wanderer, a man with more of a past than a future. He is a bit like Merlin in the Arthurian legends, sometimes good, sometimes a bit ominous, most often just commenting in his wisdom. There is even an omniscient "witch" type in Erda, the Earth Mother. At the end, there is Brünnhilde, the maiden, whose union with the hero completes his character.

For all this, there are certain difficulties to be overcome for a full appreciation of *Siegfried*. Male voices and characters are all we hear for the first two acts, except for an offstage "bird" who sings briefly, and much of what we see is brooding on the past. And there are a few *longueurs*. As one hard-core Bayreuth veteran muttered wearily after a less-than-inspiring performance of this opera's second act, "Wagner *can* go on at times."

Of course, its relative inaccessibility makes *Siegfried* the favorite opera of many who wish to be known as hyperrefined, and they are not without cause. There are great opportunities here for singers who are good character actors, and the orchestra never stops weaving magic. Seen as part of a complete *Ring*, *Siegfried* comes fully alive.

There are also many who see *Siegfried* as almost the "comic relief" of the *Ring*, like a *scherzo* or "fun" third movement of a traditional classical symphony. Wotan actually laughs in this opera, as do Alberich, Mime, and even Siegfried. Which doesn't mean you should expect to guffaw through this work. There are lighthearted touches here, but the overall feel is one of terrible seriousness punctuated by some excellent frivolities.

In general, *Siegfried* is no longer seen to be as unique, in either the positive or the negative sense, as it once was. Television, videos, and simultaneous in-house translations at the opera have all helped people to follow the subtleties of the drama. In our psychoanalytically obsessed era, many respond to Wagner's insights, which prefigured Freud and Jung. It is not uncommon for people to be introduced to Wagner by a performance of *Siegfried*, since some socialite types who have bought tickets to an entire *Ring* are frightened off by what they've heard about this one and give away their tickets.

## CAST OF CHARACTERS

SIEGFRIED *(tenor)* This is the child of Siegmund and Sieglinde, whose birth Brünnhilde prophesied in Act III of *Die Walküre*. Wotan also anticipated his arrival, telling Brünnhilde she must await "one who is freer than I, the god." After Siegfried's mother died in child-birth, he was raised by Mime the dwarf in a cave somewhere in the forest, "to the East." Mime didn't do a very good job. Siegfried is wild, untamed, "anarchic" (according to Shaw), "premoral rather than amoral" (according to Donington), and "free" (according to Wagner). Musically, the role is a killer. The sheer amount of music to be sung is enough to scare off even tenors who have mastered the role of Tannhäuser. The only rivals to this role in difficulty are Tristan (whose demands may be as much intellectual as physical) and the *Götterdämmerung* Siegfried.

THE WANDERER *(bass or bass-baritone)* This is Wotan in *Welt-schmerz*. He has apparently grown weary of Valhalla, and roams the world, seeking and dispensing wisdom. He wears a slouch hat, in the manner of pilgrims, as he did the time Sieglinde saw him at her wedding.

MIME *(tenor)* This is not quite the same pathetic victim of his brother Alberich we met in *Das Rheingold*. Here his envy, or life's cruelty, have made him an evil, plotting, and sleazy character. He also has a tendency to repeat himself. The role is written for tenor, but not the standard Wagnerian *Heldentenor*. Mime can be sung by a wide variety of tenors, including the relatively lighter-voiced variety. He must be a good actor, and must have the ability to sing, if not loud, then at least at great length.

ALBERICH *(bass)* This onetime master of the Nibelungs has spent the two generations since *Das Rheingold* in single-minded obsession—he wants the Ring back! Alberich in this opera does not have to make quite as much noise as he did in *Das Rheingold*, but he still must be a commanding presence. He must portray subtle intelligence and a certain sense of self in his scenes with Wotan and Mime.

FAFNER *(bass)* This giant from *Das Rheingold* transformed himself into a dragon shortly after walking off with the Nibelung's hoard and the Ring, so we only get to see him as a dragon in this opera.

ERDA *(contralto)* Our all-knowing Earth Mother literally pops up again in this opera, and she's more inscrutable than ever. The age of Earth Wisdom has long passed by the human history moment of *Siegfried*, and Erda's words are as murky and mysterious as the distant past. She also has a nickname, the Wala, just to confuse you even more.

A FOREST BIRD *(soprano)* This offstage role has some very pretty (and familiar) music to sing, but her singing time is quite brief. The lyric voice required is one of a very few in the *Ring*, Freia and the Rhinemaidens being the others. It was the great diva Joan Sutherland's debut role at the Metropolitan. Occasionally, the role is assumed by big-name sopranos.

BRÜNNHILDE *(soprano)* This is the same ex-Valkyrie whom we left, so poignantly, asleep on the rock surrounded by magic fire.

# THE OPERA

## *Prelude and Act I*

Setting: Mine's cave deep in the forest. Metalsmith works are visible.

*Comment: Whether the curtain is up or down during the Prelude, we have a clear musical picture of Mime alone and brooding silently on servitude, toil, the hoard of gold under Fafner, and the Ring. We can also hear him thinking about the shattered sword Notung, which he knows will be the instrument of Fafner's death once it is repaired. By this point, the leitmotivs are as familiar as our own relatives, and Wagner can really begin to play with them. It is as easy to follow Mime's train of thought as if he were singing—perhaps easier. Wagner washes the whole picture in murky tones by relying on the woodwinds in general, and the bassoons in particular, to create an atmosphere of brooding.*

Mime is despairing in his toil. Every sword he crafts is snapped in two by the wild boy Siegfried. There is one sword Siegfried couldn't shatter. That is Notung, whose fragments Mime has but cannot forge for all his skill. If Mime could ever repair Notung, Siegfried could use it to kill the dragon Fafner, and win the gold and the Ring for Mime! But until then, Mime must continue to make swords just so Siegfried can break them!

Siegfried enters the cave, hollering and leading a wild bear with which he taunts the terrified Mime. The dwarf begs not to be eaten—he has forged a new sword. Siegfried sends the bear away. The ugly old smith has done his work and gets to live—for now. Why bring a live bear home, asks Mime. I wanted a better companion than you, answers Siegfried. Mime shows him the new sword, which the boy contemptuously breaks, heaping abuse on its maker. Mime whines about ingratitude, and unctuously offers food, which the boy refuses. Mime prattles on about how he raised this little babe and nurtured him, giving him toys and warmth with never a thought for his poor self. Siegfried admits he has learned much from Mime, but has never learned to tolerate him. He loathes the dwarf and only wants to strangle him. That's why he roams the forest, where the wild creatures are dearer to him than Mime.

And yet Siegfried always returns to the cave. Why is that so? That's your heart, explains Mime. All young creatures yearn for their parents. But the young of the forest have two parents, notes Siegfried. Where is Mime's wife? "I am both father and mother to you," explains the dwarf, but Siegfried calls him a liar. The young creatures all look like their parents, and he looks no more like Mime than a fish looks like a toad. He says this is the only reason he keeps returning to the cave he hates—to find out who his parents were, and he almost strangles Mime to force the dwarf to tell him.

Mime explains that he took pity on an ailing woman in the forest, who came back to his cave, delivered a baby, and died. The story emerges laboriously, while Mime interjects his own selfless role in tenderly nurturing the babe—how Sieglinde commanded the babe be named Siegfried, and how his father, whom he never met, was killed in battle. Siegfried demands proof, and Mime shows the splinters of the sword Sieglinde left behind "as cheap payment." Siegfried orders the sword recast that very day, so he can pursue his adventures and never return to the hated cave. He runs out into the forest, overjoyed to know at last that Mime is not his father. Alone, Mime wonders how he will forge the sword and get Siegfried to kill Fafner.

*Comment: We in the audience must check ourselves to make sure our sympathies don't get confused in this scene. It's almost possible to believe Mime at face value. He has, as he claims, nurtured the boy for twenty-odd years, and Siegfried is not a pleasant person. Not until later in the drama is it made very clear that Mime has only done all of this to gain the Ring, after which he will be happy to kill Siegfried. The mawkishness of his little "poor me" song, whose repetitiveness tells us it is used daily to torture the boy, should be sufficient to cast our sympathies with Siegfried. A good modern analogy to this is the Beatles' song "She's Leaving Home," whose chorus of parental self-pity almost succeeds in making us feel for them, but ultimately ends up justifying the daughter's rejection of them in our eyes. As for Siegfried, we must focus on his horrible loneliness rather than his crassness, or this opera won't be easy to enjoy.*

Wotan enters the cave, stating in majestic lines that he is called Wanderer by the people of the world. He requests hospitality, offering wise counsel in exchange. Many times has he told people what they needed to know when they asked him. Mime tries to get rid of him, but the Wanderer sits by the fire. He asks Mime to pose any three questions to him, offering his own head if he should fail. Mime accepts, the sooner to be rid of him. He asks who dwells in the depths of the earth. The Nibelungs dwell in Nibelheim, answers the Wanderer. Black-Alberich once ruled them by means of a magic Ring, and he should have won the whole world, but failed. Then who, asks Mime, dwells on the face of the earth? The giants (*Riese*) dwell in Riesenheim. Fasolt and Fafner ruled them, but they envied the Nibelung's power and gained the Ring. Fafner slew Fasolt, and now, as a dragon, guards the hoard. Who, asks Mime, lives in the heavens? The gods, answers the Wanderer, live in Valhalla. Wotan, the Alberich of Light, rules them with the Spear cut from the World-Ash Tree, which bears marks of trust and contract (law) carved on its shaft. All obey the Lord of the Spear.

Mime is satisfied with the answers, and tells the Wanderer he is free to leave, but Wotan stays put. The dwarf should have asked him what he needed to know, rather than try to stump him with abstract questions. Now Mime must stake his head on the three questions posed to him. It is becoming clear to Mime who the Wanderer is, and he braces himself for the questions. What is the race, asks the Wanderer, whom Wotan oppressed though the dearest of all to him? This was the Volsungs, Siegmund and Sieglinde, whom Wälse sired, and from whom sprang Siegfried, the strongest of them all. With what sword, asks Wotan, will Siegfried slay Fafner? Notung is the name of the sword, answers Mime, who tells its story. Wotan flatters his wisdom, and poses the final question. Who will mend Notung's splinters? Mime's head spins. How on earth would he know that? Then that's the question you should have asked me, responds Wotan. Now listen well: Only he who does not know fear can remake Notung. By rights, Wotan has won Mime's head, but he will forfeit it to the one who comes after him—the one who does not know fear. The Wanderer leaves.

*Comment: This scene is rather ridiculous to read about. The first five of the six "questions" are startling in their banality, and give ammunition to those who find the* Ring *repetitive. Don't these people have anything else to think about but the same old mistakes of days past?*

*The answer is no, they don't. That's the point, and in performance this scene is quite powerful. It illustrates how Wotan has become, in a sense, equal to Mime—both are helplessly waiting for Siegfried to take the action they cannot take that will fulfill their destinies. Note how Wotan, in his retelling of the story of the Ring, eliminates his own role in the drama. Instead, the Ring "is lost" by Alberich, and "is gained" by Fafner. He is coming to the point where he understands even his own willful actions as predetermined by an unseen fate.*

*The back-and-forth ritualism of this scene is typical of fairy tales and
their "three questions," but is also reminiscent of the Annunciation of
Death scene in* Die Walküre *in its musical feel.*

Alone again, Mime stares out into the sunlit forest, hallucinating
that it is a monster waiting to devour him. He collapses in anxiety.

Siegfried bounds in, abusing Mime for idleness. Mime admits
that, despite everything he taught the boy, he forgot to teach him
fear. Siegfried asks what fear is, and Mime describes the blood rush
that accompanies the sensation of fear in such exquisite detail that
the boy wants to experience it for himself. Mime advises him that
he'd know fear intimately if he were to see the dragon Fafner.
Siegfried insists on going to the dragon's cave as soon as the sword is
finished. He will repair it himself. You were always lazy at your
lessons, chides Mime. Now you'll wish you paid attention. Siegfried
pushes him aside, saying there's nothing he can learn from the one
who doesn't know.

Mime stands over Siegfried's shoulder while the boy tosses tools
carelessly about the smithy. Siegfried smashes Notung's splinters
even more as he works, saying he must reduce them to mere rubble
to build them anew. Mime ponders his dilemma. Siegfried lustily
pumps the bellow, while Mime gets the idea to poison him just after
he kills Fafner and so win the Ring. He's not quite as stupid as that
Wanderer thought he was! Siegfried pours the molten metal in the
trough, and steam hisses. Mime prepares the poisoned soup, but
Siegfried's instincts tell him not to eat any of it. He hammers at the
sword, and the dwarf gloats over his future as Master of the Ring. At
last, Siegfried triumphantly brandishes the finished sword, bearing it
down on the anvil, which breaks in half.

*Comment: Siegfried is all sweaty muscle in this scene, and Mime is
revealed as the pure evil he is. His description of fear sounds to most
people like a summary of sexual love, and, in a sense, he has spent his
life "married" to fear. The juxtaposition of fear and love will be
explored beautifully in the opera's final scene. Siegfried sings long and
loud here. While pumping the bellows, his "song" is an elaboration of*

*the same two notes, "NOOOO-tung, NOOOO-tung," with which his*
*father, Siegmund, had addressed the sword before he pulled it out of*
*the tree in Act I of* Die Walküre. *Here the same notes also reflect the*
*physical action of the bellows. Siegfried becomes boisterous as he ham-*
*mers the sword. The hammering must be done onstage by Siegfried.*
*The rhythms are the same as those associated with the Nibelungs in*
Das Rheingold. *It is a test of, if nothing else, the tenor's percussionary*
*skills.*

## Act II

Setting: The forest.

A brief prelude introduces dark, quiet, threatening tones—themes
associated with brooding, misfortune, and the Curse of the Ring.

Alberich is keeping watch on the cave called Neidhöhle. Fafner
has transformed himself into a dragon, in which guise he sleeps,
guarding the hoard of gold. Alberich is convinced he will regain the
Ring one day. Is this the day?

**Comment:** *Alberich's little monologue here seems dramatically primi-*
*tive by Wagnerian standards. To have a character, alone on stage,*
*singing "Here I am and this is what I'm doing" belongs to an earlier*
*tradition. Yet the prelude and opening of this long act are appropri-*
*ately murky and disconcerting. The dark of Mime's cave has been*
*replaced with the forest, which alternates as a joyous and ominous*
*place. We are at a crossroads here, a breaking point. Alberich, Wotan,*
*Mime, and Fafner are all prisoners in a hell of their own making,*
*obsessed with gaining what they have lost or holding onto what they*
*have. They are slaves to their plans, and Wotan alone sees the futility*
*of the situation. It is time for a change, and only one who has no plan*
*can effect that change.*

Wotan appears as the Wanderer, eliciting a string of abuse from
Alberich. The god tells the dwarf to relax—he is only there to see, not

to act. Alberich declares he is no longer as gullibly impressed by Wotan's slickness as he once was, for now he can see the fear that gnaws at the god's heart. That fear is well founded, for he himself will regain the Ring and topple Valhalla! The god calmly replies that neither of them have any more role to play—events will work themselves out as they must, since it's up to Siegfried, independently, to succeed or fail. Wotan himself does not even care to affect the outcome.

Alberich is happy to hear that there's one less contestant for the Ring! This leaves his brother Mime as the chief rival. Must he fight only Mime? Wotan suggests the question be posed to Fafner himself. Perhaps if Alberich warns the dragon of impending death, he may give up the Ring in exchange for his life. Wotan calls Fafner, who warily asks who wakes him. A friend with advice, says Wotan ironically. A hero is coming to fight you, says Alberich. "I am hungry for him," is the dragon's lazy reply. He's strong, warns Wotan, and Alberich adds that he will prevent the fight if Fafner will give him the Ring. The dragon may safely sleep then with the rest of the gold. Fafner growls that he will keep all he has. "Let me sleep!" The dragon yawns and falls back into oblivion.

Wotan laughs. "Well, that didn't work!" He advises Alberich to let things go their appointed way, and to fight only with Mime. He disappears into the forest. Alberich watches him leave, repeating how he hates the gods and will live to see their downfall. He hides behind a rock.

*Comment: People look forward to this scene so they can see what effects the production staff have cooked up for the dragon. Many of the more avant-garde (read: low-budget) productions get mighty impressionistic to avoid putting a papier-mâché dragon on stage. Wagner instructed the bass-singing Fafner to be offstage, preferably under the stage, and to sing through a regular speaking trumpet like those used by carnival barkers. That's all our modern directors have to read, and they feel licensed to amplify Fafner to the rafters with all their electronic wizardry. It makes Fafner sound like Iggy Pop on a slow night, but we live in an age of overkill.*

*As fun as the dragon may be, the most interesting aspect of this scene is the one-on-one confrontation of the two alter egos, Alberich and Wotan. They have paralleled each other's paths throughout the saga to the point where it now seems logical to refer to them respectively as the Black-Alberich and the Alberich of Light. Both have renounced love for the sake of the Ring—Alberich explicitly in the first scene of* Das Rheingold, *Wotan more obliquely in his abandonment of Siegmund and Brünnhilde. Both have engendered offspring to win the Ring for them. They have come to understand each other's psychology and motivation as only adversaries can. The difference is that Wotan has developed, while Alberich, though still a commanding presence, is entirely defined by the same rage. He is a lot like Satan in Milton's* Paradise Lost, *once magnificent in his evil defiance, now a bit out of step with the times in his repetitive rantings. It is an excellent depiction of what we would call the banality of evil.*

Mime and Siegfried arrive, the dwarf insisting that this is the best place in the world to learn fear. The dragon's jaws can swallow a man in one gulp, his tail coils around and crushes, even his saliva can burn a man up. Siegfried asks if the dragon has a heart, and being told that it has, trusts Notung to stab him there. Mime tries to persuade Siegfried to fear the dragon and be wary in battle, and remember how Mime loves him. Siegfried orders him not to love him, and repeats how he loathes the dwarf. Mime says he will withdraw. It is nearly noon, when Fafner likes to slither down to the stream and drink. Siegfried threatens to make the dragon eat Mime, and Mime leaves, hoping that Siegfried and Fafner will kill each other.

Siegfried stretches out on the ground, still rejoicing that Mime is not his father. But what did his father look like? At least he couldn't have been ugly, like Mime. He never wants to see that gnome again.

The leaves of the forest murmur. Siegfried thinks about his mother. What did she look like? He can't imagine that at all. Perhaps she had eyes like a doe, but lovelier. Why did she die? Do all men's mothers die of their sons? How sad! If only he could see her!

A bird hovers over Siegfried, chirping happily. It seems to be trying to tell him something—is it about his mother? The dwarf had told him that birds have a language, if one could understand it. He impulsively cuts a reed. He'll try to understand the bird's meaning by imitating its tune. He blows in the reed, but his notes are sour, and his tune does not soar like the bird's. He admits he's too stupid to learn from the bird, but he can play a hearty woodland tune on his horn! Siegfried blows his horn, awaking Fafner, who emerges from his cave. This is a pretty playmate, the boy exclaims!

**Comment:** *The "Forest Murmurs" episode is celebrated for its sheer loveliness, which is a welcome respite in this opera of ugly dwarfs, dragons, plots, and crudeness. The music here is subtle and gossamer-thin. Do not expect the lush scene painting of, say, the meadow in* Parsifal. *The "bird" in this scene is alternately an oboe, a flute, and a clarinet. Listeners who are familiar with* Das Rheingold *will notice the Rhinemaidens' song repeated by the bird, accompanying Siegfried's yearnings for the mother he never knew (which Wagner highlights beautifully on solo violin with a single quotation of Sieglinde's "You are the spring" motif). In Freudian terms, this is the longing for the infantile state of dependence on the mother projected to a longing for a primal state of natural innocence, as in the world's various golden age myths.*

*Siegfried's efforts on his "reed" are usually played to the comic hilt. It's very amusing to see an audience of Wagnerites accustomed to full orchestral fortissimi straining to follow a single out-of-tune oboe. When Siegfried plays his unaccompanied horn, we hear variations on a tune associated with him that will be exhaustively explored throughout the remainder of the saga. He also interjects the sword motif. God knows where he learned that. The lurching bass music telling us that Fafner is stirring is every bit as comic as the "reed," although it's not clear that it was meant to be.*

Fafner wearily asks who wakes him, and Siegfried announces he is one who seeks to know fear. Are you full of bravado? asks Fafner. Bravery or bravado, you will decide, answers Siegfried. Fafner is content. He came out looking for a drink, but now he gets a meal! They taunt each other further before fighting. Siegfried stays clear of the tail and the mouth. Fafner rears up to pounce on Siegfried, who stabs him straight to the heart with Notung.

Fafner is stunned by the wound, asking who goaded the boy to this deed, since his young mind never could have conceived it. Siegfried replies that he knows very little, but asks the dragon who he is. The last of the race of giants, he replies, warning Siegfried that whoever put him up to this deed now seeks his death. Siegfried notes that the dragon seems wise in his death throes, and asks for information about himself. He tells his name, and repeating the name "Siegfried!" with a sigh, Fafner dies.

Some of the dragon's blood had spewed onto Siegfried's hand, burning it. Instinctively, he puts his hand to his mouth to lick the blood off, and suddenly notices the forest bird is speaking to him. He can understand it! The bird tells Siegfried that the Nibelung treasure in the cave now belongs to him. The Tarnhelm would help him perform great deeds, but the Ring would make him ruler of the world! He thanks the bird, and goes into the cave of Neidhöhle.

*Comment: Fafner asks Siegfried what is prompting him, and Siegfried, characteristically, does not know. The orchestra, however, repeats the Curse of the Ring theme, letting us know that Siegfried is also a pawn of fate for all his "independence." The adversary who gives wise counsel in death throes is as much a part of fairy tales as the dragon itself. The metamorphosis of the bird-as-woodwind into bird-as-lyric-soprano is excellent. We are thrilled to hear a light, lovely woman's voice after all these grumbling men. Those who enjoy understanding the* Ring *in psychoanalytical terms see great implications in the hero pulling the dangerous treasure out of a dark hole.*

Mime and Alberich both approach the mouth of the cave at the same time, each telling the other to stay away from "his" property, and arguing over who has more rights to the gold. Mime offers to give Alberich the Ring in exchange for the Tarnhelm, but Alberich insists he will have the entire treasure. Mime answers that he will likewise share none of it with Alberich, and he will call on Siegfried to kill his brother. They notice Siegfried emerging from the cave, and curse as they see him carrying both the Tranhelm and the Ring. They hide.

Siegfried regards the Ring, not sure what it signifies but trusting the bird's counsel. The bird now warns him to beware of Mime, who seeks his death. Siegfried will now be able to understand the meaning behind Mime's words as if he could read his heart, the same way he can understand birds. He nods his head in acknowledgment.

Mime comes to Siegfried, asking if he has slain the dragon and learned fear. Siegfried replies that he has not yet learned fear. The dragon's death saddens him, since there are worse creatures who still live unpunished! Mime bids him quiet, since he won't have to endure him much longer. Do you mean to harm me? asks Siegfried. Did I say that, my son? I have always hated you and your kind. Now I'll take the treasure you've won, and your life! Siegfried is glad to hear the dwarf has always hated him, but balks at giving him his life. Mime insists he is misunderstood. He only wants to give Siegfried some refreshing soup, which will put him to sleep, after which Mime will kill him and win the Ring. Slay me as I sleep? asks Siegfried. Is that what I said? asks Mime. I only want to chop off your head! Now drink this soup and choke to death so you never taste another drop! Taste this! cries Siegfried, who kills Mime with one stroke of the sword. Alberich, hidden, laughs hideously.

Siegfried casts Mime's body into the cave to rot on the treasure he envied, and stretches out again on the ground. He is hot and tired. The bird flies about, and Siegfried speaks to it. How lonely he is! The bird must have friends, brothers and sisters, a father and a mother, but he has no one. All he ever had was a detestable dwarf. Does the bird know of a companion for him? The bird says it knows a wonderful wife for him, sleeping on a rock surrounded by fire. Whoever could cross that fire would win Brünnhilde! Siegfried's heart burns at the news. Shall he cross the fire? Can he waken the bride? Only one who does not know fear can cross the fire and wake Brünnhilde, advises the bird. I am the idiot who does not know fear, replies

Siegfried, candidly. He sought fear from Fafner, but perhaps will learn it from Brünnhilde! He bids the bird to lead on—he will follow it to the mountain!

*Comment:* *Mime never shuts up in this act. Did Wagner feel a pang of guilt in killing him off this way? Siegfried has three warnings about the dwarf's intentions (his own premonition in the first act, then Fafner and the bird). Then there is the scene in which he can read Mime's thoughts, which is amusing but rather belabored. If Wagner's intention was to have Mime annoy us to death with his endless chatter, so much so that we are tempted to cheer his murder, he succeeded.*

*Not to criticize, but if there's any chunk of the* Ring *that could benefit from a prudent restructuring, Act II of* Siegfried *is it. There's no shortage of brilliant music here, nor of characterization and development, nor least of all of action, but the pacing and unfolding of events is untypically halting. Instead of the great sweeping arc of music and drama that we get in most acts of Wagner's operas, what we get here is a dramatic structure that is difficult to fathom. Siegfried has two long soliloquies—one before he slays the dragon and one after he kills Mime. That he is able to lie on the ground and pine for mother love after killing (twice) may be illustrative of his character, but it's no easier on the audience for all that.*

*Commentators have a nasty habit of implying that those who get restless in places like this are stupid, boorish, bourgeois, or some other adjective that implies it's "their fault if they're bored." People don't fall for that as easily as they once did, so another answer must be sought. Wagner, of course, is beyond reproach, so the blame usually falls on the tenor, and has since the first performance. Siegfried almost always disappoints, but we must be careful not to overindulge in this facile pastime. For a mere mortal to sing, act, and look the part of Siegfried is an accomplishment beside which the mere slaying of a dragon and walking through a fire might be regarded as paltry.*

*The end of the act also strikes many as an anticlimax. Basically, the bird says "Now go find Brünnhilde!," not bothering to explain who this Brünnhilde woman might be, and Siegfried replies, "OK, I will!" He then scampers offstage to some remarkably "cute" music, notwith-*

*standing the corpse-strewn stage. We can be forgiven if we mutter, on our way to the lobby, "Well, Wagner had to bring the curtain down somewhere!"*

## Act III, Scene 1

Setting: The base of a rocky mountain. Night.

In the Prelude, the full orchestra gives out a complex counterpoint of themes.

**Comment:** *Everything and everyone connected with the* Ring *have either just confronted each other or are just about to.*

Wotan magisterially calls Erda, the Wala, to wake and hear him. She arises from the sleep of wisdom, a frost-covered apparition emerging from a cleft in the rock, emitting a blue light. Who calls her? Wotan announces himself as one who has wandered the world in search of wisdom. None is wiser than she, the eternal woman! All is known to her—what connects mountain and valley, air and water. So he has come to her for knowledge. "My sleep is dreaming," she replies, "my dreaming meditation, my meditation the mastery of wisdom." But the Norns are awake while she sleeps, spinning what she knows. Why not speak to them? Wotan will not be put off by this. The Norns spin, constrained by the world. They can change nothing, but from Erda he must learn how to "hold back a rolling wheel." Men's deeds make her mind dusky, she replies. For all her wisdom, she was once overpowered by Wotan, to whom she bore a wise maiden. Why not go ask her? Brünnhilde flouted the Stormfather, permitting herself to do what he had wanted to do but did not permit himself. She is now punished with sleep until the chosen hero awakes her. Why speak to her?

Erda is confused—the world is wild and twisted! Does he who taught pride punish pride? Does he who is responsible for the deed punish the deed? Does the ruler of right and trust rule by lies? Oh, let me sleep, she pleads, and seal my wisdom! But Wotan retains her.

She planted the thorn of anxiety in his heart, and now she must tell him how the god may conquer his anxieties. "You are not what you call yourself!" she hurls at him, requesting sleep again. "And you are not what you think you are!" is his retort. The time of Erda's wisdom is passing, and will crumble before his will. Does she know what his will is? The passing of the gods! What he once feared, he now wills! Siegfried, his hero, will awaken Brünnhilde, and she will perform the deed that redeems the world! Erda descends to eternal sleep, and the night grows calmer. Wotan turns and awaits the inevitable in the moonlight.

*Comment: Erda freely admits that she's grown foggier at this point than she had been in the time of* Das Rheingold. *In that opera, she came to Wotan uninvited, and gave unsolicited, if murky, advice. Here she does not even recognize him.*

*Wotan has achieved a certain philosophical evolution in this scene. To align the personal will with what must be is the goal of most religious discipline.*

Siegfried appears. He has lost the bird. The Wanderer asks what he seeks. The way to the fire-belted rock and the sleeping woman, he answers. Who told you to seek the rock and crave the woman? The forest bird, he replies. How did you understand the chatter of a bird? The blood of the dragon I killed at Neidhöhle scarcely touched my tongue, and I understood bird talk, answers Siegfried. Who incited you to slay the dragon? Mime, a lying dwarf who wanted to teach me fear, he answers. And who made the sword strong enough to kill the dragon? I did myself, the boy declares. But who made the sturdy pieces from which you made the sword? How would I know? answers Siegfried, growing impatient. But they were useless splinters until I forged them again. Wotan laughs heartily, saying he agrees with the boy on that point. The laugh annoys Siegfried, who orders the old chatterbox to direct him or get out of his way. Wotan advises patience and respect for his elders, but Siegfried blows up. All his life there's been an old man in his way, and if this one isn't careful, he'll end up like Mime! Furthermore, why do you wear such a big, floppy hat? That is the custom of Wanderers, Wotan replies. But one of your eyes is missing. Was it plucked out by some other person you were annoying by standing in his way? Wotan replies mysteriously that his missing eye is now in Siegfried looking at him, but this is lost on the dumb boy.

Siegfried laughs, but demands that the old man move. Wotan replies that he has always loved Siegfried's race, but he knows how to chastise them when he has to. Siegfried tells him again to move, because he knows that this is the path to the woman. The bird told him so before it flew away. It feared for its life, answers the old man, since it saw the Lord of the Ravens. Wotan forbids passage, and points out first the glow, then the flames engulfing the mountain. Would he walk through fire? Siegfried insists he will, and the Wanderer says if the fire will not stop him, he will use his Spear. This very Spear once shattered the sword the boy carries. Overjoyed to meet his father's foe at last, Siegfried shatters the shaft of the Spear in one blow. There is a peal of thunder, and a flash of lightning running from the broken Spear up to the mountaintop. Wotan regards the broken pieces of the Spear with perfect calm, picking them up after a moment and saying, "Go. I can no longer stop you." He disappears in complete darkness.

**Comment:** *Farewell, Wotan! The once-magnificent god quietly retires from the stage at this point. (In theory, we should see him again at the end of* Götterdämmerung, *burning up in Valhalla, but few productions bother.) The confrontation of Siegfried and Wotan can be understood psychologically (the Oedipal moment), politically (the new smashing the old), or in classic terms of tragedy (the rescuer and the victim have traded roles). Whatever concept the production is emphasizing, it goes without saying that this scene should be impressively portentous.*

Siegfried makes his way up the fiery mountain, undaunted by the flames in which he "bathes." Not a single hair on his head is singed. He finds himself at the summit of the peak.

**Comment:** *The orchestra plays a magnificent interlude, juxtaposing sleep, fire, and Siegfried's horn calls, summoning a new excitement for this critical moment.*

*If the psychoanalytically inclined are titillated by Siegfried's pulling the treasure out of the cave in Act II, they are permitted a field day here. One doesn't have to be a classic Freudian to sense something going on. Siegfried's passage through the flames can be understood as an interior journey through the terrifying subconscious to the gratifying union of male and female aspects of the self.*

*Shaw saw it all in blunt socialist terms. Wotan, signifying the church, had invented the flames of hell to cower the masses and bar them from a dangerous empowerment. The fire around the mountain is as "imaginary" as the flames of hell, but only the all-free anarchist Siegfried would dare to challenge the illusion.*

### Act III, Scene 2

Once on the mountaintop, Siegfried immediately notices the sleeping, armored figure. A companion at last! He removes the helmet. How beautiful the hero is, but the breastplate is constricting his breathing. He cuts the breastplate away, but leaps back in terror at what he sees. "That is not a man!" he cries. Who can help him? He calls on his mother, begging for aid in this strange new feeling. Is this—fear? He must wake her by kissing her lips, even if it kills him. After a long kiss, Brünnhilde opens her eyes.

Brünnhilde greets the world and the gods, asking who the hero is who wakened her. Siegfried tells her his name, and she joyously repeats her greeting to the world, the sky, and the sun. He joins her in blessing the elements, since now he can see these two eyes that captivate him so. She blesses his mother and the earth that nourished him, and tells him she has always loved him, even before he was born. Siegfried asks if Brünnhilde, then, is his mother. She tells him his mother will not come back to him. But she, Brünnhilde, fought for him, defied Wotan, and was punished, all because she did not think, but only loved—Siegfried! He revels in her beauty and her words, seeing that she has caused him his first anxiety but has not taken away his courage.

Brünnhilde notices her horse, Grane, grazing nearby. It, too, was awakened by Siegfried's kiss. She then notices her armor stripped away. She has become a defenseless woman, and Siegfried's ardor is growing. No god ever came so close to her, and heroes bowed before her virginity! "I am Brünnhilde no more!" She becomes more fearful despite his urgings, pleading with him to love her by letting her be, but he continues. She must awaken to laughter and life, and be his. "Oh, Siegfried," she replies, "I was always yours!" He embraces her and she responds, wondering if her wildness does not consume him. He responds that they set each other's blood ablaze equally, and yet that fear that she so recently taught him he has forgotten. She cannot resist this childlike hero, this lordlike boy. Laughing, she will love him, and let them perish while laughing. She bids farewell to Valhalla and the gods, and let the night of annihilation descend. Siegfried loves her, he is hers in beaming love and laughing death! He hails the day and the sun and the world in which the waking Brünnhilde dwells, and repeats her sentiments that she is his in beaming love and laughing death.

*Comment: Beaming what and laughing huh? What on earth are Siegfried and Brünnhilde talking about here? This may be one instance in the* Ring *when you're actually better off not knowing what the characters are saying.*

*This celebrated scene remains popular with audiences in spite of its capacity for low comedy. The music is sublime throughout, from Brünnhilde's awakening to graceful orchestral tones to the unveiling of passion later. People recognize two melodies from the sublime* Siegfried Idyll, *one of Wagner's few nonvocal pieces and one that is heard often on the radio and in the concert hall. The climax is thrilling if both singers are in good voice, and it's a relief to hear Wagner relaxing his dogma about lovers singing at the same time and allowing them a bit of overlap.*

*This, however, is not your standard love duet. Anna Russell famously*

*called it "Anything you can sing, I can sing louder," and it does have a
competitive feel to it. The two "contestants" are famously mismatched,
with the tenor having sung at the edges of his capacities for several
hours and the soprano coming in for the last half hour and stealing the
show. There is a contrary school of thought on this subject, which says
that the advantage is actually to the tenor, since he is warmed up,
whereas she must come on cold and hope for the best. This may be true,
since Brünnhilde's role here, though brief, is no picnic. Although
it doesn't have the scope of the role in* Die Walküre *or* Götterdämmerung, *it has the highest tessitura (average pitch) of any of
the three Brünnhildes, and some sopranos insist it is the hardest of the
three.*

*To return to the dramatic situation, Siegfried is remarkably likable
in this scene. His famous declaration "That is not a man!" ("Das ist
kein Mann!") has been cracking up audiences for over a century. There
may be some people who feel uncomfortable with unabashed laughter
in this opera. When the Metropolitan Opera performed its first
Siegfrieds after installing its famous electronic translation devices, the
screens were left tastefully blank for this line. Granted, you don't need
to be a German language scholar to appreciate the moment.*

*Siegfried learns the meaning of fear from Brünnhilde's beauty, and
instinctively cries out for his mother. When Brünnhilde explains she
has loved him since before he was born, he draws a remarkably intelligent conclusion, and asks if she is his mother. Of course, Wagner
doesn't say it directly—he rarely says anything directly. The actual line
is, "Then my mother didn't die? The beloved one was only asleep?" but
the meaning is clear enough. It is shocking how many translations, in
the opera house and elsewhere, cop out on this sublime moment of pre-
Freudian insight. Newman, uncharacteristically, ignores it altogether.*

*It is harder to make sense of Brünnhilde's invocation of laughter,
and then of death, and finally of laughing death. Laughter begins as
an emblem of true living, but ends up rather more associated with
death. Does Brünnhilde know that her union with Siegfried means the
end is coming? And does she welcome that as part of a move toward
Nirvana, or annihilation of the self according to the Buddhist ideal? (If
so, what's all the laughing about?) Or is it Wagner's murky way of*

invoking the old operatic cliché "*Let's live and die together*"? It is often hard to fathom just how much Brünnhilde does know, and what she says usually only complicates matters. One is welcome to ponder these mysteries at length and write academic essays on them, but most prefer to enjoy this scene for its sheer romantic excitement, and attribute Brünnhilde's impenetrable words to her justifiable giddiness in the moment.

## BASICS: WHEN TO EAT, DRINK, AND VISIT THE RESTROOM

Like *Die Walküre*, performances of *Siegfried* usually begin at 6:00 or 6:30 p.m. This is deceptive. *Siegfried* is considerably shorter than its predecessor, and the extra time is usually given to long intermissions for the singers to rest, pray, or generally collect themselves. The second intermission is usually a bit longer. The set for Act III is complicated, and the tenor must be given ample time to reattach any sound-producing organs he may have severed in the second act. Each of the acts is roughly the same length, with the last being a bit longer, so standard common sense will suffice here.

## ROUGH SPOTS AND HOW TO GET THROUGH THEM

In Act I it's just Siegfried, Mime, and Wotan, so hope the artists are actors as well as singers. The score should carry you through here in any case. Like the first act of *Die Walküre*, this first act has the feel of a single mighty crescendo, even though there are only three people in it. It begins conversationally (Siegfried/Mime), becomes ritualistically confrontational (Mime/the Wanderer), and concludes boisterously (Siegfried at the forge/Mime).

The best way to approach Act II is not to assume that slaying the dragon marks the climax of the action. If you do, you're guaranteed to find the rest of the act long. Think of the death of Fafner as midpoint apex, actionwise, and know ahead of time that there's a lot left to happen. There is usually an embarrassing miniature exodus out of the theater by the infirm and the faint of heart at the conclusion of Act II. While no amount of reasoning will work on such people, this is good to know if you have decided to economize and buy standing-room tickets. Even the ushers of New York—more Nibelungs than Rhine-maidens—will usually look the other way at this point when standees snarf up the empty seats for the remainder of the performance.

Wagner is often easiest to appreciate in his third acts (*Die Meistersinger* being a possible exception), and this is true in *Siegfried*. Those who equate opera with prima donnas are thrilled to hear a real live diva at last, while the rest of us can enjoy all the fabulous music.

◆

# GÖTTERDÄMMERUNG

Premiere: Bayreuth, 1876.

## THE NAME

*What to call it and what it means*  This is one of those German words formed by compounding, which can make their words so incredibly long. *Götter* means "of the gods," and *Dämmerung* means "sunset," "twilight," or "dusk." It's best to call it by its German name, unless you want to be mistaken for George Bernard Shaw, who called it everything from "Night Falls on the Gods" to "Gods' Gloaming."

*How to pronounce it*  Even though we are again plagued with those pesky little umlauts, they are less of a problem this time around than they were in *Walküre*. The best compromise is to treat them both as if they were the English vowel *e*. Thus, "Get-tehr-DEM-ehr-oonk," or anything near it.

## WHAT IS *GÖTTERDÄMMERUNG*?

*Götterdämmerung* is the massive, awesome conclusion to the *Ring*, the first of the series to be conceived and the last composed. It is the longest of the *Ring* operas, and the most demanding in terms of production. Partly because of its earlier conception, it has many features from the standard operatic war chest that we haven't yet seen in the *Ring*, including a duet, a trio, a battle call, a chorus or two, and a really big "suicide aria" for the diva at the end. Shaw, for one, was frankly disappointed with *Götterdämmerung*, seeing it as mere grand opera (!) compared to the allegorical music drama of the *Ring*'s first three parts.

Shaw was correct from his own point of view, but it's sad that his own theories of what Wagner was about interfered with his full appreciation of *Götterdämmerung*'s glories. And beyond all the formal theorizing, which was so much more important a hundred years ago than it is today, *Götterdämmerung* is definitely a part of the *Ring*. We have Siegfried, Brünnhilde, Alberich, and even the Rhinemaidens and a Valkyrie, as well as a host of new characters. All the musical themes we have been following for three nights will be found here, developed and even "resolved" in dramatic terms. This opera contains much of Wagner's most magnificent music, presented through a mastery of the orchestra that may have been the greatest he ever achieved. Only a pedant today could take exception to the choruses and the trio. Indeed, considering the dramatic impact of this opera's second act, Wagner may have discovered, at this late date in his career, that there was more "truth" in such operatic conventions than he and his fellow artistic reformers had ever imagined.

## CAST OF CHARACTERS

SIEGFRIED *(tenor)* Our young hero has grown up quite a bit since we last left him on Brünnhilde's rock. Apparently his night, or year, however long he was with her, taught him some self-confidence and greatly improved his language skills. This role is insanely difficult, demanding range, volume, and stamina.

BRÜNNHILDE *(soprano)* She's back and she's angry! If you thought you had heard everything a soprano could do on the previous two nights, well, you ain't heard nothing yet. One of the great diva roles, the *Götterdämmerung* Brünnhilde gets to sing of love, have fights, swear vengeance, leap on a horse, and burn down the universe.

ALBERICH *(bass)* The Obsessed One returns, in a dream sequence with his son Hagen. We are not sure if he is dead or alive at this point in *Ring* history, and it doesn't really matter. He has become nothing more than a vindictive idea.

WALTRAUTE *(mezzo-soprano)* One of the Valkyries, making a rare "solo" appearance. This is a definitive role for aging mezzos who aren't quite ready to turn it in yet.

GUNTHER *(baritone)* The son of a man named Gibich and a woman named Grimhilde. He is a sort of chieftain of a Rhineland tribe called the Gibichungs. In the whole Wagnerian canon of loser baritones, Gunther is probably the sorriest one of all.

GUTRUNE *(soprano)* Gunther's sister. She has sweet music accompanying her entrances and exits, but Gutrune is either incredibly stupid or knows how to play helpless. She is more of a plot device than a person.

HAGEN *(bass)* One of the true bad guys of the *Ring*, whose father, Alberich, is the other contender for the title. His mother, the same Grimhilde who bore Gunther and Gutrune, once slept with Alberich for gold, and Hagen was the result of this rather grotesque encounter. Mrs. Gibich's (Grimhilde's) extracurricular activities do not seem to have harmed the family's zealously guarded reputation. Hagen, whose father was a dwarf, is inevitably played by an enormous bass. The role requires volume and stamina, particularly in the Act II "Call to the Vassals," but it also requires much subtlety and intellect in his "dream" sequences.

THE THREE RHINEMAIDENS Our watery friends from *Das Rheingold* are back, a bit more melancholy than they were, but still more agreeable than anyone else in this grim tale. They have even developed a certain philosophical patience at this point, a wisdom from which the others in this opera could benefit.

WOGLINDE *(soprano)*, WELLGUNDE *(soprano)*, FLOSSHILDE *(mezzo-soprano)*.

THE NORNS These are the Nordic equivalent of the Fates in Greek mythology, who spin the rope of destiny. In their strangeness, they are also like other sets of three sisters in literature, not least the witches in *Macbeth*. These Norns are three of the drabbest women you'll ever meet on a stage.

## THE OPERA

### *Prologue*

Setting: Brünnhilde's rock.

The three Norns arise slowly to spin the rope of destiny. The first one sings of how she once wove the rope around the World-Ash Tree, next to a spring that whispered wisdom as she worked. One day, Wotan came to the spring, taking a drink and leaving one of his eyes as payment. The god then cut a branch of the tree to make his great Spear, and the tree withered from the wound as the spring dried up. Now she must use the simple fir tree for her work. She asks her sister if she knows what happened. The second Norn sings of Wotan's Spear, covered with the marks of contracts with which he ruled the world, until a bold hero shattered it. Then Wotan commanded his heroes to hew the dead trunk of the World-Ash Tree and pile the logs around the base of Valhalla. She asks the third sister if she knows what will happen.

The third Norn sings that Wotan sits in his hall surrounded by gods and heroes, awaiting the flame that will catch the logs around them and burn them, ending their reign. They must spin more to know more. The first Norn asks if she sees fire or daybreak. Her sight has grown dim, and Loge does not flare as he once did. Do the sisters know what happened to him? The second explains that Wotan tamed him, and Loge tried to gain his freedom by gnawing at the Spear, but it overpowered him and held him to Brünnhilde's rock. What will happen to him? The third Norn says Wotan will one day plunge the shattered Spear shaft into the fire and ignite the logs around Valhalla with it. What then will be? The first Norn says she is confused and her rope is tangled. She remembers that Alberich once stole the Ring; what happened to him? The second can see the Ring rise—its curse tangles her threads. The third says the rope must be stretched, and then, to their shock, it snaps. In utter resignation, they descend to their mother Erda.

**Comment:** *Trying to make literal sense out of the Norns is as hopeless as deciphering Led Zeppelin lyrics. Their words are really sound, mystery, and ritual. Their formulaic questions, such as "Do you know what happened?" and "Do you know what will be?," are never clearly answered, but are strangely echoed by Brünnhilde at the end of the opera.*

*This scene probably gets dissed more than any other in the* Ring. *The complaints usually echo those aimed at Wotan's monologues—it is dreary, and we know all this already. Those who have a dangerously limited knowledge of the* Ring's *creation will tell you that the Norns' original function was to explain what happened before the beginning of* Siegfrieds Tod, *the original, solo form of Götterdämmerung. Later, they will tell you, Wagner wrote the three prequels to Götterdämmerung and this became superfluous, but his arrogance prevented him from cutting it.*

*Not quite. The Norns are telling the story as they see it, and there are some interesting deviations from what we have seen. There is that very confusing story of the World-Ash Tree. Everyone points out that Wotan couldn't have lost his eye there, since he had already lost it to pay for his marriage with Fricka. Did Wagner forget this detail? Improbable. The Norns could have faulty memory (they admit as much), marrying Fricka may have been involved in drinking from the spring and cutting the tree, or perhaps Wotan "put one over" on everybody each time he recounted how he supposedly lost an eye.*

*The whole Loge saga seems bizarre, although it helps explain why Wotan was pounding his Spear on the rock at the end of Die Walküre. Also, the piling of the logs around Valhalla is a fascinating touch that usually eludes producers and audiences alike. The conflagration at the*

*end of this opera will be something in which Wotan has actively partic-*
*ipated, beyond merely accepting it.*

*While there are contradictions in the words, there are nothing but*
*answers in the music. The Norns' scene runs through many of the*
*important leitmotivs of the* Ring, *an elegant example of television's*
*"Last week on* Dynasty. . . ." *In typical Wagnerian fashion, the themes*
*are recognizable, yet changed, as if warped through yet another lens of*
*memory.*

After an orchestral interlude, Siegfried and Brünnhilde emerge
from the cave.

*Comment: A lovely cello line erupts into themes associated with*
*Siegfried, which are then stated in broad, heroic terms in the brass. The*
*message is blunt: Siegfried has become a man!*

Brünnhilde hails Siegfried, proving her love by sending him forth
to adventures and glory. She has passed her magic onto him—all that
remains to her now is desire. He is grateful for all she has given him,
and now he will think only of her, but she chides him to think of
himself and his deeds and their vows to each other. He consigns her
to the custody of the flame-surrounded rock, and, as a sign of his
pledge, takes the Ring from his finger and places it on hers. She
delights in the gift, and, in return, gives him her horse Grane. The
horse no longer flies, since it lost its power when she lost hers, but the
steed will serve Siegfried valiantly. They sing each other's praises in
rapture as he takes leave.

*Comment: The first question one asks here is, How long have*
*Siegfried and Brünnhilde been together on the rock? They certainly*
*seemed surprisingly ready to part company. Later, in the first act, Wal-*
*traute will say that Wotan "recently" ("Jüngst") returned to Valhalla*
*with his Spear shattered, but what does "recently" mean in Valhalla*
*time? Wagner does not really answer this question. What matters here*
*is not how or how long, but that these two who were allegorical con-*

*cepts have now become a man and a woman as Wagner understood those terms.*

An orchestral interlude depicts Siegfried's journey up the Rhine River.

**Comment:** *This symphonic interlude, famous from concert performances, is a masterpiece of Wagner's ability to tell a story by means of the orchestra alone. First we hear Siegfried, represented by horn calls, descending the mountain back through the fire. Eventually, we know he is journeying on the Rhine as we hear music of the river and its Maidens. Lastly, we hear dark themes of the Ring and the world of the Nibelungs, telling us where Siegfried is headed. The hero is borne along by people and events he does not understand. Incidentally, people always say "Siegfried's journey down the Rhine," but Hagen's comments later make it clear that he is headed up the Rhine. Remember, you read it here first.*

## Act I, Scene 1

Setting: The Hall of the Gibichungs, near the banks of the Rhine.

Gunther, seated on a throne as king of the Gibichungs, with his sister Gutrune beside him, asks his half-brother Hagen for news of his own reputation along the Rhine. Hagen gruffly replies that he envies Gunther's legitimate title, which their mother Grimhilde commanded him to respect. Gunther is shocked—he, for his part, envies Hagen's wisdom, and bids him say what he should do to improve his fame. Hagen advises Gunther and Gutrune to find spouses. But who would be the bride to best profit Gunther's position? Brünnhilde, surrounded by fire on a rock, is the best woman Hagen knows, but Gunther could never pass through the fire and win her. Only one man could—Siegfried, who slew the dragon at Neidhöhle and won the Nibelung's hoard. Whoever truly knew how to use that hoard could become master of the world. Gunther is bitter at the news.

Why would Hagen tell him of something so unattainable? Hagen suggests Siegfried could be persuaded to bring Brünnhilde to Gunther if Gutrune had previously won the hero's heart.

The shy, unassuming Gutrune is aghast at this. What could she possibly do to win the world's greatest hero? Hagen reminds her of the potion they have stored in a chest. One drink of it and Siegfried would forget any woman he had ever seen and love only Gutrune. Gunther praises his mother who gave him such a brother, and Gutrune wishes she could set eyes on Siegfried. Just then, a horn is heard from the river, and Hagen calls the hero to shore.

**Comment:** *The Gibichungs' family conference that begins the actual drama of this opera (the scenes at the rock were a prologue) establishes their characters effectively. Gunther is worthless, Gutrune is malleable, and Hagen is scheming. Still, the scene is full of confusing information. No wonder people can't tell the Ring from the hoard, since Hagen makes no mention of the former and says that controlling the hoard is what gives power. (Of course, he doesn't want to tell Gunther the whole truth.) The fact that the Nibelungs are now Siegfried's slaves may be technically true, since he has the Ring, but this has no bearing on the drama. Presumably, Siegfried doesn't even know it himself. Newman and others thought this was another holdover from* Siegfrieds Tod *that Wagner never updated.*

*Siegfried's sudden appearance on the river is a bit of mythological camp we must accept at face value, like the old magic potion gimmick.*

Siegfried bounds ashore, seeking the famous Gunther and offering, according to chivalry, friendship or combat. Gunther greets him and they swear friendship. Hagen asks about the hoard of gold, but Siegfried says he had almost forgotten about it. It's still in the cave of Neidhöhle, guarded by the dead dragon. He only took the helmet, although he doesn't know how to use it. Hagen tells him about the magic of the Tarnhelm, and asks if he didn't take anything else. Yes, answers Siegfried, a ring, which a sublime woman keeps. Brünnhilde! mutters Hagen, to himself. Gutrune offers Siegfried a drinking horn, which he lifts to his lips, toasting Brünnhilde. As soon as he drinks, he becomes inflamed with passion for Gutrune, who withdraws from the room in modesty and agitation.

Siegfried asks Gunther if he is married, but Gunther replies that he is incapable of winning the only woman who would satisfy him. Siegfried immediately volunteers to capture this woman using the Tarnhelm, and, drugged into forgetting the past, asks where he can find her. Gunther explains that she is on a mountaintop surrounded by fire, which causes Siegfried to stir with vague recollections, but he promises to win the woman for Gunther in exchange for Gutrune's hand. He and Gunther take a drinking horn and cut their forearms, dripping blood into it and swearing blood brotherhood. Siegfried asks Hagen why he does not join in the oath, but Hagen explains that his cold blood would taint the drink. Gunther tells Siegfried to ignore the joyless one, and he and Siegfried run to the boat for the journey to Brünnhilde's rock. Hagen is told to keep watch over the palace.

Gutrune comes back into the room, asking for news, and leaves again, dreaming of Siegfried as her husband. Alone, Hagen keeps watch, musing on his hate and his longing for the Ring, which will make these high-born Gibichungs serve him, the son of the Nibelung!

**Comment:** *Although reading this scene makes Siegfried look like one of the bigger idiots ever to hit the operatic stage, the music is full of nuance. After he drinks the potion, his words are at odds with the orchestra, which breathes reminiscences of his love for Brünnhilde. It is a good example of the orchestra as the subconscious, striving, yet unable, to put a certain longing into words.*

*Hagen's watch is as somber and bitter as the man himself. Wagner is practically daring the spectator to fall asleep, but try not to.*

After an orchestral interlude, the scene returns to Brünnhilde's rock.

**Comment:** *For the "Rhine Journey" interlude, the mood went from exuberant and loving to dark and somber. The journey is now, in a*

*sense, reversed, beginning in the mood of Hagen's ruminations and
ending with Brünnhilde thinking of her love and covering the Ring
with kisses. The circle is imperfect, however, because music of the Ring
and its curse naturally intrude on Brünnhilde's musings.*

### Act I, Scene 2

Brünnhilde hears the once-familiar sound of a winged horse, and is
hailed from afar by her Valkyrie sister Waltraute. Perhaps she is
Wotan's messenger, coming with news of her punishment's reprieve!
Or was Waltraute coming in envy to share in the unexpected delights
her punishment brought her with Siegfried's love? Waltraute asks her
to control her excitement and listen to her carefully.

Wotan no longer sends the Valkyries to battle; even the heroes of
Valhalla hardly see him, since he has been roaming the world as the
Wanderer. Recently he returned with the pieces of his Spear, a hero
shattered. He sent the heroes out to hew the World-Ash Tree and pile
the logs around Valhalla, then summoned the gods and heroes in
rings of council around his throne. So he sits, not touching Freia's
apples, sending only two ravens out into the world for news. The
Valkyries clasped his knees, but he thought only of Brünnhilde,
dreamily whispering that the world would be free if only she would
return the Ring to the Rhinemaidens. Waltraute slipped out of the
hall and rode to Brünnhilde to ask her this one thing—return the
Ring!

Brünnhilde bluntly asks her sister if she is out of her mind. One
glance at the Ring gives her more joy as a token of Siegfried's love
than all the splendor of Valhalla. She will never renounce love, even
if it means the end of the gods! Waltraute flies away, crying woe to her
sister and Valhalla.

**Comment:** *Waltraute makes most of her case in a single narrative,
which is most beautiful when she quotes Wotan thinking of
Brünnhilde. She is like an expression of Brünnhilde's reflective consciousness. Commentators find it easy to call Brünnhilde an embodiment of Wotan's will and Fricka a personification of his conscience, but*

*it isn't typical to see Waltraute spoken of in this way regarding Brünnhilde. Perhaps women aren't permitted singing character aspects in commentaries. It would explain the emotional, rather than rational, appeal of Waltraute's case, which she drops as soon as Brünnhilde balks. This one would never make a name for herself as a courtroom attorney.*

The fire around the mountain flares up again, signaling that someone approaches. Brünnhilde hears the familiar horn call, and rises ecstatically to greet Siegfried—but an unfamiliar form appears through the now-receding fire. It is Siegfried, but with the Tarnhelm on his head, in the guise of Gunther. Brünnhilde declares herself betrayed, and asks who this is who violates her. A mortal, or one of hell's warriors? Siegfried says he is a Gibichung, and Gunther is the name of the hero she must follow. She lashes out at Wotan, who, she imagines, has decreed this as her final humiliation. Siegfried orders her into her cave, but she holds out the Ring at him for protection. He pounces on her and, after a violent struggle, wrests the Ring from her finger. She withdraws humbly into the cave. Alone, and in his natural voice, Siegfried draws his sword Notung, which he will lay between himself and Brünnhilde to witness his chaste faithfulness to his oath with Gunther.

**Comment:** *Here Wagner indulges in the sadistic and prolonged humiliation of women that comes so naturally to creators of opera. It is painful to watch.*

*It's a wonder Wagner didn't let the underutilized Gunther actually take the stage in this scene and give the tenor much-needed rest. Siegfried is supposed to be disguising his voice to sound like Gunther (as if this role weren't already hard enough), and much of his music is lower than his usual range. All this with a stupid helmet on his head!*

*It's also strange that Siegfried can remember his sword's name but can't remember his wife. This scene ends with a remarkable lack of fuss considering the gargantuan chunk of theater that it concludes. To call it anticlimactic is not overstating the case.*

## Act II

Setting: An "exterior shot" of the Gibichungs' Hall, with Hagen leaning against a pillar where we left him. There is an open space, and the banks of the river. In the background are three stone altars for Wotan, Fricka, and Donner, respectively.

Hagen is leaning on his spear maintaining his watch, perhaps asleep even though his eyes are open. It is night. As moonlight appears, we see Alberich approach and crouch before Hagen. He asks if Hagen his son is sleeping, or can he hear his father whom sleep and rest have long betrayed? Hagen mutters that he hears the hateful gnome, and asks what message he bears him in his sleep. Alberich advises Hagen to remember his might, if he has inherited strength from the mother who bore him. Hagen says he has his mother's strength, but little reason to thank her. She was a victim of the gnome's evil plans, and now he, Hagen, is prematurely old and hates those who are happy. Hate the happy! echoes Alberich, and thus love me! He no longer fears Wotan, who was overthrown by his own offspring and must soon perish. Who inherits the gods' power? asks Hagen. I—and you! replies Alberich. The Volsung (Siegfried) gained authority when he won the Ring, but he does not know its power and therefore even the curse is weakened. He must be destroyed. He is already heading toward his doom, answers Hagen. Alberich exclaims that there must be no delay. If the wise woman who loves him ever persuades him to return the Ring to the Rhinemaidens, all would be lost; but Hagen, bred to hate, can win it in defiance of Wotan and the Volsung. Does Hagen swear it? Hagen advises calm; he will have the Ring. But swear it, urged Alberich. I have sworn it to myself, counters Hagen. Alberich withdraws, repeating, "Be true, my son!"

**Comment:** *This bass-to-bass encounter is excellently swarmy, with both characters trying to outdo each in evil. The narcoleptic Hagen tries to assert his independence from his father while simultaneously submitting to him. Later in the act, it will be seen that his stupendous*

*"Hoi-ho" cry to the vassals is really an amplified echo of Alberich's parting notes, where he says "Be true!"*

The sun rises, and Siegfried bounds out of the bushes, greeting Hagen. Hagen asks where he came from, and Siegfried answers that he came directly from Brünnhilde's rock, from which he "wished" himself, by means of the Tarnhelm, back to the Gibichungs' Hall. Gunther and Brünnhilde are following in a boat. But where is Gutrune? Hagen calls her forth, and she asks Siegfried for details of his adventure. She is particularly anxious to know exactly what went on between Siegfried and Brünnhilde on this trip to the rock, but Siegfried assures her that Notung formed a barrier between their bodies. Hagen spots the sail of the boat coming up the river, and Gutrune excitedly bids him call the vassals to the hall for the wedding feast, while she leaves with Siegfried to gather the women.

Hagen ascends a rock in the middle of the open space and calls the vassals to gather, using his horn and his voice, as if to battle. Bring weapons and make haste, for there is great danger!

The men gather in great excitement. What is the danger? Who is the foe? Gunther arrives with a bride, proclaims Hagen. Does danger threaten him? ask the vassals. Hagen replies that Gunther brings a formidable wife. Does her family pursue? ask the vassals, still not grasping Hagen's peculiar sense of humor. No, they come alone, unfollowed. Then why assemble the warriors? Why the call to arms? You must slaughter a steer for Wotan, kill a boar for Froh, and a goat for Donner, but kill sheep for Fricka, that she may bless the marriage. And then what? ask the vassals. Then you must let your wives fill your drinking horns and revel until you pass out! The vassals finally understand that Hagen is calling them to celebrate, and it must be a special day indeed if ever the grim Hagen can be so merry. They laugh and carouse until Hagen sees the boat approaching, bidding the vassals to welcome their new queen. Greet her and be quick to avenge her if she is ever harmed!

**Comment:** *Here we have Hagen trying to start a party among a crowd of Gibichungs who are as slow-witted as he is dour. No matter. This* *scene can raise the dead. Fantasies of singing Hagen's "Call to the Vassals" keep basses alive through years of music school and provincial tours. When the vassals come onstage, we are treated to the first chorus in the entire Ring (not counting two collective screams from the Nibelungs in Das Rheingold). And what a chorus it is! The power of the men's voices, singing* fortissimo *almost the whole time, is overwhelming after all the intimate confrontations of the Ring. Within the exuberant revelry, listen for hints of doom and disaster in the orchestra.*

Gunther presents Brünnhilde, who remains with her eyes downcast, to the Gibichungs amidst noisy acclamations. Gutrune and Siegfried arrive followed by the Gibichung women. Gunther hails the two happy couples by name. Upon hearing "Siegfried," Brünnhilde raises her eyes and trembles violently. Gunther lets go of her hand and wonders, with all the others, if she is demented. "Siegfried, here! Gutrune?" she mumbles. Siegfried answers that Gutrune won him as Gunther won Brünnhilde. "You lie!" she exclaims, and then staggers as if fainting. Siegfried helps her as she staggers, calling Gunther to help his bride. Brünnhilde sees the Ring on his finger and cries out. Hagen advises the vassals to listen well to the woman. The Ring does not belong to Siegfried, she cries, but to Gunther who wrested it off her hand! She tells Gunther to claim the Ring he took from her back from Siegfried, but he is confused and knows nothing about any ring. Suddenly, Brünnhilde understands that it was Siegfried who tore the Ring from her finger, and she calls him a liar. Siegfried says he won the Ring from the dragon he slew at Neidhöhle, but Hagen urges Brünnhilde on. If she truly recognizes the Ring, then there must some deceit in this matter. Brünnhilde screams that there is a treachery, deceit more vile than any ever known! She asks the gods if this, too, was part of her punishment, and calls on them to aid her in her vengeance. Gunther begs her to be calm, but she casts him aside, calling him a "betrayer, self-betrayed." She announces to the assembly that she is already married—to Siegfried!

The hero steps forward to proclaim his innocence. Though he wooed Brünnhilde for Gunther, his sword remained between them.

She craftily says that his sword remained in its sheath when its master won his beloved (which was true, the first time around). Gunther and Gutrune both beg Siegfried for reassurance, while the vassals demand an oath. Hagen offers his spear as voucher for the oath, and Siegfried puts two fingers on its tip, saying the spear may strike him dead if he has broken faith with Gunther. Brünnhilde then grabs the whole spearhead in her hand, dedicating its point to the death of the shameful liar who has perjured himself. Siegfried calls on Gunther to control his wife, whose wild mountain ways will calm in time. Enough of scolding women! he says, but privately he confesses to Gunther that perhaps the Tarnhelm only half hid him. Still, women's anger abates quickly. He invites the vassals and the women to join him at the festivities, and leaves with the assembly.

**Comment:** *Apparently, the medieval Germans conceived of marriage as a sort of rape with choral accompaniment. Here we get "Brünnhilde Ballistica," and the score includes all the vocalizing to be expected from a violated diva. We also finally hear a chorus of women singing along with the men in this scene.*

Hagen, Gunther, and Brünnhilde remain, silently pondering the situation. Brünnhilde asks, as if to herself, what devilry is afoot here. She has passed her power and her wisdom to Siegfried. Who will vindicate her and break her bonds to the traitor? Hagen offers himself as her champion, but she is unimpressed. What could Hagen do against Siegfried? One flash of his heroic eyes could defeat Hagen. Craftily, he agrees with her, but asks if there is no way in which Siegfried is vulnerable. No, she answers, she used all her runes to protect his body in battle. However, he could be struck in the back. She knew he would never show his back to a foe, so she neglected to shield it with magic. "That's where my spear will strike him!" exclaims Hagen. He urges Gunther to the deed, who does not stir. That would be shameful. He is caught in his own fraud. What will he do? He asks Hagen for advice, but Hagen replies that nothing can help him, no brain nor hand, nothing but Siegfried's death!

Brünnhilde and Hagen take turns urging Gunther and shaming

him with cowardice, until at last Hagen tells him in an aside that killing Siegfried means infinite power through the Ring. This convinces Gunther, whose only concern now is for Gutrune. Brünnhilde has no concern for Gutrune, while Hagen advises telling her nothing of the plot. There will be a hunting party in the morning, and Siegfried will be killed by a boar. The three join in an oath, Gunther and Brünnhilde calling on Wotan to avenge their wrongs, while Hagen calls on his father Alberich, the Lord of the Ring, whom all will obey once more.

The procession of vassals and women appear bearing Siegfried and Gutrune on shields. Gutrune tries to smile in a friendly manner to Brünnhilde, who does not respond. At last, Gunther takes hold of her as they are likewise carried off by the Gibichungs toward the altars of the gods for the wedding sacrifices.

**Comment:** *The chorus does not sing at the end of this exciting act, yet there is still a tremendous feeling of climax after the "oath trio." Almost everyone loves Act II of* Götterdämmerung *for its unceasing drama and sweep. Shaw, of course, griped about the trappings of grand opera, such as the chorus and, gasp! an oath trio, while Newman found himself able to call this act "in some ways Wagner's supreme achievement in the art of music drama." This just goes to show that facts can be arranged to agree with whatever agenda the writer is promoting. All we need to know is that it is thrilling, be it grand opera, music drama, or whatever.*

### Act III, Scene 1

Setting:  A wooded valley on the banks of the Rhine.

The three Rhinemaidens appear in the river, swimming while they sing a pretty but melancholy song to the sun. How bright Lady Sun's rays appeared when they danced on the Rhinegold at the bottom of the river! If she would only send them the hero who would return the Ring, then the Rhinemaidens would envy her rays no more! Woglinde hears Siegfried's horn, and the three sisters dive under the water to await him.

Siegfried appears in the clearing by the river. An elf led him astray, and now he has lost both his hunting party and the bear he was chasing. The Rhinemaidens surface, and tease Siegfried flirtatiously. He asks them if they are hiding the bear he was chasing. If the bear is their lover, he is happy to leave it to them. Woglinde asks what Siegfried will give them if they give him the beast, but he says he has nothing to give. His hunting bag is empty. Wellgunde points out the Ring Siegfried wears on his finger, and the Rhinemaidens together ask for it as a prize. This Ring, he explains, I won in battle with a dragon—too great a prize for a meager bearskin! The Rhinemaidens ask him if he is always so cheap. He should be generous with women. But then, he answers, his wife would scold him. Does she beat you? they ask, laughing. Laugh if you will, he says, but you're not getting the Ring. So handsome, so strong, so attractive, they each say. What a pity he's so cheap! They laugh as they dive underwater.

Siegfried runs to the riverbank and holds the Ring over the waters. The Rhinemaidens may have the Ring if they want it! They resurface, much more serious than before. Let Siegfried keep the Ring until he learns of its curse! He calmly puts it back on his finger as they warn him of its dangers. As he slew the dragon, so he shall be slain—this very day! Only the Rhine can wash away the curse. The Norns have decreed this in their rope of destiny. Siegfried is unmoved. Notung slew the dragon, it will do the same to the Norns' rope. He will not be threatened into surrendering the Ring. The sisters agree to leave the doomed madman who does not keep oaths and who does not value secret wisdom. A proud woman will give them their Ring that day. They swim off, singing.

*Comment: The Rhinemaidens' song in this scene sounds very close to Brünnhilde's love theme at the end of* Siegfried, *but the commentaries never say so. It's a hard observation to work into a systematic analysis, so perhaps it's better left alone. One could always say it is another manifestation of the eternal feminine, and hope that means something.*

Hagen and the vassals are heard in the distance, calling Siegfried with characteristic "Hei-hos." Siegfried answers their call with a "Hei-ho!"

*Comment: It was at this point, a good five hours into a most vocally demanding evening, that Wagner thought it would be a nice idea to give the tenor a cute little high C to sing. It is the first note of his "Hei-ho!" and is completely unsupported—that is, it comes out of nowhere as the first note of a phrase. Nine times out of ten it is a complete disaster and elicits a chorus of "ughs!" from the audience! Even if the tenor manages it, it sounds funny. God knows what Wagner was thinking, but his arguments with Unger, the opening-night Siegfried, are well documented. Perhaps Wagner was just getting even.*

Hagen and the vassals come to the clearing, asking for news of Siegfried's hunting adventures. Siegfried shyly admits that he has bagged nothing, although there were some waterfowl he would have liked to catch! They sang to him that he would be slain that very day. He asks for drink, and Hagen hands him a horn, asking if it is true that Siegfried can understand birdsong. Siegfried replies that he hasn't listened to birds since he has heard women's voices. He drinks and offers the horn to Gunther, who is strangely grim. To cheer him up, Siegfried offers to sing songs of his boyhood. Gunther accepts the offer.

Siegfried tells of the evil Mime who raised him in envy, and how he was able to forge the sword that Mime couldn't. The dwarf led him to the forest, where he killed the dragon. Having tasted its blood, Siegfried tells how he understood the bird, who told him to take the treasure and the Tarnhelm, and the Ring, which would make him master of the world! He took the Ring and Tarnhelm, and the bird then told him to beware the evil Mime, who was plotting his death. With one blow of Notung, he slew Mime. What he could not forge, he could still feel, comments the grim Hagen. The vassals ask him what else the bird told him, but Hagen bids him drink more before telling. Into the horn he has put the juice of an herb, which will refresh Siegfried's memory. Siegfried drinks and recalls the bird telling him that if he crossed the fire around the mountain, Brünnhilde would be his bride. He did as the bird advised and aroused the slumbering woman with his bold kiss, while she embraced him passionately.

Gunther is shocked. Two ravens fly out of a bush and circle over Siegfried's head, then fly away. Hagen asks Siegfried if he understands what the ravens are saying, because to his ears they are calling for vengeance. He stabs Siegfried in the back with his spear. Gunther and the vassals are aghast, demanding to know what Hagen has done. "I have avenged perjury!" he replies. Siegfried, dying, remembers Brünnhilde, and greets her. He falls back and dies.

*Comment: When Siegfried offers to sing of his boyhood, there isn't one member of the audience who doesn't think, "Oh, God! Here we go again!" Yes, he goes through the story one more time, singing, as part of his narrative, almost everything the Forest Bird had sung over the course of the second act of* Siegfried. *Now it's one thing to hear a lovely and refreshed lyric soprano from offstage singing a pretty tune (it's also the Rhinemaidens' original song from* Das Rheingold—*remember?), but quite another to hear a tenor struggle at the end of the all-time vocal marathon. If the tenor can manage it, and muster the nuance necessary to depict reemerging memory, he is an operatic god. Don't count on this happening, however.*

The vassals put Siegfried's body on a shield and carry him back to the Hall of the Gibichungs.

*Comment: This is the other, more famous "tone-poem" in* Götterdämmerung, *familiar to many as "Siegfried's Funeral." It is not so much a march as a symphonic reconfiguration of themes associated with Siegfried. The famous two chords, played* fortissimo *by almost the entire orchestra, are one of the great musical depictions of the absoluteness of death. Heard on the radio or in the concert hall, they are impressive and memorable. Within the context of a complete performance of the* Ring, *they are searingly unforgettable. They entwine with Siegfried's themes and eventually metamorphose, through barely per-*

*ceptible gradations of rhythm and tone, into a convincing statement of victory. If your heart does not pound in mournful cadence with this, perhaps the saddest moment of the Ring, well, maybe music isn't for you after all. It isn't about grief for the death of Siegfried. You probably don't care that much about him anyway—who does? The music demands that each member of the audience consider the inevitability of death—their own and everybody else's.*

### Act III, Scene 2

Setting:  The Hall of the Gibichungs.

Gutrune is alone, waiting for the hunting party to return. Where is the sound of Siegfried's horn? She cannot sleep. Brünnhilde frightens her. Where is she? Did Gutrune see her walking by the river? From afar, she hears Hagen calling for torches. He brings the spoils of the hunt.

**Comment:** *Gutrune's solo moment is dark and somber. This is another of Wagner's attempts to lower the collective blood pressure, so to speak, between climactic moments. Most people find it unnecessary. Wieland Wagner almost started another revolution with his 1965 Bayreuth production when he cut this brief scene altogether.*

Hagen enters with Gunther and the vassals, cruelly urging Gutrune to welcome home her hero. The procession enters bearing the body. Gutrune faints. Gunther revives her, but she accuses him of killing Siegfried. He says it was Hagen who did it. Hagen boasts of the deed, saying Siegfried's life was his since he swore falsely on Hagen's spear. He adds that the Ring is likewise his by right, but Gunther claims it as his property. They exchange words, the vassals try to come between them, and Hagen strikes Gunther dead with a single blow.

Demanding the Ring, Hagen approaches Siegfried's body, but Siegfried's arm miraculously raises itself threateningly. Hagen and the vassals recoil in horror. Brünnhilde emerges solemnly from the background, commanding silence. Gutrune accuses her of bringing disaster upon the house. Brünnhilde calmly advises Gutrune to be silent. Gutrune was merely Siegfried's lover, but she was his wife. Gutrune curses Hagen for urging her to steal this woman's husband.

*Comment: The "threatening arm" gimmick demands much of the audience's credulity, but, really, what else could Wagner do to prevent Hagen from taking the Ring off Siegfried's dead hand? In most productions, Hagen must then stand sheepishly aside and await his own watery demise at the end. Gutrune, likewise, does not move until the end. The hope is that Brünnhilde will hold the audience's attention sufficiently to make these matters irrelevant. Indeed, if the audience is busy watching Hagen and Gutrune during the subsequent Immolation Scene, the performance is not to be considered a success.*

Brünnhilde addresses the assembly in a solemn and commanding voice. Build a funeral pyre by the banks of the Rhine to consume his heroic body. She orders Grane brought in, to follow her and Siegfried in glorious death. She praises Siegfried's loyalty and honesty in spite of his unwilled deceiving, and asks (to no one in particular) if they know how this could be.

Looking upward, she invokes Wotan, whose guilty gaze she now bids look on her grief. He sacrificed Siegfried to his own cause, and the hero had to betray her so that she could gain wisdom. Does she now understand Wotan's will? Yes, she understands everything. All is clear to her. She wishes rest for the god.

Brünnhilde takes the Ring off Siegfried's dead hand and puts it on her own, looking at it thoughtfully. Addressing the Rhinemaidens, she tells them to take their Ring back from her ashes after the fire has purified it, and wash it in the waters of the river. The curse will be broken.

Seizing a torch from a vassal, she tells the ravens to fly home and tell what they have heard here, and, on the way, to pass the rock where she had slumbered and direct Loge to Valhalla, for now is the end of the gods. She heaves the torch at Siegfried's pyre, but says she throws it at Valhalla's glittering walls. The pyre bursts into flame. The ravens fly away.

Grane is brought in, and Brünnhilde speaks to it as to an old friend. Does Grane know where she is leading it? Does the steed not champ to join Siegfried in the flames, as she does? Her heart burns to embrace Siegfried. Does Grane see? With a war cry, Brünnhilde mounts Grane and they leap into the funeral pyre, telling Siegfried his wife greets him in joy.

*Comment: This, of course, is the big soprano moment in all history. It's listed in* Guinness *as the world's longest aria. There is hardly one shade of the human experience that Brünnhilde does not have to depict in this grandest of grand scenas. She is grieving for her love, her life, everything she knows, all of which will shortly pass, yet at the same time she is every inch the heroine, taking a supreme action. Good luck to those who attempt this!*

The flames flare high as the Gibichungs recoil. When they are at their height, the Rhine overflows its banks and floods the fire. The Rhinemaidens appear above the pyre. Hagen, as if insane, orders them back from the Ring, and jumps into the water to claim his prize. Woglinde and Wellgunde entwine their arms around him and drag him down to his death in the river. Flosshilde holds the Ring aloft in triumph before the river subsides to its natural banks. A glow in the background increases. The fire around Valhalla is growing. The gods and heroes assembled within calmly await the end. Valhalla crumbles. The world begins anew.

*Comment: Obviously, this is no standard "slow curtain, the end" type of conclusion, and what you see on the stage will depend greatly on the specific agenda (and budget) of the production you are attending. Wagner was very clear in his stage directions. The Gibichungs, representing humanity in general, are unscathed by the cataclysm, although their hall has collapsed. The gods have burned up. In theory, we should watch them burn, but very few productions take this literally*

*and we are expected to infer this from the information in the orchestra
(Valhalla motif + fire motif = Valhalla burns up). The message as
Wagner conceived it was that the passing of the gods is a good thing,
inaugurating the new age wherein people and love are the supreme
beings. Whatever the production in question is trying to say (see "Productions of the Ring," p. 303), the effect should at least be impressive.*

## BASICS: WHEN TO EAT, DRINK, AND VISIT THE RESTROOM

Act I of *Götterdämmerung* is long, famously long. It is often pointed
out that the first act of this opera is longer than all of *La bohème*.
While most people agree that this act does hold one's interest, the
fact remains that two and a half hours is a long time to sit in one
place. The problem is exacerbated by the fact that it is the first act
that is so long. This means that unless you are at Bayreuth or another
festival, you will probably be running across town at rush hour to
catch a six o'clock curtain. Try to eat something light before the
opera begins and plan on another snack at the first intermission.

The real problem is the bathroom situation. Unlike *Parsifal*, the
intermissions for *Götterdämmerung* are not extended, and you may
count on a hysterical crowd scene at the restrooms during the first
intermission. If at all possible, take care of this before the opera
begins (preferably before you arrive at the opera house), and do not
drink diuretic fluids before the first act. That cup of coffee or tea can
wait till the next intermission.

Act II is relatively short—just over an hour. If you cannot get near
the restroom during the first intermission, judge whether or not you
might be able to "bite the bullet" for another hour. The lines will
practically disappear.

People don't usually worry about falling asleep during the second
act because it is so intensely dramatic and "in your face." Remember,
however, that the act begins with Hagen taking another of his naps,
with appropriately murky music. Those who have eaten or drunk too
much at the first intermission will undoubtedly fall dead asleep at

this point, which is a shame. That would mean missing the full spectrum of drama Wagner has created in this act, from somber brooding to vehement passion.

Act III is tricky. It's slightly longer (lasting about an hour and a half) than people expect after the wham-bam second act. Audiences sometimes find themselves in physical discomfort at this point. Just make sure to take care of your bodily needs at the second intermission, and all will go well. There's no need to torture your body any more than necessary—your nerves will be sufficiently tested watching the tenor and soprano struggling with those throat-busting notes in their respective final scenes.

## ROUGH SPOTS AND HOW TO GET THROUGH THEM

Practically everybody gripes about the Norns in Act I, but we have already dealt with them. In any case, the whole damned scene lasts only about ten minutes, and a budding Wagner fan ought to be able to withstand ten minutes of just about anything.

The rest of the first act (all right, *Prologue* and Act I) is more of a challenge to our physical constitutions than to our attention spans. A great deal happens in this act, and the scenery changes frequently. Having Hagen doze off in the middle is daring on Wagner's part, but the scene is not long and is delightful in its slinking evil. The Waltraute scene is best approached as pure opera in the grand manner rather than intellectual conflict. Watch to see how well the mezzo (usually aging) projects cosmic despair. Brünnhilde and Siegfried-as-Gunther on the rock make for an exciting and pathetic, if cruel, scene. The only dullness in this part is the strangely uneventful ending, but before you have time to be annoyed by it you will be applauding or running up the aisle toward the restroom, cafe, or bar.

Act II will not give your mind a moment to wander.

Act III, as noted above, is a bit long, but there is certainly enough to hold your attention. The universe burns up, for one thing. Before that, the Rhinemaidens are a delight as always. Siegfried's scene with the hunting party can be long if it's one of those dreadful nights when the tenor opens his mouth and nothing—simply nothing—comes out! Conversely, there is sometimes a perverse excitement in the house if one is waiting to see if the tenor will actually die before he is "killed." Such nights do not provide for great music, but they can make good opera.

The only potential lull after Siegfried's death might be Gutrune's little scene. If the soprano is not keeping you riveted during her seventeen lines, just take the time for deep breathing and meditation exercises. You'll need it for what follows. Perhaps this is what Wagner had in mind in the first place.

Whether or not you find your mind wandering during parts of *Götterdämmerung* depends largely on your circumstances. If you are attending a performance of this opera alone, much will seem superfluous. If, on the other hand, you are concluding your attendance at an entire *Ring*, chances are it will fly by with many fewer *longueurs*. If your *Ring* tickets are for performances done the way they were meant to be done (that is, all within a single week), you will be amazed at how quickly the time passes. *This is the central paradox of the* Ring *as theater: When seen one opera after the other, the whole seems quite short, economical, and unrepetitive!* There is no logical explanation for this, but it is so. Wotan's monologues, Siegfried's retellings of his life, and even the Norns all make perfect sense when taken as part of the whole experience. Any veteran of live *Ring* performances will corroborate this.

## LOBBY TALK FOR *GÖTTERDÄMMERUNG* (WHAT, EXACTLY, HAPPENS TO BRÜNNHILDE AT THE END?)

The great, soaring theme that ends the *Ring* gives us the final comment on the action. It tells us what we are to make of the whole confusing conclusion. Unfortunately, this theme is, in itself, the source of much confusion. The theme was heard once before: in Act III of *Die Walküre*, when Sieglinde blesses Brünnhilde before fleeing

Wotan's wrath. She addresses Brünnhilde as "Greatest miracle, noblest woman!" ("*O hehrstes Wunder! Herrlichste Maid!*"). The theme is broad enough to be memorable, in the hands of a good soprano, but it is not repeated through the subsequent operas until this point at the very end.

For years this was known as the Redemption through Love motif, and there was a good reason for believing this as its true definition. The program for the Bayreuth premiere of the *Ring* in 1876 included a guide to the leitmotivs of the work—all two hundred plus of them listed, numbered, and defined. This handy bit of hard science was compiled by a junior associate of Wagner's named Wolzogen, and he listed this theme as "Redemption through Love." (It's number 89, if you're interested.) Newman and the other great scholars accepted this and dissected it accordingly. After all, Wagner certainly knew of Wolzogen's guide, and he did nothing to change this entry.

The idea of redemption through love is nothing new. It is the notion that, whatever faults a person may have committed, their love alone is great enough to "save" them. This resonates in Christianity as well as mythology. In opera, it is practically a cliché. It is the basic premise of *Tristan* (albeit in a very complicated form) as well as *The Flying Dutchman* and *Tannhäuser*, not to mention *Manon Lescaut*, *La fanciulla del West*, *Aïda*, *La traviata*, and a host of other operas rarely compared to Wagner. It is the raison d'être for every whore on the operatic stage, forgiven because of a capacity to love. Perhaps the cue came from the Gospels, where Jesus forgives the many sins of the woman who washes his feet, saying "she has loved greatly" (Luke 7:47).

All very interesting, of course, but how are we to understand "redemption" in the supposedly non-Christian world of the *Ring*? It's not Brünnhilde who is redeemed, but the world in general and the Ring in particular. But is it really? Does the ending of the *Ring* really deliver the same sort of fulfillment message as, say, *Parsifal*? No, it doesn't, and even if it did that would not explain Brünnhilde as the basis of all this redemption.

Shaw, predictably, had no use for this theme at all, whatever one calls it. He saw the music itself as "of no great merit: it might easily be the pet climax of some popular sentimental ballad," and adds that Wagner only used it because it "gushed" and "for convenience' sake." He then devotes two chapters to explaining this as a *political* choice on Wagner's part. Poor George! He always got loopy when things didn't agree perfectly with his ideals.

Had Shaw lived until 1976, he would no doubt have jumped all over Cosima's just-published *Diaries* and found more to write about, particularly concerning this one, climactic theme. In the *Diaries*, Cosima notes that Wagner referred to this theme as the Apotheosis of Brünnhilde rather than the Redemption through Love. This is a different matter altogether.

The dictionary defines "apotheosis" as "the act of raising a person to the status of a god," or, in a word, "deification." This has given a new spin to our understanding of the *Ring*'s conclusion, and commentators since 1976 have twisted themselves into pretzels attempting to deconstruct it anew. In fact, so intensely do they emphasize that this theme is *not* to be called what it used to be that we might as well now call it the Not-Redemption through Love motif. In any case, it opens new interpretations that are beginning to be seen on stage. The Metropolitan's 1989 production of the *Ring* concluded with an image of a star rising to the heavens, looking also like an ascending drop of water or perhaps even a single sperm, and signifying the continuance of life after the cataclysm. But why Brünnhilde?

Unlike Fricka, Brünnhilde has comprehended the universal import of the situation beyond her own personal needs, and, unlike Wotan, was able to take the necessary action to effect what had to be. In this way, she earns, or proves, or demonstrates, or manifests her own latent divinity. That is, she is "bigger" than herself. The alignment of personal will with the universal destiny (Wotan's elusive goal) is, in itself, a marker of divinity.

In the Hindu conception, one great cycle of time follows another as one lifetime follows another. Brünnhilde's literal action causes the end of one cycle and, presumably, the dawn of the next one, even if it means sacrificing her own life. Her ability to relinquish her "will to life" (in Schopenhauer's phrase) breaks her out of the Karmic cycle that has trapped everyone else (including Wotan, who talks a great deal about "the end," but cannot make it happen himself). Brünnhilde's action moves her up a notch in creation to the sphere of those not bound to time and its cycles. She is divine.

# Facets of the Ring

◆

## PRODUCTIONS OF THE *RING*:
## WHAT YOU MIGHT EXPECT TO SEE

When Wagner first produced the complete *Ring* in 1876, his goal was to present a *Gesamtkunstwerk*, a total work of art. His genius as a composer of music was well known, but he wished the *Ring* to represent the acme of all the arts, including acting and poetry. The physical dimensions of the production were to herald a new era as well, and clearly the Bayreuth Festival House represented achievements in theatrical architecture and acoustics. The one aspect where Wagner's genius seemed to have let him down was in the areas of scenic and costume design.

The *Ring* called for advances in the field of production that were unheard of in 1876 and still make producers gasp. For starters, the drama is meant to begin *underwater*. Then there are vast and rapid scene changes, characters changing into dragons and toads and God knows what else, rings of fire, flying horses, and so on. A very capable crew of mechanics and engineers was assembled for the first production, and no doubt they worked wonders. The Rhinemaidens, for example, were placed atop bobbing contraptions that were wheeled around by stage hands. With a bit of waving silk to hide the mechanisms, the illusion actually came off rather well. All were pleased with this, including the Rhinemaidens themselves, who were originally quite dubious, and had to be coaxed, cajoled, and threatened into the infernal vehicles.

Other effects were less well received. The character transformations were achieved by means of "curtains of steam." Shaw said it made the theater smell like a laundry. There was no way to get the Valkyries, let alone their horses, to fly, and a pantomime dragon is a pantomime dragon, no matter what great music accompanies him. The glitzy audience at the premiere had been told to expect a revolution in stage production, and there was a vague sense of disappointment in this regard.

Nobody is a genius in all fields. The fact is that Wagner, for all his revolutionary aesthetic innovations, had a rather conventional design sense. His dream house, Villa Wahnfried, is pleasant but utterly bourgeois. While he was busy telling his singers to look at each other rather than at the audience, like conventional opera singers of his (and, alas, our) time, he was quite content to see them "act realistically" in front of a painted backdrop, whose natural representations and time-honored illusory perspectives would undulate with every passing breeze.

The artist in him must have sensed this dichotomy. "Next year, we will do it all differently," he said after the premiere, but he died before he could restage the *Ring.* He also made a remark that has puzzled and titillated subsequent generations. Having invented the invisible orchestra (a reference to the famous covered pit at the Bayreuth Festival House), he said he wished he could invent the invisible stage. "And," he added with a smile, "the invisible audience."

Many have taken this comment to justify sitting home and listening to compact discs on the latest stereo systems as the "best" way to hear the *Ring,* but nothing replaces live theater, as Wagner well knew. Remember that he didn't put a lot of effort into writing oratorios or presenting "concert versions" of his works. Cosima noted in her *Diaries* that they couldn't see how Edison's new phonograph invention could be of any use to them. Wagner clearly wanted all the magic of opera, even if he didn't always know how to make it happen visually. Also, it is odd that movies, which have tackled so many grand operas so successfully, have thus far steered clear of the *Ring*, even in installments or, God forbid, highlights. (Fritz Lang made two movies based on the original *Niebelungenlied*, but avoided the *Ring*.) The *Ring* is obviously meant for the stage, even if it can then be enjoyed on a video or a telecast. The question is, How do you present it on stage? Do you try to make it as "realistic" as possible, knowing that it will always be slightly disappointing visually but at least possible to understand? Or do you reject any attempt at realism and jump headlong into symbolism or abstraction? And, if you make the second choice, what sort of symbolism or abstraction will best unfold the *Ring* for the audience?

This is the basic issue at stake in *Ring* productions today. To see where we are, it is necessary to take a quick look at what has happened between 1876 and now.

The question remained moot for a long time. Even though theatrical innovators like Adolphe Appia dreamed of bringing their new ideas to the *Ring*, no house would invest in them. Opera houses throughout the world, when they staged the *Ring* at all, were slavishly faithful to the original production. One saw blond women in braids and breastplates, horned helmets, faux-Teutonic costuming and decoration, and so forth. Occasionally, there were attempts to "improve" certain aspects, but always along the lines of what Wagner had conceived. The Valkyries, for example, were sometimes hurled around the stage on winged carousel horses, daring the audience, one imagines, to explode with laughter. True innovations were slight for many years. In 1924, Siegfried Wagner replaced the traditional "flats" with three-dimensional sets at Bayreuth and actually got flack for it in certain quarters.

This was nothing compared to the uproar that greeted the Bayreuth production of 1933. Heinz Tietjen, the manager of the Prussian State Theaters, and his favorite designer Emil Preetorius staged a new production with new sets and costumes. The Valkyries' rock, most notably, looked somewhat cubistic. This was a very tame development compared to some of the truly ravishing design innovations Germany had seen in the 1920s, but the battle lines were drawn by 1933. Change was Jewish or Bolshevik, while tradition was pure and Aryan. Bayreuth was intended by the Nazis to be a bastion of ideals amidst a corrupted world. How could such aesthetic decadence permeate the fortress? Preetorius modified his designs and costumes in subsequent years.

The political implications of tradition versus innovation plague the theater today. In Germany, it is quite possible to divine people's political orientation by whether they applaud or boo any given production.

This explains the reopening of the Bayreuth festival after the war in 1951 as a political and historical, as well as theatrical, event. Never in history has the relatively discrete art of stage design borne such significance.

Wieland's famous postwar production had to strip the *Ring* of all associations with the Third Reich. Since the Nazis had insisted on realistic representation of details and faithfulness to original stage directions, all as part of their broader cultural ideology, the new production opted for basically *no* representation of details and hardly any stage direction at all. The main feature of the stage was a sort of disk, a metaphor of both the Ring and the world, on which the action unfolded. Imaginative lighting set the emotional tone for each scene. The characters, who could hardly be presented in the tainted trappings of Norse mythology, were dressed in rather neutral outfits that suggested, if anything, Greek mythology. All the traditional props, from Donner's hammer to those blasted drinking horns, were gone. Even stage directions were ignored. For example, Wotan and Fricka were standing rather than lying down at the beginning of the second scene of *Rheingold*. Wieland justified this by referring to his grandfather's "invisible stage" comment.

Traditionalists howled, signed petitions, and threatened. Wieland persevered. Fortunately, he was a genius, and his productions held up to critical analysis. When lesser minds attempted to copy his style in other theaters, they tended to fail. Without Wieland's gift for lighting and other details, all they were left with was a blank stage.

There was little need to worry about cheap Wieland imitations, since not too many *Ring* productions even tried to copy Wieland's 1951 masterpiece. As astounding and radical as the New Bayreuth production of 1951 was, it was not the most influential. After all, where does one go from virtual nothingness? Wieland's second *Ring* production of 1965 was far more influential. After Henry Moore declined to design the sets, Wieland designed them himself with more than a nod toward Moore. Totemistic and ritualistic shapes abounded, speaking of an inner-psychological world. (Donington's groundbreaking Jungian analysis of the *Ring* was published in 1963.)

This set the tone for several years after, and the world was treated to an abundance of productions that looked as if they were taking place either at a papier-mâché Stonehenge or in your local modern art museum's sculpture garden. Look at any album cover of the *Ring* from this period, and you'll feel as though you are being subjected to a Rorschach test. But, hey, at least you couldn't mistake the people on stage for Nazis.

In the 1970s, directors and designers finally started having a spot of fun with the *Ring*. The then-extravagantly funded midsized theaters of West Germany took the lead in this regard. A well-received production in Cassel in 1974 came to be called the Space-Age *Ring* from its use of those motifs. British companies were taking chances at the same time. The Sadler's Wells company produced a *Ring* in English that was part outer-space, part everything else. This toured the country for a few years and surprised audiences pleasantly. London's Covent Garden hired Götz Friedrich to direct and Josef Svoboda to design a major *Ring* production in 1974. Friedrich had astronauts where he wanted them, but also other touches: tribal ritual motifs, cadaverous beings—you name it. The era of postmodernism had arrived. In other words, a little of this, a little of that . . . Images from the world of comic books and science fiction and fantasy, which owed a great deal to Wagner in the first place, also began, in turn, to influence *Ring* productions in this period.

The next important step would be a very concrete presentation of the *Ring*. The year 1976 marked the centenary of the *Ring*'s premiere, and all Wagnerian eyes were on Bayreuth. Wieland was dead, and few expected true innovation from his brother Wolfgang. Bucking expectations, Wolfgang commissioned Pierre Boulez to conduct and Patrice Chéreau to produce the new *Ring*. Two Frenchmen, of all things, were shocking enough to the old guard, but traditionalists were further disturbed by Boulez's musical iconoclasm and Chéreau's unfamiliarity with opera. What they presented is still hotly debated, but no one would deny that it was one of the important moments in Wagnerian production.

Chéreau looked to George Bernard Shaw's book *The Perfect Wagnerite*, and basically staged the *Ring* as face-value Marxist analysis. Wotan was the Capitalist, complete with top hat; Hunding's hut was a row of Victorian houses; and so on. This was the *Ring* as thematic statement. The effect was enhanced by the excellent, unconventional (for opera) direction of the performers, who set a new acting standard for the operatic stage. In this regard, Chéreau's unfamiliarity with opera served him well. Many were shocked at the time, but have since come to remember this as one of the definitive productions of the *Ring*. It was televised in the United States in the early 1980s with surprising success.

Meanwhile, *Rings* were popping up everywhere. San Francisco looked back to Wieland's 1951 production, where the gods were draped in vaguely Greco-Roman costumes, and produced a neoclassical *Ring* in the 1980s. But a "themed" *Ring* is a relative rarity in the United States. Most productions of the *Ring* in the last generation have been a synthesis (some would say hodge-podge) of the styles outlined above. There is realism when the production staff can manage it, historical reference when convenient, and abstraction of one sort or another the rest of the time. Inherently surreal moments, like "The Ride of the Valkyries," are done however they can be to create an impression, and contemporary audiences are especially fond of groovy dragon machines. The Seattle Opera has made quite a name for itself with good syncretic productions along these lines. American opera companies tend to rely on team effort more than the authoritarian, hierarchical European systems do, and productions reflect this. It is therefore harder for American companies to present productions that clearly represent the visions of a single creator. One needs an absolute dictator in the manner of Wieland Wagner to bring such efforts off.

In 1989, the Metropolitan Opera presented its own first new production of the complete *Ring* since 1948. (The *Ring* presented in the 1974–75 season was patched and borrowed. Also, the whole *Ring* hadn't been presented at the Met within a single week since 1938!) The 1989 production was of the "realistic" type of *Rings*—modified, of course. The Valkyries did not wear horned helmets or ride flying horses, but there was the rainbow bridge, the tree in Hunding's hut, drinking horns, and so forth. Europeans and American hipsters clucked their tongues in disapproval: here was a perfect example of American operatic traditionalism and political-aesthetic naiveté, they said. But the Met knew what it was doing. There having been no complete *Ring* production in over a generation, there was no point in presenting a radical reassessment of the work. Furthermore, the Met must have had an eye to the televised performances. The millions of people who watched (or claimed to watch) it were best served by this sort of a production.

There was more. The Mighty Met, with its legendary production capabilities, knew it was probably the only house in the world that could hope to approach anything like Wagner's stage directions and not look ridiculous. The opening Rhinemaidens' scene alone, always a nightmare for directors and designers, utilized the moving stages ("wagons," as they're called), to create the illusion that the audience was *bobbing* in the water. The descent into Nibelheim, the magic fire, and, especially, the *Götterdämmerung* finale also blew everyone away. "Let's see Bayreuth top that!" was the basic message. There were some silly painted backdrops of the old tradition to contend with as part of the price for all this, but the lighting and staging were fine-tuned in subsequent years. Audiences, live and over the television, were quite pleased. The Met can take much credit for its role in making the *Ring* the popular entertainment it is today.

The Met production, however, may have put the lid on any other "realistic" presentations of the *Ring*, at least for a while. There isn't much any other American company could do to top the Met in the realm of spectacular realism, short of setting the theater on fire and diverting the local river, so the other companies have been pushed further into experimentation and innovation. This has been another salubrious effect of the Met production. The Chicago Lyric Opera produced its long-overdue first complete *Ring* in 1995, and scored successes with its most imaginative details. The bungee-jumping Rhinemaidens were a particular hit.

The future of *Ring* productions seems to belong to the designer. In the earlier years of the century, the conductor reigned. One speaks of Mahler's *Ring* or Furtwängler's. The next phase was the ear of *Regietheater*, when the director was supreme, as witnessed by references to the Wieland Wagner, Friedrich, or Chéreau *Rings*. Now we hear more and more of the *Ring* by Rosalie or Eiko Ishioka.

This, of course, is to be expected in our fashion-obsessed era of visual superficiality, but there is an exciting and promising aspect to this development. Design, by definition, is concerned with appearances even at the expense of substance. Whereas directors are trying to tell people how to interpret a piece (Götz Friedrich, for one, is very clear that contemporary audiences need to be told what to think), design-driven productions tend to *suggest* more than define. As exciting as the director-versus-Wagner clash of egos can be, *Regietheater* must of necessity limit the scope of interpretation. Even Wagner sensed this when he was his own *régisseur*. The new trend promises to open a wide world of possibilities to the next batch of *Ring* devotees, and Wagner would have approved of that. After all, the goal has always been the same: Finding a way to unpack the limitless delights of what remains, in the final analysis, *Wagner's Ring*.


## PERFORMANCE HISTORY AND ESSENTIAL
## LORE OF THE *RING*


*Artistic temperaments (1876)* Of all the roles in the *Ring*, few were as hard to cast in the first production as Grane, Brünnhilde's trusty steed. Legend has it that all necessary arrangements to rent a performing horse had been made with a dealer of circus animals; then Wagner was informed, at the eleventh hour, that the dear creature had a nasty habit of breaking into dance steps whenever he heard music! Ludwig, as usual, saved the day, loaning the valuable black stallion Cocotte from the royal stables, who behaved in a more seemly fashion. In fact, Cocotte was so impressive that Wagner changed his stage directions for the Annunciation of Death scene in *Walküre*, instructing Brünnhilde to "park" him in the cave beforehand lest he steal the show.

*More critter crises* (1876) Grane, it turned out, was less of a problem than Fafner, whose dragon outfit had to be made in London. The middle part never showed up, and some pretty quick patchwork had to be done between the head and tail sections. Supposedly, the shipper on the London side misread the order, and had sent it to Beirut rather than Bayreuth. It is impossible to verify this story, but it is entirely believable, since people constantly confuse these two very different places. Tell your friends you are going to the Bayreuth festival, and see how many are disappointed not to receive postcards from Lebanon.

*Inhospitable Bayreuth* (1876) The pretty town of Bayreuth can assault visitors with an array of tortures, many of which are still part and parcel of attending the festival today. Heat and dust one day, rivers of mud the next, and, most of all, accommodations that can never meet the demands of the admittedly strange horde that descends on the small town every summer. Apparently, this was so from the first festival. Tchaikovsky, who always had problems with the whole affair anyway, wrote that the main topic of conversation that first year was not music or theater, but where one might find a restaurant that hadn't run out of food.

*"And what do you do for a living?"* (1876) One person who managed to get a hotel room that year was Dom Pedro II, emperor of Brazil and longtime admirer of Wagner. When instructed to sign the hotel's guest register, he wrote his name; when asked to fill in his occupation, he calmly wrote "Emperor."

*Great ways to say "Hello"* (1876) If Ludwig ducked out of town before anyone could see him, Kaiser Wilhelm I had other ideas. Wagner met the imperial train at the platform with marching bands, fluttering banners, and cheering throngs. The gruff old kaiser, once merely king of Prussia, stepped off the train and approached Wagner, saying, "I never thought you'd pull it off!"

*Sound advice* (1876)  August 13 was the first day of the actual festival. Excitement was running high, with half the crowned heads and most of the musical notables of the world in attendance. Wagner wrote out a final urging to the cast and posted it backstage. It read: "Clarity! The big notes will take care of themselves; the small notes and the text are what matter. Never address the audience but only one another; in monologues always look up or down, never straight ahead. Last request! Be faithful to me, dear friends!" These words should be written in bronze and placed in the wings of every opera house in the world.

*Beyond Bayreuth* (1881)  Angelo Neumann, a singer who became a sort of manager-agent, got Wagner's permission to produce the *Ring* at Leipzig in 1878. He faithfully followed details of the Bayreuth production, and had the good sense to have his sets and costumes photographed, so we have some idea what the first *Ring* looked like. The Leipzig production was successful, and Neumann hired the Viktoria Theater in Berlin for another *Ring* production, which was given in May 1881. Neumann persuaded Wagner to come and supervise rehearsals. It was a triumph. The most singular aspect of this *Ring* production was that *Das Rheingold* was given with an intermission, since the urban audiences were perceived as requiring one. (Perhaps they needed to visit each other at intermission, since they managed to survive Act I of *Götterdämmerung* with no recorded fatalities.) What is even more surprising about this is the fact that Wagner appeared not to mind at all. There were times, after all, when he could be accommodating.

*Rams versus Vikings* (1896)  Animal issues continued to dog Bayreuth after Wagner's death. For Cosima's new production of the *Ring* at the 1896 festival, her extremely literal commitment to her late husband's stage directions led her to find two live rams to draw Fricka's chariot in *Die Walküre*. They worked better than the children on hobbyhorses behind a scrim she tried for "The Ride of the Valkyries," which fooled no one. Both experiments were subsequently abandoned.

*The* Ring *as politics (1918–45)* The *Ring*, or at least snippets of it, is too powerful not to be used for propaganda purposes. "Siegfried's Funeral" was played at Lenin's state funeral in 1924. This has some logic to it, since Siegfried was the new creature who smashed the old to bits, but the juxtaposition of Lenin and Wagner is a strange one. On the other hand, is there any better funeral music?

The heroic imagery of the *Ring* always had a special appeal to military propagandists. In the First World War, the German generals had their Operation Walküre, and the great defensive line against the 1918 Allied offensive was named the Hunding Line. Why? What is so heroic about Valkyries, who never really fight but just pick up dead bodies from the battlefield like loud vultures? And *Hunding*? He's killed off without even a hero's death! It doesn't matter. People rarely think through their pet images, least of all in wartime.

After the swift German surrender of 1918, General Ludendorff circulated the "stabbed in the back" theory, which said that the German armies were invincible at the front and must have been sold out back home. Hitler picked up this image from the *Ring* in *Mein Kampf* when he wrote the warlike German Siegfried (meaning the army) had been stabbed in the back by the Reichstag. Years later, Francisco Franco asked Hitler to send air support to the Fascist side in the Spanish Civil War. Hitler complied, and, having just attended a performance of *Walküre* at Bayreuth, named the operation *Feuerzauber* ("Magic Fire"). Again, what does Wotan's Farewell have to do with an air raid?

Either the German generals of 1944 hadn't learned their lessons from 1918 or they hadn't read their librettos, but they couldn't resist naming their Western front defensive system the Siegfried Line. This line held longer than the Hunding Line had in 1918, and seriously impeded the American forces during the last winter of the war, but it eventually failed. Life imitates art yet again.

Several accounts of Berlin in the last days of the war record that the state radio was given to endless repetitions of music from, of all things, *Götterdämmerung*. God knows how this was supposed to inspire the people to a final resistance, but there's no point questioning Nazi logic. Throughout the Third Reich, propagandists had used the immolation imagery of *Götterdammerung* for their purposes, portraying a great conflagration that would bring about a new world order. So it did, of course, but those making the speeches were, in fact, what had to be swept away first!

*Clash of the titans* (1968) Conductor/director/dictator Herbert von Karajan was, by 1968, accustomed to doing what he wanted when he wanted, and merely handing his bills over to the local government. When he was invited to New York to produce a *Ring* at the Met, everybody rightly predicted doom. Besides everything else, he would have to work with the legendary Rudolf Bing, general manager of the Met and no less an autocrat than Karajan. Heedless of union overtime, Karajan scheduled scores of rehearsals for every detail of the production, including several dozen for the lighting alone. When Bing saw the results, he sniffed that he could have made the stage pitch-black in just one rehearsal!

Karajan's *Ring* at the Met got as far as *Walküre*. The rest of the production was worked out and performed at Salzburg, where Karajan answered to nobody except, perhaps, God. It was later sent to the Met as a *fait accompli*, where it was successfully given in the 1974–75 season and then promptly packed away.

## ORIGINS OF THE *RING*

The conventional understanding of the writing of the *Ring* goes as follows. First Wagner wrote the libretto for a grand opera to be called *Siegfrieds Tod*, or "Siegfried's Death," the germ of what we now know as *Götterdämmerung*, the final opera of the series. It began with the Norns telling the story of all that had previously happened. Later, Wagner realized he would need a whole separate opera to serve as an introduction, and wrote *Der junge Siegfried*, or "The Young

Siegfried," which corresponds to the opera we know simply as *Siegfried*. In that work, the character of the Wanderer explained all that had happened previously in his scenes with the dwarf (who wasn't yet named Mime) and Erda. Unable to contain himself, Wagner then wrote *Die Walküre*, where Wotan must explain what had happened previously in his long Act II monologue. Eventually the composer was so unsatisfied with stopping there that he penned *Das Rheingold*. The *Ring*, then, was effectively written backward, which explains why there is so much repetition in "flashback" of what we have already seen.

Like much of the conventional wisdom on Wagner, there is just enough truth in this summary to make it truly misleading. There are two major errors. First, it could only be plausible at face value if Wagner had *completed* (including the music) *Siegfrieds Tod*, or *Götterdämmerung*, before deciding it needed a "prequel," and then had done the same each time until he had the entire *Ring* as we know it. Only then could we believe that this is why he had "repeated" himself so often in the saga. Yet the same people who propound this tale know perfectly well that the entire poem was completed and published before he wrote one note of music (well, he had written down a couple of measures here and there as they popped into his head, but the basic point stands). Are we to believe that he merely composed the music and never noticed such recapitulations as the Norns' scene and Wotan's monologue? Hardly.

The second problem with this interpretation of events is that it ignores the fact that Wagner had written a prose outline called *The Nibelung Myth as Scheme for a Drama* in 1848, that is, before he had written *Siegfrieds Tod*. This outline covers the same ground as the *Ring*, from the beginning of time to Brünnhilde's immolation, albeit with many differences from the work we know. However, it is important to understand that Wagner had conceived the work as a vast tetralogy (four-parter) from the start, and then produced the librettos incrementally. And, yes, those librettos were written in reverse order.

Still, we may put to rest the notion that the *Ring*'s repetitions, if that's what they are, result from sloppy planning or egomania on Wagner's part. He basically knew what he was doing from the start, even if he only admitted it to himself and the world one libretto at a time. Indeed, Father Lee, in his book *Turning the Sky Around: An Introduction to the Ring of the Nibelung*, points out that Wagner had no need to stop at *Das Rheingold*. He might just as well have added a fifth opera to precede the four we know, showing actions referred to in the subsequent operas. This, he suggests, would have been called *The World-Ash Tree*, and would have traced Wotan's rise to power. As excellent an idea as this may be, we must admit we have quite enough to deal with in the *Ring* as we know it.

Oddly, however, for all Wagner's rewrites and revisions, a surprising amount of the original outline for the drama creeps up in various places in the *Ring*. He had originally conceived this drama in terms of groups rather than individuals. There were *many* giants. *All* the gods contracted them to build Valhalla. There were *many* Volsungs, which was the name of one of the races of humans. And so on. The Volsungs were the most heroic of the human races, but they were in danger of corruption through breeding with inferior races. (You can surely see where *this* is heading.) Siegmund and Sieglinde were each married to another, but those unions were sterile, and the twins paired off to produce a real Volsung. Wotan was not, originally, their father. Much of this carries over to the *Ring* in strange ways. The giants are constantly referred to as a "race," with a homeland of their own, and yet there are only two of them for all we know. The same is true of the Volsungs. "Race" seems like a big word to refer to a single set of twins, but it's used time and again, and their child Siegfried is once referred to as "the strongest Volsung of them all!" All *three* of them? While Wagner was careful, in most cases, to revise facts and details as his story evolved, much of the *spirit* overlapped between versions.

The main difference between Wagner's drama outline of 1848 and the *Ring* as he wrote it is the ending. Originally, Brünnhilde's sacrifice purified the Ring, as it does in *Götterdämmerung*, but this had the effect of ensuring the rule of the gods rather than ending it. Siegfried's spirit soared to a rejuvenated Valhalla. Wagnerites have made much of this about-face, seeing a change in Wagner from an optimistic to a pessimistic world view between the years 1848 and

1854, when the completed poem as we know it was published. At this point in the commentaries, we are usually reminded of Wagner's discovery of the philosopher Schopenhauer, whose pessimistic writings had such an effect on him, but this is not an explanation. Wagner picked up Schopenhauer in 1854, by which point he had already found the original ending of the *Ring* unsatisfactory. Most scholars now agree that the philosopher Schopenhauer did not so much affect Wagner's thinking as provide him with a vocabulary to express what he already believed.

The standard explanation for Wagner's change of heart relies on political history. Certainly the Europe of 1854 was a very different place from what it had been in 1848, when idealistic aspirations exploded in a series of revolutions across the continent. Wagner, as we have seen, was an active participant in this movement in 1849, and the failure of the revolutions affected him not only in practical matters (he was exiled from Germany), but intellectually. In fact, he took it all rather personally, and tended to see the revolutions' failure as a failure of will on the part of the people to support the revolutionary art he was creating. This is evident in several of the pamphlets he produced around 1850. The revolutionary movement was killed off where it had started, in Paris. When the elected president Louis Napoleon declared himself dictator and subsequently Emperor Napoleon III in a December 1851 coup, everything was over. Wagner said he was stunned by that development.

Newman has demonstrated that Louis Napoleon's December coup cannot be held responsible for Wagner's move toward a cataclysmic ending to his saga, since he had already written of the self-annihilation of the gods in his sketchbook in May of that same year. Newman deduces that the cumulative sense of doom pervading the onetime revolutionaries after 1849 had more to do with the changed ending of the saga than any single event.

Fine, but are we any closer to an answer? Why would a hotheaded radical like Wagner wish to portray the preservation of the old order in his first rush of revolutionary fervor, only to will its destruction later in his bitterness? The problem is that the scholars have looked at the time line of history and the time line of Wagner's creative life and assumed too great a correlation between the two. Nobody seems to have suggested the obvious: that having Valhalla and the world burn up at the end of the *Ring* is better theater than having it purified in some vague manner, and Wagner's theatrical instincts told him so. One might even say it's better *opera*, but you'd really be playing with fire, excuse the expression, with that one. It is more agreeable for idolators to believe that historical events and Wagner's great artistic achievements naturally sprang from the same source.

Clearly, there was great upheaval in Wagner and in Europe within these years. But how, exactly, did the *Ring* get written? While still modifying the texts of *Der junge Siegfried* and *Siegfrieds Tod*, Wagner began working on the texts of *Rheingold* and *Walküre*—simultaneously! By the end of 1852, he had the entire poem pretty much together, although many alterations were yet to come. The following year, he began to compose the music, starting at the beginning of *Rheingold*. By August 1857, he had written up to the end of Act II of *Siegfried*, and then he abruptly stopped. (Finding the exact spot where he left off kept scholars busy for years.) He then turned his attentions to *Tristan* and *Meistersinger*. He orchestrated Act II of *Siegfried* in 1865, and then put it aside again. He resumed the work in March 1869 and finally finished it in November 1874.

## LOGICAL INCONSISTENCIES IN THE *RING*

Even though Wagner worked on the *Ring* for about twenty-eight years, there are still plenty of confusing details in the story. You may as well know this right from the start. Well, what of it? *Hamlet* doesn't exactly "make sense," but it's no less great for all that. In fact, that's an important part of why it still is compelling.

Here is a list of ten logical inconsistencies in the story of the *Ring*, some with possible (if far-fetched) explanations, others without. This is by no means a complete list, they're just the first ten that came to mind. They are here not only so you won't spend too much time pondering the impossible or wondering if you read the summaries wrong, but also to accustom you to the idea that music drama is not an exact science. Perhaps you'll want to add your own favorites to the list—such a sport is considered popular parlor entertainment in some circles.

1. *Das Rheingold*, Scene 1 What is a dwarf doing at the bottom of a river? Possible explanation: Wagner had originally conceived the river as having a sort of air tunnel underneath it. This is why Alberich sneezes and complains of the "damp," something of an understatement for a river bottom. Later, Wagner seems to have forgotten this detail, as he has the dwarf chase and almost catch the Rhinemaidens. By the way, do the Rhinemaidens have a mother? It's not Erda. She says she was only overpowered "once," although that was an exceedingly fertile encounter (*Siegfried*, Act III, Scene 1).

2. *Das Rheingold*, Scene 4 What are we to make of Erda's advice to Wotan? She says a dark day is approaching for the gods; Wotan must surrender the Ring! Will giving up the Ring save the gods? Apparently not. Would keeping the Ring hasten their downfall? Probably. Would returning it to the Rhinemaidens have helped? So it is hinted many times subsequently, yet Erda does not address this solution. Granted, she is meant to be mysterious, but she really goes over the edge in that department.

3. *Das Rheingold*, Scene 4 Does the Ring itself actually have any power whatsoever? Why can't Wotan, for the brief period when he wears it, compel the giants to submit to his will?

4. *Die Walküre*, Acts I and II Why do Siegmund and Sieglinde flee? Naturally they want to make love, but Hunding is drugged and manages to sleep through their Act I duet. It's hard to imagine he'd wake up even for their big "moment of truth." Siegmund has the sword and intends to fight. He even goes offstage looking for Hunding in the second act. So why did they run away in the first place? Why not have a nice breakfast, let Hunding sleep off his drugs, and then kill each other right there like civilized people? Possible explanation: the people in the land around Hunding's house are Hunding's kin, who "protect his honor," as he says in Act I. Siegmund must get far away to have a one-to-one combat. Likelier explanation: dra-

matic license. It's more sensible having the twins show up at the mountain pass in Act II than having Wotan and Fricka argue in Hunding's living room.

5. *Siegfried*, Act II Why doesn't Wotan simply kill Alberich? It wouldn't be morally right, but he kills Hunding off without a second thought. Dwarfs aren't immune to murder, as Siegfried demonstrates.

6. *Siegfried*, Act II Who, exactly, is the Forest Bird in *Siegfried*? If it's a voice of primal nature, as the score and all the commentators tell us, or some other manifestation of the "eternal feminine," why doesn't it tell Siegfried to return the Ring to the Rhinemaidens? Then everyone can live happily (or miserably) ever after.

7. *Götterdämmerung*, Act I In *Das Rheingold*, Fricka was told that a woman who wore the Ring could be assured of her husband's fidelity, which was apparently the apex of nineteenth-century notions of feminine power. Yet when Brünnhilde is wearing the Ring, a mere spiked cocktail is enough to send her husband reeling off into the arms of, literally, the first woman he sees. Once again, the Ring is not merely fatal, it's useless as well.

8. *Götterdämmerung*, Act II Where does Alberich get the gold to buy Hagen's mother for the night? And what was the going rate for "one-nighters" in those days?

9. *Götterdämmerung*, Act III Siegfried says the "Nibelungs are his vassals." Who on earth told him this? Brünnhilde? Why would she even want him to know? Newman suggests this was a holdover from Wagner's earlier conception of *Siegfrieds Tod*, which was more akin to the original *Nibelungenlied*, and that Wagner merely forgot to change it. Imagine staring at a libretto for twenty-eight years and "forgetting" to make a change!

10. *Götterdämmerung*, Act III Why is Gunther so eager for his brother-in-law's wedding ring that he dies for it? Did someone tell him that it was *the* Ring? If so, who? When?

# *RING* TIME LINE

Some people find the durations of the events and the intervals between them to be very confusing, and with good reason. It seems that Wagner left some room for interpretation on this subject. By doing so, he was reflecting the traditions of the classical and medieval epics, which were deliberately vague about time. The events they described did not occur on our plane of reality, chronological or otherwise.

Still, one needs to have some bearings, so the following outline is provided to help give some idea.

*Das Rheingold*
Scene 1: From the beginnings of time to a point in legendary history.
Scene 2: An unspecified amount of time since the end of the first scene, but not very long afterward.
Scene 3: The same day as Scene 2.
Scene 4: Evening of the same day.

*Die Walküre*
Act I: One evening, at least one generation past the end of *Das Rheingold*. Wotan has spent some time worrying in Valhalla, some time roaming the earth, and Siegmund and Sieglinde have grown up since they were born at the time when Wotan was abiding with the mortal woman.
Act II: The following evening.
Act III: The next day into evening.

*Siegfried*
Act I: One day, after exactly one generation has passed since the end of *Die Walküre*. We can assume this to be about twenty years.
Act II: That night, into the following day.
Act III: That evening, into the following day.

*Götterdämmerung*

Prologue: Good question. Siegfried and Brünnhilde may have only spent a single night together, in which case he has certainly learned a lot very quickly, including restlessness.

Act I: This takes however long it took Siegfried to sail up the Rhine. His trip back to the Valkyries' rock, with Gunther lumbering along, does not seem to have taken more than a few hours. Waltraute says that Wotan "recently" had his Spear shattered, so the time span from the end of *Siegfried* to the beginning of *Götterdämmerung* is meant to be understood as brief.

Act II: That night, into the following day.

Act III: That day, into the night.

The time frame of the *Ring*, then, is very unusual. It covers vast expanses of time, but the actual action occurs in swift moments. In this way, it is very much like the original *Nibelungenlied*, which focuses the action on busy moments scattered over long historical spans. Basically, once chronological time begins (somewhere in the first scene of *Das Rheingold*), we get twenty-year stretches of nothing, punctuated three times by extremely eventful single days.

## "NONCHARACTERS" IN THE *RING*

These days, you're likely to see the gods costumed as astronauts or Hunding's hut represented as a shopping mall in New Jersey. This is all fun, of course, but the synopses and commentaries still read as if productions were faithful to Wagner's original specifications. This leads to much confusion, as audiences strive in vain to find the ravens, Grane the horse, or even the rainbow, which they have read about, on the actual stage. In addition, several people and objects are referred to that are important but are never seen. Third, there are objects in the *Ring* that are practically characters in themselves. This list of "Noncharacters" is provided to help make sense of the story, in spite of any bizarre interpretations you may see onstage.

THE SPEAR This is Wotan's symbol of authority. He carved it from the World-Ash Tree (in other words, he violated the natural order to impose his system, based on law). He carries it about everywhere until it is smashed by Siegfried.

NOTUNG This is the sword Wotan plants in the tree in Hunding's house, intending it to be found by Siegmund one day when Siegmund really needs it (hence its name, "Needful"). Notung is shattered by Wotan while Siegmund fights Hunding, but the pieces are picked up by Brünnhilde and given to Sieglinde, who gives them to Mime the dwarf. That's how Siegfried inherits the pieces of his father's sword. Once he forges the sword, a feat only he can accomplish, he uses it to shatter Wotan's Spear. Either this is a form of unconscious vengeance for his father's death or it tells us that Wotan's will to self-annihilation has been present in his plans from the start.

THE TARNHELM This is the magic helmet that Mime forges out of the Nibelung gold (not the Rhinegold) on Alberich's orders in *Das Rheingold*. It can do a lot of cool things for its owner—let him change shape, become invisible, or wish himself to another location. Nobody, least of all Siegfried, seems to understand or utilize the full power of the Tarnhelm.

THE RING This, of course, is the central prop of the whole affair, although it disappears from the stage from Scene 4 of *Rheingold* until Act II of *Siegfried*. Although it's hard to manifest on stage, we are to imagine the Ring as melting in the final immolation, after which it is tempered by the waters of the Rhine and then taken back down to the river's depths by the Rhinemaidens.

THE RHINEGOLD This is the original lump of gold in the Rhine, and then it is the Ring.

THE HOARD OF GOLD This is what the Nibelungs have mined out of the earth as slaves of Alberich. One of the biggest question marks left at the end of the saga concerns this hoard. When we last left it, it was in a cave under two corpses. At the end of the story, no one who knows about it is left alive, with the possible exception of Alberich, who may or may not still be alive. Hmmm . . .

GRANE Brunnhilde's flying horse. There is some debate about the sex of the horse. At present, there is an Internet chat group furiously debating the subject. Whatever. Grane loses the ability to fly when Brünnhilde loses her godhead (at the end of *Walküre*), and apparently falls asleep on the mountaintop when she does. Grane also is awakened by Siegfried's kiss to Brünnhilde—a detail whose comic potential has never, to my knowledge, been exploited. In theory, Grane burns up with Brünnhilde on Siegfried's funeral pyre.

THE TWO RAVENS I don't think you'll ever actually see two pantomime ravens on stage, but they're not without some importance. Wotan is, among other things, "Lord of the Ravens," and these two become his eyes and ears to the world as he sits in Valhalla waiting for *das Ende*. They make several theoretical appearances in *Götterdämmerung*, although they also have an important reference, often overlooked, in *Siegfried*. When Siegfried is looking for the fiery mountaintop, he gets lost, having lost his little bird. He runs into the Wanderer, who explains that the bird fled the presence of his ravens.

GIBICH The founder of the "race" of Gibichungs, apparently brave, strong, and proud in a way his pathetic son Gunther never will be. We know this because Brünnhilde calls Gunther an "unworthy scion of a noble race," one of several such references to racial deterioration throughout Wagner's works.

GRIMHILDE The mother of Gunther, Gutrune, and Hagen, and presumably the wife of Gibich. If Gunther lacks his father's bravery, then surely the shy, retiring Gutrune lacks her mother's grit. Grimhilde once bit the bullet and slept with a gross Alberich for gold. The story of the *Ring* does not tell us why she did this, but Grimhilde's memory is never spoken of shamefully because of this act. Perhaps we are meant to admire her bravery.

THE HEROES OF VALHALLA If you die gloriously in battle, your spirit gets to go to Valhalla. In Wagner's conception, this is Wotan's fortress castle, and the heroes are kept on hand to defend the citadel in case of enemy attack. One of Wotan's concerns about the Ring is that its owner would be able to compel the heroes' loyalty. According to the stage instructions, we also are supposed to see the heroes burn up in the general conflagration of the finale. Before that, they feast eternally in the Great Hall, with maidens who perform their every wish. Siegmund might be said to alter the course of history by preferring to remain with his sister/wife rather than ascending to macho paradise.

HELLE   This is where Siegmund will go if he turns down the Valhalla offer, the underworld kingdom of the dead. Helle is a female deity in Norse and Teutonic mythology.

THE WORLD-ASH TREE   This mysterious plant is all over the story. The people of pre-Christian Northern Europe worshipped trees as deities, and remnants of the tree cult are found throughout the medieval epics—and even later. Witness Hans Sachs and his vaguely hallucinogenic elder tree in *Meistersinger*, to say nothing of the ubiquitous modern Christmas tree. The World-Ash Tree takes on various meanings in the *Ring*, but basically it is a symbol of the prelegal, Erda-based system that existed before the era of the gods (or, in Robert Graves's terminology, the matriarchal society before it was *supplanted* by patriarchy). Wotan cut a branch off the World-Ash Tree to make his famous Spear, causing the tree and its neighboring spring of wisdom to dry up and die. The Norns, as leftovers from the matriarchal times, have never quite been themselves since this violation occurred. This tree comes back in the story of the *Ring*. Wotan orders his heroes to cut up the dead trunk and pile the logs around Valhalla, which is how everything burns up at the end.

SIEGFRIED'S LIME TREE   All right, this may be a very minor detail, but it can cause some unnecessary confusion. The tree that Siegfried sits under in Act II of the opera bearing his name is indeed a lime tree, but there are no little green citrus fruits growing on it. The English language uses the same name for the fruit tree and the tree Germans call the *Linden*. Germans simply adore *Linden* trees, as seen in the name of the showplace avenue of Berlin, *Unter den Linden*. Hitler, in a very un-Germanic moment, chopped down all the trees along that street for better military parades. The *Linden* trees are presently being replanted, and, *no*, they will not have limes hanging from them.

THE TREE IN HUNDING'S HOUSE  This, too, is an ash tree, but if there's any significance in that fact, it is very arcane.

THE VOLSUNGS' MOTHER  This poor creature never even warrants a name. She was merely used by Wotan as a twin factory for his plan to have offspring recapture the Ring. She was killed in the attack on her house when Sieglinde was abducted.

WOTAN'S MISSING EYE  This disembodied organ pops up all over the place. Wotan paid for his drink at the Norns' spring with it, and also pays to marry Fricka with it. (Shaw and others see much significance in the second of these payments.) When Siegfried asks the Wanderer what happened to his missing eye, Wotan replies with what must be the single creepiest line in all opera: "It is now [in you] looking back at me." Wes Craven could hardly improve on that one.

# ◆

# PARSIFAL

PREMIERE: BAYREUTH, 1882.

## THE NAME AND HOW TO PRONOUNCE IT

*Parsifal* is named for its lead character, and it's pretty much pronounced as it's written. If you want to show off your German, hit the *r* with a slight glottal fricative. British people, perhaps to emphasize their distinctness from Continentals, tend to mispronounce it "Parsifull."

## WHAT IS *PARSIFAL?*

*Parsifal* is Wagner's final masterpiece, a depiction of a corrupted society renewed by an innocent young man who becomes wise through compassion. The story of the individual, that is, the "coming of age" of the hero, is as old as storytelling itself. The interesting thing about this example of the genre is the community where the hero becomes himself, for Parsifal stumbles (literally) upon the knights of the Holy Grail. These worthy men live in a castle in northern Spain, sustained by and devoted to the Grail itself.

The legends of the Holy Grail are complicated, numerous, and extremely far-reaching, embedded in the Euro-American consciousness by such diverse sources as the troubadours, Sir Walter Scott, and even Monty Python and Indiana Jones. The definition of the Grail changes in each of these manifestations. For the purposes of *Parsifal,* the Grail is the cup that Jesus used at the Last Supper, and that was used to catch his blood when he was pierced on the cross by the Spear. The Grail and the Spear were both transferred by angels to Monsalvat in northern Spain where, in the Middle Ages, the Christian and Muslim worlds were slugging it out for the domination of Europe. A king, named Titurel, was chosen by God to head a brotherhood of knights, and a castle was built that none can find but those called by the Grail. At the castle, the knights are sustained spiritually and physically by the Grail, which is uncovered by the king in a ritual very closely resembling Holy Communion. Thus renewed, the knights embark on adventures for the greater glory of their faith, carrying the Holy Spear with them to battle the heathen and other enemies.

If all this strikes you as a bit much for the opera house, you are not alone. Many people object to the Christian particularism of the work (Nietzsche, for one, threw a world-class fit), while others find the liturgical language and enactments truly blasphemous. Wagner himself could not bear to call it a music drama, much less an opera, and called it, instead, a *Bühnenweihfestspiel*, or "stage-consecrating festival play." From the start, it was intended to be performed only at Bayreuth. *Parsifal* has always had a certain aura surrounding it, a sort of uniqueness perpetuated by fans and detractors alike.

Yet for all its rituals and otherworldliness, *Parsifal* has a powerful story to tell. All is not well in the kingdom of the Grail. The Holy Spear has been lost to an evil magician, the king lies incapacitated with a wound that won't heal, and the land itself is enveloped in gloom. Wagner used a dark palette in his scoring to depict this, which is part of the reason many people find this work heavy and dull.

Such people are not merely being obtuse. In a word, *Parsifal* is slow. There is very little external action. The score even includes directions for periods of complete silence. *Parsifal* is not for the impatient, nor for those who need to be hit over the head with loud sound bites every few minutes to stay awake. In a way, the experience of *Parsifal* is akin to that of a no-hitter in baseball. It is the very pinnacle for the devoted fan, who writhes in ecstasies of tension and delayed gratification, while the casual spectator languishes in boredom waiting in vain for "action" (hit tunes or home runs).

For all its static nature and its otherworldliness, there is little that is obscure in the score, and it can be appreciated by any open-minded operagoer with the ability to sit still for a few hours. There is no need to sweat out details of the score beforehand. As Cosima put it well in her *Diaries*, "It is all so direct!"

## CAST OF CHARACTERS

PARSIFAL *(tenor)* A "guileless fool," which is the literary way to say a young man who has done nothing and knows less. Parsifal has lived on his own since running away from home as a young child. He does not even know his own name. In many ways, he is similar to the all-free and unsocialized Siegfried, although, being somewhat more surreal and somehow less human, he is considerably less obnoxious. Parsifal actually does very little throughout this work in the usual sense of heroic action, beyond the admittedly impressive feat of catching a spear in midair. His growth is largely internal.

KUNDRY *(soprano or mezzo-soprano)* The "wandering Jew" of medieval legend. Kundry is generally cited as Wagner's most enigmatic, and most interesting, female character. As a young woman, she laughed at Christ suffering on the cross, and was condemned to wander the earth until saved, seeking but never finding rest or death. In Acts I and III, she is a wild unruly penitent performing service to the knights of the Grail, while in Act II she is a beautiful seductress and slave to the evil magician Klingsor. Divas, therefore, love to take on the role of Kundry, since they get to assume three of the best poses in the soprano arsenal: madness, seduction, and piety. She has a foot, so to speak, in each world, and is really the most human character, philosophically speaking, in this drama.

TITUREL *(bass)* The original king of the knights, he is burdened by his years and has made his son Amfortas king. Titurel is kept alive only by the annual uncovering of the Grail (a sort of celestial life support), a duty he is too weak to perform himself. He has a grand total of ten lines to sing in *Parsifal*, and they are sung offstage. In fact, his only stage appearance is as a corpse. The role, however, is important in terms of the story, and his brief vocal appearances must be impressive.

AMFORTAS *(bass-baritone)* Titurel's son, the current king of the knights, languishing because of his sin. He was seduced by Kundry several years before, and, while he lay with her, Klingsor stole the Holy Spear and stabbed Amfortas in the side. The wound bleeds yet. The loss of the Spear and the "wound that won't heal," beyond psychological implications, are the signs of decay in the knights' community and the kingdom of the Grail.

GURNEMANZ *(bass)* The "nice guy" of the story, Gurnemanz is the first to see the possibility of a savior in Parsifal. He is something of the mentor figure familiar from coming-of-age literature. This role is demanding in terms of the sheer amount of music to be sung, for Gurnemanz does all the explaining (and there is plenty to be done) in this tale.

KLINGSOR *(bass)* The bad guy. Klingsor had once aspired to be a knight of the Grail himself. Titurel refused him, and Klingsor, in desperation to prove his aptness for service to the Grail, castrated himself. This act guaranteed his exclusion from the brotherhood, but also (somehow) gave him power in the arts of black magic. He lives in a magic castle with a garden he has conjured out of the desert on the southern slope of the same mountain range as the Grail Castle at Monsalvat (in other words, he faces Moorish Spain, while the knights face Christendom).

FLOWER MAIDENS *(sopranos and mezzos)* These are Klingsor's most effective weapons, lovely maidens (although the term "maiden" is probably not to be taken literally) who seduce chaste men. Members of the audience usually assume these ladies to be supplied by the chorus, but in fact the six Flower Maidens are soloists with separate billing in the program. Their music is semi-individuated, not unlike some of the music of the townspeople of Nuremberg in *Meistersinger*, and it is not unusual to find star singers in these roles.

## THE OPERA

### *Prelude*

**Comment:** *Wagner described the meaning of the Prelude as "faith— suffering—hope?" The first part portrays faith in simple majestic themes, including a "borrowed" one. Many listeners will recognize the famous "Dresden Amen" from church services, where it remains standard to this day. Wagner must have heard it thousands of times when he was Kapellmeister at Dresden. It was also used by Mendelssohn in his Reformation Symphony. The suffering theme is an expansion of one of the central measures of the faith motif, which is an excellent theological observation (i.e., spiritual suffering is central to faith), made by means of music and therefore appealing more to the subconscious than to the intellect. For "hope?" we are given a brief moment of the strings playing softly in marvelously unresolved ambiguity. The Prelude is often heard on the radio and in the concert hall, where it is moving, yet annoyingly incomplete. All of the themes heard here are fully explored and resolved in the reset of the score. It is, in effect, an "executive summary" for the entire subsequent drama.*

### Act I

Setting: A shady forest in the domain of the Castle of Monsalvat, in northern Spain, in the Middle Ages.

Gurnemanz, an elderly but vigorous knight of the Grail, and two young squires are awakened by trombones from the offstage castle. They pray silently. Gurnemanz tells the squires to prepare for the king's bath in the nearby lake. Two knights enter. Gurnemanz asks if the latest potion found by the knights has eased the king's pain. A knight responds that the pain has returned, and is worse. Gurnemanz says mysteriously that only one man can help the king, but when they ask him the name of the man, he gruffly orders them off to prepare the bath.

The knights and squires see Kundry racing madly on a horse toward them. She rushes in, dressed wildly, hair everywhere, eyes alternately flashing and staring lifelessly. She hands Gurnemanz a potion for the king, saying merely, "If this doesn't help, there's not a potion left in Arabia to help him. Ask no more! I am weary!" She throws herself on the ground. Amfortas is brought on, in pain. He forbids the knights to seek out more potions for him, since the only help he can expect will come from an "innocent fool," as he was once told. Gurnemanz persuades him to try one last remedy, the potion that Kundry has brought from Arabia. When Amfortas thanks her, she snaps back, "Don't thank me! It won't help! Go to your bath!"

Amfortas is carried to the lake. The knights and squires harass Kundry, still lying on the ground, but Gurnemanz rebukes them. She may be strange, but she has never harmed the knights. In fact, she has given much service to the brotherhood. Who knows what sin she may be expiating in service to the knights? Prompted by more questions from the squires, Gurnemanz tells them what he knows. Klingsor, rejected for knighthood by Titurel, had built a magic castle and garden to corrupt the knights, and their king Amfortas had been ensnared by a seductress. Never guessing that the wild Kundry lying on the ground could have been the same woman in a different state of being, he asks her why she didn't help the knights on that fateful day. "I never help!" she growls back at him.

Gurnemanz then repeats the details of the story to the squires: how Titurel had received the Grail and the Spear from angels, how he built the Castle of Monsalvat and formed the brotherhood of knights, how Klingsor's garden had seduced many other knights to their damnation even before Amfortas, and how Titurel had grown old and relinquished the crown to his son, whose fate the squires already know. The squires remark that the one who retrieves the Spear will win lasting honor, but Gurnemanz explains that Amfortas, praying in atonement after the incident, was told in a revelation that he must wait for "an innocent fool, enlightened through compassion" to retrieve the Spear and heal the wound. The squires repeat "an innocent fool . . . ," as if in prayer. There is silence.

*Comment: The whole first part of Act I is slow, stately, expository, and a bit glum. The curtain rises on three sleeping bodies, which sets the tone. Even the passing back and forth of Amfortas is pained. Kundry's entrance provides a little flurry of musical activity, but it quickly fades as she falls asleep on stage. Gurnemanz's long (fifteen minutes) narrative gives us important information for what follows, and includes many seeds of subsequent themes that, if followed closely, will reveal subtle beauties. The problem is that it's rather dull. Newman assures us that this narrative is superior to others in opera: "It is not a hoary operatic device dragged in willy-nilly, as in* Il Trovatore, *to tell the audience what it needs to know under the pretext of one character telling another on stage." Actually, it is exactly that, all "psychological justifications" notwithstanding. George Martin is much more direct. "This is the spot to snooze," recommends his* Opera Companion. *While there may be wisdom in both these opposing points of view, they both miss the point. Wagner, who was a genius of the theater above everything else, knew he had to lower the audience's collective blood pressure, so to speak, to put us in a receptive frame of mind for what was to follow. He did this by giving the know-it-alls some arcane leitmotivic titillations for their amusements, and putting the remainder of the audience fast asleep.*

A commotion is heard among the knights—a swan has been wounded in flight by an arrow! The swan flies overhead, and dies onstage. A boy is dragged in carrying a bow. "Did you do this?" asks Gurnemanz. "Yes!" replies the boy, proud of his shooting skill. The knights and squires call for punishment. Gurnemanz explains that wildlife and humans live together in this holy forest. The swan was seeking its mate to circle over the lake and consecrate the king's bath, and now look at him! The boy breaks his bow in shame. How could he commit such a crime? "I didn't know," replies the boy. Where are you from? asks Gurnemanz. Who is your father? Who sent you here? The boy replies that he doesn't know to each question. What is your name? "I once had many, but I don't know them anymore." Gurnemanz mutters that this is the dumbest person he's ever met, besides Kundry.

Gurnemanz dismisses the knights and squires, and asks the boy if he knows anything at all. He knows his mother's name, Herzeleide ("Heart's Sorrow"). Since you look noble, why didn't your mother teach you about better arms than bow and arrow? Kundry answers that his father had been slain in battle before he was born, and Herzeleide had reared the boy in seclusion to spare him a similar fate. This triggers some memory from the boy, who remembers leaving his hermitlike home to follow some knights he saw one day. He never could find them, however, and he had to forge his own way in the world with only his handmade bow and arrows. Gurnemanz says that the boy's deserted mother must grieve, but Kundry answers that she grieves no more. Herzeleide has died of her broken heart—she saw it herself as she rode by. The boy grabs Kundry by the throat at the news, and Gurnemanz rebukes him for his violence. The boy passes out, and Kundry fetches spring water. Gurnemanz commends this act of goodness, but Kundry characteristically says, "I never do good!" She crawls off into the forest, moaning how she wants to sleep forever, without nightmares, just die.

*Comment: Our introduction to the character of Parsifal is a difficult scene to stage. First of all, there is the problem of the swan. Sensible productions treat this moment as allegorical, but it is surprising how many opera companies still insist on having a stuffed swan (whose white feathers become increasingly gray as the production wends through the years) tossed on stage from the rafters. Then there is Parsifal himself. Wagner meant for us to see him as an impetuous twelve-year-old boy at this point in the drama, but there are very few tenors who can pull off the requisite illusion of innocence and latent wisdom (let alone physical youth) in the character. Judging by the ample proportions of Winkelmann, the tenor whom Wagner chose as his first Par-*

*sifal, we should probably not waste too much time worrying about the issue.*

Gurnemanz notes that the king has done with the bath, and the time for the love feast of the Grail has arrived. "Who is the Grail?" asks the dumb boy. Gurnemanz replies that he cannot explain, but all will be revealed if the boy is called to its service. The boy notes that he is standing still, but seems to be moving. The old man explains that time and space are one in this holy place. The two disappear, and the scene is transformed to the Great Hall of the Castle of the Grail.

**Comment:** *Wagner's directions for his original production called for a painted scene on rollers moving from one side to the other to achieve the visual effect for this Transformation Scene. These days, audiences are generally treated to a sort of impressionistic light show rather than any vaudeville-style moving backdrops. In either case, the music is what matters here. The Transformation Scene is a five-minute-long tone poem of ravishing beauty whose uninhibited emotionality is in marked contrast to the barrenness of the previous scenes. The themes of holiness and suffering are richly and recognizably depicted in the orchestra, while backstage trombones and trumpets, tympani, and reverberating bells create an impression of the Grail Hall as a unique spiritual environment.*

The two reappear, and Gurnemanz tells the boy to watch what is about to happen. The boy moves to the side of the Hall and remains there, silent, until the end of the act. The knights of the Grail enter the Hall in procession, singing of the meal that will renew them. Amfortas is carried in along with a small shrine covering the Grail, which is set on an altarlike table in the center of the Hall. An unseen chorus of youths from halfway up the dome sings of the redeeming blood of the Savior. After them, a boys' chorus from the summit of the dome sings, urging the assembly to take the bread and wine of life. This is followed by complete silence.

The voice of Titurel is heard from offstage, as if from a tomb, urging Amfortas to uncover the Grail, that he, Titurel, may live and have divine guidance. Amfortas protests that he is unworthy, as the only sinner among them, to perform the duty. He wails of his lot in life, of his sin, of the pain his wound never ceases to give him, and sinks back, semiconscious. The chorus of boys and youths from above sing of the prophecy of the innocent fool who will end the suffering, and the knights urge Amfortas to uncover the Grail. Heavenly voices urge the taking of body and blood in token of God's love. In great pain, Amfortas prays before the uncovered chalice. The boys' choir sings, the Hall darkens. A dazzling ray of light falls from above onto the chalice, turning it blood-red. Amfortas, momentarily strengthened, holds the cup aloft, and blesses the bread and wine on the table with it. The knights kneel. Titurel sings in gratitude at the Lord's bright greeting. Amfortas puts the Grail back on the table, and the divine glow fades while light returns to the Hall.

The Grail is covered again. The squires begin distributing bread and wine from the altar. The boys' choir sings of the Lord's transformation at the Last Supper. The knights take the bread and wine. The youths sing of the continuing consolation of the bread and wine. Half the knights sing of the bread, then the other half sing of the wine. Finally, there is an expression of blessedness in faith and love, beginning with half the knights, then the other half, then the youths, and lastly, the boys. The knights embrace solemnly. Amfortas, bleeding again, is carried out with the shrine containing the Grail, and the knights follow him out. Gurnemanz, alone with Parsifal on stage, asks the boy if he has any questions about what he just saw, but the boy is too overcome to speak. Assuming him to be dimwitted and uninterested, Gurnemanz shoos the boy out. Alone, he hears a heavenly voice repeat the prophecy of the innocent fool.

**Comment:** *This is the controversial scene of the work. Reading about it, listening to a recording of it, and experiencing it live are three separate matters. When reading a synopsis, such as this, one is struck by the appropriation of the externals of the Communion sacrament for operatic use. Christians of various denominations, non-Christians, post-*

*Christians, and anti-Christians have all expressed problems with it. There is no doubt that Wagner laid it on thick here. He laboriously depicts a procedure that the Roman Catholic Mass covers in a few sentences. But comparing this scene too directly with the Eucharist does a disservice to both. Here Wagner has embodied the essence of a religious experience without specifically re-creating one. A person of any religious bent, or none at all, can appreciate the spiritual core at the center of the weighty symbology.*

*Wagner accomplishes this deconstruction of a spiritual process by musical means. The knights are divided into "choirs" of basses and tenors, while the youths (boy altos) are meant to be "half-way up the dome" and the boys (boy sopranos) are meant to be "at the summit of the dome." The architecture of the score sends the music up and down, so to speak, throughout the scene, punctuated by Amfortas and Titurel. The "Blessed in faith, blessed in love" exclamation is a single upward figure beginning in the lower basses, carried by the tenors to the altos and finally to the sopranos. In a well-rehearsed production, it is a simple but magnificent effect, a vocal ladder of faith uniting all life. On the extreme ends of this vocal scale are the bass Titurel (singing off-stage "as from the grave") and the heavenly (female) voices. The grave is united to the heavens by vocal intercession.*

## Act II

Scene: A tower in Klingsor's magic castle. Klingsor is on one side, surrounded by a magician's paraphernalia.

Klingsor invokes Kundry, using her many names, including Herodias and Rose of Hell. He causes smoke to rise and tells her to obey her master. She rises, screaming, then wailing, and finally croaking, calling for sleep, deep sleep, and death. He torments her for roaming among the knights, who are all weak and venal. But today, she will face her greatest challenge, one who is shielded by his simpleness. She refuses. He insists she obey. She must do Klingsor's will in any case, since he alone is immune to her powers. She laughs at him, asking if he is "chaste." He is furious at this reference to his self-

castration, throwing scorn at the world and claiming that he will soon
own the Grail himself. The boy will be his means to victory—already
he is drawing near. Kundry still refuses to seduce the boy. Klingsor
blows a horn and summons his knights to defend the castle walls,
which the boy is already storming. Kundry laughs hysterically, then
wails, and finally vanishes. Klingsor comments on the boy's defeating
each of his knights and mounting the wall to the garden, predicting
that the boy will be his slave once he falls from purity. The tower disappears, instantly replaced by a lush garden of great beauty.

*Comment: This scene is a swirl of musical action compared to any-
thing in Act I. Kundry screams, moans, and wails, while Klingsor ful-
minates at the top of his bass lungs. It's all rather deliciously sleazy.
This, and a brief spear-wielding moment at the end of the act, are
Klingsor's only appearances in this opera, however important he is to
the story. Count on him to chew up the scenery while he can.*

The boy appears on the wall overlooking the garden. The Flower
Maidens rush in, wondering what was the commotion that caused
them to wake up alone, without their lover knights. They see the boy,
and are terrified that he has come to harm them. When he speaks,
they are soothed by his simplicity and begin to notice how handsome
he is. They invite him to stay with them, adding that he's highly
preferable to their usual lovers. He walks among them, telling them
how beautiful they are.

*Comment: The music of this scene could come from any French
romantic opera—even the kitschiest. Still, it is pleasant to hear lively
women's voices after the heavy maleness of the first act, and without
this scene the work would be more narrow in its scope and less balanced. Besides the singing Flower Maidens, there is the nonvocal corps
of ladies who paw Parsifal. Sometimes they dance a ballet, in other productions they lie about trying to look sultry. Wagner's first production
called for twenty-four ladies in this scene, but many subsequent stagings have greatly increased this number.*

Kundry appears on the wall, calling out the name "Parsifal." He freezes at the sound of his own name, which he had forgotten. It reminds him of his mother. Kundry dismisses the Flower Maidens, who withdraw reluctantly. Kundry says she herself chose the name from the Arabic *"Fal Parsi,"* meaning "innocent fool." She tells him how she saw Herzeleide nurse her baby, swearing to protect him from his father's fate of death in battle. How gently she held him! Did he perhaps fear her kisses? He certainly didn't consider her sadness when he left her pining, until, in her grief, Herzeleide died.

Parsifal rebukes himself for being so heartless and stupid, but she tells him he can atone through the passion that once engulfed his parents. She herself will give him his mother's last blessing, a kiss. While she is kissing him in anything but a motherly fashion, Parsifal jumps up and doubles over in pain. "Amfortas! The wound!" he cries. He feels the same wound, the torment of love and longing, bleeding within himself. He falls into a trance, remembering the blood he once saw flowing into the Grail, and Amfortas's desperate pleas before it, and all he could think to do was walk away and pursue childish things! How, he asks the Redeemer on his knees, can he purge his guilt? Kundry begins caressing him. Yes, he exclaims, "I recognize these caresses, and these lips, that kissed away Amfortas's soul's salvation! Corrupter! Away from me forever!" Kundry tells him to have a thought for her in his newfound empathy. He is her redeemer, for whom she has waited eternities. If he only knew the curse upon her! Once she saw him—and laughed! Now she seeks him from world to world, but each time she finds him, there is nothing but cursed laughter, and each time the sinner falls weakly in her arms. She cannot weep, only shout, rage, storm, rave for eternity. If she could unite with Parsifal for one hour, and weep on his breast, she would be redeemed!

But Parsifal understands that they would both be damned if he were to lie with her for one hour. He is, indeed, her redeemer, but in a very different way. She counters that it was her kiss that made him understand the world. Let her love him for an hour, and he will be like a god! Then, godlike, he can redeem her. He tells her that love and redemption are already hers if she shows him the way to Amfortas. "Never will you find him!" she hurls back, furious. And she will call on the same Spear against Parsifal if he insists on finding the king and abandoning her! He casts her away. She calls for help, and invokes the spirit of wandering, whom she knows so well, to descend on Parsifal. At that moment, Klingsor appears on the rampart, and hurls the Spear at Parsifal. It freezes above Parsifal's head. He seizes it and uses it to make the sign of the cross. The castle and the garden vanish. Kundry collapses, screaming. He mutters to her, "You know where you can find me again," and hurries off.

*Comment: The Kundry-Parsifal scene is usually called the emotional "crux" of the drama, and, indeed, it is practically the only scene in the work containing real human interaction and character development. It is masterly on every level. Kundry certainly knows how to appeal to men; first by mothering, then by promising deification. Her tale of Herzeleide is some of the most lyrical music in the opera, and many in the audience who have overindulged at intermission drift off. Parsifal's "Amfortas!" cry and subsequent narrative are the tenor's big moment. Anyone who is still asleep after that is fair game for Kundry. Telling of her plight, Kundry wallows in the lower registers until she hits a high Z on the world "laugh" (memories of Isolde!), which comes out of nowhere and can usually peel the wallpaper. Sometimes it's done lyrically, more often it's ghastly, but either way it's entirely effective.*

*In actuality, Kundry preps with a B-flat below middle C, inhales for two and a half beats, and blasts a high B, followed directly by a C-sharp below middle C. In other words, up one octave, down two octaves. Musicians of the time were startled, since they couldn't possibly assign this series of notes to any known scale (a common criticism of Wagner). In fact, it still sounds startling. These two measures are among the most insane in all music. Historians credit this moment as a major influence in what would be called the expressionist music of the subsequent century—those pieces by Alban Berg and others that sound to many people like notes flying all over the place. There's no doubt that Kundry's music opened many possibilities that would have just sounded "wrong" before Wagner came along. Perhaps even the octave* leaps in the Beatles' "I Wanna Hold Your Hand" and other popular songs owe something to this.

Kundry is often considered the "motivator" of this scene, which is true, but she also reveals much of her own psychology through her words and actions. Her segue from the death of Herzeleide to offering her own body to Parsifal as consolation illustrates her situation perfectly. Her sex instinct is part of her "will to life," which has kept her trapped in the Karmic cycle of birth/death/rebirth for a millennium. This is in opposition to Parsifal's offer of freedom through renunciation. Commentators usually understand this in terms of Schopenhauer's pessimistic denial of the life instinct, and, indeed, Parsifal advises her to "turn away" from her desires. He is offering her Nirvana through the transcendence of desire, a concept she cannot yet understand.

By the way, the Arabic source of the name Parsifal is pure, shall we say, invention on Wagner's part. Don't bother looking it up in your Arabic dictionary. It's just another one of Wagner's many name games.

The "Spear trick" at the end of the act is a nightmare for directors. Many choose this moment to shift from realism to impressionism, even if they had been super-earthy in the previous Flower Maidens scene. Wagner obliges by a trick of his own in the orchestra. When Klingsor appears, the lower strings are sawing in muddy tones appropriate to the evil magician. When he flings the Spear, there is a run from the harp. Musicians sometimes point to this as an uninspired moment on the part of Wagner the orchestrator, but what they fail to consider is that the effect works on the audience. The jarring intrusion of sweet harp sounds causes the spectators to "blink," so to speak, thus making them more vulnerable to whatever visual magic the production crew can conjure. This is a good example of an average operagoer being in a better position to judge something than the experts, who are often limited by the needs of their own field of expertise. The Spear trick, if done well, can still make the audience gasp.

## Act III

Scene: A beautiful spring meadow in the land of the Grail. There is a spring of water and a small hermit's hut.

### Prelude

**Comment:** *The sad, tired strains of the Prelude are meant to suggest all the wearisome years of Parsifal's wanderings that have passed since the end of the second act. The Prelude also sets the tone for Kundry, exhausted beyond all human endurance, and Gurnemanz, heavy with age. Even the brotherhood itself, we will find out, is spent. The music is Wagner at his most subtle and masterly.*

### Act III, Scene 1

A hideous groan is heard. Gurnemanz emerges from his hut to investigate, and finds Kundry half-buried beneath a thicket of winter thorns. He bids her to wake up and greet the spring, but she is motionless. He drags her out of the thorns, and tenderly chafes her to get some sign of life. At last she revives, gets up, and sets about doing small tasks like a serving woman, though still quite out of it. Gurnemanz asks her if she has nothing to say to him, not even thanks for having brought her back from death. Hoarsely, she croaks, "To serve! To serve!" He comments, more to himself than to her, that there's not much serving to be done these days. The knights don't go on glorious crusades anymore, so there are no messages to be carried. Every knight scours the forest for his own herbs and roots. He notes how changed the strange woman is. Perhaps the holiness of the day has brought this about. As she is carrying water from the spring, she silently draws his attention to a wanderer who has appeared, a knight in full armor, his face hidden by a visor.

**Comment:** *This brief scene can be quite touching. The reunion of Gurnemanz and Kundry is that of two very old people who, if they are not exactly friends as we understand the word, have come to under-*

*stand one another as central to each other's lives. Kundry's vocal role consists of two groans, one of her signature screams, and the single line "Dienen! Dienen!" She remains onstage through the entire third act without uttering another sound. It is "Diva as mime" from here to the end.*

Gurnemanz asks the knight who he is and, receiving no answer, assumes him to be under a vow of silence. The old man then says that he, too, has vows, and must tell the knight that it is blasphemous to appear in the realm of the Grail fully armed, and most of all on this holiest day. Among what heathens has the knight been living not to know that this is Good Friday? The knight complies, planting his Spear in the ground, removing his helmet, and kneeling in prayer before the Spear. Gurnemanz instantly recognizes the boy he once drove away, while Kundry nods that she, too, remembers Parsifal.

The knight and the old man greet each other gently. Parsifal explains that he has been wandering for years in search of Amfortas, and is probably still lost, since everything here seems so changed to him. He has been through numerous conflicts and battles, and suffered many wounds, but never did he strike back, and now he can truly claim to bring back, unprofaned, the Spear of the Holy Grail. Gurnemanz bursts out in rapture at the return of the undefiled Spear, and tells Parsifal how badly in need of its healing the knights of the Grail are. Amfortas, longing for death, has long since ceased to perform his holy duty of uncovering the Grail. The knights wander around the forest, living on common food, he himself is merely waiting for the end, and Titurel, denied the sight of the Grail, has already died. Parsifal bitterly accuses himself of causing all this distress, and almost faints.

Kundry fetches water, but Gurnemanz says he must be refreshed by the holy spring, and purified from his years of wandering. The armor is removed. Gurnemanz says Parsifal will be led to Amfortas this day, who has promised to uncover the Grail one last time to sanctify Titurel's funeral and atone for his death. Kundry, meanwhile, washes Parsifal's feet and anoints them with a phial of oil she has kept

in her bosom. She dries his feet with her hair. Gurnemanz anoints
Parsifal's head, greeting him as king. As his first act, Parsifal scoops
water out of the spring and baptizes Kundry, who appears to weep.
He looks at the meadow, wondering why it seems so uniquely beautiful today. "That," explains Gurnemanz, "is the magic of Good Friday." Parsifal asks why it is that every living thing does not weep on
this day of utmost grief. "You see that it is not so," replies Gurnemanz. Rather, all creation rejoices at the Savior's sign of love, and
gives thanks that nature itself regains its innocence on this day.
Kundry looks up at Parsifal. He sees that she, too, longs for redemption today, and kisses her on the forehead. Bells peal, and Gurnemanz says it is time to go to the Castle. Parsifal takes up the Spear,
and the three slowly walk on as the scene changes.

**Comment:** *By this point in the drama, the character of Parsifal has
transformed. He has now achieved wisdom through compassion—not
just for Amfortas, but for all. Yet the character remains his usual static
self throughout this scene, his one gesture being to baptize Kundry. A
tenor who can act, of course, can persuade us through gesture and
expression of Parsifal's growth, but a tenor who can act is only slightly
less rare than a flying chicken. (There have been some recent positive
developments in this area.) The score, however, leaves no doubts. This
scene is imbued with a sense of resignation and acceptance that is hard
to resist.*

*Kundry's washing of Parsifal's feet is a direct reference to Jesus.
Whether or not we are to see Parsifal as an analogue of Jesus, and there
is much debate on this point, it is clear that Kundry sees him as such.
This act is her atonement for her ancient sin. Seeing an actual baptism
on stage is difficult for people whose feelings about Christianity, pro or
con, run to the extreme but most can appreciate its relevance to the
drama.*

*Gurnemanz's discourse on the meaning of Good Friday dominates
this scene. The "Good Friday Spell" music is familiar from the radio
and the concert hall, albeit usually in its nonvocal form, which is a*

*great loss. Here Wagner has abandoned himself to an almost volup-*
*tuous expression of lyrical beauty.*

### Act III, Scene 2

The scene transforms again, as in the first act, to the domed Great
Hall of the Castle of the Grail. The knights enter the Hall, half of
them carrying Amfortas in his chair and the other half carrying the
coffin of Titurel. Both are placed in the center of the Hall. The
knights demand Amfortas perform his duty and uncover the Grail,
for the last time!

**Comment:** *The music for this transformation is reminiscent of the*
*first one, except that everything has gone haywire. There is a loud and*
*repeating descending figure in the orchestra, full of doom. The bells,*
*which were eerie but beautiful in Act I, are now menacing. The music*
*continues unbroken as the double procession of knights enters, their*
*voices seemingly out of tune with each other as their various choral*
*divisions repeat "For the last time!" in a state of near-hysteria. Wagner*
*comes very close to atonality in this scene, and the effect can be deeply*
*terrifying.*

Amfortas rejects the pleas, and, in bitter self-recrimination, tears
the lid off Titurel's coffin. The knights turn away with a cry, while
Amfortas begs his dead father to intercede with heaven and grant
him death. He tears open his garment and displays his bleeding
wound, begging the knights, who shrink away, to plunge their swords
into him and end his misery.

Parsifal, accompanied by Kundry and Gurnemanz, steps forward
and touches Amfortas's wound with the tip of the Spear. Amfortas is
healed instantly. Parsifal steps among the knights, holding the Spear
aloft, announcing, "The Holy Spear I bring back to you!" All gaze in
rapture. Parsifal commands the Grail be uncovered. The knights
kneel as the Hall grows dark, lit only from above, and the Grail itself
begins to glow. Quiet voices from the dome sing of the redemption of

the Redeemer. Kundry, gazing at Parsifal, falls lifeless to the ground. Parsifal waves the cup in blessing over the knights.

**Comment:** *A summary such as this can only suggest the mystical beauty of this scene. Its effect is heightened by contrast with the preceding scene of almost cosmic terror. All is fulfillment and completion here. The musical themes of the work that are associated with suffering and fear are transformed, while those representing faith are resolved. Shimmering strings accompany delicate harps to create the feeling of a new and sublime spirit descending on the Grail and its servants. (For more ideas about this implications of this scene, see "Lobby Talk for Parsifal," below.) It must also be remembered that this was Wagner's final creation. Certainly, after this scene, there could not have been much else to say.*

*It seems unfair, if typical of Wagner's stories, to kill Kundry off so gratuitously in the scene. Certainly Amfortas has longed for death as much as she, but the libretto clearly states that she dies while he lives. Many productions take liberties with this detail, either killing off Amfortas or keeping Kundry alive. Indeed, there are many ways to interpret the ending of Parsifal. Some show true insight into the music, others border on the insane (see "Productions," below).*

## BASICS: WHEN TO EAT, DRINK, AND VISIT THE RESTROOM

Face facts: You're going to have to shuffle your routine a bit for this one. Tell your office you're having an emergency (spiritual, if they must know), and leave by four o'clock (assuming it's a six o'clock curtain, which it usually is). Eat a light but high-protein meal, such as fish. Anything heavier is guaranteed to wipe you out cold for most of Act I. Have your coffee or tea early enough to avoid any unforeseen emergencies during the first act.

Which brings us to an important point. Whatever else you do, make sure you visit a restroom before arriving at the opera house. The line there will be around the corner, especially at the ladies' room. Even people who don't really need to go will stop in for form's sake ("just to be sure"), causing a panic or (in extreme cases) a stampede when the first bells summon the audience to their seats. If you haven't been to a restroom before you arrive, then you'll just have to get in line with the rest, even if it looks like the "last train to Marseilles" scene from *Casablanca*.

The first act of *Parsifal* is probably the single chunk of Wagner requiring the most attention in this department. It's true that both Act III of *Meistersinger* and Act I of *Götterdämmerung* are longer than this act, but they are different cases. The *Meistersinger* marathon is at the latter part of the evening, when the body has had a chance to settle down and relax, to put it mildly. For *Götterdämmerung* and *Parsifal*, the long stretch is at the beginning, when people have generally just arrived in their seats, out of breath after a dash through rush-hour traffic, and are attempting to sit perfectly still (perhaps for the first time that day) for more than two hours. The body has a way of sneaking its needs up on a person in such circumstances. *Parsifal* is the harder, though slightly shorter, of the two. Some fidgeting is expected in Act I of *Götterdämmerung*, with no real loss to the spectator. The Grail scene in Act I of *Parsifal*, however, is meant to be almost an out-of-body experience. The last thing anyone needs for full appreciation of the moment is the body's baser instincts reminding them so directly of their carnality.

There will be a reverse stampede to the restroom at the end of Act I, which may have been the real reason for the "no applause" tradition in the first place. Outsmart the hordes: find out from the usher or bartender beforehand how long the first intermission will be, and plan accordingly. Chances are there will be no need to rush. The first intermission tends to be very long—up to forty minutes—ostensibly to allow people time for refreshment. Another possible reason for the long intermission is that the soprano playing Kundry must be transformed from hag to vamp, and backstage personnel have been known to work overtime on this project.

Whatever the house's real reasons may be, the first intermission is an excellent time for an overpriced sandwich, cocktail, or cup of coffee. A refreshment of some sort at this point in the evening is an excellent way to move from the spirituality of the first act to the earthiness of the second. A word to the practical: even the most affected socialites have been seen pulling homemade sandwiches and snacks out of purses and jacket pockets at this juncture. It is a perfectly acceptable practice. Bananas, for some arcane reason, are always particularly in evidence. Some yuppies may think you are being cheap to follow this example, but most people will recognize you as a seasoned and smart operagoer. The problem is that the buffets in the opera houses often run out of food on such nights, in which case those who were too cool to pack their pockets with food are to be seen wolfing down mints or begging matrons for their sandwich scraps.

A Saturday matinee performance has its own pitfalls. Usually people tend to err by overindulging in morning coffee before the performance. You don't want a case of the jitters for this work any more than you want to overshoot your mark with alcohol or other sedatives. Basically, the same approach as the evening strategy will serve you well here: high-protein light food before, sustenance snacks for intermission, sensible consumption of both coffee and alcohol throughout the day.

If you happen to be attending a performance at Bayreuth, it need hardly be added, none of this is an issue.

## ROUGH SPOTS AND HOW TO GET THROUGH THEM

For many people, *all* of *Parsifal* is a "rough spot," and no guide in the world can help them get through it. For others (and they are a large number), the very idea that there are *longueurs* in *Parsifal* is unthinkable. For these, remember, this work is like a religious ritual, and to complain of dull parts would be akin to censuring the Sistine Choir for going on too long at a papal mass. What makes *Parsifal* unique is that there is hardly anybody in between these two camps. It remains either the pinnacle or the nadir for most operagoers.

Which is not very helpful to the newcomer. This guide has already pointed out a few places where the music is, shall we say, mellower than in other spots, and suggested strategies for approaching such scenes as Gurnemanz's first narration and the beginning of the Kundry-Parsifal encounter. There aren't really any recondite musical developments to listen for, as in *Tristan* or the *Ring,* nor are there many subtle dramatic developments to look for. Everything is *right there* in this work, if you are awake to hear it.

What *Parsifal* really requires for full enjoyment is a certain mindset. Rule number one: Relax! Wear comfortable clothes. Tell yourself that you are about to experience something that has no analogue, and don't compare it to other operas—even Wagner's. Savor the stillness. If you are an alpha-type personality who can never relax your brain, meditate on everything you know about the concept of Nirvana. If you still can't plug into this sort of world, listen to your own breathing during the parts that have lost you. When was the last time you did that? It may even create a heightened state of awareness, causing the transcendental scenes of this work to catapult you into a new dimension.

Don't laugh. There have been several instances of people having "experiences" of one sort of another during *Parsifal.*

## PRODUCTIONS: WHAT YOU MIGHT EXPECT TO SEE

Anything. Or, perhaps, nothing at all.

*Parsifal* is the story of a closed, crystallized community renewed by the spiritual development and compassion of an innocent individual. The success of any production depends on how well the contrasting states of decay and renewal are depicted in the course of the work. Obviously, there is much leeway.

Wagner chose the settings for the first production. He was moved by the interior of the Siena Cathedral when he saw it, thinking it the finest room in the world. The painter Paul von Joukovsky sketched the interior and designed the sets of the Grail Hall based on this space. The most notable features were a high dome (from which, in theory, the boys' choirs sang), supported on a circle of columns. This was the painted backdrop conservatives were ready to go to war to preserve in 1934. Klingsor's magic garden was based on the garden of the Palazzo Rufolo in Ravello, near Naples. In other words, the first production was a naturalistic re-creation of actual places (one could hardly expect otherwise in 1882), and yet a certain spiritual atmosphere was undeniable.

Nothing much changed in *Parsifal* productions until Wieland Wagner famously cleared off the stage in 1951, giving what amounted to a sound-and-light show. Although this was radical, it was clearly within the parameters of the work. In this case, darkness gave way to light. Nor are you likely to see any other approach to *Parsifal* than one in which dark/closed/dying give way to light/open/living. The details depend largely on which pet symbols the director and designer choose to use for this portrayal.

The moribund knights of the Holy Grail may be depicted as fascists, ecclesiastics, or others who are instantly recognizable as "arch-conservatives." This is almost too obvious to shock anybody any more. Most often, the production likes to create a new mythological space in which the eternal battle of old and new can be played out. Outer space, inner psyche—it's all been done, and it usually makes perfect sense.

Sometimes details of the libretto are altered to fit the statement being made. The biggest question mark in the whole affair, Kundry, is often the focus of these changes. As pointed out above, there's really no reason for her to die in the last scene, and some productions like to see her alive and participating in life at the end. Some take it another step, and have doors open, allowing women into the temple. Nice idea.

As for the Flower Maidens, well, kitsch remains kitsch, whether it's 1882 or the new millennium. Directors can never resist a little T & A in this scene, and the score truly begs for it. Expect lots of color, floating gauze, and female flesh in this scene, no matter what concept is being explored in the rest of the opera.

The meadow scene is invariably . . . a meadow, in one form or other. Karajan's famous Salzburg production of 1980 would be hard to beat for surreal realism. The meadow was studded with flowers— real ones, whose scent pervaded the auditorium through the scene.

The "Good Friday Spell" music has often been called "perfumed," but this performance was truly a multisensory treat.

## PERFORMANCE HISTORY AND ESSENTIAL LORE OF *PARSIFAL*

*The odd couple* (1880–82) King Ludwig arranged for the Munich Opera orchestra to go to Bayreuth for the *Parsifal* festival, which meant the conductor would be Hermann Levi, the Munich Kapellmeister. Wagner was irked that Levi, the son of a rabbi, would be the conductor for his most sacred work, yet he knew that Levi was the best man for the job. Some of the more fanatic Wagnerians were not so easily swayed, and they began to write letters and sign petitions against this "sacrilege." (As bad as Wagner was, a lot of his devotees have always been even worse.) In fact, Wagner thought himself quite enlightened about the whole question, even though he commented to Cosima that if he were a member of the orchestra, he would not want to be conducted by a Jew. Worse yet, Wagner sadistically made sure that Levi knew how much opposition there was to him. Levi offered his resignation. Wagner wrote one of his "why is everybody so temperamental?" letters, asking Levi to come to Wahnfried and get to know the Wagners "as we really are." He added that perhaps the experience of conducting *Parsifal* might occasion a great change in Levi's life (i.e., baptism), but continued to say, "In any case, you are my *Parsifal* conductor."

Apologists for Wagner's anti-Semitism often point to Levi in their defense of Wagner, usually omitting too much reference to this twisted letter. It should also be pointed out that Levi, although remaining true to his origins, was not immune from the self-loathing syndrome, and had publicly defended Wagner's pernicious pamphlet "Judaism in Music." But whatever Wagner's and Levi's *mishegoss* (the Yiddish term for craziness seems the only word for it), the superb fact remains that *Parsifal* was brought to life by a rabbi's son.

*Filling in the cracks* (1882) Wagner had determined that the Transformation Scenes in Acts I and III would be represented on stage by means of a cyclorama, one of those long painted canvas scrolls rolled from one drum to another to create the illusion of motion. The stage mechanics couldn't get the drums to move quickly enough, and informed Wagner that they needed four minutes of music to effect the scene change. At first, Wagner was amused. It wasn't often he was asked to make his works *longer*! Later, he complained about "composing by the yardstick," and handed the task over to a musical assistant. The assistant, who happened to be Engelbert Humperdinck (later the composer of *Hansel and Gretel*, not the Las Vegas singer), was mortified, but did his job. To his surprise, Wagner accepted the extra four minutes of music for inclusion in the first Transformation Scene. The mechanics eventually got the drums rolling faster, and Humperdinck's contribution was excised.

A *very special event* (1882) *Parsifal* was given at Bayreuth for sixteen performances in the summer of 1882, the first time the Festival House had been used since the *Ring* festival of 1876. Everything was different this second time. While there were fewer royals and glitzy types, musical Europe was there, and the rest of the audience was filled out with hard-core Wagnerians. Nor was there the same sense of disappointment that pervaded 1876. *Parsifal* was truly unlike anything anybody had seen or heard. Even the critics had nothing but superlatives for the singers, the chorus, the orchestra, the production, and, most of all, for Levi. Wagner called the conductor's performance "beyond praise." Perhaps most shocking of all—there was a profit left over after the festival!

A *Bayreuth exclusive* (1882–1903) Wagner always intended that *Parsifal* should be performed at Bayreuth—and absolutely nowhere else! The thought of this sacred work sharing a stage in repertory with other operas was more than he could bear. In fact, his greatest fear in accepting the Munich orchestra was not Levi, but the implication that the Munich opera would then have the right to perform the work in the capital. Ludwig, as usual, accommodated Wagner. *Parsifal* was only produced in Munich as one of the "private" performances for which Ludwig was becoming notorious. But nothing, not even the private entrance Wagner built in the Festival House to ensure the royal privacy, would get Ludwig to Bayreuth again. Pity. He never got to hear *Parsifal* in the house for whose miraculous acoustics it was specifically composed. Nor, if Wagner and Cosima had gotten their way, would anybody else have heard it outside of Bayreuth. There were concert performances in London in 1884 and New York in 1886, but Cosima held the copyright until 1913, and keeping *Parsifal* in Bayreuth became something of an obsession with her.

*Piracy* (1903) The United States was not bound by German copyright agreements, and only consideration for Cosima's sensibilities prevented the Metropolitan Opera of New York from producing *Parsifal*. This consideration bit the dust with the new century, and the Met prepared to present the work. Cosima went ballistic, writing letters, initiating law suits, appealing to honor—all to no avail. *Parsifal* was premiered at the Met on Christmas Eve, 1903 (as festive holiday entertainment, presumably). It was repeated for over 350 performances all around the United States over the next two years. Cosima effectively banished anyone who had anything to do with the New York production, and her wishes counted for something in her adopted country. The Met conductor, Alfred Hertz, was never again invited to conduct in Germany.

*Guarding the treasure* (1913) Well, there wasn't much one could do about America, but Germany was another matter. With the copyright on *Parsifal* set to expire on the last day of 1913, the Bayreuth forces went to war to save the work as a Bayreuth-only presentation. A petition to change the law specifically for *Parsifal* gathered thousands of signatures, including that of the ever-unpredictable Toscanini, and Richard Strauss lobbied the Reichstag in Berlin. Nothing changed, and the copyright lapsed. Now anybody was able to produce *Parsifal* anywhere and under any circumstances.

Many companies were waiting to see what would happen before investing in a *Parsifal* production of their own. Once the copyright expired, theaters scrambled to put together new productions from scratch, but by then it was too late. The war would soon shut down the theaters, and most cities had to wait quite a long time before seeing *Parsifal*.

*A delay in Saint Petersburg* (1913–97) Czar Nicholas II was one of the many fans who looked forward to seeing *Parsifal* at home, finding it rather inconvenient to attend a Bayreuth festival. He ordered a production to be mounted at the Maryinsky Theater after the copyright expired. The Maryinsky fudged a bit, and a rehearsal was given as a private performance for the czar and a few courtiers in 1913. The production never happened. The war put an end to all new productions, and then came the revolution. The Soviets, predictably, had no taste for *Parsifal*. The Russian premiere of the work was delayed until 1997.

*The ravages of time* (1934) Even with the copyright expired, the Bayreuth *Parsifal* remained authoritative. Nobody dared alter a single detail of the sacred original production, except for the Flower Maidens scene, which was constantly revised, never satisfying anyone. But the Grail Hall set was considered perfect. To change it would be sacrilege—especially at the very shrine committed to opposing such blasphemies!

Never mind that production values and capabilities had changed drastically in the previous half-century, and that the old painted backdrops, fluttering in the breeze, were embarrassingly out-of-date. Never mind the supreme irony of *Parsifal*, the story of a petrified community in need of renewal, becoming similarly fossilized. The old guard could not stomach the idea of a new *Parsifal*. (Photographs of the original sets are used in the 1982 film *Parsifal*, directed by H. J. Syberberg, making some sort of statement or other.)

The new head of the festival, the notorious Winifred Wagner, saw that a new production must be mounted, no matter what anybody, Wagners included, might say. Alfred Roller, a great designer of the Vienna Secession movement (and aesthetic idol of Hitler) was personally recommended by the Führer for the new production. It bombed. Those who wanted real innovation were disappointed, while there was never any pleasing the arch-conservatives.

*Try, try again* (1937) Winifred scrapped Roller's production and gave the job of designing the next *Parsifal* to her twenty-year-old son Wieland. The result was no more successful. Wieland's original *Parsifal* was hopelessly traditional to the point of being "retro." Within fifteen years, people would laugh at the thought of ever calling Wieland a conservative.

*Ideologies* (1939) It was all a moot point within two years of Wieland's production. The Nazi bureaucracy banned *Parsifal* in Germany for the duration of the Third Reich, without stating a reason. Hitler might have intervened, but never did. *Parsifal* was not one of his favorites. The result was that, once again, it was possible to see this work in New York but not in Germany—not even in Bayreuth this time!

*The clueless conductor* (1951) When Wieland Wagner staged his revolutionary *Parsifal* in 1951, one assumed he would have worked closely with the conductor, who would naturally have been in complete agreement with the spirit of the production. Such was not the case. Hans Knappertsbusch was a worthy conductor, but utterly out of synch with Wieland's intentions. When the famously conservative Knappertsbusch was asked how he could participate in such an "abomination," he replied that, all during rehearsals, he assumed the sets had not yet arrived. Winifred Wagner, who had been banished from the running of the festival because of her association with Hitler, said she assumed her son Wieland was out of money, and therefore left the stage empty.

## LOBBY TALK FOR *PARSIFAL* (BOY MEETS GRAIL)

If people have come up with wildly differing meanings for the *Ring*, they have pushed all bounds of sanity with their interpretations of *Parsifal*. The bare bones of the story are beyond dispute: this is the tale of a community whose once lofty ideals are now fossilized in decadence, subsequently renewed by contact with an innocent individual who has become wise through compassion. After that, one can think anything.

One traditional interpretation is plausible yet difficult to consider. The last line of the libretto has heavenly voices proclaiming that "the Redeemer is redeemed." What could this possibly mean? Does it refer to Parsifal as the redeemer, and, if so, had he not already been redeemed earlier in the drama? Or has something changed in the nature of *the* Redeemer, Jesus? The latter is implied, at the very least. Wagner, in his later years, spoke much of Jesus, to the consternation of Nietzsche and many others. He even ultimately rejected the racial theories of Count Gobineau because they did not take into account the transcendental power of Jesus to unite humanity.

However, the Jesus of Wagner's imagination is very different from the one familiar through Christianity. Wagner's Jesus was an individual who was godlike because of a perfect compassion, quite unique in essence and not specific to a historical setting. In other words, Wagner had to disconnect Jesus from Judaism. For all his admiration for Jesus, or whoever he imagined Jesus to be, Wagner could not accept any Jewish identity of Jesus, and felt that Christianity would be flawless if limited to the Gospels. While many modern Christians feel more comfortable with the voice of the Gospels than that of, say, the warlike Book of Joshua, Wagner was letting his prejudice overpower his intellect. He didn't know the Old Testament, nor did he want to. Cosima's *Diaries* record that Wagner's entire study of the Old Testament amounted to two days of cursory reading, after which he pronounced the whole work as worthless. Parsifal succeeds Amfortas, who is weak from having "screwed around" with Judaism in the form of Kundry. The community to be renewed is Christianity itself, and the renewal is based on a blind disregard for history and context that borders chillingly on genocide. This particular interpretation of *Parsifal* as a plea for the purging of Judaism from Christianity (an undertaking that is like purging water from the ocean) can be and has been supported by various citations of Wagner's writings, and there may well be some truth in it.

Yet it is an insufficient summary of the work. If Wagner had wanted us to see the work in this way, it seems likely that he would have said so explicitly in one of his many writings. And if this be the "message" of *Parsifal*, then we may be thankful that Wagner's thoughts on the subject were incomplete and ambivalent enough to be shrouded in a symbology that is so open to other interpretations. Nor was this interpretation enough to make *Parsifal* acceptable to the ideologues of the Third Reich, who banned the work anyway.

Besides the racial theories that people have seen in *Parsifal*, there is also a sexual reading of it that won't go away. Charles Osborne thought the work was possibly "a celebration of high-minded homosexuality." It's hard to know how he and others who agree with him arrive at this conclusion, unless it's because Parsifal does not perform the conventional tenorial function of screwing the prima donna when he has the chance in Act II. More likely, those who suspect a latent homosexuality of *Parsifal* are thinking of the closed, all-male world of the knights. Certainly *Parsifal* is guilty of misogyny (as is every other opera—bar *none!*), but to equate misogyny with homosexuality is pernicious, ignorant, and at least fifty years out of style. One must also ask why Wagner, of all people, would glorify homosexuality. One hopes these scholars are not basing this on the composer's weakness for pink satin. No, the likelier explanation is that Wagner was despicable, so he must have been homosexual also. Well, he wasn't. Yet the otherwise lucid Robert Gutman is able to see a connection between the monastic knights and "the fellowship of Ernst Röhm's troopers," referring to the Nazi Brownshirts. Such are the dangers of reading history backward.

Yet *Parsifal*, as has been stated, is pleasing to people of various religious backgrounds, including no religious background whatsoever. What is it that Wagner has hit upon with his piece that gives it such universality? One answer is in the myth behind the story, and in Wagner's treatment of it.

It is an ancient and universal belief that the virility of the sacred king is directly related to the fertility of the land. If the king is impotent or sterile—that is, if he is incapable of insemination—the land itself will be barren. This is a theme of T. S. Eliot's *The Waste Land*.

The regeneration of the land is echoed in the heavens as well. One of the most universal and primal fears is the fear that the sun won't rise. This is merely the fear of darkness, felt by everyone at one time or another, projected to the cosmic level. To ensure the daily regeneration of the sun, societies instituted sacrifices. Performing the sacrifice guarantees regeneration of the sun. Each sunrise and each springtime awakening of the land is an analogue and promise of resurrection. In Tenochtitlán, Aztec priests performed human sacrifices before sunrise to sate the serpent god Quetzalcoatl so he would not feed off Huitzlipochtli the sun god and so diminish the sun's life-giving power just when it is about to rise again.

In ancient, Egypt, a culture plainly obsessed with the afterlife, the festival of Opet was celebrated by the Pharaoh and his consort in the spring, when they entered the precincts of the Temple of Amon-Ra at Luxor, and the consort masturbated the Pharaoh, spilling his sacred seed on the grounds of the inner sanctum to ensure the fertility of the land. Note that this was done in the Temple of Amon-Ra, the sun god. The continuum was obvious to the Egyptians: the sustained virility of the king—the regeneration of the land—the daily rising of the sun—and the resurrection of the body.

This association of phenomena is only slightly less obvious in the Christian tradition. The implicitly sexual language used in the Roman Catholic liturgy, including the word "resurrection" itself, bears witness to the ancient and persisting fears about darkness, barrenness, and the death from which there is no sequel. The mystery of faith, intoned by the congregation, assures that "rising, You restored our life," or, alternately, "Christ has died, Christ is risen, Christ will come again." Christ is the "sacrifice" whose blood has "conquered darkness." The blood sacrifice that ensures the sunrise and the life-giving virility of the sacred king are both united in the person of Christ. For the faithful who seek resurrection for themselves, the "Sacrifice" (so it is called three times in the Catholic liturgy of the word) of the Eucharist must be performed repeatedly.

In *Parsifal*, Amfortas the sacred king is impotent in his own person (he has lost the Spear, for starters) and is furthermore incapable of performing the sacrifice of the Eucharist for the benefit of the community. In Act I, Titurel commands Amfortas to perform the office of the love feast because he himself is too feeble ("*schwach*") to do it. By Act III, the situation is critical. Titurel is dead, the land is barren, there is no chance of resurrection for the knights or the land, and the Great Hall is dark. The knights, in near-panic, command Amfortas to perform the service "for the last time." The stage directions inform us at this point that Amfortas can only "raise himself a little" ("*ein wenig aufrichtend*"). The terror depicted in the music, with near-atonality and the bells pealing with finality, is not the mere terror of personal death, much less annoyance at Amfortas for failing his duty. It is the all-encompassing fear that the sun won't come up.

Parsifal, a type of Christ (which he clearly is, no matter what waffling Wagner did on the subject), restores the community by returning the sacred Spear. A transformed suffering motif is then heard. The suffering motif is developed out of the first theme heard in the Prelude (which Wagner called "faith") and one continually associated with Amfortas and the barrenness of the land. It is a progression up a minor scale for six notes, "falling" back down several notes before it can resolve itself in the climactic seventh note, which would complete the scale. At the point in the opera when Parsifal returns with the upheld sacred Spear, the motif continues to rise up the scale and breaks through, so to speak, to the climactic seventh note, which the orchestra then celebrates with the shimmering cascade figures of a pure faith motif. It is an elegant orgasm in slow motion.

It is also a great deal more. The libretto specifies that Parsifal's ability to perform the sacrifice causes the Great Hall to be suffused with brilliant light shining from above. The continuation of life is assured. The sun will rise again. By addressing these issues of eternal significance to people, and by doing so in a musical idiom that had never been previously employed and that has not been equaled since, and by daring, in our modern era, to present a picture of hope and fulfillment, *Parsifal* can be an experience unlike any other in the performing arts.

## ENDNOTE: WHEN TO APPLAUD

A very wise friend once gave the following advice to a person attending her first performance of *Parsifal*. "Oh, it's easy," he said. "All you need to know is don't applaud after the first act and don't laugh if the Spear trick doesn't work." Setting aside flippancy for the moment, the issue of applause in this work is important because it gets to the nature of the work itself. What, exactly, is *Parsifal* and what is the most plausible response to this most unusual piece?

The standard custom is to allow the curtain to fall on Act I in silence. In New York, the conductor approaches the podium in total darkness before the Prelude and is not greeted by an ovation. (In Bayreuth, the conductor is never greeted by the audience for the simple reason that he is not visible in the covered pit.) Both subsequent acts are treated conventionally. The conductor is greeted by an ovation upon entering the pit, the orchestra rises, and there are the standard curtain calls after the acts are finished.

How did this all come about?

Wagner felt the first act, with its Hall of the Grail scene, was too sacred to be applauded. Moreover, he did not intend to part the curtain for bows at the end of Act I. This was interpreted by his devotees to mean that there would be no applause at all in *Parsifal*, which was never his intention. Whatever the many defects of the man's character, he was often generous in his praise of the singers who went to such lengths to create his music dramas. *Parsifal*, with its extraordinary length, assuredly warranted applause.

In fact, Wagner was so impressed with the singing of his Flower Maidens at the first performance that he shouted a lusty "Bravo!" People in the audience turned to shush the Philistine who would so desecrate this sacred experience, unaware that it was Wagner himself!

Wagner was not the last person to get hissed for making inappropriate noise at *Parsifal*. It often happens that some poor suckers who didn't do their homework begin applauding as the curtain descends, only to be quelled by the control freaks around them who end up making a lot more noise shushing than the applauders themselves

would have made. Occasionally, there is someone who likes expressing disapproval of the silence tradition by shouting "Bravo!" at the top
of his lungs, whether the performance warranted it or not. Then
there are the no-nonsense people of Houston and a few other places,
who happily applaud every curtain and every entrance of the conductor and don't give a second thought to silly old taboos.

At Bayreuth, as you may well imagine, there is never any need for
anyone to shush an applauder at the end of Act I. The silence is profound and all-encompassing. Nobody seems to breathe, much less
applaud. The audience floats out to intermission in pious stillness as
if transfigured.

The tradition has fluctuated at Bayreuth over the years. After Wagner attempted to clarify the situation, the festival audiences held their
applause at the end of the first act, but then applauded at the end of
Acts II and III. In the 1920s and 1930s, there was no applause whatsoever. (The "no applause at all" rule was traditional in New York in the
first three decades of the century. Perhaps Met audiences felt a tinge
of guilt over their "pirated" production.) No one was sure what to do
through the 1950s, until finally the program for the 1967 Bayreuth festival printed an outline of what was expected. The original "first act,
silence; everything else, standard" policy became the norm there as
well as in Vienna, London, New York, and other cities, which had
also fluctuated.

Many people understandably find all this tradition and reverence
ridiculous. Why should such foolishness be reserved for this opera
(whatever else it may be), alone among all those written since 1597? If
it is so sacred, they say, then let it be sung in a church and let Holy
Communion be extended to the audience at the appropriate
moments in the score. After all, they rightly point out, overtly sacred
music is applauded after it is performed, sometimes even in religious
buildings.

Once again, one must fall back on the excuse that this line of reasoning is based on logic, which does not often apply in the opera
house. The experience of attending an opera—any opera—is
drenched in traditions and customs that are in no way necessary to
the appreciation of the work itself, as is the experience of attending a

baseball game or a rock concert, for that matter. The reverent silence at the end of Act I of *Parsifal* is of the same order.

Furthermore, it works, or it never would have become a tradition in the first place. The Grail scene is quite otherworldly, with its long silences, eerie lighting, and unseen choirs and bells. Applause at the end would feel superfluous and unnatural. It's a better idea to save your excitement for the beginning of Act II, when the conductor and orchestra are usually greeted with a stirring ovation (unless, of course, it's Bayreuth), which is wholly in keeping with the very earthy ambience of the following act.

If Act I is too ethereal for conventional methods of appreciation, why then does the audience applaud after Act III, which is, if anything, even farther removed from mundane reality than the first act? Apparently, silence was practiced in New York for a while at midcentury, but it simply didn't work. For one thing, the audience wants to show its appreciation for the artists on stage and in the pit, who have at the very least been working hard for six solid hours. More important is the need to break the spell, so to speak, of the final scene. While something approaching an out-of-body experience may be delightful in the opera house itself, one must prepare to reenter the real world. Whatever Wagner's lofty goals may have been, we are the people who must face the hazards of driving home, taking a city bus or subway, or even walking down the treacherous Green Hill of Bayreuth after the performance. A gut-level "Bravo!" or two shouted from your seat in the house is a good way to get ready for life after *Parsifal.*

# PART THREE

# EXPLORING

# WAGNER

# Wagner Issues:
## Vegetarianism, Antivivisectionism, and Anti-Semitism

◆

The personality of any other artist may or may not be relevant to a full appreciation, but with Wagner, there is no getting around the issue. His life and his thought are all over his art. Knowing something about him is crucial to the experience of his work.

By all accounts, Wagner was an impossible human being. Even his devotees acknowledge this, although they allow him his defects as attributes of one who was too great to be judged by mortal standards. In the popular imagination, Wagner has been judged guilty of every sin known. People who know little about his music can tell you that he had an uncontrollable libido (not true), that he used everyone in his path (somewhat true, although most were begging to be used), and that he felt entitled to whatever he desired (absolutely true).

There is a problem in dismissing Wagner as pathologically antisocial; he was much more interesting than that. His virulent anti-Semitism, his prodigality, and his genius for alienating people, for example, are rendered even more twisted, and much more fascinating, by his obsessive relationships with Jewish people, his financial generosity, and his ability to charm people. He was a complicated and deeply disturbed individual.

Books have been written on the subject. Besides the biographies, there are scores of character analyses by psychologists and others who have tried to come to terms with his personality. The reader will find some of these outlined in the "Wagner in Print" chapter. What follows here is the barest summary of various aspects of Wagner as a person. It is not going to be pretty.


## NATIONALISM

Wagner wrote constantly about the meaning of being German, contradicting himself several times along the way. German identity has always been a puzzle, especially before there was any actual country by that name. What is Germany? More specifically, *where* is Germany? This issue remains on the front pages of newspapers today.

As a kind of parlor game, Wagner and Cosima were in the habit of discussing the greats of art and history, and debating who was greater than whom. Was Shakespeare greater than Dante? How did Calderón and Lope de Vega stack up? And what about in music? Who's on top, Gluck or Weber? The *Diaries* are filled with this stuff. You might ask, Who cares? Well, they cared a great deal. They appeared to be quite incapable of appreciating various artists for their diverse accomplishments. Everything had to be understood as part of a hierarchy, they were only interested in "the greatest."

This comes through in their "ranking" of races and nations. The historic problem with German nationalism always lies in the fact that the homeland must be praised at the expense of other nations. In other words, the loudest German patriots have only rarely been able to glorify their own nation and leave it at that. This is not unique to Wagner. Nietzsche, Goethe, Luther, and countless others have indulged in the same vice. Gutenberg's Bible proclaims on its frontispiece that it was printed in Germany, the land that God has graced "above all others" in art and learning. This problem goes way back.

For Wagner, the issue was one of culture rather than pure politics. His obsessive nationalism was founded on one idea—that the Italians and the French had developed true cultures whereas the Germans had been thwarted from fulfilling their cultural destiny by slavish imitation of Italian and French models. His next notion was that Germans in his time were being further retarded by the influence of the Jews, whose infiltration into German society was stunting "true" German culture before it had any chance to develop.

Wagner was not imagining German cultural debasement. The Germany into which he was born was in many ways a cultural colony of France and Italy. Throughout the eighteenth century, German courts spoke French, ate French food (when possible), and lived in buildings intended to be, in some sense, French. The problem was that it was never very convincing. Anyone who has toured the Neue Schloss at Potsdam or Schloss Charlottenburg in Berlin can concur that there is nothing quite so bizarre as Prussians imitating the French. Those German buildings never quite soar the way their French models do. The right spirit is missing.

Then there are the Italians. While the Italians did not present the military threat to Germany that the French did, their cultural supremacy was at least as great. First, there was the question of religion. Wagner was zealously anti-Catholic, but not because he was any model Protestant. His gripe was that Catholicism was inherently Latin and therefore fundamentally un-German. For an Italian to pray in the Latin language was an affirmation of heritage, while for a German to do so he perceived as a rejection of heritage. Consider the kingdom of Saxony, where Wagner was born. Due to the bizarre edicts of the various peace treaties concluded by the European powers over the years, the king of Saxony and his court were Catholic, while the Saxon people were entirely Lutheran. It was an insane situation. Then there was the elegant Saxon capital of Dresden, where Wagner was in charge of music at the theater as well as at the court (Catholic) chapel. Dresden was famed for its collection of Italian art, its Italian-designed palaces, and its largely Italian opera company. All this on the banks of the Elbe River!

Now think of Hans Sachs's final monologue, where he warns about "foreign influences." The German word is *welscher*, which implies foreign in a Latin (French or Italian) sense. Sachs's nationalism may be noxious, but his caution against foreign influences under which "no prince will understand his people" is no idle paranoia. (Incidentally, it is the word *welscher* that one commentator, Charles Osborne, translates plainly as "French." Osborne goes on to say that this line is especially evil since it inspired Hitler's policy of eradicating French culture. This is exactly the sort of irresponsible nuttiness that keeps us from truly confronting the evil in Wagner's thought. Furthermore, it shows an ignorance of the character of Hitler, who, for all he may have damaged French culture, loathed Berlin, worshipped Paris, and said bluntly that his favorite building in the world was the Paris Opéra!)

A nation without geographical borders must be defined by race, a fact proven by the continued existence of the Jews. The Germans tended to attribute their cultural debasement to political realities, but the flourishing of Jewish culture was a reproof to gentile Germans.

## ANTI-SEMITISM

If you mention the name Richard Wagner to the average person, the first adjective they will associate with it is "anti-Semitic." This is not a gratuitous association. Wagner was intensely and obsessively anti-Semitic, growing more so as the years passed until it appeared to be almost the only thing he thought about. History is full of anti-Semites, but few who made it so much a part of their lives as Wagner.

The first targets of Wagner's anti-Semitism were individuals, but this quickly devolved into a pseudo-theory of everything that was wrong with Judaism, and the problem this posed for Germany. We have already seen how Wagner's resentment of Meyerbeer (and, to a certain extent, Mendelssohn) found expression in the pamphlet "Judaism in Music." The composer Halévy also informed Wagner's demonography. Halévy and Wagner were on agreeable social terms during the Paris years, and the agreeable and modest Halévy once said he had no idea why he was so successful with the Parisian public. Wagner understood this comment to mean Halévy was merely composing for the money, and praised him for being the first Jew he had ever met who was honest enough to admit it. The publisher Maurice Schlesinger and the critic Eduard Hanslick came within the sights of Wagner's guns, and Wagner disparaged Heinrich Heine, a witty writer to whom Wagner was indebted for, among other things, much of the story of *The Flying Dutchman*.

These were among Wagner's perceived Jewish enemies from real life. In Wagner's characters, there is the case of Beckmesser in *Meistersinger*, who is clearly a dig at Hanslick but who was also dangerously perceived as an implied dig at Jewish music in general. (Here, logic really begins to fall apart. Some early listeners perceived a satire of synagogue singing in Beckmesser's serenade. That's a stretch. Besides, Beckmesser's defining characteristic is pedantry. What is so pedantic and rule-bound about Jewish music?) About *Parsifal*, one can say anything and get away with it, so we cannot hope to summarize anti-Semitic views of that work. Suffice to say that many have seen it, and continue to see it, as a plea for a purification of the world from Jewish influence. The last important Wagner character of this category is Alberich. Many anti-Semites chose to see Alberich as the prototypical Jewish capitalist, sworn off love and dedicated solely to wealth and power. (Again, Marx's view of the Jewish role in European society was dangerously close to this as well.) In each case, Wagner had of course written fictional characters, and people read their own agendas into them. However, and this point must be stressed, Wagner never lifted a finger to contradict any of these hypotheses.

Many apologists for Wagner point to his several important friendships with Jewish individuals: Samuel Lehrs, Catulle Mendès, and Karl Tausig, his companion and copyist in the Vienna years. In the Bayreuth years, there was Wagner's invaluable assistant, the brilliant Josef Rubinstein, who lived at Wahnfried, and of course Hermann Levi. Rubinstein and Levi both seem to have some conflicts about their backgrounds, so they might not be the best alibis available. There was also the impresario Angelo Neumann, who did so much to promote Wagner's works outside of Bayreuth. This interesting person seems to have been comfortable with his own Judaism, even to the point of making gentle jibes on the subject in his letters to Wagner and Cosima (who were not amused). As invaluable as Neumann became to Wagner, however, he never became part of the Bayreuth inner circle.

The fact that "some of his best friends were Jewish" does little to exculpate Wagner from his anti-Semitism. It does, however, make us wonder what the exact nature of his problem was. Psychologists and cultural historians struggle with the issue to this day.

It is also interesting to note how Wagner distanced himself from the institutionalized anti-Semitic movement in Germany in the 1870s and 1880s. There was a famous incident in which Pastor Stroecker, an insanely anti-Semitic and enormously popular and influential Lutheran preacher in Berlin, circulated a petition asking the Reichstag to rescind Jewish emancipation laws it had recently passed. Wagner refused to have anything to do with Stroecker's petition or his movement, and said so publicly. Wagner was evasive on his motivations, however, stating merely that he had lost all faith in governments and that the problem was not one that had a political solution. One person who did sign the petition, expecting Wagner and the whole Bayreuth crowd to follow suit, was Hans von Bülow, who was especially embittered by Wagner's noncompliance. It was around this time that Bülow made his miserable joke that he would have had more professional success with Wagner if he had gotten himself circumcised.

Whatever else was going on in the murky mind of Richard Wagner, his main point, made over and over again in his writings, was that Germans had failed to develop their own national culture. In other words, the same problem that Germans faced regarding the French and the Italians was magnified with the Jews, who actually lived among the Germans. Personal and communal insecurity of identity is at the root of his whole problem. This is not intended to exonerate—there is no exoneration—but merely to understand the problem in context. It explains how Wagner was able to say, in his 1881 essay "Know Thyself" (which is yet another exhortation to the Germans to identify and nurture a national culture), that the Jews were "probably the noblest race of all." Jews, Wagner understood well, *knew* who they were.

## VEGETARIANISM

When Friedrich Nietzsche first arrived for dinner at Wagner's home in Tribschen, he announced that he was a vegetarian. "You are an ass," was Wagner's typically blunt reply. In the following years, vegetarianism, or at least the concept of it, began to loom large in Wagner's life and thought. In fact, it became one of the mainstays of his confused, confusing creed.

Wagner's view of history (based on the intense study of everything other than history itself, which he rarely read) led him to believe that the two main causes of racial degeneration were intermarriage and meat-eating. There's no use wondering where he got these ideas—they don't come from anywhere. But this is what he thought. His private newspaper, the *Bayreuther Blätter*, and the essays of his last six years base much of their arguments on this assumption.

This has led people to assume, naturally, that Wagner was a vegetarian. Biographers tend to write around the issue, but people remember that two of Wagner's foremost fans, George Bernard Shaw and Adolf Hitler, were both vegetarians. Now that Cosima's *Diaries* are available, it is apparent that Wagner never actually became a vegetarian himself. He talked about it, but continued to eat meat. At one point, he considered an all-dairy diet, surely the most unusual remedy ever devised against the chronic flatulence from which he suffered.

The interesting point here is the huge disparity between what Wagner wrote and what he actually did, a disparity that plays into his anti-Semitic writings as well. Wagner always appeared to be shocked when Jewish people expressed concern about working with him. Remember his letter to Levi after the critical point of the *Parsifal* fracas—a fracas that Wagner went out of his way to rub in Levi's face: "Come [to Wahnfried] and get to know us as we really are." Wagner felt no more compunction about writing this line than he felt about eating steak while preaching the evils of meat-eating. He was, as was stated at the beginning of the chapter, utterly impossible.

Cosima's *Diaries* are strangely reticent on the whole subject of food. Of course, she writes about art and music and the creation of great masterpieces, so one forgives her for omitting such mundane details as what was on the lunch table. Yet she does spend paragraphs telling us what medicines everybody in the family was taking, other trivia such as disagreement with the gardener, and an excruciatingly detailed account of the daily progress of Wagner's digestive system. It is almost as if she were more interested in food as it left the body than as it entered.

The few references she does make to eating are strange. Once, she records that Richard ate a beefsteak for lunch, and makes no further mention of the matter. The two other references to flesh-eating are intriguing, and she only makes them because Wagner felt unwell afterward. The first was after he ate salami in Pisa, and the second after he ate shellfish in Palermo. Both times she refers to these meals as "dietary lapses."

It's enough to make one wonder if Wagner was secretly keeping kosher for some diabolical reasons of his own! Certainly, many people who keep kosher, when eating with nonkosher people, simplify the whole matter by saying that they are "basically vegetarian." This is not meant as a serious suggestion based on years of scholarship—merely a passing observation on the strange lives of the Wagners. Besides, it would explain a lot, wouldn't it? At the least, it would explain what Wagner meant to Levi when he said "as we really are," and why he would even consider an all-dairy diet.

## ANTIVIVISECTIONISM

The third mainstay of Wagner's pseudo-philosophy, after anti-Semitism and vegetarianism, was antivivisectionism. This debate over whether it was ethical to dissect live animals in the interests of science was a huge issue in Wagner's time, and is scarcely less so even in our own. Wagner prided himself on his love of animals (notwithstanding that his dog Robber, it will be recalled, ran away from him *twice*). Those who advocated scientific progress at any price, and they were many in the late nineteenth century, thought antivivisectionism was an unaffordable sentiment. Wagner came to loggerheads on this issue with the crown princess of Prussia, who was firmly in the camp of the vivisectionists. They had previously disagreed over the Jewish issue. Apparently, they were not the only two in Germany who sensed a connection between these issues.

Wagner said there was no hope for the German Reich as long as vivisectionism continued. His ideal of Germany was an Aryan brotherhood without Jews, without meat, and without live-animal dissections. One wonders why he didn't seek his Utopia somewhere in northern India, where he might have found such a place already in existence, but this never occurred to him. In any case, given the disparity between his words and his actions on the first two subjects, we might wonder if Wagner also secretly dissected live animals in the basement of Wahnfried.

## RICHARD WAGNER, ARCHFIEND

The poet Auden summed it up best when he called Wagner "a regular shit." Yes, this is the same Auden who concluded that Wagner probably was, all things considered, the greatest artist in history. Auden did not make either of these remarks irresponsibly; he thought about the subject a great deal before arriving at these conclusions. The subject requires serious thinking, and the reader is urged to consult the "Wagner in Print" chapter for more information. Arriving at ill-informed conclusions on the subject of Wagner is all too easy, and presents its own dangers.

Wagner, the man, has become symbolic of everything evil in the world. His anti-Semitism and his Aryan chauvinism, bad as they were in and of themselves, can hardly be separated now from the atrocities committed by the Third Reich. In addition to this, he is notorious, even among people who do not listen to his music, as little more than a thief, a user of men for their money and their wives, and the supreme example of the artistic megalomaniac.

No argument from this writer. The problem, however, arises in isolating Wagner as *the* archfiend of modern cultural history. This has the unhealthy effect of exonerating everyone else. For example, as long as we unthinkingly associate Richard Wagner with Nazism (anachronistic as this may be), then we don't need to worry so much about such composers as Carl Orff (whose music we hear in every other film score and TV commercial) and Richard Strauss, who was, by all accounts, such an agreeable fellow. In all fairness, there is an occasional buzz about the political associations of Strauss and Orff, but it is hardly on the Wagnerian level. The next production of *Der Rosenkavalier* in your area will probably not be accompanied by any apologia in the local paper. The next production of *Die Meistersinger* will. The 1995 Metropolitan production of *Meistersinger* was greeted by the local papers with articles seeking to separate the journalists' love of the music from their hatred of the man. Fine, even though nothing new or helpful was said. What is ironic about this is that Charles Dickens's *A Christmas Carol*, whose entire premise, it could be argued, is implicitly anti-Semitic, was playing at the same time just down the street, and was marketed as "perfect family entertainment." There were no articles questioning this. *A Christmas Carol* was acceptable as long as *Meistersinger* was decried.

Was there a newspaper article decrying Debussy's treatment of women the last time his music was performed in your area? The fact is that he abused his feeble mistress to death, even while he composed stunning music. Would anyone blame women, or even men, for boycotting his music because of this? Yet one never reads about this. Nor does the issue stop at artists. Do people who drive Ford automobiles question the anti-Semitism of Henry Ford? It was there, God knows. What about Mercedes-Benz and its active role in the Holocaust? And yet owning a Mercedes remains the goal of many yuppies who wouldn't be caught dead at a Wagner opera.

As long as you know you're supposed to disdain Wagner, you can get away with a lot of other sins. This is the real problem with isolating Wagner as the archfiend of history.

## SO WHAT DO WE DO WITH ALL THIS?

Many people no doubt wish Wagner's operas would just disappear, taking the memories they carry of the entire painful twentieth century along with them. This will not happen. The work of Richard Wagner is too good—that is, it still speaks humanely to too many people.

There is concern that the music itself carries a toxic message, and that repeated listening cannot fail to produce an evil effect. This is giving Wagner too much credit. Art does not create good or evil. Worrying about the effect of Wagner's music is the same sort of reverse thinking that accuses the Beatles and the Bible for the murders committed by Charles Manson.

Most people just say they appreciate the music, and ignore any messages they don't like. The artist who created it is a separate issue from the art. The critics are always seeking to exonerate themselves from suspicion if they praise Wagner. It's getting tiresome. Also, we have seen in the work of Robert Gutman and others that the "love the art, hate the artist" position is only tenable up to a point. History is full of good people but there's only one Wagner, and this is more than a damned unlucky quirk of fate. Productions that cosmetically address the issues of racism, chauvinism, and anti-Semitism aren't helping either. Denial never solves anything for long.

It would be great if Wagner's operas became the touchstone for real, meaningful dialogue about the issues they bring up. In other words, instead of writing holier-than-thou articles in the papers condemning the horrific thoughts of Richard Wagner, wouldn't it be excellent if people questioned how much of this toxicity has permeated the rest of our culture? For example, if flag-waving is pernicious at the end of *Lohengrin*, why is it acceptable at the Democratic and Republican national conventions? Is Hans Sachs's final monologue fundamentally different from any immigration debate on the floor of Congress? What do people really mean when they use such words as "nation," "people," and "freedom" (or *Reich, Volk,* and *Freiheit*)? Under what guises do people express anti-Semitism today? Have we really superseded assumptions about racial theories? After all, most of

Wagner's racial theories were based on ideas developed by the French aristocracy, who bear no small responsibility for the development of proto-fascist racial notions. But don't most Americans still subscribe to these same ideas? Don't people still talk about coming from a "good family"? If there is any doubt about this, let the reader consider the popular obsession with royalty and titled celebrities. Those titles are based on the same racial theories that led Wagner to some of his worst notions.

Imagine if people would attend performances of Wagner operas and ask themselves, What was there in this that made me uncomfortable? Then, instead of just attributing it to the fact that Germans are impossible (a racist notion), they might ask themselves, How am I implicated in all this? What outmoded assumptions still shape my thinking? Do I let myself be taken in by people who mask hateful thoughts under patriotism, national security, "what's good for the people," or "the safety of my family"? The greatest lesson we could learn from the experience of Wagner is that pretty surfaces often mask senseless and evil content.

Of course, it's not yet that kind of world. In the meantime, how much easier to assume that Wagner was a proto-Nazi who happened to write pretty music, that Nazis are fundamentally different from you and me, that all German culture is suspect, and thank God we're so much better!

# *Wagner on CD*

♦

Opera on recording is a vast, confusing world characterized by a strident minority of shrill partisans amidst a great majority who feel at sea with the whole issue. Walking along the opera aisles of your record store's classical department can be intimidating: rows and rows of expensive little box sets with no information except some cover art and, perhaps, a familiar name or two. These days, the Internet is abuzz with newcomers to the world of Wagner asking for advice on which recordings to buy. This is understandable, considering that a new-release CD set of a Wagner opera can put you out as much as ninety dollars. Who wouldn't need some guidance? Yet taking advice off the Internet is risky. There are too many weird people with individual axes to grind, determined to win converts to their arcane causes—a favorite diva, usually, or some other personal issue. It is frightening which recordings are recommended in this manner.

The debate over which are the best recordings opens up the Pandora's box of singers and their interpretations of roles. This is a very personal matter, and no one can tell you how to react to a certain voice. This doesn't mean people won't try, however, so keep this in mind when someone is in raptures about a particular recording.

There are three general categories of opera recordings: studio, live, and highlights.

*Studio*: For most people, studio recordings are the best choice. They are usually made in conjunction with a series of live performances, and the soloists are sufficiently involved in their roles to communicate their characterizations through the technology. Other advantages include clarity of sound and high quality from the soloists, who can, of course, always rerecord a difficult passage if they lay an egg on the first take. (For many "experts," this represents a compromise of artistic integrity, but for most of us, it just means good singing.) Studio recordings of Wagner operas are extremely expensive to produce and are becoming rarer and rarer.

One disadvantage to listening to studio recordings is that they tend to spoil people for the unpredictabilities of live performance. The phenomenon of eternal disappointment with the singers at a live performance, as old as opera itself, has only been made worse by studio recordings. There is no way a flesh-and-blood Walther or Siegfried is going to sound as fresh after five hours of howling as your CD analogs sounded. And you may never hear Brünnhilde trill after her war cries the way she did on your recording (where she may well have recorded that single note after a week's rest). Just remember that recordings and performances are two distinct art forms, or you may end up becoming one of those long-faced people in the lobby of the opera house who look hopelessly disappointed by life.

*Live*: Many single performances of Wagner operas have become legendary in the annals of theater history—those rare nights when it all came together and something truly sublime happened—and a surprising number of these are available on recording. These are the recordings all the experts recommend. What they don't tell you is that live recordings are always a compromise. While Frau Lederlung may have lit the house at that legendary performance in Magdeburg in 1909, you'd have to be almost psychic to know that from the recording made on a wax cylinder underneath the stage. In recent years, of course, recording techniques have improved, and live recordings are the order of the day. (They're a whole lot cheaper to make, for one thing.)

The Bayreuth festival has been issuing live recordings for years, and they have always been at the forefront of sound technology.

Bayreuth live recordings tend to be better than most for a few reasons. First, no place on earth has the acoustical properties of the Festival House. All the great singers will tell you that it is an ideal place to sing, since the orchestra pit is covered and the singers do not need to "push" as much as in standard opera houses. Also, singers on stage are able to hear their own voices while singing, and can adjust accordingly.

That's the theory, at any rate. There are plenty of live Bayreuth recordings where the singers sound just as tired and hoarse toward the end of the evening as if they had been barking all night at the Met. Still, there is no arguing that the warmth of the Bayreuth acoustics tends to complement the singers. The true best reason to buy the Bayreuth recordings is the legendary chorus. There's nothing like it anywhere.

*Highlights*: Any sane person would naturally assume that the many highlights recordings are the logical place to start a collection, but don't count on it. For one thing, these highlights are the reason everybody thinks of Wagner as bombastic and ham-fisted. Listening to "The Ride of the Valkyries," "Siegfried's Funeral," and the Over-ture to *Tannhäuser* all in succession would send anybody over the edge. As for the highlights of a particular opera, it's much the same. Either you're going to like what you hear and want to buy the com-plete opera or you'll hate it and never listen to it. Either way, you've wasted your money. The highlights are best for people who already have a complete recording of the opera in question but want to judge a particular aspect of a recording—a singer, a conductor, or the sound quality. While highlights recordings are generally marketed toward the newcomer, they are, in fact, more appropriate for the expert with gargantuan CD collections.

*The Flying Dutchman (Der fliegende Holländer)*
Antal Dorati, conductor. London, Rysanek, Tozzi, Liebl. Royal Opera House Chorus and Philharmonic (Live, 1960). Decca 417 319-2DM2.
Sir Georg Solti, conductor. Bailey, Martin, Talvela, Kollo. Chicago Symphony Chorus and Orchestra (1985). Decca 414 551-2DH3.

Herbert von Karajan, conductor. Van Dam, Vejzovic, Moll, Hofmann. Vienna State Opera Chorus and Vienna Philharmonic
Orchestra (1982). EMI MVD99 1311-3.

James Levine, conductor. Morris, Voigt, Rootering, Heppner. Metropolitan Opera Chorus and Orchestra (1994). Sony S2K66342.

The George London/Leonie Rysanek performances of *Dutchman*
remain legends in operatic circles, and this recording will give you an
idea of the sheer electricity they generated. The production quality
is, predictably, primitive, however. Don't buy this as your only *Dutchman* unless you're only interested in vocal characterization. Bailey
makes a compelling Dutchman, but Solti's recording is remarkably
dry, without any of the spookiness that is key to this work. Karajan, on
the other hand, goes for effects bordering on camp. The quiet passages are mere sea breezes, while the Sailor's Chorus will probably
blow your speakers out. José Van Dam is an excellent Dutchman of
the introverted variety, while Djuna Vejzovic is uneven as Senta.
Levine and the New Yorkers have answered an urgent need with
their *Dutchman*; intense yet controlled, and brilliantly recorded.
James Morris is as weary as the ocean. You actually want to *help* this
guy. Deborah Voigt, today's most promising Wagner singer, is dead-
on with her Senta, although some may quibble with her portrayal of
Senta as a real girl with romantic tendencies rather than an out-and-
out drooling psycho.

*Tannhäuser*

Wolfgang Sawallisch, conductor. Windgassen, Silja, Waechter,
Bumbry. Bayreuth Festival Chorus and Orchestra (Live, 1962).
Philips 434 420-2PM32(2).

Solti, conductor. Kollo, Dernesch, Braun, Ludwig. Vienna State
Opera Chorus (with Vienna Boys' Choir) and Vienna Philharmonic Orchestra (1986). Decca 414 581-2DH3.

Giuseppe Sinopoli, conductor. Domingo, Studer, Andreas Schmidt,
Baltsa. Royal Opera Chorus and Philharmonia Orchestra (1989).
Deutsche Grammophon 427 625-2GH3.

The Sawallisch *Tannhäuser* (using the Dresden edition of the score) captures all the excitement of the 1962 performances at Bayreuth, where Grace Bumbry made such a splash as *die schwarze Venus*. This opera, for no one reason in particular, sounds especially good at the Festival House. Wolfgang Windgassen is both heroic and melodious as the title character, while Silja is interesting if occasionally bizarre. Eberhard Waechter is always a lesson in German vocal technique. Solti is at his masterful best with this score in his recording, contrasting frenzy with refinement, and the Vienna Philharmonic responds magnificently. Dernesch and Braun are excellent, and Ludwig excels, as always. René Kollo, however, is not quite up to this almost unsingable role. The Giuseppe Sinopoli recording blew away the nay-sayers on many fronts. The conductor himself refrained from the quirkiness that defined much of his early career, and delivers a strong reading of the score. Placido Domingo was said to be headed for early retirement when he announced plans to record this role, but his performance is awesome. While not the stentorian Tannhäuser of earlier generations, Domingo projects the contrasts of the role's personality, from sexual to pious. The "Rome Narrative" is amazing. Studer is solid as Elisabeth, and Baltsa goes for a bit of camp as Venus. The Royal Opera Chorus surpass themselves under the direction of Norbert Balatsch, who is also the current resident choral genius of the Bayreuth festival.

*Lohengrin*

Rudolf Kempe, conductor. Thomas, Grümmer, Ludwig, Fischer-Dieskau. Vienna State Opera Chorus and Vienna Philharmonic Orchestra (1963). EMI CDS7 49017-8.

Rafael Kubelik, conductor. King, Janowitz, Gwyneth Jones, Stewart. Bavarian Radio Chorus and State Orchestra (1971). DG 449 591-2GX3.

Karajan, conductor. Kollo, Tomowa-Sintow, Vejzovic, Nimsgern. Berlin Deutsche Oper Chorus and Berlin Philharmonic Orchestra (1976). EMI CMS5 66519-2.

Solti, conductor. Domingo, Norman, Randová, Nimsgern. Vienna
    State Opera Concert Chorus and Vienna Philharmonic Orchestra
    (1985). Decca 421 053-2DH4.
Claudio Abbado, conductor. Jerusalem, Studer, Waltraud Meier,
    Welker. Vienna State Opera Concert Chorus and Vienna Philhar-
    monic Orchestra (1992). DG 437 808-2GH3.
Sir Colin Davis, conductor. Heppner, Sweet, Marton, Leiferkus.
    Bavarian Radio Chorus and State Orchestra (1995). RCA 09026
    62646-2.

The good old Kempe recording holds up remarkably well, with good
remastering on the CD, firm conducting, and Jess Thomas actually
interesting in the title role. Elisabeth Grümmer is right-on as Elsa;
hers is a forthright portrayal from a bygone era, but loses none of the
pathos this character needs. And any recording featuring Christa
Ludwig is automatically a good bet. Still a good first choice. Rafael
Kubelik knows his Wagner, but this recording is most notable for the
"meow-mix" combination of Gandula Janowitz and Gwyneth Jones.
These two go at it like stars of daytime soaps. Karajan hardly allows
his singers' characterizations to interfere with "his" orchestra on his
recording. Solti, on the other hand, gives full rein to the vocalists, and
they rise to the occasion. Domingo can portray sanctity like no one
else. Look no farther than his rendition of Lohengrin's final monologue on this recording if you want to know what people mean by
Domingo's "Holy Grail" voice. Jessye Norman, not an automatic
choice for Elsa, colors her voice intelligently. Tenor Ben Heppner is
the best feature of Sir Colin Davis's offering.

· There's no shortage of *Lohengrin* recordings, and half of them feature Cheryl Studer as Elsa. Of these, the best is Abbado's recording.
He and the legendary strings of the Vienna Philharmonic positively
*drip* in piety. Jerusalem is intelligent and sensitive in the title role,
and Waltraud Meier is sufficiently bitchy as Ortrud.

*Tristan und Isolde*

Solti, conductor. Uhl, Nilsson, Resnik, Van Mill, Krause. Vienna
   Singverein and Vienna Philharmonic Orchestra (1960). Decca
   430 234-2DM4.

Karl Böhm, conductor. Windgassen, Nilsson, Ludwig, Talvela,
   Waechter. Bayreuth Festival Chorus and Orchestra (Live, 1966).
   Philips 434 425-2PH3.

Karajan, conductor. Vickers, Dernesch, Ludwig, Ridderbusch,
   Berry. Deutsche Oper Chorus and Berlin Philharmonic Orchestra
   (1972). EMI CMS7 69319-2

Leonard Bernstein, conductor. Hofmann, Behrens, Minton, Sotin,
   Weikl. Bavarian Radio Chorus and Symphony (1981). Philips 438
   241-2PH4.

Daniel Barenboim, conductor. Jerusalem, W. Meier, Lipovsek,
   Salminen, Struckmann. Berlin State Opera Chorus and Berlin
   Philharmonic Orchestra (1994). Teldec 4509-94568-2.

Basically, buy the Karajan recording. His conception of the work is
clear: It's about sex. This is the best recording Jon Vickers ever made,
and he made some great ones. One friend of mine swears he can
actually hear the blood spurting out during the Act III monologue.
Helga Dernesch is a sublime Isolde—more introverted than other
great Isoldes of the past, but thoroughly convincing. If you're one of
those people who think this opera should be called *Isolde (und ein
bissel Tristan)*, you'll settle for none but Birgit Nilsson in the title
role. Although the Böhm recording is live, it's the better of the two
choices featuring the legendary Swede. Not only is she as strong and
agile at the end of the evening as she was in the beginning, but she
actually is even more involved than on the studio recording. Wolfgang Windgassen wowed them for a generation at Bayreuth, and you
won't be disappointed here. Solti's studio recording is also excellent,
but it's missing something—sex. While the Bernstein recording is not
quite the disaster everyone predicted it would be, it remains a curios-
ity and not the ideal first choice. Barenboim takes an unhurried (to
put it mildly) approach to this score, wallowing in rich, deep tones.
He leaves it to the singers to create a sort of inner excitement. While

both Jerusalem and Meier do some of their best singing ever on this recording, he is more successful than she at communicating psychic urgency.

## Die Meistersinger von Nürnberg

Hermann Abendroth, conductor. Schöffler, Suthaus, Scheppan, Dalberg, Kunz, Witte, Kallab. Bayreuth Festival Chorus and Orchestra (Live, 1943). PREI 90174.

Karajan, conductor. Adam, Kollo, Donath, Ridderbusch, Evans, Schreier, Hesse. Dresden State Opera Chorus and Leipzig Radio Chorus, Dresden State Orchestra (1970). EMI CDS7 49683-2.

Silvio Varviso, conductor. Ridderbusch, Cox, Bode, Sotin, Hirte, Stricker, Reynolds. Bayreuth Festival Chorus and Orchestra (Live, 1974). Philips 434 420-2PM32(1).

Ernst Jochum, conductor. Fischer-Dieskau, Domingo, Caterina Ligendza, Lagger, Hermann Laubenthal, Ludwig. Berlin Deutsche Oper Chorus and Orchestra (1976). DG 415 278-2GH4.

Sawallisch, conductor. Weikl, Heppner, Studer, Moll, Iorenz, van der Walt, Kallisch. Bavarian State Opera Chorus and Orchestra (1993). EMI CDS5 55142-2.

Solti, conductor. Van Dam, Heppner, Mattila, Pape, Opie, Lippert, Vermillion. Chicago Symphony Chorus and Orchestra (Live, 1995). Decca 452 606-2DHo4.

Jochum's recording of this opera is a fine accomplishment—he never loses control of the orchestra or the chorus, and that's half the battle with this behemoth. Dietrich Fischer-Dieskau is bitch-elegant as Hans Sachs, making the role sound like the longest song Schubert never wrote. This is perfect for Sachs-as-philosopher, but this guy never made a pair of shoes in his life. Caterina Ligendza is refreshingly full-throated as Eva, rather than the vanilla Twinkies who are often thrust into the role. Domingo's Walther is a revelation: his vast non-Wagner experience has taught him something about singing in ensembles, which is crucial here.

Sawallisch's *Meistersinger* was the first to be recorded in digital sound, and full sound is what this recording is all about. Bernd

Weikl's famous portrayal of Sachs captures all the world-weariness of the "been there, done that" cobbler. Any exhaustion in the voice only adds to the characterization. Cheryl Studer is vocally firm as Eva, though pure-music fans tend to appreciate her more than others, as she can come across as cold and uninterested. In the Act II duet with Sachs, she might as well be singing about shopping on Fifth Avenue. One can appreciate all of Ben Heppner's vocal splendor on this recording, without any of the physical stiffness that sometimes marks his live appearances.

Unless you're a serious student of Wagnerian performance history, you'd have to be nuts to buy a live recording of this opera. The 1974 Bayreuth recording, well conducted by Silvio Varviso, is a mistake. The innumerable choristers tumble on- and offstage like a tryout for the Calgary stampede, and there's not much left of tenor Jean Cox's voice by the excruciating second scene of Act III. The quintet sounds like a convocation of cats in a moonlit alley. Pass it up, even though it's everywhere and usually on sale (and now you know why). One other live recording of interest to the ghoulish is the 1943 Bayreuth festival recording, loaded with names you've never heard of and never will. Although the sound production is predictably compromised, the musicianship is of a very high standard throughout. The soloists, orchestra, and chorus (which was filled out with members of the SS on leave) perform well—and all this as the German war machine was collapsing in flames! If you ever wondered why many people cannot forget the evil bond between Bayreuth and the Third Reich, this recording will provide answers. The production was one of Wieland Wagner's first for the festival. Characteristically, he never, ever referred to it.

## The Ring

Solti, conductor. *Rheingold* (1958): London, Flagstad, Svanholm, Kuen, Neidlinger, Watson, Kmentt, Waechter, Madera, Kreppel, Böhme, Balsborg, Plümacher, Malamut. *Walküre* (1958): King, Régine Crespin, Nilsson, Hotter, Ludwig, Frick. *Siegfried* (1962): Windgassen, Hotter, Nilsson, Stolze, Neidlinger, Höffgen, Böhme, Sutherland. *Götterdämmerung* (1964): Nilsson, Windgassen, Frick,

Fischer-Dieskau, Watson, Ludwig, Popp, Jones, Guy. Vienna State Opera Chorus and Vienna Philharmonic Orchestra. Decca 455 555-2DMO14.

Böhm, conductor. *Rheingold* (Live, 1966): Adam, Burmeister, Windgassen, Wohlfahrt, Neidlinger, Silja, Esser, Nienstadt, Soukupová, Talvela, Böhme, Siebert, Dernesch, Hesse. *Walküre* (Live, 1967): King, Rysanek, Nilsson, Adam, Burmeister, Nienstadt. *Siegfried* (Live, 1966): Windgassen, Adam, Nilsson, Wohlfahrt, Neidlinger, Soukupová, Böhme, Köth. *Götterdämmerung* (Live, 1964): Nilsson, Windgassen, Frick, Neidlinger, Fischer-Dieskau, Watson, Ludwig, Popp, Jones, Guy. Bayreuth Festival Chorus and Orchestra. Philips 446 057-2.

Karajan, conductor. *Rheingold* (1968): Fischer-Dieskau, Veasey, Stolze, Wohlfahrt, Kéléman, Mangelsdorf, Grobe, Kerns, Dominguez, Talvela, Ridderbusch, Donath, Moser, Reynolds. *Walküre* (1966): Vickers, Janowitz, Crespin, Stewart, Veasey, Talvela. *Siegfried* (1968): Thomas, Stewart, Dernesch, Stolze, Kéléman, Dominguez, Ridderbusch, Gayer. *Götterdämmerung* (1970): Dernesch, Brilloth, Ridderbusch, Kéléman, Stewart, Janowitz, Ludwig, Rebmann, Moser. Berlin Deutsche Oper Chorus and Berlin Philharmonic Orchestra. DG 435 211-2.

Levine, conductor. *Rheingold* (1988): Morris, Ludwig, Jerusalem, Zednik, Wlaschiha, Gustafson, Baker, Lorenz, Svendén, Moll, Rootering. *Walküre* (1988): Gary Lakes, Norman, Behrens, Morris, Ludwig, Moll. *Siegfried* (1988): Reiner Goldberg, Morris, Behrens, Zednik, Wlaschiha, Svendén, Moll, Kathleen Battle. *Götterdämmerung* (1991): Behrens, Goldberg, Salminen, Wlaschiha, Weikl, Studer, Schwarz, Hong, Kesling, Parsons. Metropolitan Opera Chorus and Orchestra. DG 445 354-2.

The easiest way to start a fight among opera people is to ask the seemingly innocent question, Which is the best recording of the *Ring?* Everyone has *really* strong opinions on this one.

The fact is that all available recordings of the *Ring* are excellent, but you'll want to listen to a few before you sink the couple of hundred dollars into this investment. The Solti *Ring* (the first full-length recording) was a historic achievement in recording history, and many people still prefer it to all others. It's easy to see why. Solti understood that the listener would be lacking all the visual information of a live performance, and somehow got his singers to communicate great nuance of characterization solely through their voices. For example, Alberich's laugh at the end of the first scene of *Das Rheingold*, as rendered by Gustav Neidlinger, is the vocal definition of "villainous." The Solti *Ring* is what we used to call "vinyl theater." Any recording that features Joan Sutherland as the Forest Bird is a classic by definition. On the downside, the orchestral passages range from excellent to serviceable. There are times when it seems that Solti is just pushing through to get to the next exciting vocal scene (the orchestral transitions in Act II of *Walküre*, for instance). This problem was made worse when the collection was first transferred to CD. Apparently, mistakes were made in the process, and much of the orchestral texture sounded even muddier than it needed to. Fortunately, the entire collection has been remastered and rereleased. If you opt for the Solti *Ring* (and it remains the "standard" choice), make sure you are getting the remastered edition.

Karajan's complete *Ring* was released shortly after Solti's. Vocally, it's hit and miss. Régine Crespin, a notable Sieglinde of her day, sings Brünnhilde in *Walküre* (a mistake), and then is replaced by the excellent Helga Dernesch in the subsequent two operas. Dietrich Fischer-Dieskau sings Wotan like one who was born to rule the universe rather than an ambitious political leader. This pleased some listeners and annoyed others. As for the orchestra, let's face facts right away: no one else has ever come close to Karajan and the Berliners, and probably never will. Sunlight *shimmers* in the Rhine, the Valkyries' horses *fly*, and you can feel flames around you when Siegfried goes up the mountain. When Siegfried swallows Hagen's potion, the orchestra does not fade away, it *forgets*. Karajan, whose career was dogged by accusations of Nazi collaboration (or worse), clearly knew something about power. The *Rheingold* finale is as majestic, colossal, and, yes, totalitarian as Wagner intended it to be.

If there were ever a case to be made for a live recording, Böhm's recording of the *Ring* at Bayreuth is surely it. The Philips label has always had exceptionally high standards for recording quality, and nowhere are the legendary acoustics of the Bayreuth Festival House better represented than here. You're in good hands with Böhm, one of the leading Wagnerian conductors of all time. If the cast looks suspiciously close to Solti's, this was a conscious choice. Nilsson, Windgassen, and Neidlinger are more mature and, if possible, even more expressive here than in the studio recording. Perhaps it's that quintessence of a live performance that just can't be reproduced in the studio. Böhm knew that the best Bayreuth performances of the 1960s would be remembered by future generations as a vocal golden age, and we are lucky to have these performances preserved for us. If you find these recordings on sale, as they often are, snatch them up.

James Levine basically "owns" the score of the *Ring* at this point. It's all there—subtlety, control, magnificence, color. In the places where Solti tolerated the score, Levine blossoms. (Compare their orchestral interludes in Act II of *Walküre*, for example.) Many people would shoot me for saying that (particularly British critics, who have steadily maintained a snotty attitude toward Levine), so be warned. By *Götterdämmerung*, the orchestra is incomparable.

Vocally, Reiner Goldberg is hardly the ideal Siegfried, but, really, who is? Hildegard Behrens has rabid fans and violent detractors, but this woman can communicate feelings like few other Brünnhildes. Her Immolation Scene in *Götterdämmerung* is a true catharsis, giving the whole cycle the air of Greek tragedy that Wagner intended from the start. James Morris has been spoiling audiences for so long now that his achievement is often underrated. The man has a limitless vocal palette from which he colors the various aspects of Wotan—wet dreams of power in Scene 2 of *Rheingold*, the ritualized voice of the Father God in the "Three Questions" scene with Mime in Act I of *Siegfried*, and good old operatic heartwrench in his Farewell in Act III of *Walküre*. You will even want to listen to his reading of the *Walküre* Act II monologue, and that's no small accomplishment. Gary Lakes and Jessye Norman are more comfortable here than they were on stage. Christa Ludwig is Christa Ludwig. The smaller roles range from excellent (Kathleen Battle as the Forest Bird) to serviceable.

Many people mix and match their *Rings*, with this *Rheingold* and that *Walküre*, and so forth. This is perfectly acceptable for those who lack unlimited financial resources (not to mention shelf space). Just don't admit this too freely at intermission.

Of course, you'd never dream of buying anything like an "Orchestral Highlights of the *Ring*" CD, so you wouldn't need to know that Karajan's is the most majestic, and Levine's probably the most subtly recorded.

*Parsifal*

Solti, conductor. Kollo, Fischer-Dieskau, Frick, Ludwig, Kéléman. Vienna Boys' Choir, Vienna State Opera Chorus, and Vienna Philharmonic Orchestra (1972). Decca 417 143-2DH4.

Karajan, conductor. Hofmann, Van Dam, Moll, Vejzovic, Nimsgern. Berlin Deutsche Oper Chorus, Berlin Philharmonic Orchestra (1980). DG 413 347-2GH4.

Barenboim, conductor. Jerusalem, Van Dam, Hölle, Meier, von Kannen. Berlin State Opera Chorus, Berlin Philharmonic Orchestra (1991). Teldec 9031-74448-2.

Levine, conductor. Jerusalem, Weikl, Moll, Waltraud Meier, Mazura. Metropolitan Opera Chorus and Orchestra (1992). DG 072 435-3GH2.

Levine, conductor. Domingo, Morris, Moll, Norman, Wlaschiha. Metropolitan Opera Chorus and Orchestra (1991). DG 437 501-2GH4.

Solti and the Viennese are, of course, superb, but the conductor seems to have opted for a remarkably secular reading of the score. The cast is excellent. Karajan, on the other hand, chose to make his recording as otherworldly as possible. His managing of the Act III Transformation and the entrance of the knights of the Grail plays like the soundtrack to the End of the Universe. Truly harrowing. Critics called the Karajan recording of *Parsifal* "spiritual," and there's really no other word for it. Tenor Peter Hofmann has good points and bad points vocally, but his involvement in the role is beyond question. Djuna Vejzovic is nobody's favorite Kundry. The rest are brilliant.

Everybody complained that Levine's conducting was too slow on his recordings, but people in a rush shouldn't be listening to *Parsifal* anyway. Levine out-Karajans Karajan in savoring the silences and resonances that are so central to this score, and the recording quality is of the highest standard. Domingo's Parsifal is nothing short of a spiritual achievement for many of us—this guy has the Holy Grail in his throat! Jessye Norman is right there with him the whole way in what is one of her finest performances on CD, and the rest of the cast is absolutely top-notch.

Siegfried Jerusalem also blossomed in the role of Parsifal, and his intelligence and pathos are well captured on the Barenboim recording. The conductor opts for a characteristically smooth and seamless reading of the score. Waltraud Meier is an excellent Kundry, at her best when she's shattering the crystal in Act II.

# Wagner in Print

◆

Now that you have a guidebook to the subject of Wagner, you will also need a guidebook to the other guidebooks. There is no limit to the scope of books available on this subject. There are, however, a few that are particularly helpful. This list is meant to help you through the groaning shelves at the bookstore or library. It is in no way meant to be complete.

## BIOGRAPHIES

*The Life of Richard Wagner,* by Ernest Newman. 4 volumes. New York: Knopf, 1933–46.

Newman's *Life* ranks not only as the Everest of the subject of Wagner, but as one of the great achievements in the art of biography itself. The research is awesome. Every letter, conversation, date, and receipt that he could lay his hands on was questioned and analyzed critically. We are particularly indebted to Newman for clarifying the confusing information previously collected. There is no analysis of the music, which Newman saved for his book *The Wagner Operas.*

Not that Newman's *Life* is perfect. In fact, much of the scholarship done since the publication of these volumes has been in response to certain details in Newman, which only underscores the importance

of his work. Much direct information has come to light since Newman worked, most notably Cosima's *Diaries*, to which Newman had
only partial access.

The first volume of the *Life* appeared in 1933, the last in 1946. The
intervening years saw cataclysmic developments in Germany that
demanded a response from anybody writing on a subject so central to
German identity. This is evident in the progression of the book. For
example, he says very little in the first and second volumes about
Wagner's budding anti-Semitism, and virtually nothing about the
notorious pamphlet "Judaism in Music" except that several Jewish
people were upset by it. By the fourth volume, all guns are blasting.
True, Wagner's character became more overtly unattractive as he
grew older, a fact that would be reflected in any chronological biography of him, but it seems clear that Newman's perception of the situation was affected by contemporary events. When quoting from
Wagner's pamphlet "What is German?," where Wagner is dismissing
the desire for war and domination as innately foreign to the German
spirit, Newman drily comments, "This makes interesting reading in
1940."

Such statements are typical of Newman's urbane style and
restrained irony throughout the *Life*. He can also be quite hilarious,
in a potty British professor sort of way. Many of his pronouncements
have become legendary in Wagner circles. They have a cumulative
effect of revealing a biographer who can see his subject critically
while remaining obviously and passionately dedicated to it.

*Richard Wagner: His Life. His Work. His Century*, by Martin Gregor-
Dellin. New York: Harcourt Brace Jovanovich, 1980. 575 pp.

This biography, written in a readable, anecdotal style, includes
long digressions on philosophical and historical tangents pertinent to
the subject. True to its subtitle, it gives a good picture of the "world"
of Wagner, and spends less time analyzing issues within Wagner's
operas than the effect those issues had on other people of the time.
Gregor-Dellin loves his details; he has fun recording such matters as
where Wagner stayed in his many travels, when (exactly) he arrived,
and how much he spent on an almost daily basis. The author also

edited Cosima's diaries (see below) for publication, and is an inexhaustible archivist. His access to unpublished letters and other documents gives him some interesting stories to tell, and he gives a thorough and credible account of the Wagner-Nietzsche rift. According to Gregor-Dellin, Nietzsche was diagnosed as being a chronic masturbator, which was considered quite serious. Wagner, as usual, gave opinions about this to Nietzsche's doctor and others, and Nietzsche never forgave him. Quite plausible.

Others have faulted Gregor-Dellin for whitewashing Wagner's life. Indeed, the author forgives much. His glib glosses on Wagner's anti-Semitism amount to an apologia, which was denounced as criminal by the succeeding generation of Germanists.

*My Life (Mein Leben)*, by Richard Wagner. Translated by Andrew Gray, edited by Mary Whittall. New York: Da Capo, 1992. 811 pp.

Normally, it would be logical to begin learning about an artist's career by reading his or her autobiography, but all the usual rules fly out the window with Wagner. It's not that it's dull, for all its length (hey, the guy could tell a story). This memoir was written in 1864 at the command of King Ludwig, who wanted to know everything about his idol. Wagner dictated it to Cosima. It is therefore cagey regarding matters that might have raised the eyebrows of Cosima or the king, which basically means sex and politics are unreliably recorded here. Also, by the 1860s Wagner had begun to believe some of his own fictions about his musical influences. Separating fact from fancy in this volume has become a specialized science of its own. This is a long read for the very unreliable information it contains. Put it toward the end of your reading list.

*Richard Wagner's Visit to Rossini and An Evening at Rossini's in Beau-Séjour*, by Edmond Michotte. Translated from the French and annotated, with an introduction and appendix, by Herbert Weinstock. Chicago: University of Chicago Press, 1982. 144 pp.

When Wagner was attempting to scare up enthusiasm for his work in Paris in the late 1850s, Rossini, the retired, well-loved composer, was reputed to have made disparaging comments about him. Rossini denied this vehemently in public letters, and Wagner called on the venerable old man to thank him, if not for his support, then at least for his nonopposition. This charming book purports to be a record of their conversation at that visit, covering such topics as Beethoven, Weber, "the music of the future," and the nature of opera. Whether the conversation ever took place and whether this is a faithful record of it remain highly debatable (this is discussed in the good introduction). However, the conversation is very believable and certainly makes for a good read.

## WAGNER STUDIES

*The Wagner Operas,* by Ernest Newman. New York: Knopf, 1984. 724 pp.

This is the definitive book on the works themselves, an exhaustively thorough account of their origins and sources and a note-by-note analysis that has not been surpassed since it was first published in 1949. Father Owen Lee blithely says that "every good Wagnerian knows it by heart," and he's only slightly exaggerating. That's the good news. The bad news is that its age is showing. Things were a bit different in Newman's day. First of all, he could assume that any reader of his book would have the ability and the inclination to sit at the piano and play through the over 550 musical examples that form the basis of his analyses. Nor are those musical examples simple enough for anyone who remembers "do, re, mi" to whistle through; they are full measures from the piano-vocal scores. Newman spends about half of his space brilliantly systematizing the various leitmotivs in each of the operas, and the other half warning against too systematic an approach to Wagner's leitmotivs. Second, the libretto translations he employs (all his own except *Lohengrin*) are archaic and either unreadable or hilarious ("No more far'st thou forth warriors to seek . . ."). Such texts are not without value, and often echo Wagner's original sounds and archaisms, but they don't make for easy going. This book remains indispensable to the Wagner fan, the undisputed "desert island book." Just make sure you are a Wagner fan before leaping into it.

*Bayreuth: A History of the Wagner Festival*, by Frederic Spotts. New Haven: Yale University Press, 1994. 334 pp.

Run, do not walk, to buy this invaluable book. Spotts's book is true to its title, telling the history of the festival from Wagner's first fantasies to the present day. In the course of this tale, the author succeeds in explaining the history of the whole Wagnerian phenomenon. His remarkable accomplishment lies in presenting the story, warts and all, without any special agenda beyond an obvious love for the subject. Spotts is able to analyze the role of the Third Reich in Bayreuth, and vice versa, responsibly, informatively, and with remarkable aplomb. With Cosima, Siegfried and Winifred Wagner, Wieland, and today's leader Wolfgang, the author gives credit where it's due and critiques where appropriate. A thrilling read.

*In Search of Wagner*, by Theodor Adorno. Translated by Rodney Livingstone. New York: Schocken Books, 1981. 159 pp.

Adorno was one of the guiding lights of the Frankfurt School of philosophers, and a person for whom Wagner had special significance. This Jewish writer fled the Third Reich and taught at the New School in New York. The book is a compendium of essays based on lectures given there and in Germany. Adorno is credited with a philosophical style that does not jump to conclusions. He will point out the uniqueness of a single turn of poetic or musical phrase in Wagner, and analyze it for what it is, refusing to create whacked-out theories from such details. This is probably Adorno's greatest gift to the realm of Wagner scholarship—especially after the Nazi years. As for what he does say, I leave that to the philosophy students to unpack, but I can inform you that he says it, whatever it is, very well.

*The Perfect Wagnerite*, by George Bernard Shaw. New York: Dover, 1966 (reprint of the 1923 edition). 136 pp.

Shaw's brilliant, important, and vastly amusing analysis of the *Ring* is a pleasure to read. He deconstructs the tetralogy as an allegory of class struggle, using Marx's theories when they are convenient but dispensing with them just as fast when they get in the way. *The Perfect Wagnerite* is loaded with quotable gems in the best Shavian manner, perfect for cocktail party chatter—even, or perhaps especially, when they are downright wrong. Read this!

*The Darker Side of Genius: Richard Wagner's Anti-Semitism*, by Jacob Katz. University of New England Press, 1986. 158 pp.

You may think this is too specific for a reader with only a general interest in Wagner, but everyone needs help getting perspective on this aspect of his life and work. This manageable volume is a good place to start. Dr. Katz presents a reasoned analysis of Wagner's anti-Semitism in his operas and writings within the context of the movement as a whole. He concludes that Wagner's anti-Semitism is quite culpable on its own without the additional "burden" of subsequent history. It is a lucid and responsible work.

*Wagner's "Ring" and Its Symbols*, by Robert Donington. London: Faber & Faber, 1974. 342 pp.

This psychoanalytical run through the *Ring* is considered a classic among Wagner fans. Donington uses the tools of Jungians and post-Jungians to present a solid system for interpreting the saga. Most impressive is the fact that he addresses the entire tetralogy, from beginning to end, within the framework of his system, rather than just culling the parts that agree with his point of view. You don't have to be an expert on psychology to read this book, but Donington does presuppose a little knowledge of the *Ring*. He sticks very close to the music, and takes every leitmotiv apart like a scientist. (Written musical examples are included in a large appendix.) You'll never hear the *Ring* quite the same way again after reading this book.

*Wagner's Ring: Turning the Sky Around*, by M. Owen Lee. New York: Proscenium Publishers, 1994. 122 pp.

Father Lee is familiar to listeners of the Met Saturday matinee radio broadcasts, where he consistently gives fascinating analyses of the works in question. In fact, he may be the world's only opera commentator who can be far-reaching and sensible at the same time! This will come as a great relief to people wishing to read more about the *Ring*. Father Lee's book, based on his Wagner talks during the 1988 and 1989 seasons, covers the stories of the four operas and looks into their deeper meanings. His view includes psychological, political, and other aspects used to deconstruct these works, but manages to remain coherent and, well, sensible throughout. The written musical examples are thoughtfully simplified so you don't have to sit at the piano (with Vladimir Horowitz at your side) to get through them. Highly recommended.

*Pro and Contra Wagner*, by Thomas Mann. Translated by Allan Blunden, with an introduction by Erich Heller. Chicago: University of Chicago Press, 1985.

This is a large collection of Thomas Mann's various writings about Wagner, covering fifty years of the famous novelist's thoughts on the subject. Mann struggled with Wagner his whole life, never resolving his conflict, and never able to accept his inability to resolve it. He also idolized Nietzsche, which hardly simplified matters. Inner turmoil aside, Mann makes searing observations about every aspect of Wagner, and anyone can enjoy his celebrated prose. This anthology also contains the famous essay "Sorrows and Grandeur of Richard Wagner," which got him thrown out of Germany for the duration of the Third Reich. You'll wonder what all the fuss was about when you read this balanced critique. If this book served no other purpose, reading this essay while knowing what ensued will convince anyone who still needs convincing just how insane Germany was in 1933.

*Richard Wagner: The Man, His Mind, and His Music*, by Robert Gutman. New York: Knopf, 1990. 491 pp.

Although this book is a biography, presenting all its information chronologically, it is groundbreaking for its bold look at the issues involved in the study of Wagner. While most scholars of Wagner settle for the old formula "the man was dreadful, the music sublime," and leave it at that, Gutman had the radical idea that Wagner's personal problems were integral to his art. It is not possible, in Gutman's view, to study Wagner as a phenomenon separate from his effect on the world. Occasionally, he takes this point of view into the intellectual twinkie-zone, and many of his arguments can be deconstructed. But we remain indebted to Gutman for this book and the more holistic genre of scholastic inquiry that it inspired.

*The Complete Operas of Richard Wagner: A Critical Guide*, by Charles Osborne. New York: Da Capo, 1992. 304 pp.

The best thing that can be said about this book is that it's usually on sale. Osborne has great credentials, as literature director of the Arts Council of Great Britain and chief theater critic of the *Daily Telegraph* in London. The problem is that he goes off the deep end trying to be morally superior to Wagner. Along the way, he makes more than a few mistakes and unscholastic leaps of faith. (This is the guy who translates *welscher* as "French" in *Meistersinger*, and then discusses Hitler's vendetta against French culture. He's also the one who sees homosexuals lurking around the dark recesses of the Grail Hall in *Parsifal*.) The book purports to be a biography as well, with a narrative of Wagner's life running through the summaries of each opera. This means we are treated to in-depth looks at the early operas *Die Feen*, *Das Liebesverbot*, and *Rienzi*, all presented as if anybody cared. Skip it.

*Confessions of a Jewish Wagnerite*, by Lawrence D. Maas. With a Foreword by Gottfried Wagner. London: Cassell, 1994. 268 pp.

The subtitle of this book is *Being Gay and Jewish in America*. It's a shame "Gay" wasn't on the cover, because this fascinating memoir is largely a coming-out story written by a Jewish Wagnerite, and, yes, self-loathing plays a large part in the author's early struggle.

The basic tone of the book is "This is who I am and this is what Wagner makes me feel." The beauty of this tale is that Maas has the courage to state his personal thoughts and feelings in plain English, without faux-scholastic ellipsis, and, best of all, without hiding what he's really thinking behind an elaborate aesthetic or political theory.

If other scholars had been able to do the same, they probably would have made more sense. This may be the book Thomas Mann or Theodor Adorno wanted to write, but couldn't.

## COSIMA

*Cosima Wagner*, by Richard du Moulin-Eckart. Translated by Catherine A. Phillips. 2 volumes. New York: Da Capo, 1981.

This was the authorized biography of Cosima, written while she was (barely) alive in 1928. It is an entirely worshipful tome, written by a man who clearly idolized her. Whenever du Moulin-Eckart comes across problematic or potentially unpleasant episodes in her life, he employs the simple solution of lying through his teeth. As a source of direct information, it is fraught with hazards. Until the publication of Cosima's *Diaries*, however, this was where researchers had to go to get glimpses of that vital document. It is not recommended for normal people. The refinement of its writing style is completely in keeping with its elegant proto-fascist author.

*Cosima Wagner*, by George Marek. New York: Harper & Row, 1981. 291 pp.

This biography is chatty, anecdotal, and pleasant to read, even if it does sometimes lapse into flights of purple passion. The author spends a great deal of time emphasizing the obvious; namely, that Wagner was self-obsessed, Bülow was neurotic, Liszt was a failure as a father, and Marie d'Agoult (Cosima's mother) was an elegant mess. There isn't, unfortunately, a great deal more information in this book that couldn't be found in most of the standard Wagner biographies. If this book isn't enough for you, you can always go to . . .

*The Diaries of Cosima Wagner*, edited and annotated by Martin Gregor-Dellin and Dietrich Mack, translated by Geoffrey Skelton. 2 volumes. New York: Harcourt Brace Jovanovich, 1980.

. . . all 2,200 pages of them. Cosima began keeping a daily diary in

1869 and ended it on the day of Wagner's death in 1883. If you want to know how well Richard Wagner slept on any given night in that period, or the state of his digestive system, this is the place to go. The first volume (1869–78) focuses largely on the move to Bayreuth and the efforts involved in launching the first festival against the imagined opposition of "all the world." The second volume is a daily celebration of marital bliss (best line [R. to Cosima]: "If only everybody knew how self-contained we are!"). Cosima supposedly kept these diaries as a form of instruction and inspiration for their son Siegfried, and never intended them for publication. They are tedious, smug, hateful, and devoted to every utterance from the Wagners' mouths, including some very stupid observations. For example, we are informed that Shakespeare and Dante are better in German than in their originals. (Wagner never came close to mastering English or Italian.) Italians, by the way, lack the natural sunniness and humor of the Germans. Every page contains, among other such drivel, at least one paranoid delusion about Jews.

The *Diaries* are also, unfortunately, quite indispensable to people who wish to untangle Wagner's convoluted character for themselves. Every recent biography of Wagner quotes from them at length but selectively, depending on the scholar's agenda (and they all have one). If daily life at Villa Wahnfried strikes one as crashingly dull between frenetic moments, there is information of value here, particularly Cosima's faithful records of what Richard and others played on the piano for entertainment. Liszt is hardly heard at all, except when he shows up in person to remind everyone of his own music. There are also surprising moments when a well-concealed humanity slips in. Reading the newspapers, Richard and Cosima blast the British for their imperialist wars. "After all," she says, "the Zulus are people, just like us." When Bismarck's government ratifies repressive anti-socialist laws, Cosima responds, "Imagine passing laws against a specific group of people!" Imagine indeed.

These volumes are well translated and the notes are helpful, but they are still not for casual readers who are neither insomniacs nor masochists.

*Richard and Cosima Wagner: Biography of a Marriage,* by Geoffrey Skelton. Boston: Houghton Mifflin, 1982. 319 pp.

Skelton was the translator of Cosima's diaries (a three-year task) and had mounds of information at his fingertips. He boiled down information from that mammoth job, as well as other books he had written on Wagner, to create this manageable volume. His years of study on the subject appear to have had the unusual effect of giving him sympathy for these two hard-to-love individuals, and he is remarkably forgiving of their darker sides. Beyond this, there is plenty of interest in this book that won't be found in other books, although in packing in the facts Skelton must sometimes dispense with the incidental information that gives color to the history.

## LUDWIG II OF BAVARIA

Don't be surprised if you find yourself drawn to the enigmatic character of King Ludwig as you read more about Wagner's extraordinary career. Many Wagnerites have also become "Ludwigites." Conversely, there are people who became interested in Wagner's works by touring Ludwig's fantasy castles in Bavaria. The two men are inextricably linked. *The Swan King: Ludwig II of Bavaria,* by Christopher McIntosh (London: Robin Clark, 1986, 218 pp.), is a fascinating account of Ludwig's life, including details of expenditures that shed much light on the historic actualities of Ludwig's career. The analyses of Ludwig's building program from a psychological point of view are nothing short of brilliant, but it seems a shame to read about Ludwig's life without the benefit of photographs. It might be worth exchanging a few of the details provided by this book for color pictures of Ludwig's castles, which explain so much more. *The Dream King: Ludwig II of Bavaria,* by Wilfrid Blunt (with a chapter on Ludwig and the arts by Dr. Michael Petzet, Penguin Books, 1973, 264 pp.), is remarkable for its magnificent color photographs of the irresistible places in Ludwig's life. The informative text is unabashedly devoted to Wagner and the role he played in Ludwig's life. Unfortunately, this book is currently out of print and hard to find. It is worth combing the libraries and secondhand shops for.

## FRANZ LISZT

Even the slightest interest in the career of Richard Wagner will lead one to the subject of Franz Liszt, Wagner's eventual father-in-law and fellow herald of the "music of the future." Any biography of Liszt is also a social and musical history of the nineteenth century, since he was perhaps the world's first pop star, and knew everybody. Despite some less-than-perfect behavior (especially to a few women), he was always charming, urbane, gregarious, and generally appealing. Accounts of his life make for extremely pleasant reading, particularly after spending time reading about Wagner. *Franz Liszt*, by Alan Walker (Volume 1, Cornell University Press, 1983, 481 pp.; Volume 2, Knopf, 1989, 626 pp.; Volume 3, Knopf, 1996, 594 pp.), is the place to go if you want the whole story—a look at Liszt's music, excellent details of his astounding social life (and the life of basically everybody else in nineteenth-century Europe), and illustrations. Walker even went through the newly rediscovered Vatican documents pertaining to the famous case of the annulment of Princess Carolyne's marriage and presents what he found in the second volume. (Oddly, the new evidence only makes the whole affair more mysterious than ever.) This massive undertaking, which has received praise and awards everywhere, would take you through a long winter—in Alaska. Walker is erudite and stylish, and clearly dedicated to the subject. It's clear he has no patience for Wagner or Cosima, frankly calling them leeches, users, and all-round opportunists, which may be overstating the case slightly. (Then again, it may not.) *Liszt*, by Derek Watson (New York: Schirmer, 1989, 404 pp.), is a smart book aimed mostly at musicians. Only 161 pages chronicle Liszt's life story, and the author avoids details to prevent his book from becoming a social history of nineteenth-century European high society. This is commendable for musicologists but a loss to the rest of us, since Liszt's life story is better than a prime-time television soap opera. After a brief summation of

Liszt's character, the balance of the book is dedicated to an analysis of his enormous and diverse musical output. It is useful for people who are trying to navigate their way through Liszt's work, which has gone in and out of fashion several times, and is, at present, rightly considered worthy of serious attention. In *Liszt,* by Sacheverell Sitwell (New York: Dover, 1967, 400 pp.), the famous scion of the literary Sitwell family amuses himself with a highly stylized account of Liszt's life and work. Wagner himself is given full status as central to Liszt's life, but his role is summarized rather briefly, since, as the author notes, his story is so fully chronicled elsewhere. The style of the writing is, for better and for worse, exactly what you'd expect out of a guy named Sacheverell.

## WIELAND WAGNER

The elusive but important figure of Wieland Wagner is best approached in *Wieland Wagner, the Postive Skeptic,* by Geoffrey Skelton (New York: St. Martin's Press, 1971, 222 pp.). Wieland was a notoriously reticent person—almost a recluse. He remains a bit shadowy even after you've read this book. Skelton was a trusted friend of the Wagner family, so you won't find much criticism of Wieland or any scandal here, although his matter-of-fact look at Wieland's long-term affair with singer Anja Silja must have been considered very impartial at the time. You will find great photographs and also a rare look at Wieland's important career in and outside Bayreuth.

# Wagner-Oriented Films

◆

The story of Wagner makes "good copy," as a number of movie pro-ducers have discovered. Below is a list of movies about Wagner's life or work, or in which the character of Wagner plays a central role.

*Wagner* (1982), directed by Tony Palmer. 300 minutes.

This docudrama was culled from a nine-hour series first seen on BBC. Some critics thought Richard Burton was "painful to watch" as Wagner, but those who have read a Wagner biography or two might find him surprisingly on the money in the role, obnoxious but entirely mesmerizing. Vanessa Redgrave is staunch as Cosima, Marthe Keller poetic as Mathilde Wesendonck, Gemma Craven almost too sympathetic as Minna. Laszlo Galffi is handsome and oth-erworldly as Ludwig, while Ekkehard Schall as Liszt makes us won-der how any woman ever flipped over this fussy old man. The rest of the cast is filled out with the likes of John Gielgud, Laurence Olivier, Ralph Richardson, Joan Plowright, Gabriel Byrne, Prunella Scales, and Franco Nero. On the operatic side, we get glimpses and sound bites of Manfred Jung, Jess Thomas, and several others. Gwyneth Jones displays considerable acting ability (and a tasteful bit of flesh in the bathtub) along with some of her wild sounds as Malvina Schnorr, while the hunky Peter Hofmann is shamefully padded to play Lud-wig Schnorr. Sir Georg Solti conducted the musical snippets.

Judging from the list above, it's obvious that *Wagner* was a high-budget extravaganza, complete with an elaborate production sensibility. It follows the life of Wagner in the manner of a long documentary, with occasional but distinct flights into surrealism. The soundtrack is a nonstop string of greatest hits, especially the anvil-pounding Nibelheim theme from *Rheingold*, played every couple of minutes no matter what's going on. This must have been very effective in engaging television viewers who were flipping channels, but it can drive you crazy if you've been watching it through for five hours.

There are a few fudges with the facts, but they are not too numerous and are in most cases unavoidable for narrative purposes. (For example, the exterior shots of the Paris Opéra are filmed at the Palais Garnier, which hadn't yet been built at the time of the *Tannhäuser* premiere. Still, the filmmakers could hardly be expected to reconstruct the old Opéra, and the point gets across in any case.) The massive research and the respect for the subject are blatant. In fact, the film placates the know-it-alls with many in-jokes and oblique references to Wagner trivia. The dragon costume for *Siegfried* is shown with its neck section missing, while a mysterious placard says "Beirut." At another point, Wagner is discussing Nietzsche's betrayal, saying nothing more than "he masturbates, you know." Neither of these references is explained further. (See p. 311 for the Beirut thing and p. 393 for the Nietzsche incident).

Any film about Wagner must present aspects of his complicated character selectively, and this one is no different for all its length. His borrowing and his debts, for example, are well depicted, but there is no hint of his well-documented prodigal generosity, which tells us much about the man's core relationship to money. Similarly, the movie shows Wagner running around screaming about the "dirty Jews," which he certainly did, but fails to show us the disproportionate number of Jews who held central positions in his life, which makes the subject so much more interesting. Levi, Neumann, and Rubinstein are never seen. Other characters are oversimplified. Bülow comes off as a rather nice chap, and Ludwig is basically all wrong. Still, the movie is a major accomplishment. It is perhaps best approached after, rather than in lieu of, reading one of the standard biographies. The performers are all interesting, and often spellbinding. Burton is monumental when he isn't asleep. At the very least, the camera work and the art direction, in the capable hands of a mostly Italian crew, are breathtaking.

*Parsifal* (1982), directed by Hans Jürgen Syberberg. 255 minutes.

File this one under the heading of "Very Deep." Director Syberberg had previously filmed a notorious interview with Winifred Wagner shortly before her death in 1976, where she made the famous remark that she would kiss Adolf Hitler if he walked in the room today. He had also been noted for the film *Our Hitler,* a lengthy production with many marionettes dealing with contemporary Germany's soul-wrenching relationship to the Third Reich experience. You can expect a bit of the same here, since he seems to need to come to terms with Wagner as he had with Hitler. Much of the action takes place on or in a giant death mask of Wagner, and the final resolution implies an inner psychological victory of cohesion rather than a world-redeeming metamorphosis.

To accomplish this, Syberberg uses a self-conscious theatricality, complete with marionettes, deliberate in its anti-magnificence. The Flower Maidens are deformed. The knights are vaguely sinister (and you know what that means: their hall is filled with battle flags, including, yes, the Nazi one). The acting is stylized beyond that of the Grand Kabuki, and there is no shortage of the bizarre. Kundry's Act I ride is on a carousel horse. She then emerges from a primal fjord— with a gondoliers' post in it (presumably an allusion to Wagner's life and death). And so on.

Musically, it's hit and miss. The Prague Philharmonic Choir and the Monte Carlo Philharmonic are conducted by Arnim Jordan, who also lip-synchs the role of Amfortas, sung by Wolfgang Schoene. This is meant to be profound, but comes off as a case of conductor ego run amok. The chorus (which uses women's voices instead of boys') should have spent less time rehearsing tortured expressionist poses and more time rehearsing vocalizing in unison. The venerable

Robert Lloyd is impressive singing and acting Gurnemanz. He alone among the principals plays it at face value. Edith Clever acts Kundry well, considering everything, to the good singing of Yvonne Minton. Titurel is King Ludwig trapped in a leaky basement. Whatever.

The most controversial touch was the role of Parsifal. Sung well by Reiner Goldberg, it is portrayed in the film by a boy who looks about twelve, and then, after Kundry's kiss, by a young woman. She looks no stranger "singing" the tenor lines than the twelve-year-old did, and it all makes sense by the end of the movie. She and the boy come together in Wagner's head, representing the union of *animus* and *anima*, while Kundry and Amfortas lie down and die together. Odd, but much more satisfying than most endings of this drama.

Don't see this movie as your intro to *Parsifal*. Rent a video of a stage production instead, and save this one until you're jaded by standard representations. If hallucinogenic drugs play any role in your life, this movie would be an excellent place to employ them.

*Ludwig* (1973), directed by Luchino Visconti. 248 minutes (!).

This film is discussed by a great many Wagner fans, few of whom have ever actually seen it. It's not currently available on video, and only makes rare appearances in arty retro movie houses. It also crops up on European television periodically, and devotees pass around pirated copies like rare contraband. *Ludwig* holds a place in film history as Visconti's last work, made when that famous director was well beyond any such mundane considerations as audience appeal. Here we have the story of our favorite king of Bavaria from the time of his coronation to his death in 1886. At least, we think that's what this film is about, since it's filmed almost entirely in the dark! This was considered "heavy" by stage and screen directors in that era (cf. Karajan's "pitch-black" *Ring*). What you can see is gorgeous. Helmut Griem unravels beautifully as the title character, Trevor Howard is weird as Wagner, and Romy Schneider stunning as the Empress Elizabeth. The film is so guarded emotionally that one never really plugs in. The net result is rather disappointing, all things considered.

*Lisztomania* (1975), directed by Ken Russell. 106 minutes.

By the same guy who had Ann Margret swimming in baked beans in the movie *Tommy*. Ken Russell makes that movie look positively understated in this over-the-top extravaganza. This film purports to tell the life story of Liszt as something of a rock star, with all the mid-1970s excesses associated with that milieu, including a heavy dose of T & A. Although *Lisztomania* is unmitigated trash, it is not without some entertainment value to the Wagner fan. An early scene shows Liszt (Roger Daltrey) playing variations of *Rienzi*—interspersed with "Chop Sticks"—to an audience of hysterical teenyboppers. When Wagner (Paul Nicholas) gets furious, Liszt says, "Well, we are in show business, Dickie." Very plausible. The film cops out toward the end by simplistically turning Wagner into Hitler and misogynistically blaming it all on Cosima. Until that point, however, the movie is remarkably faithful to history amidst all its deliberate anachronisms. Perhaps the truth was more bizarre than Russell's superficial shock value. The Wagner fan will also note that this movie, supposedly about Liszt, is ultimately about Wagner. One other note: Ringo Starr plays Pope Pius IX. Pretty rich.

*Song Without End* (1960), directed by Charles Vidor and George Cukor. 130 minutes.

Dirk Bogarde, as Franz Liszt, heaves his shoulders elegantly while pounding the ivories (music played by Jorge Bolet) amidst lush settings in this schmaltzfest directed by Charles Vidor (who died during the filming). *Song Without End* is, in its own way, even sloppier with the facts than *Lisztomania*. The gorgeous actress Capucine reinterprets the Princess von Sayn-Wittgenstein, Liszt's "longtime companion," as a virginal beauty (she was neither). There are at least two classically camp moments in the movie. During an imaginary meeting between the princess and Marie d'Agoult, the former Mrs. Liszt in all but name, the princess asks cattily, "Tell me, did he drive you to Paradise?" Marie answers, "Your Highness, he does not know the road." Later, Martita Hunt as the grand duchess of Weimar delivers one of the all-time great truths when she warns the princess, "My dear, no man is worth half the Ukraine."

Wagner is treated shabbily in this film, which focuses on Liszt's relationship with the princess at the expense of other aspects of his life. The movie ends circa 1864 with Liszt taking holy orders while Capucine strikes a pious pose in Saint Peter's wearing a drop-dead ensemble by Jean Louis. Cosima is never mentioned by name. Perhaps, as the title suggests, a sequel was being considered. In Wagner's two appearances in the film, he is rude and vaguely gross, which is an overstatement. Whenever Liszt champions the Wagner cause, he precedes it with tired apologies about the music redeeming the man.

The main attraction of this movie for the budding Wagnerite lies in two of the perversely (or perhaps teasingly) selected location shots. Linderhof, King Ludwig's creamy chateau with a Venusberg grotto, substitutes for the ducal court of Weimar, where Liszt was a sort of music director. The scenes that were supposed to be at the Court Theater of Weimar were actually filmed at the beautiful old Margravine Opera House of Bayreuth. Liszt is seen conducting the Pilgrims' Chorus from *Tannhäuser*, during which the princess is served divorce papers in her box. Later, Dirk runs up and down the peculiar lobby of that old theater, and we can see the strangely tacky setlike cardboard balustrades of the grand staircase.

*Meeting Venus* (1993), written and directed by Istvan Szabo. 121 minutes.

All right, so Glenn Close lip-synching Kiri TeKanawa sounds more like a bad drag revue than a major motion picture, but this flawed, interesting film is well worth seeing anyway. The setting is a mythical multinational institution called "Opera Europe," located in Paris and where, they say, one can be misunderstood in six languages. Their attempt to put together a production of *Tannhäuser* is seen through the prism of contemporary European politics and becomes a metaphor for the contentious political, cultural, and linguistic issues of European unification.

The characters are all parodies, but anyone who has worked around opera can tell you that these parodies have a basis in fact. Along the way, there's actually a lot of *Tannhäuser*. The Venusberg scene in S & M fetish gear is superbly corny, and accurate, Eurotrash. The opening night is threatened when the unions call a strike and the fire curtain cannot be lifted. The diva (Close) suggests singing in front of the fire curtain. At the finale, the chorus of oppressed peasant pilgrims (very Götz Friedrich) carry the flowering staff through the opera house, having such an effect that the conductor's baton blooms, while Close glows in fabulous white chiffon! What's not to like? Well, plenty. The reductive stereotypes are tiring. But if you can enter the surreal spirit, this is a rewarding movie. The very idea of *Tannhäuser* in Paris is an excellent forum for these issues—personalities and politics destroyed the 1861 production, and matters have only superficially changed since then. Besides TeKanawa, René Kollo, Hakan Hagegard, and Waltraud Meier provide the main voices, demonstrating that the music is given pretty fair due for a movie.

*The Fisher King* (1991), directed by Terry Gilliam. 137 minutes.

The title refers to the ancient source myth of *Parsifal*, and this neomyth shows us Robin Williams as the innocent fool and Jeff Bridges as the ailing king. Williams's alienation from society is that he is a homeless man (nice touch), while Bridges's "wound that won't heal" is alcoholism (very nice touch). The action takes place in contemporary New York, where the Holy Grail is in a private collection on the Upper East Side. In all, the movie is more interesting than satisfying, from a Wagnerian point of view, because in trying to make a universal myth "relevant" it becomes the story of individuals rather than of communities.

The film depicts Bridges's downfall (literally) from hot-shot radio host in an uptown penthouse to impotent souse in a downtown flophouse whose faith in life and love is restored by the compassion of the homeless man. Lovely, but how exactly does this save the planet? In a way, the film suffers from being too devoted to the myth as Wagner saw it, whereas Wagner himself did whatever violence necessary to the old myths to tell the story he wanted to tell. Since we must have conventional romance in our films, this film has a love interest (Amanda Plummer) who is fun but, unlike the eternally enigmatic Kundry, ends up also being brought out by contact with the homeless man. Instead of the question marks left behind by Kundry, we have something of an homage to family values. Mercedes Ruehl (who won an Oscar for this) plays Bridges's girlfriend, and she is her usual brilliant self. Interesting to note that she is the most successful character in the film, and is the only one without an analogue in *Parsifal*.

*What's Opera, Doc?* (1957), directed by Chuck Jones. Music arranged by Milt Franklyn, lyrics by Michael Maltese.

It's hard to know what category to place this cartoon in, except probably that of the greatest single union of Wagner and film. In case you don't already know, this is Bugs Bunny (as Brünnhilde, sort of) and Elmer Fudd (as Siegfried, sort of) sending up Wagner in a big way. The music used is as follows: the *Dutchman* Overture, "The Ride of the Valkyries" (using the immortal Iyrics "Kill da wabbit," etc.), Siegfried's Horn Call, the Tarnhelm theme from *Rheingold*, some Venusberg music from *Tannhäuser* followed by the Pilgrims' Chorus (containing the unforgettable dialogue "Oh, Bwünnhilde, youah so wovewy!," "Yes, I know it, I can't help it!"), the Immolation Scene from *Götterdämmerung*, and ending, as Wagner himself had, with a reprise of the Pilgrims' Chorus. This cartoon has permanently defined Wagner for most Americans. Tell people you are planning to attend a performance of Wagner opera, and count how many will sing "Kill da wabbit" at the mere mention of the name.

Attentive viewers will also note the use of the *Lohengrin* Act III Prelude in that other minor masterpiece of this genre, *Long Haired Rabbit*.

*Twilight of the Golds* (1996), directed by Ross Marks. Screenplay by Jonathan Tolins and Seth Bass, based on the play by Jonathan Tolins. A Showtime presentation. 95 minutes.

A gay Jewish artist (Brendan Fraser) is staging a "people's" version of the *Ring*, lasting only seven hours and financed by corporate tie-ins. His uneasy relationship with his family explodes when his pregnant sister (Jennifer Beals) and her genetic researcher husband (Jon Tenney) discover in prenatal testing that their child will be gay. Moral crises ensue. The artist and the girl's parents (Garry Marshall and Faye Dunaway) are at sea trying to provide guidance.

This classic modern Jewish family, portrayed by one of the most relentlessly *goyische* casts ever assembled in Hollywood, struggles with the issues at stake until all works out. Sis keeps the baby, loses the husband, and practically marries her brother. The brother's "relevant" *Ring* premieres, the reunited family attends, and he leaves us with some interesting, if a bit "warm and fuzzy," observations on the meaning of Siegfried crossing the magic fire. Obviously, there are some major issues at stake here, and all miraculously resolved in ninety minutes! Rosie O'Donnell is excellent fun as Sis's buddy, and Jack Klugman entirely steals the show in five minutes as the doctor's Orthodox Jewish father, who is almost the only moral compass available. Interesting.

*Pandora and the Flying Dutchman* (1950), written and directed by Albert Lewin. With Ava Gardner, James Mason, and Nigel Patrick. 123 minutes.

What *were* they thinking? More Carmen than Pandora, Ava Gardner plays a tanned and tarty saloon *chanteuse* in Spain in the 1930s. She's not interested in any of her many suitors except James Mason, who plays a Dutch sea captain named, if you can believe it, Hendrick van der Zee. *Oy!* As luck would have it, he's *that* Dutch sea captain, condemned to wander until . . . well, you read about it several chapters ago. There are car races (why?) and matadors and you name it, all filmed in psychedelic Technicolor. Late-night TV viewing at its most bizarre.

*Interrupted Melody* (1955), directed by Curtis Bernhardt. With Eleanor Parker, Glenn Ford, and Roger Moore. 106 minutes.

This is a big-screen adaptation of Marjorie Lawrence's autobiography of the same name. Lawrence was a great diva of the 1930s, primarily noted for her Wagner performances. She was stricken with polio in 1941, and, though confined to a wheelchair for several years afterward, resumed her career by singing first to the troops and eventually on the operatic stage in specially staged performances. You can imagine what Hollywood producers of the 1950s could do with that! The movie cheerfully blends fact and fancy to achieve a high-gloss tearjerker. At her first *Götterdämmerung* at the Metropolitan,

Lawrence argues to follow the libretto's instructions for the Immolation Scene, which say to leap on the bareback horse and ride into the flames. Come opening night, by golly, she does just that, and makes history. This much is fact. Lawrence was from the Australian outback and had no trouble with this feat. After the polio, she is seen making her "comeback" as Isolde, arranged in elegant immobility on the stage. While singing (you guessed it) the *Liebestod*, she rises to her feet and stands, and right at the moment of the climactic key change! This, alas, is not what we can call fact, but it is perhaps the single most messianic use of the *Liebestod* in film yet. This movie has many snippets of Wagner's music in it, and is also interesting for the glimpses of operatic production values of that time. The singing was done by Eileen Farrell.

# Wagner Soundtracks

◆

Wagner's music has seeped into the communal subconscious, and it's easy to see why moviemakers are so often tempted to borrow a few grand effects from the composer and save themselves a lot of work. The list below is by no means complete; "The Ride of the Valkyries" alone has made casual appearances in at least ten movies not included here, and if one were to include the Bridal Chorus from *Lohengrin*, another entire volume would be needed. This is meant as a demonstration of how deeply this music is embedded in our culture, even among people who think they've never heard a note of it. Or, as you might prefer to say to friends who question your new interest in Wagner, "Relax, you're soaking in it!"

A *Farewell to Arms* (1932) The stirring scenes depicting the collapse of the Italian army and its retreat after the battle of Caporetto in the First World War are accompanied by music in which the thunder motif from *Das Rheingold* is repeated—and repeated and repeated. You won't want to hear it again for some time after seeing this Gary Cooper/Helen Hayes film.

*Humoresque* (1946) Whoever cast John Garfield as a concert violinist obviously held nothing sacred, so don't be too surprised when you hear the *Liebestod* from *Tristan* played as a violin solo (!) in the score of this famous tearjerker while Joan Crawford kills herself. Isaac Stern played the off-camera fiddle. This film stylishly reduces the whole issue of Eros/Thanatos to its lowest common denominator in the simplistic imagination: Love Kills.

*The Great Dictator* (1940) Few people remember that one of filmdom's most sublimely twisted scenes owes much of its impact to an ingenious use of Wagner's music. Charlie Chaplin plays Adenoid Hynkel in this fierce satire of Hitler. When fantasizing about world domination, Hynkel dances dreamily with a helium-filled globe as his partner—to the exquisite strains of the *Lohengrin* Prelude. The globe bursts and ruins the sobbing dictator's reverie, brutally interrupting the music as well.

Using Wagner as Hitler's soundtrack is plausible enough (especially when this film was made, so soon after Hitler went into raptures over the famous 1936 Bayreuth *Lohengrin* production), and any lesser filmmaker would have left it at that. Not Chaplin. The end of the film has the Jewish barber (also Chaplin), mistaken for "der Phooey," broadcasting a speech on the radio, urging resistance to brutality and promising the dawn of a new era. His girlfriend Hannah (Paulette Goddard) hears the miraculous message and gazes skyward—to the now-swelling strains of the same *Lohengrin* Prelude. This double-edged use of the same music amounts to a manifesto on the power—and powerlessness—of art. Satan and the angels can be equally inspired toward their divergent ends by the same work (be it music, literature, even Scripture). The individual is responsible for the outcome. Shakespeare, Oscar Wilde, and countless others have said the same thing, but using Wagner to illustrate this truth was an eloquent statement in 1940, and no less so today.

*William Shakespeare's Romeo and Juliet* (1996) It's hard to tell whether the creators of this movie, filmed in the great postmodern tradition of MTV, decided to employ the *Liebestod* from *Tristan* for the final tableau of the dead lovers as a bit of tongue-in-cheek sentimentalism or because it remains the best music to depict dead lovers. Buyers of the soundtrack (as opposed to the "Songs from the Movie" recording) are no doubt surprised when they hear several cutting-edge songs by the Butthole Surfers and others followed by this heavy dose of psychoeroticism.

*Help!* (1965) In this movie, the Prelude to Act III of *Lohengrin* is played while the hooded subcontinental fanatic bad guys raid and trash the Beatles' ultracool flat—the one with John's book-lined sunken bed. The producers of the album, Capitol Records, oblig-ingly included this piece of music on the soundtrack album at the end of side one, presumably so those who had no taste for it could lift the needle before it played. Those who heard their first Wagner this way are probably as baffled as the rest of us to learn, on attending an actual performance of *Lohengrin*, that this is intended to be wedding music.

*Apocalypse Now* (1979) This is the most famous, influential, and, frankly, overrated use of Wagner's music in film, showing American helicopters dropping napalm on Vietnam to a tape loop of "The Ride of the Valkyries." The creators of this movie managed to manipulate a great deal of popular mythos in this scene, using Wagner's music to associate the American Airborne Cavalry (as in "flying horses") with the Third Reich and thus make an antiwar statement that has seared itself onto the national subconscious. The odd thing is that it hadn't been done before. It is also interesting to note that, while Wagner is always accused of overkill, this entire scene takes only three minutes in the opera house, while the movie producers, who aren't often enough accused of overkill, repeat the music for seven minutes for their purposes. Thanks to this scene, you can count on someone, attempting wit, to make reference to "napalm" and "victory" when you tell them you are attending a performance of *Die Walküre*.

*The Lady Eve* (1941) This sophisticated comedy has Barbara Stan-wyck as a gold digger and Henry Fonda as her "mark." She eventually falls for him, and we have the classic confrontation of corrupting ver-sus redeeming love, all with fabulous costumes by Edith Head. In one surreal passage, Fonda gives Stanwyck a half-sincere speech for-giving her supposedly lurid past, while the soundtrack plays the beginning of the *Tannhäuser* Overture, with its Pilgrims' Chorus of penitents! Some studio executive amused himself frightfully with this in-joke.

*Excalibur* (1981) The soundtrack to this movie is almost entirely snippets of Wagner hits. Not a bad idea, especially for a movie about knights, fayre laydies, and evil sorcerers, but the problem is that the music takes over the story at a certain point, and becomes something of a story of its own. Confusion arises because of a too-facile association between the legends of King Arthur and Wagner's myths. The two are certainly related in many cases, but this movie attempts to conflate them all together, as if the one or the other weren't confusing enough on its own. Starting from the formula that Arthur = the Holy Grail = Parsifal, the whole Wagnerian canon is eventually employed to tell the familiar story of Lancelot and Guinevere. Arthur is abandoned by Guinevere and becomes impotent. *Parsifal* music abounds while the camera pans images of devastation. Excalibur being a sword, we must naturally have the sword motif from the *Ring* at every chance. This theme is very convenient, since it is used in the Funeral March from *Götterdämmerung*, whose two insistent chords are played whenever the director wants your total attention. When the sword is cast into the lake by the repentent Lancelot, we get the Rhinemaidens' music because, well, it is water. Lancelot stabs himself (à la Klingsor—more music). When Guinevere joins him to die at his side, you earn no extra credit points for guessing that the musical accompaniment is the *Liebestod*. Perceval (the Arthurian forerunner of Parsifal) rides in to save the day, and so on and so forth. This is a movie, so we can never have more than a few seconds of this great music at a time, and the Wagner fan will leave this movie teased to distraction as well as confused by too much reference. Too bad. It's a thoroughly enjoyable movie on its own merits.

*The Big Broadcast of 1938* (1938) This extravaganza from a very bygone era features a flimsy plot meant only to frame a cavalcade of star performances, including one you have to see to believe. Bob Hope is emceeing an elegant shipboard cabaret, and introduces Kirsten Flagstad to sing an "aria" (!) from "The Valkyrie" (accent on the second syllable, "Vahl-KEE-ree"). The curtain opens, and *voilà!* There she is, replete in winged helmet and shield (costumes by Edith Head) and working that spear like a professional baton twirler. The singing performance is equally fascinating. Flagstad sings Brünnhilde's brief scene at the beginning of the second act, with all the "*Hojotoho's.*" The trill is wanting, the high C's are not held, and yet she makes it totally convincing, further evidence that Wagner expected variations and perhaps wildness in this moment. This clip is interesting and utterly bizarre, explaining once and for all why Wagner has never replaced Cole Porter on the cabaret circuit. The scene directly following features W. C. Fields.

*Aria* (1987) This movie featured segments by ten different famous directors, each choosing an aria or operatic segment and filming a story to go with it. The music itself provides almost all of the sound. Interesting idea, with varying results. The film was quite popular when it came out, especially with those arty types who like to be up on things but would never be caught dead in an opera house, since it provided a *Reader's Digest* approach to opera with a terminally hip sensibility. The Wagner segment, featuring the *Liebestod* (of course), was directed by Franc Roddam. Bridget Fonda made her film debut with James Mathers as—now this is a real stretch here—a pair of young lovers. They drive to Las Vegas, find a motel room, get naked, make love (he enters her at the moment of the key change; good editing), land in the bathtub, and slice their veins open. There is a cut to an exterior shot at the moment of Isolde's final octave leap. Finally, we see (or think we see, since it's all very vague) the lovers driving back across the desert, so, gosh, maybe it was all a fantasy and maybe all of us die a little every time we make love. People get *paid* for this? Leontyne Price sings beautifully, but everybody already knows that.

*The Damned* (1971) If you think Luchino Visconti could have filmed this intense analysis of National Socialism's psychosexual pathology without at least one reference to *Tristan*, you haven't been paying attention. You'll never hear the *Liebestod* sung worse than here, where actor René Koldehof plays an SA commander at a rally of the Brownshirts. While his fellow carousers lie in poses of drunken

debauch, festooned with swastika armbands and black fishnet stock-
ings, Koldehof rasps his way through just enough of the score to send
a "message" to the savvies in the audience. As dawn arrives (read daylight—someone did their homework), so do the storm troopers with
machine guns, and all the naked brownshirts are vividly massacred in
an orgy of bloody male flesh. Brief but unforgettable, this sequence
may be filmdom's most horrific use of Wagner's music, reinforcing
the verdict of Nietzsche and others that this music was "diseased,"
"decadent," and ultimately fatal.

*The Bachelor and the Bobby Soxer* (1946)  Shirley Temple daydreams
about her knight in shining armor and hallucinates Cary Grant in
full armorial drag while the Prelude to *Lohengrin* plays. Funny in-
joke.

*The Silver Chalice* (1954)  Paul Newman's film debut was in this
overblown biblical saga, where he played a silversmith who makes—
yes—*that* chalice. When it is held aloft and glowing, the soundtrack
plays the "Dresden Amen." I guess they couldn't resist. Now, of
course, Wagner didn't write the "Dresden Amen" himself, but it's
used here because of its chalice-associated role in *Parsifal*, not
because Mendelssohn also used it in his *Reformation* Symphony.

*Seven Beauties* (1975)  Lina Wertmüller's harrowing film of one
man's will to survive uses "The Ride of the Valkyries" as background
music to our first views of life inside a German concentration camp.
While this is not the most strikingly obscure choice of music (and,
really, what other music could she have used?), Wertmüller deserves
credit for this scene's directorial deftness. Expect shots of suffering,
hopelessness, and no shortage of naked, mangled bodies, both dead
and alive, all seen as if through the unforgettable eyes of Giancarlo
Giannini. Wertmüller also should be praised for being able to make
her unforgettable statement without having to repeat herself, or the
music, *ad infinitum.*

*Un chien andalou* (1928)  What student has not seen this eighteen-
minute silent classic, directed by Luis Buñuel with Salvador Dalì as
his co-screenwriter? Who can forget the opening sequence, where

the woman's eye is sliced open by the barber's razor? And what music could accompany all this depravity and dismemberment other than the *Liebestod?* Actually, Buñuel cuts between our favorite *Tristan* music and a perky tango to make his statement on the pointlessness of everything (I think). The soundtrack was not added until 1960. The end of the film features a corpse carried out of a beautiful springtime park, while the *Liebestod* mercifully concludes (after much teasing). For some reason, David Bowie showed this movie in lieu of an opening band during his 1976 American tour, creating yet another unusual venue where people heard Wagner's music.

# *Making the Hadj:*
## *An Insider's Guide*
## *to Bayreuth*

◆

The Wagner Festival at Bayreuth is elitist, expensive, difficult to get tickets for, hard to get to, and uncomfortable when you finally arrive. Why would anyone in their right mind go to it?

Because it is the ultimate operatic experience. The festival offers interesting productions given in a civilized format inside a unique theater for people who take this stuff *very* seriously. Five or six cycles are given between late July and the end of August, with each cycle usually consisting of a performance of the *Ring*, *Parsifal*, and two other Wagner operas. One production is new every year.

### TICKETS

Tickets to the festival are expensive, but at this point they're less than opera tickets in London and scarcely more than the Met. The problem is not the price, it's the availability. Hundreds of thousands of people every year send away for them, and the house only seats about 1,800. Everyone will tell you there's no possibility of getting in, and that the waiting list is about fifteen years.

Not entirely true. Tour packages are one way to manage it. Contacting your local Wagner Society is another. Post on the Internet. Use your imagination. If worse comes to worst, there are always a few people standing in front of the Festival House waiting to buy any no-show tickets that may appear. Get a piece of cardboard and write *"Ich suche Karte"* on it.

## GETTING THERE

Once you scare up your tickets, you will need to get yourself to Bayreuth. Remember that Wagner chose this town specifically because of its inconvenient location. He didn't want anybody "dropping by" his festival on their way to other activities. Most people outside of Germany fly into Frankfurt, take a train to Nuremberg, and transfer to the train to Bayreuth. The same can be done from Munich. On the map, Prague appears to be the closest major city. So it is, if you are a bird, but if you are counting on trains, Frankfurt or Munich are much better options.

## ACCOMMODATIONS

Good luck! The hotel situation has hardly improved since the first festival in 1876. Make sure you have reservations, and a year is not too far in advance to book them.

If you haven't been invited to stay at the nearby Palace of Regensburg with the Thurn-und-Taxis crowd (you really should have sent them a Christmas card), the Bayerischer Hof is the best address in town. You'll be competing for rooms with the conductors and stars of the festival, so book early. It's also remarkably convenient to the train station (next door, in fact). The Goldener Hirsch and the Hotel Königshof across the street are almost as good. All three of these hotels by the train station are good spots for people-watching late at night since most of the festival crowd will pass by them on their way home from performances. The Treff Hotel Rheingold is the schmaltziest choice inside the attractive older part of town.

Many have found themselves homeless for the festival by assuming that there will be accommodations at the local university, since the festival is in summer and school is out. Big mistake. The University of Bayreuth hosts several summer programs, and their dorms are full. Nice try.

If you're doing the backpack-and-hitchhike thing to the festival (and, yes, there are those), don't expect to camp out in the park or the bus terminal. This *is* Bavaria, you know.

## THE PERFORMANCES

Wagner intended the Festival House to present perfect performances of his works. By about twenty minutes into the first night of *Das Rheingold*, he had to admit that there are no perfect performances in live theater—not even at his Bayreuth! This house has no monopoly on singers. The soloists you will hear at Bayreuth are basically as good, or as bad, as those you would hear in any other major opera house. One difference, however, is that you will hear them better at Bayreuth. The acoustics of the Festival House are nothing less than a miracle. The famous covered orchestra pit, the wooden structure, and the shape of the raked auditorium all contribute to this. That tenor you heard choking on *Tannhäuser* in New York or London might just blow your socks off at Bayreuth.

The chorus at Bayreuth will certainly have this effect on you. The festival has always boasted a truly great chorus, and the particular acoustics of the house make their sound unlike anything you've ever heard. For some, the chorus alone is reason enough to make the trek. The scale progression from basses to boy sopranos in the first act of *Parsifal* is absolutely hallucinogenic in this house.

Performances at the Festival House begin at 4:00 p.m., except for *Das Rheingold*, which begins at 6:00 p.m. Intermissions last between an hour and an hour and a half. It is ideal. All those problems of eating, running to the restroom, and dashing across town to make the curtain in time simply disappear, allowing you to focus on the music and the theatrical experience.

## THE SCENE ON "THE HILL"

Bayreuth attracts a diverse assortment of people these days. Germans remain the largest contingent, with local Bavarians well represented. There are also a good many British and Americans, followed in number by French, Japanese, Italians, Spaniards, and South Americans. People from all parts of the globe are to be seen there, with the local, university's Center for African Studies increasing the number of visitors from that continent as well.

The crowd at Bayreuth is made up of business people and artists, politicians and notables, students, celebrities, and, yes, various nobles and royalty, displaced or otherwise. Yet no one is there simply to "make the scene." All are intensely focused on the works being given. (The programs do not include synopses. The idea is that you already know every note and word of the work in question if you are there.) Although the Bayreuth festival is expensive and has a certain glamour, there are much easier places to be chic than the Green Hill.

Because, you see, one should not expect comfort at the Festival House. The seats are unupholstered wood, and there are no arm rests. It takes the body quite a bit of shifting to find a way to sit through the long operas without doing permanent damage to yourself. And the seats are the least of it. The inside of the house is famously hot and airless. Ventilation is out of the question—the acoustics could be disturbed, and what is more important? (Airplanes are rerouted away from the skies over Bayreuth during the festival.) Heavy velvet drapes are drawn across the doors to the auditorium to prevent any sound (or air) from entering. The beauty of this is that total silence— the famous Bayreuth hush—reigns. The music truly emerges from quiet. The extremely serious audience never utters a sound, a cough, or a sneeze. It just doesn't happen.

That's the upside. The downside is that you can pass out. It happens all the time. Just make sure you pass out quietly.

So what does one wear to such a marathon? What else but black tie or evening gowns? Yes, formal attire is more popular than ever these days. White tie is not unheard of. The idea is that *anybody* could wrench their back, sweat, and pass out in a T-shirt and jeans, but to do it in evening wear—well, that shows devotion! Of course there are the dress-down types in early Grateful Dead ensembles, and yes, a simple suit will do, but why bother? You wouldn't be comfortable in the infernal Festival House even if you went bare-butt naked, so why not dress up a bit? And don't worry about overdressing. It's almost impossible.

If your tickets are for the first cycle of performances, the opening night will be a regular gala. White tie, decorations, even swords will be seen. Bring your camera. Everyone else does.

Lately, the ladies have been wearing a great deal of what they call national costumes from their various countries, and dirndls, saris, kimonos, fabulous creations in kinte cloth, and beautiful outfits from all over have blended well with the usual assortment of Chanel suits and evening gowns. And a word to the gentlemen: it is perfectly acceptable in these less disciplined times to remove the jacket once you take your seat. This simple procedure will greatly increase your comfort, and will save your jacket from getting ruined.

All this dressing up makes the long intermissions a world-class promenade. The grounds around the Festival House are beautifully maintained, and walks through the relatively cool gardens and woods are crucial after the operatic sauna you've just experienced. Nobody is "reading up" on anything at intermission—you know everything already, remember? Enjoy the people-watching. A curt nod of the head and a breezy Bavarian *"Grüss Gott!"* are sufficient conversation with strangers, wherever they're from. It is also *very* fashionable to have your small dog held for you during the performance (by one of your personal staff, presumably) and to play with it at intermission.

These observations might make the Bayreuth festival experience sound stuffy, but in fact there's a certain country-casual style going on at the same time. While there is a full restaurant and good cafe adjacent to the theater (whose prices are high but not at all outrageous, and certainly lower than their counterparts in urban opera houses), most people opt to snack during the long intermissions and have a leisurely supper after the performance. It's nothing to see an elegant European lady eating bratwurst standing up, careful not to drip mustard on her *couture* creation, while the promenaders favor ice cream cones. Champagne is available, but beer is much more *comme il faut*. The restaurant, with its full meals, generally attracts the elderly, the infirm, and those who have always dreamed of the day when they could face Wagner's later acts on a full stomach.

Another rather fun feature of the intermissions is the group photograph tradition. People mysteriously begin to gather directly in front of the house about twenty minutes before the next act begins. A photographer appears on the balcony over the rather small front door to the house, snapping a series of pictures until the whole crowd in this area has been photographed. Later, the pictures are made available (at about eight dollars apiece) at the Tscheitschonig stationery store in town (see below). While the terminally hip are appalled at this, or pretend to be, everyone else joins in, and it's part of the fun. Also, it puts you in a good position to hear the beautifully harmonized horn choir that replaces the photographer on the balcony, playing a selected theme from the act to be given at fifteen, ten, and five minutes before the end of intermission, and reminding everybody why they're there.

Throughout all this, the talk is Wagner, Wagner, and more Wagner. The Bayreuth audience is the most intensely focused group of people you're ever likely to see.

The long intermissions, the promenades in the woods and the gardens, and the conversations with people who have the same interest all make a lot of Wagner fans wonder what heaven has in store to top a good week at the Bayreuth festival.


## AFTER THE PERFORMANCE

It would be a pity to run back to your hotel directly after the performance, especially if you've dressed. Besides, you'll want to "come down" from the experience in a relaxed atmosphere, even if this entails arguing over nuances of the music or production with other opinionated Wagnerians. Many people head farther up the Green Hill to the pleasant gardens of the Hotel Bürgerreuth. Many of the orchestra and chorus go there to eat, drink, unwind, and argue. They are instantly recognizable by their casual attire (the orchestra members play in the covered pit, which is said to make the auditorium of the house seem cool and airy by comparison, while the chorus will have changed out of their costumes). Pricey Italian/French/local cuisine is served under Japanese lanterns. It can be lovely, but also a bit hectic, as the staff struggles to serve clients clamoring for food in about fifteen languages.

A very select group, including many of the stars and glitterati, heads for the dining room of the Bayerischer Hof Hotel. The excellent food is, believe it or not, a sort of *nouvelle haute*-Franconian.

## FREE TIME

There isn't a lot of it. Bear in mind that the performances usually start at 4:00 p.m., which means you'll probably start getting dressed by 2:30 or 3:00, and you probably won't get home from your smart *après-théâtre* supper until after midnight. Add to this the fact that even the most modest pensions in this part of the world ply you with a classically hearty breakfast, and you can see that you'll hardly have time to breathe.

### *Wahnfried*

There are a couple of "must sees" in this town. Without any doubt, you have to go to Wahnfried, which houses the Richard Wagner Museum these days. The museum has an impossible task: to present Wagner and his family to the world in a way that will please everybody. They do a decent job of it, all things considered, and the exhibitions in the house are required viewing for any fan. There are also archives and study centers at Wahnfried.

The house itself, basically planned by Wagner, will bring you very close to the ghosts of Richard and Cosima, even if it is not a spectacular architectural achievement. The famous salon sometimes has musical presentations, and one must pay homage to the piano given to Wagner by Steinway & Sons of New York (yes, you read that right) on the occasion of the first festival in 1876. Wagner himself preferred other pianos in the house, but Liszt loved the Steinway. It is lucky to be still in existence. Wahnfried took a direct hit in the last days of the war and was two-thirds destroyed, along with much of its contents. Wieland Wagner reconstructed the house, predictably along clean, modern lines. When the house was sold to the city of Bayreuth in 1973 (for a pretty penny), Wolfgang and his mother, Winifred, worked with historical architects, reaching back into their memories to restore the house as closely as possible to its original appearance.

Liszt spent as much time as he could at Wahnfried in his later years, and Cosima had a house built for him next door. This house is now the site of the Franz Liszt Museum. While not as elaborately funded as the Wagner Museum, it is well worth a visit, if only as an homage to this remarkable man.

The front of Wahnfried has a bronze bust of King Ludwig, as well it should. In the back are the attractive gardens where so many notables promenaded in 1876. Richard and Cosima are buried in relatively tasteful graves there. (Liszt, who died at Wahnfried in 1886, is buried in the municipal cemetery of Bayreuth, next to his grandson Siegfried Wagner.) The back gate opens on to the Hofgarten, the once royal preserve of the Neue Schloss, and now an attractive park. Swans are abundant.

### The Markgräflisches Oper

This theater with the near-unpronounceable name was the attraction that first brought the Wagners to Bayreuth in search of a suitable site for the festival. It was built by the Margravine (roughly equivalent to "Countess") Wilhelmine of Bayreuth around 1740. This interesting lady was the sister of Frederick the Great. When she was sent off to dull Bayreuth, she decided to liven things up a bit, and started building. This was the height of the period we now call rococo, and Wilhelmine went hog-wild with it. Stop by this building (confusingly known as the Opera House of Bayreuth) and see what you think of German rococo.

### *Evenings in Bayreuth*

Chances are you will be at the Festival House in the evenings, but there is the occasional night off. The House, for example, is dark one night between performances of *Walküre* and *Siegfried*, as well as the night after *Siegfried*.

There is usually a concert at the old Opera House on one of these off nights. By all means, go. While eighteenth-century interior design is not above criticism, you will experience what sort of intimacy was achieved in these smaller, ornate theaters. Sit in the first or second tier of faux-boxes if you want to be seen. At intermission, walk through the strange lobby to the cafe-salon. French doors open onto a balcony overlooking the cobbled plaza and fountain. Flowers are everywhere. Take your coffee out on the balcony and imagine your-self waving to your cheering subjects below.

The concerts are usually of pre-Wagnerian music, with Mozart in abundance, played by the splendid musicians who have gathered for the festival. At the very least, spending your festival off-night at a con-cert will establish you, once and for all, as a *very* serious music lover.

If time permits, stop in at the Zollinger Conditerei Operncafe next door to the old Opera for coffee and pastry before the performance. Gilt-and-white walls with mirrors, chandeliers, and starched linens abound. You simply don't find places like this outside of central Europe.

For late-night entertainment, including after performances, you may want to explore the Rathskeller-type establishments in the city's oldest part of town. These are to be found in the casbahlike cobbled streets around Sophienstrasse, behind the main square and transit center. These establishments will amuse you if your idea of a fun night out in Germany was formed by seeing *The Student Prince*. If you like to think of yourself as more up-to-date, a few trendy cafes, boutiques, and bars have opened on the very narrow Badstrasse, directly behind the old Opera. This area is Bayreuth's very modest answer to Soho or Kreuzberg. Wear black. If you're gay, or you want a truly interesting place to go, check out Judy's Pub on the Tunnel-strasse just off the main Bahnhofstrasse. Judy's may be the only place in the world where you can see white tie and tails mixing with neon lycra in one small room.

### Other Stops in Bayreuth

After breakfast, trot over to Tscheitschonig stationery and magazine store, where the pictures taken from the balcony of the Festival House at the previous day's performance will be on display in the window. Even if you don't intend to buy any, the window is something of a late-morning gathering spot and gossip center for festival-goers. Also, there will be pictures of celebrities attending the festival in the window, and you can make fun comments on how everybody looks. (Don't bother pointing out that the prime minister of the republic is overweight—everybody already knows that.) The stationery shop is right on the Bahnhofstrasse, near the Parsifal Apotheke (pharmacy).

The Eremitage is a must if you have fallen in love at the festival (not likely), or if you want an elegant baroque stroll. The Eremitage is a lovely, pointless folly across the Autobahn, built as, well, a pretty place to stroll in the eighteenth century. It's not really a palace, just a backdrop in stone with statues. Ludwig stayed here during the first festival.

On Sunday mornings, the Lutheran and Catholic churches in the old town offer *extremely* multilingual services where the level of music is, predictably, fairly high. Dress as if for an important business meeting.

The town of Bayreuth, attractively reconstructed after being obliterated in the last days of the war, has worked hard to make itself welcoming to strangers, and perhaps to transcend its swastika-bunted past. The main streets are festooned with international flags among the blue-and-white Bavarian banners and flags of the Federal Republic. The university stresses international culture and relations, especially in music. The whole town celebrates the festival that put it on the map. Bookstores sell a wide array of musical and Wagner-specific literature, and signings by the star musicians are frequent. Plays, some quite funny or avant-garde, and concerts are given in several venues. Souvenirs, even tacky ones, are sold everywhere. Even those who have no interest in Wagner celebrate the importance of the festival.

# GLOSSARY

◆

**abbé** A vague title of the Roman Catholic church, referring to a man who has taken holy orders but is not fully a priest. Franz Liszt famously became an abbé in 1864 within the order of Franciscan friars. His ecclesiastical duties were extremely light and seemed primarily limited to the private sphere. This allowed him to appear in society in the costume and collar of a Catholic priest, saving a good deal of money on clothes while at the same time annoying his son-in-law Wagner.

**alliteration** The poetic device of using the same consonant sound repeatedly, especially at the beginning of words, as in "Peter Piper picked a peck . . ." Alliteration was a required element of Old Germanic poetry, and Wagner, in his attempts to sound archaic, was positively, even maddeningly, addicted to it. Alberich in *Das Rheingold* often uses alliteration, as in his line *"Garstig glatter glitschriger Glimmer!"* (rough translation: "Grossly glimmering glittering goo!")

**aria** (from Italian, literally, "air") A set piece of solo vocal music in an opera. "Song" might be a good way to say this, but, for some reason, nobody does. It is a given that Wagner never wrote arias in his operas after *Tannhäuser*. The fact that "Elsa's Dream," Isolde's *Liebestod*, and Siegmund's Spring Song are not arias must be taken on faith, like the emperor's new clothes.

**atonality** Music that does not have any key as its center. The twentieth century has been obsessed with this concept, primarily in the work of Arnold Schoenberg, but many see the phenomenon foreshadowed in the works of Liszt and Wagner. The strange harmonies of *Tristan* and parts of *Parsifal* are particularly notable in this regard, but all of Wagner's mature music is loaded with accidentals (notes outside of the key being used), which points toward atonality.

**Bavaria** (in German, Bayern, as in BMW) Formerly a kingdom, now a state, of southern Germany, including the cities of Munich, Augsburg, Nuremberg, and Bayreuth. Bavaria is considered prosperous, conservative, attractive, and Catholic (except for its upper area of Franconia).

**Bayreuth bark** Wagner's famous advice to his singers, urging them to pay attention to the text and the small notes, devolved, under Cosima's guidance, into an unlovely mannerism known by this name. The term "Bayreuth bark" was common before the First World War, which tells us something about what we might have heard had we attended the festival in that time. Wagnerian singers are often accused of "barking." In fact, barking is all but gone today. Remind your older friends of this when they rhapsodize about the supposed golden age of Wagner singing.

**Bayreuth hush** This refers to a phenomenon unique to the audiences at Bayreuth, who, after a brief period of chatter while getting to their seats, fall into a deep and respectful quiet *before* the house lights are dimmed. Explanations for this range from a desire to observe an honorific meditation on the subsequent miraculous music to the infamous lack of air in the Festival House. Whatever its reason for being, the Bayreuth hush is eerie but effective, allowing the music to emerge from absolute silence.

It is perfectly permissible among Wagnerites to use this term in other contexts as well. For example, by saying, "Our guests observed a Bayreuth hush," you can imply that your recent party was not of the "swing from the chandeliers" variety. The phrase is used incorrectly in reference to the tradition of not applauding after Act I of *Parsifal*. Don't make this mistake. The proper term to describe the quiet of the Bayreuth audience after the first act of *Parsifal* is not "hush," but rather "sepulchral silence."

***Bildungsroman*** (German) A "coming of age" story, of which Goethe's *The Apprenticeship of Wilhelm Meister* is the definitive example. The term is often applied to *Siegfried* and sometimes, obliquely, to *Parsifal*.

***Bühnenfestspiel*** (German, "stage festival performance") This is the term Wagner used for the *Ring*, since "opera" would never do and even "music drama" hardly seemed a sufficient description. The word recalls the ancient Athenian drama festivals, or at least those festivals as Wagner imagined them, where the entire populace attended a day-long trilogy of plays that were part history, part mythology, and part religion.

***Bühnenweihfestspiel*** (German, roughly, "stage-consecrating festival performance") Wagner's term for *Parsifal*. Since the *Ring* defied existing nomenclature, Wagner did backflips to one-up himself for *Parsifal*.

**cavatina** A formal and stately operatic aria without repetitions. Erik sings a cavatina toward the end of *Dutchman*.

**crescendo** (from Italian, literally, "growing") This handy word is used in English and other languages to describe music, vocal or instrumental, that gets steadily louder. The Prelude to *Rheingold* is one single crescendo.

***Entrümpelung*** (German, literally, "cleaning out attics") The style that characterized Wieland Wagner's productions, with their almost-bare stages, at Bayreuth in the 1950s, and many other lesser, creativity-challenged productions since then. A good analogy in the field of graphic arts might be the famous cover of the Beatles' White Album.

***Fach*** (German, literally, "compartment," "shelf," or "department") This is the word Germans and know-it-alls use for vocal range, as for a tenor or a soprano. It is also popular among arty types in a more general sense, as in "She shouldn't have danced that macarena at the wedding—it's really not her *fach!*"

**Franconia** (in German, Franken) Region and former duchy of south-central Germany, including Nuremberg and Bayreuth. Staunchly Protestant, it was casually handed over to severely Catholic Bavaria by

Napoleon in 1806, and it remains mostly in the state of Bavaria in the current Federal Republic. Walther von Stolzing in *Meistersinger* is a Franconian knight.

**German Confederation** The loose organization of the many smaller kingdoms, principalities, and free cities of Germany from the fall of Napoleon in 1815 until the declaration of the German Empire in 1871. Each of these independent political entities (from the larger kingdoms like Prussia, Saxony, and Bavaria, to the tiny states like Weimar, to independent city-states like Frankfurt) had its own laws, currency, army, and bureaucracy. It is best to consider this untenable feudal situation when confronting the nationalist strains (which sound so noxious now in view of subsequent history) in *Lohengrin* and *Meistersinger*.

The various states often quarreled and sometimes fought, as did Prussia and Bavaria (causing major trouble for Wagner) in 1866. Occasionally, they could agree on something. Wagner's banishment from his native Saxony in 1849, for example, was cheerfully upheld by the other members of the Confederation until 1861. Confusingly, all the various heads of state kept their titles and some of their privileges after the unification of 1871 right until the fall of the German Empire in 1918, making Germany a land of much hollow pomp and ceremony surrounding the figurehead kings and princelings. The Bayreuth festival is a good place to spot the descendants of those people today.

*Gesamtkunstwerk* (German, literally, "total work of art") Wagner coined this much-used, and misused, phrase in his essay "The Art-Work of the Future" in 1849. He was thinking of a new form of theater that would unify drama, music, dance, and design to become something greater than the sum of its parts. Primarily, he was projecting an ideal production of the *Ring*, which was beginning to brew in his head at about that time. The term has since been used in other fields. The important architects Otto Wagner (no known relation) and Josef Hoffmann used it to describe their work in turn-of-the-century Vienna, which was meant to be a synthesis of urban planning, architecture, and interior design, down to the last detail. The term can also be used jocularly by sophisticates, as in "My dear, it was more than a dinner party, it was a *Gesamtkunstwerk!*"

**grand opera** A term with a specific and a general meaning. In its specific sense, grand opera refers to an opera in four or five acts on an epic or historical subject. These were the rage in nineteenth-century Paris. They are characterized by star-turn solos and prominent choruses, and invariably have a longish ballet toward the middle. Wagner claimed to loathe the grand operas of Paris, although he was favorably impressed with the attention given to production details and the excellence of the musicians involved. Meyerbeer's operas, such as *Les Huguenots* and *Le Prophète*, are the definitive types of this genre, although another good example might be Wagner's own early success *Rienzi*. (Bülow, in a rare attempt at humor, once called *Rienzi* the best opera Meyerbeer ever wrote. Wagner was not amused by this comment. He told Bülow to write a better opera if he could.)

In its general sense, grand opera refers to any big sprawling opera, the type that cannot be done effectively by a good college ensemble. In this sense, the term definitively applies to Wagner's mature works. Anna Russell makes a delicious and provocative reference to *Die Walküre* as grand opera in her analysis of the *Ring*. Speaking of Siegmund and Sieglinde's illegal, immoral liaison, she says, "But that's the beauty of grand opera — you can get away with anything so long as you sing it!"

**Heldentenor** (German, literally, "heroic tenor") A tenor whose voice is exceptionally powerful (read "loud"). Virtually all of Wagner's lead roles for tenors require voices of this type. Unfortunately, a true *Heldentenor* is rather like the proverbial ghost: often talked about, never actually encountered. It is best to use this word in sentences such as "Alas, there are no more . . ." Apparently, this has been a safe thing to say since Schnorr died in 1865.

**Holy Roman Empire** The most confusing political entity in history. Founded by Charlemagne in A.D. 800, it came to refer to Germany and Austria and whichever lands they happened to control at a given moment. It was finally laid to rest by Napoleon in 1806, leaving Germany in more of a political vacuum than usual and greatly affecting all subsequent history. By Wagner's time, it becomes part of the pervading nostalgic mythology in art and literature. The Empire figures in *Meistersinger* ("Even should the Holy Roman Empire dissolve into vapor, we would still have Holy German Art!") and *Lohengrin*, where King Henry the

Fowler is also emperor, confronting the eternal challenge of uniting Germany.

**kaiser** (from German, literally, "Caesar") Emperor, related to the Russian word "czar." This word is used for any emperor, be he Austrian, Holy Roman, or (from 1871 to 1918) German. When the king of Prussia was declared German kaiser in 1871, Wagner, the onetime revolutionary, composed a potboiling *Kaisermarsch* in his honor. In English, *the* kaiser has long referred to Wilhelm II, the bad guy of the First World War with the pointy helmet (who, in fact, used the thunder motif from *Rheingold* as his limousine's horn call).

**Kapellmeister** (from German) Basically, conductor. The confusion arises from the fact that *Kapelle* in German can mean both "chapel" and "orchestra." Indeed, the relation of these words in German is an indicator of their common heritage. In the princely courts of old Germany, the same man was usually responsible for music both in the theater and at worship. Wagner was Kapellmeister at Dresden, the capital of the kingdom of Saxony, from 1843 to 1849.

**leitmotiv** (from German, literally "leading motive") The most overused word in Wagneriana. It is a short musical phrase that describes a person, place, or thing. Anna Russell called it a fancy way to say "signature tune." The term was coined by a scholar writing on Weber in 1871. Wagner himself avoided the term, although he had previously used the term *Hauptmotiv*, *haupt* meaning "head." The *Ring*, we are told, is constructed on a system of over two hundred leitmotivs, which have been dissected, analyzed, and scrutinized for over a century.

**libretto** (from Italian, literally, "little book"; plural, libretti) The written play of an opera, comprising words and stage directions. There is no other word for this in English. The term "book" has come to mean "story." Opera composers have traditionally collaborated with librettists, some of whom were famous poets or playwrights on their own. Wagner wrote all his own libretti, considering himself a genius in that field as well. Libretti are almost always available with translations in recordings, or they can be purchased or borrowed from most libraries. Contemporary audiences, for some reason, seem to think it a presumption on their time to read libretti before a performance and prefer to be surprised, or clueless, during the performance. Hint: It only takes a few minutes to read through an opera libretto—even one of Wagner's.

*forte, fortissimo* (Italian, literally, "strong" and "very strong," also the adverbs "strongly," etc.) Musical directions indicating, basically, "loud." Wagner was not afraid to use these liberally throughout his scores.

*longueur* (French, literally, "length," "slowness") A long boring part. This is a useful word. You can admit to be being bored without sounding uneducated. No one will argue that there are some *longueurs* in Wagner's operas, but they become fewer and shorter as the works become more familiar.

**Nirvana** In Buddhism, the state of perfect blessedness achieved through the eradication of individual existence and the abnegation of passions and desires. This ideal appears frequently in Wagner's thought in his flirtations with Buddhism. He in his writings and Cosima in her diaries make repeated references to self-annihilation, presumably meaning Nirvana. *Tristan* approaches the issue philosophically, while *Parsifal* is soaking in it. Incidentally, it is also the name of one of Hans von Bülow's few compositions, written before he began his own special program of self-annihilation.

**Opéra** When it's spelled like this, capital *O*, accent over the *e*, this word refers to a building and an institution: the Opéra of Paris. In the nineteenth century, this mecca was where composers went to make money and a splash, including the child Liszt in 1825 and Wagner, disastrously, in 1860. The Opéra was then on the Rue Lepeletier, the present celebrated building (also called the Palais Garnier) not opening until 1875. Wagner never saw the building we know as the Opéra, but it is safe to assume he would have hated it.

*piano, pianissimo* (Italian, literally, "quiet" and "very quiet," also the adverbs "quietly," etc.) Musical directions indicating soft playing or singing. Although many people, including musicians, will not believe it, Wagner used these instructions frequently in his scores. Do not confuse this with the instrument we call a piano, earlier called a pianoforte, meaning it can play soft and loud. (There is also an instrument called a "fortepiano," but let's not worry about that now.) The issue is further complicated because *piano* is also, for reasons known only to God, the Italian word for a floor (because it's *low*, perhaps?). First-time tourists in Italy are invariably taken aback when they are told their hotel room is on the *primo piano*, and they imagine they will be sleeping in the first musical instrument they can find. They are hardly less confused to discover that the *primo piano* happens to be the *second* floor.

**Prussia** (in German, Preussen) Formerly a kingdom, then a state, of northeastern Germany, including Berlin and Königsberg (Kaliningrad). Traditionally the most militaristic of the German states, Prussia was formally abolished in 1949. Prussia and Bavaria have always been, at best, rivals. The fact that Hans von Bülow was Prussian did not help Wagner's career in Munich.

**recitative** In classical opera, these are the parts where characters are "talking" in between arias and ensembles. The vocal line follows speech inflections very closely. When opera began, it was almost all recitative, and it could be argued that contemporary opera has returned to this. Wagner worked hard to blur the line between recitative and aria, though the distinction is apparent in *Tannhäuser* and other earlier works.

*répétiteur* (French) Excellent French term, used in other countries as well, for a rehearsal pianist or other musician. It comes from the French verb *répéter*, "to repeat," as in "Let's try that again."

*Saxony* (in German, Sachsen) One of the several smaller kingdoms that formed the German Confederation and later the German Empire. Saxony, the southern part of former East Germany, includes the cities of Leipzig and Dresden. Wagner was a native of this kingdom, whose significance had greatly faded since the Middle Ages. Henry the Fowler, whom we meet in *Lohengrin*, was king of Saxony before he was elected Holy Roman Emperor.

**synopsis** The short plot summary usually provided in the free program at the opera house and also found in books and recordings. Newcomers to the opera must be reminded to read at least the synopsis so they don't gasp during the performance when they read the supertitles and discover, for example, that Siegmund and Sieglinde are twins.

*tessitura* (Italian, literally, "texture")  Musical term referring to the average pitch of notes in a given role in relation to the voice for which it was written. It is commonly noted that the role of Brünnhilde has a higher *tessitura* in *Siegfried* than in *Götterdämmerung*, though she hits some pretty high notes in both.

**trill**  The rapid alternation of a note with the note directly above it, sustained (one hopes) in regular intervals of pitch and time. The same term is used by singers and instrumentalists. It is a very difficult ornamentation for a singer to achieve, and extremely difficult to do well. Wagner's score for Act II of *Walküre* asks the soprano to sing a trill for two measures *after* her octave-leaping *Hojotohos*. Very few ever manage this in performance; most are too relieved about hitting the previous high note to concern themselves with vocal ornament. If the Brünnhilde accomplishes a real trill, and can be heard above the full orchestra, applaud her lustily (at the end of the act, of course).

**Vorabend** (German, literally, "fore-evening")  Introduction or first night. This is the term used by pedants for *Das Rheingold* as the "Prologue" to the *Ring*.

**yelpentenor** (mock-German)  A tired old expression for a wannabe *Heldentenor* who hasn't quite got the goods.

**Zukunftsmuzik** (German, literally, "music of the future")  A term used in the mid-nineteenth century, especially describing the music of Wagner and Liszt. Wagner, although he had written a famous article called "The Art-Work of the Future," tried to distance himself from the term. This term, and its French equivalent, *la musique de l'avenir*, formed the locus of "the" mid-nineteenth-century debate among critics. Berlioz, too, was drawn kicking and screaming into the fracas.

**Zwischenfach** (German, literally, "between categories")  A role, such as Kundry in *Parsifal*, that is sung by both sopranos and mezzo-sopranos. Venus in *Tannhäuser* and Ortrud in *Lohengrin* are also, more controversially, sometimes filed under this term. Use this word at intermission and score major points with the know-it-alls.

# THE TYPES IN THE AUDIENCE

Audiences for Wagner operas are a lot like other opera audiences, only more so. Here is a rundown of different types you can expect, and how to deal with them.

**The Know-It-Alls**  If the second bassoon missed an eighth note during a full orchestral *fortissimo*, these people will notice, will let you know they noticed, and will attempt to disgrace you for not having noticed or for enjoying the performance in spite of it. Do not attempt to engage such a person in conversation or (God forbid) argument: it's what they want, and you can't win. Pretend you've just spotted a long-lost uncle across the lobby, and run. They'll forget you were there as soon as their next victim appears, and, oddly, there's always another Know-It-All within earshot for them to debate.

**The Seen/Heard-It-Alls**  These people will try to convince you that you, you unfortunate newcomer to Wagner, cannot possibly know the meaning of real Wagnerian singing, since you didn't hear (for example) Birgit Nilsson in 1968. Interestingly, these same people, or their clones, were saying the same thing at that very performance about Kirsten Flagstad in 1938, and so on back to the dawn of (Wagnerian) time. Don't let these people upset you. Unlike the Know-It-Alls, they are not deliberately trying to belittle you. It's actually their own lost years they are mourning. This nostalgic vocal mythology is as much a part of the opera world as expensive seats and curtain calls. Smile indulgently, say "Ahh, yes!" and try to look upon them more with pity than with disapproval.

**The "We Came for *Kunst*" crowd**  Aubrey Beardsley once did a famous lithograph called "The Wagnerians," showing an affected, humorless, and vaguely hostile crowd gathering in a theater before a performance of one of their idol's works. Alas, little has changed over the last hundred years with this section of the crowd except details of fashion. These are the people for whom Wagner is more of a religion than an art form, and their severity is proverbial. Any reference to these works as "opera" might elicit violence from them. They complain if Siegfried holds his final high C in *Götterdämmerung* ("*Hoi-ho!*") for more than the quarter note designated in the score, despite the fact that only a miracle can get the poor tenor to reach that note at all after what he's sung. They probably won't bother you much at intermission or after the performance, since all conversation is beneath them and they probably have their upturned noses in a score anyway. They invariably return home by public transportation even though some of them have more money than the boxholders, this being part of the penitential pose appropriate to this life style. These people can be readily identified by the well-worn paperback edition of Nietzsche always in the coat pocket.

**The Armchair Conductors** Air-conducting at home can be educational and fun, but waving one's arms about in the opera house is an act of self-aggrandizement and unbridled hostility. Therefore, these guys (and they are always men) need to be shamed publicly at intermission if they don't respond to your pleading whispers and gestures during the performance. Try, if you can, to suggest that they are making errors in their conducting (". . . and furthermore, *adagio* means slow, not dead!"), since this will totally humiliate them. Lastly, recommend a workshop for people with control issues, and laugh when their wives or dates nod knowingly.

**The Sing-Alongs** No jury in the world, or at least in those parts of the world with opera companies, would convict you for the murder of one of these, provided you have warned them once before killing them. Anyone can get carried away by the moment, but repeat offenders must by stopped by any means available.

**The Traditionalists versus the Avant-Garde** The Traditionalists insist on seeing everything manifested on the stage that they've read in the libretto. There must be a dead *Schwann* in *Parsifal*, a live one in *Lohengrin*, a flowering staff in *Tannhäuser*, and so on, ad infinitum, or they will rail on about the collapse of Western civilization all through intermission. The *Ring*, in particular, provides fertile ground for these types, since they never can and never will see everything Wagner wrote in the libretto. (Wagner himself dispensed with such impracticalities as Fricka's chariot drawn by live rams for his own production.) Conversely, members of the so-called avant-garde feel violated if anything recognizable from real life, or the libretto, finds its way onto the stage. If anything concrete does show up in the production, it must be in the context of a Searing Critique of Bourgeois Society, or they will howl. In Germany and some other European countries, these two factions are split directly along political lines, with the Traditionalists representing the right (or worse) and the avant-garde representing some notion of the left. In English-speaking countries, personal preference may play some role, this being a possibility that does not seem to have occurred to the Continentals. Avoid both the Traditionalists and the avant-gardists. With Wagner even more than with other subjects, dogma is the enemy.

# INDEX

♦